The Princeton Companion to Jonathan Edwards

The Princeton Companion to Jonathan Edwards

Edited by Sang Hyun Lee

PRINCETON UNIVERSITY PRESS   PRINCETON AND OXFORD

Copyright © 2005 by Princeton University Press
Published by Princeton University Press, 41 William Street,
Princeton, New Jersey 08540
In the United Kingdom: Princeton University Press, 3 Market Place,
Woodstock, Oxfordshire OX20 1SY

All Rights Reserved

Library of Congress Cataloging-in-Publication Data
    The Princeton companion to Jonathan Edwards / edited by Sang Hyun Lee.
        p.   cm.
    ISBN 0-691-12108-7 (cl: alk. paper)
        1. Edwards, Jonathan, 1703–1758.   I. Lee, Sang Hyun, 1938–

BX7260.E3P75 2005
230′.58′092—dc22   2004050560

British Library Cataloging-in-Publication Data is available

This book has been composed in Sabon

Printed on acid-free paper. ∞

www.pupress.princeton.edu

Printed in the United States of America

10 9 8 7 6 5 4 3 2 1

*This volume is dedicated
to the community of Edwards scholars,
here and abroad*

Contents

Acknowledgments	ix
Introduction	xi
Note on References to the Yale Edition of The Works of Jonathan Edwards	xxi
Chronology of Edwards' Life and Writings	xxiii
One Jonathan Edwards: A Theological Life —*Kenneth P. Minkema*	1
Two Edwards' Intellectual Background —*Peter J. Thuesen*	16
Three Being and Consent —*Richard R. Niebuhr*	34
Four The Trinity —*Amy Plantinga Pauw*	44
Five God's Relation to the World —*Sang Hyun Lee*	59
Six Christology —*Robert W. Jenson*	72
Seven The Bible —*Robert E. Brown*	87
Eight Religious Affections and the "Sense of the Heart" —*John E. Smith*	103
Nine Freedom of the Will —*Allen C. Guelzo*	115
Ten Grace and Justification by Faith Alone —*Sang Hyun Lee*	130
Eleven Christian Virtue and Common Morality —*John E. Smith*	147

Twelve
The Church   —*Douglas A. Sweeney*   167

Thirteen
Typology   —*Janice Knight*   190

Fourteen
History   —*John F. Wilson*   210

Fifteen
Eschatology   —*Stephen J. Stein*   226

Sixteen
The Sermons: Concept and Execution   —*Wilson H. Kimnach*   243

Seventeen
Missions and Native Americans   —*Gerald R. McDermott*   258

Eighteen
The Puritans and Edwards   —*Harry S. Stout*   274

Nineteen
Edwards' Theology after Edwards   —*Mark Noll*   292

The Works of Jonathan Edwards (Yale Edition)   309

List of Contributors   311

Index   313

Acknowledgments

I AM GRATEFUL to all the contributors to this volume for their participation in it and their personal encouragement. My greatest debt, however, is to Kenneth P. Minkema, the executive editor of *The Works of Jonathan Edwards*. He provided with unfailing grace and efficiency the information and advice which I sought, even when, for about a month or so, I interrupted him with almost daily phone calls. His knowledge of Edwards is nothing less than astonishing. I also want to thank Harry S. Stout, the general editor of *The Works of Jonathan Edwards*, for his support and encouragement with all of my Edwards projects.

I am deeply indebted to Thomas W. Gillespie, former president of Princeton Theological Seminary, and Eun H. Kim-Nam for their financial assistance, without which the publication of this volume would not have been possible.

My gratitude also goes to the staff at Princeton University Press: Fred Appel, religion editor, for his confidence in this volume and his wise counsel from its inception onward; Debbie Tegarden, production editor, for her meticulous and caring guidance throughout the editing and production phase; and Jennifer Nippins, an editorial assistant, for her thorough and friendly reminders. I am also indebted to Vicky Wilson-Schwartz for her expert and resourceful copyediting.

I want also to thank Kil Jae Park and Jeffrey Waddington for helping me in preparing the manuscript. I am thankful to John E. Smith for permission to reprint here his essay "Christian Virtue and Common Morality," which was originally published in John E. Smith, *Jonathan Edwards: Puritan, Preacher, Philosopher* (London: Geoffrey Chapman, 1992); to the editors of *William and Mary Quarterly* for permission to reprint Janice Knight's essay on typology, originally published in that journal in 1991 as "Learning the Language of God: Jonathan Edwards and the Typology of Nature"; and to Oxford University Press for permission to reprint Harry S. Stout's essay "The Puritans and Edwards" from *Jonathan Edwards and the American Experience*, edited by Nathan O. Hatch and Harry S. Stout (Oxford University Press, 1998).

Without the support and cooperation of one's family, it would hardly be possible to accomplish scholarly research and publication. I would like to thank my wife, Inn Sook, for her frequent words of encouragement, and my son, Cy Suh Hyong, for his genuine interest in my writing and publishing endeavors.

Sang Hyun Lee
Princeton, New Jersey

Introduction

JUST AS Jonathan Edwards is being studied more than ever before, the availability of his writings for scholars as well as the general public has dramatically increased. The historic publication of *The Works of Jonathan Edwards*, Yale's twenty-seven-volume letterpress edition, is almost complete, and all of his writings, both those already issued in the letterpress edition and those that remain to be issued, will soon be electronically searchable. Scholars continue to add to the already enormous literature on Edwards, as M. X. Lesser's two-volume annotated bibliographies impressively testify. The reading and teaching of Edwards, as well as scholarly discussion of his thought, will probably increase for the foreseeable future.

The present volume is intended to be a source to which interested students, scholars, and others can turn and find a brief and yet instructive and authoritative introduction to the key ideas in Edwards' theology. Edwards' life and writings are multifaceted, and so is the interest in him today. He is studied as a theologian, a philosopher, a leader of the Great Awakening, a Puritan pastor, a literary figure, and certainly as a major influence in American culture and history. It would be agreed widely, however, that Edwards was most fundamentally a theologian. For this reason, the essays in this volume focus on his major theological ideas. It is hoped that scholars not directly working with Edwards' theology will find these essays a helpful and reliable source for his religious ideas. At the same time, it is also hoped that this volume may contribute to a more vigorous discussion of the theological and doctrinal issues in Edwards' thought.

Each of the essays includes at least some solid, though succinct, exposition of Edwards' views on a given theological topic. When there are interpretive debates or disagreements, authors were encouraged to mention them. Each essay, of course, reflects the interpretive point of view of the writer. All of the writers, however, are scholars who have worked on Edwards material for many years and are now recognized as experts. Their interpretive perspectives, therefore, are assumed to be certainly worthy of consideration. Readers could turn to this volume for a quick but reliable exposition of Edwards' views on the Trinity, freedom of the will, or typology or for an introductory orientation on Edwards' views on a particular topic before they do further research. There are also many other uses to which the essays in this volume could be put. It should be noted that in presenting Edwards' key theological ideas, the writers in this volume use three slightly different styles or approaches. The first is a kind of intellectual history in which Edwards' ideas on a given subject are explicated in relation to other aspects of his thought and, as appropriate, to other thinkers of his times. All of the authors, except those of the essentially historical essays at the beginning and end of the collection, employ the intellectual history approach. A few of them, however, add to this basic strategy two others: the history of doctrine approach, in which Edwards' ideas are related to the classic Christian formulations of the faith, such as creeds, and the constructive approach, in which his ideas are considered as a resource for constructive efforts in our own time. Robert Jenson, writing on Edwards' Christology, for example, utilizes both the intellectual history and history of doctrine approaches and also discusses the relevance of Edwards' thought for today's concerns. Allen Guelzo, writing on the freedom of the will, also points out the relevance of Edwards' perspective for today's intellectual context. Mark Noll, writing on Edwards' influence for his posterity, appropriately combines a historical approach with a history of doctrine strategy. Amy Plantinga Pauw, writing on the Trinity, and Sang Hyun Lee, on God's relation to the world and soteriology, utilize both intellectual history and history of doctrine strategies.

We now move on to a brief description of the content of each of the essays in this volume. The first three provide a biographical and chronological context for the others. In "Jonathan Edwards: A Theological Life," Kenneth P. Minkema offers a succinct outline of the major events in Edwards' life, indicating when, and under what circumstances, his major works were written. The essay provides the reader with a brief and reliable account of Edwards' life and career as well as the background against which his theological works can be better understood. Minkema's account of how Edwards' shift of emphasis from justification and sola gratia to Christian practice and sanctification correlates with the ups and downs of the revival movement of the 1730s and 1740s is especially enlightening.

In "Edwards' Intellectual Background," Peter J. Thuesen takes a quick but balanced look at Edwards' rich and wide-ranging reading. Thuesen sees the "competing influences on Edwards as a thinker": on the one hand, the traditional sources (the Bible, Reformed scholastics, and Puritan writers, among others) and on the other, such representatives of the Enlightenment and the new learning as Locke, the Cambridge Platonists, and, of course, the deists and Arminians who were Edwards' lifelong opponents. Throughout his career, Edwards' reading thrust him, according to Thuesen, into "the fertile in-betweenness." But, Thuesen observes, this "conflicted" intellectual heritage "never developed into a simple 'either-or' proposition" for him but was instead utilized in his formulation of his own creative philosophical and theological perspective. Enriching Thuesen's essay is his

INTRODUCTION   xiii

judicious use of Edwards' "Catalogue," a list of some 720 books Edwards had either read or hoped to read.

Before plunging into a discussion of Edwards' major doctrinal focuses, this volume introduces the reader to his most fundamental philosophical concepts in Richard R. Niebuhr's "Being and Consent." After a half-century of studying and teaching Edwards, Niebuhr presents in a tightly constructed paper his observations on Edwards' ideas of being, consent, and plurality and draws some cautious but challenging conclusions about Edwards' overall metaphysical vision. Niebuhr's discussion of Edwards' most basic perspective on the nature of being leads naturally to the theological doctrine of the Trinity.

"The Trinity," by Amy Plantinga Pauw, begins a series of essays on the major elements of Edwards' theology. Pauw begins by noting how for Edwards the Trinity is not an abstract or merely speculative doctrine but rather a living doctrine about God's inner life, the foundation for God's redemptive activity in the world and thus for Christian piety and practice. Pauw then outlines the two analogies that Edwards uses in his articulation of the Trinity: the Augustinian personal and the Vitorine or social. Pauw also explains how both of these models function, sometimes harmoniously and sometimes rather disjunctively, in Edwards' understanding of the triune character of God's redemptive activity in the world. Pauw ends the essay with a discussion of how Edwards' doctrine of God as triune has to be understood as essentially related to his conception of being as self-communicating beauty or excellency.

Traditional western theology conceived of God as affecting the world or what happens in the world but not as being affected in any way by the world. Through this conception, theology tried to assert God's perfection and self-sufficiency (aseity). What is unsatisfactory in this way of thinking is that but a God who is absolutely unaffected by the world would not be consistent with the picture of God in the Old and New Testaments, and it becomes difficult to explain how such an impassible God is capable of activities such as creation and incarnation. "God's Relation to the World," Sang Hyun Lee argues that Jonathan Edwards conceived of God as at once perfect in actuality and self-sufficiency and also disposed to enlarge or repeat his internal fullness outside of himself—that is, in and through the world of time and space. Thus, for Edwards, the world increases God's being and beauty, and thus affects God. What Christians do in the world by God's grace, therefore, matters to God and participates in God's own life in time and space. Temporality and spatiality, concludes Lee, are taken seriously in Edwards' theology.

In "Christology," Robert W. Jenson focuses on the astonishing way in which Edwards regards as one agent the human Jesus who is also Son of God. First, according to Jenson, Edwards' soteriological concerns (atonement and justification) made it inevitable that the one who comes in Christ to justify and sanctify the sinner is none other than God himself. So God the Son is Jesus, the historical human being, and Jesus is the eternal Son of God, the Second Person of the Trinity. Thus, Edwards cross-predicates, as Jenson shows, "doings or characteristics ontologically appropriate to Jesus as a man to God the Son and doing and characteristics ontologically appropriate to God the Son to the man Jesus." For Edwards, there was a "communion of attributes" in Jesus Christ. Finally, Jenson analyzes Edwards' various discussions of the question, "*How* is the man Jesus thus one with the Logos?" Jenson offers his interpretation of Edwards' answer to this question. In this "postmodern" era, Jenson concludes, the church urgently needs Edwards' kind of Christology.

Robert E. Brown, in "The Bible," notes that Edwards not only made frequent references to the Bible in his writings but also wrote on the nature and authority of the Bible and used it as an essential source for constructive theological arguments. When Edwards writes *about* the Bible, Brown points out, Edwards' main concern is to answer the deistic challenges to the veracity of biblical religion. Brown also discusses the question of to what extent Edwards practiced modern historical critical analysis in his biblical interpretation. Brown shows that Edwards involved himself in critical historical analysis (e.g., on the question of whether Moses wrote the Pentateuch) but was typical of theologians of his times in that his primary attempt was to harmonize Scripture with the human knowledge of his day. Brown ends his essay with a call for further study of the various ways in which the biblical content influenced Edwards' constructive thought.

Edwards' understanding of the knowledge of God is taken up in John E. Smith's "Religious Affections and the 'Sense of the Heart.'" Smith stresses the holistic character of Edwards' view of human being and human knowing and demonstrates that, for Edwards, the understanding and the affections, the head and the heart, simply cannot be separated from each other. Smith carefully goes over what Edwards means by "understanding," "inclination," "will," and "affections," and his contrast of "notional" or "speculative knowledge" with "sensible knowledge." But Smith gives the greatest attention to what is perhaps Edwards' most important epistemological idea, "the sense of the heart." Drawing mainly from "Miscellanies," no. 782, *Religious Affections*, and the sermon called *A Divine and Supernatural Light*, Smith analyzes that concept from many different angles. He also does not fail to put Edwards' ideas in their historical contexts as well as in the context of Edwards' overall theological perspective.

Allen C. Guelzo begins his essay, "Freedom of the Will," with a brief discussion of the general philosophical problem of free will and also of the background, especially the challenge of Arminianism in New England, that led Edwards to write his book on the subject. Guelzo then discusses Edwards' central theses as they are elaborated on in the four parts of the *Freedom of the Will*. According to Edwards, if the will determined itself (as the Arminians maintained it did), then the determining cause would have to be determined by another cause, and so on ad infinitum. The will is always as determined as the motive or the "greatest apparent good" is and is "free" in the sense that the person has the liberty to will as he is pleased to will. Edwards is a "compatibilist": liberty and necessity are compatible with each other. In regard to the question of moral responsibility, Edwards' own position, he argued, makes praiseworthiness and blameworthiness possible, while the Arminian position would only lead to the rule of chaotic contingency. Edwards on the will, Guelzo believes, is worthy of being heard again today.

As the title suggests, "Grace and Justification by Faith Alone," by Sang Hyun Lee, treats two topics which are inextricably related but also distinguishable, both of which received special emphasis in the Reformed theological tradition. Lee focuses on Edwards' contention that saving grace is none other than the Holy Spirit himself indwelling in the regenerate "after the manner of" a disposition and points up the difference between this idea and the Roman Catholic (e.g., Thomistic) doctrine of "created grace." For Lee, the Holy Spirit acts in the regenerate according to a "general law" especially established by God. Edwards' idea of saving grace as a newly infused disposition, concludes Lee, must be distinguished from Thomas' idea of "created grace." A question also arises as to whether or not Edwards' doctrine of justification by faith alone is true to the Reformed tradition, for the latter stresses the Pauline doctrine that God's justification is of an entirely unmeritorious sinner while Thomas' view implies that prior to justification there is in the sinner a new qualification for it. Lee argues that Edwards held to a "forensic" doctrine of justification and that the new disposition does not count as a qualification for the imputation of Christ's righteousness to the sinner. Lee admits that Edwards has enlarged the meaning of sanctification but argues that his emphasis on the reality of the change in the regenerate has to be viewed in light of his larger perspective: that God created the world, and also redeems it, in order to repeat his glory in creation.

In "Christian Virtue and Common Morality," John E. Smith offers a quite comprehensive exposition of Edwards' ethical thought as represented in the sermon series *Charity and Its Fruits* and his treatise *On the Nature of True Virtue*. Smith carefully discusses Edwards' subtle handling of the relation between the love of God and "self-love." Edwards' central argument, as Smith points out, is that true virtue is the consent of beings to the Being in general, that is, to God. If this true virtue is the morality of grace, there is also the morality of nature, or the "common morality," such as a sense of duty, gratitude, conscience. Smith carefully discusses the continuity and discontinuity between these two moralities.

In spite of Edwards' long involvement in the pastorate, he never wrote a separate work dealing with ecclesiology. Perhaps this is one reason why Edwards scholars have given relatively little attention to this aspect of his thought. Douglas A. Sweeney's essay "The Church" is the result of his wide-ranging study of the relevant passages in Edwards' works. Edwards, according to Sweeney, had a strong doctrine of the church: the church is the "mystical body of Christ," the gathering of all those who were elected by God to participate in God's own activity of repeating in time and space God's internal glory or fullness. As such, the church has an ultimate significance. This high doctrine of the church is the theological background in light of which, according to Sweeney, Edwards' stand on the qualification for the communion and other ecclesiastical issues can be fully understood.

Typology, most narrowly defined, was a method of biblical interpretation. Old Testament events would be seen as types or prefigurations of those in the New Testament, centrally the event of Christ, and thereby a unity between the two Testaments would be established. Edwards used typology in this sense, but he astonishingly extended typology to the natural realm, beyond Scripture and beyond history. "External things are intended to be images of things spiritual, moral, and divine," declared Edwards. Perry Miller's interpretation, late in the 1940s, of this typologizing of nature, sparked a lively debate that continues to this day, and Janice Knight, in her essay "Typology," quickly reviews this debate and moves on to argue her own position. Knight's thesis is that Edwards' extension of typology to nature must be viewed in the context of Edwards' overall theological perspective, according to which God's inherently self-communicating nature moved him to create the universe. What God is moved by his nature to communicate in the finite realm is his own glory, and God's typological communications of the divine things in history and nature is part of what God is doing in and through his creation. This way of reading Edwards' typology, according to Knight, is consistent with his dynamic conception of God and God's relation to the world.

In his "Letter to the Trustees of the College of New Jersey," in which Edwards explained why he could not accept their invitation to be the College's new president, he mentioned an important writing project he still had to work on, "a body of divinity in an entire new method, being thrown into the *form of an history.*" Ever since Perry Miller wrote about it in his 1948 *Jonathan Edwards*, scholars have debated what Edwards meant by "history" in this letter and what the term meant in Edwards' thought as a whole. John F. Wilson, in his essay "history" takes up the issue and articulates his own interpretation. Wilson discusses why Edwards did not mean by "history" what the concept has come to mean in the modern times. For Edwards, argues Wilson, history is the process in and through which God's project of self-glorification is carried out and thus gains its meaning entirely from outside of itself. Wilson concludes that in Edwards' "Letter to the Trustees," "there was no suggestion that history per se held special meaning." In the last part of the essay, Wilson goes over the interpretations of the issue by various other scholars, including Perry Miller and Peter Gay.

In "Eschatology," Stephen J. Stein discusses Edwards' views of "the last things" in the three main phases of his adult life: his "early years of theological reflection, from the time of his schooling to 1733; the years dominated by his involvement with local revivals and with the Great Awakening in New England, from 1734 to 1748; and the last decade of his life, the period often identified as his most productive. Stein connects Edwards' views on eschatology with his personal and historical circumstances. At the end of the essay, five summary statements are offered.

"The 1200 or so sermons and the attendant sermon notebooks, scripture notebooks, and miscellaneous manuscript writings now collected at Yale Beinecke Library vividly illustrate the day-to-day working life of a great, but not unrepresentative, New England preacher," writes Wilson H. Kimnach in "The Sermons: Concept and Execution." These sermons not only illustrate the day-to-day working life of Edwards the preacher but are also important places to look for Edwards' elaborations on many of his theological ideas. Kimnach first discusses the form of the Puritan sermons which Edwards basically followed: text, doctrine, and application. He then analyzes the various ways in which Edwards combined his sermons when he had to repreach a sermon in a different setting and at a different time. Kimnach also discusses various preachers who influenced Edwards and analyzes some important individual sermons, including *Sinners in the Hand of the Angry God*.

In "Missions and Native Americans," Gerald R. McDermott, shows that Edwards' mission work with the Native Americans between 1751 and 1757 was not just a result of circumstances but rather an activity that had a central importance in his theology. For Edwards, argues McDermott, missions are God's chief means for carrying out his work of redemption in history. Conversion is what starts the redemptive process, and without missions people would not be called to conversion. Therefore, missions are at the center of all that God and believers must do to accomplish the very end for which God created the world. It is not surprising, therefore, that Edwards was actively engaged in the affairs of the missions to Native Americans well before 1751. Edwards was the first to argue that missions was a vocation of all individual Christians. Also, through the widely read *Life of David Brainerd* and other books, concludes McDermott, Edwards played a formative role in the emergence of the modern missionary movement.

Edwards was a Puritan theologian—probably no one would quarrel with this statement. However, it is quite another matter to explain exactly in what sense Edwards the theologian is a Puritan. Harry S. Stout begins his essay "The Puritans and Edwards" with a brief discussion of the recent attention that scholarship has given to the interrelationship between the two, especially Perry Miller's almost unchallenged revisionist interpretation that Edwards had rejected the "federal theology" of the Puritans, which taught that God's covenantal relationship, with its attendant rewards and punishments, existed not only with individuals but also with nations. Stout then does a probing analysis of the occasional and weekday sermons, delivered on days of fasting and thanksgiving, that earlier scholars did not take into account. In these sermons, Stout finds Edwards making references to New England's corporate identity as a special people with a messianic destiny. Edwards, too, Stout concludes, was an heir to "that quintessentially Puritan notion of a righteous city set high upon a hill for all the world to see."

In "Edwards' Theology after Edwards," Mark Noll discusses the influence of Edwards on those who followed him. Noll begins with two of Edwards' own students, Joseph Bellamy and Samuel Hopkins, who modified some of their teacher's major ideas as well as vivified them. The students of Edwards' students—Jonathan Edwards, Jr., Nathanael Emmons, Asa Burton, and others—appropriated Edwards' ideas also for their own purposes. Noll then discusses nineteenth-century thinkers who were influenced by Edward, especially Timothy Dwight and Nathaniel William Taylor, both at Yale, and Lyman Beecher, the revivalist and social reformer. Noll pays particular attention to how Princeton theologians (Archibald Alexander, Charles Hodge, and Lyman Atwater) and those at Yale vied with each other with their own emphases in their interpretation of Edwards. In the final section, Noll describes the resurgence of interest in and studies of Edwards, especially since Perry Miller's 1949 intellectual biography. Noll concludes, "In the breadth of his learning, piety, and intellectual rigor, Edwards is more comprehensively alive today than ever in his own lifetime or since."

Kenneth P. Minkema's "Chronology of Edwards' Life and Writings," which leads off, is a result not only of Minkema's meticulous labors but also of years of research by many scholars, most prominently Thomas A Schafer. No chronology of Edwards' writings such as this has ever been either compiled or printed before. Edwards' major writings, especially the individual items in his "Miscellanies," are dated often down to the month as well as the year. This chronology will be an indispensable tool in placing Edwards' writings in their right relationship with each other and in discerning signs of movement and development in his thought.

INTRODUCTION   xix

No doubt many readers will think of some other topics that should have been included in this volume. Space and other practical considerations prevented the editor from pursuing an even greater comprehensiveness in coverage and confined him to focusing on some of Edwards' key ideas. It should be noted here that in addition to the many monographs and articles on Edwards' thought, the two important resources in Edwards studies are the extensive editors' introductions to all of the volumes of the Yale edition and M. X. Lesser's two-volume annotated bibliographies of all the secondary materials published from 1729 to 1993.

Note on References to the Yale Edition of The Works of Jonathan Edwards

In this volume, all references to Edwards' published writings are to the Yale edition of the works. Parenthetical references consist of volume numbers and page numbers. For example, (9:267) indicates volume 9 of the Yale edition, *The History of the Work of Redemption*, page 267. When a reference to the "Miscellanies" is made, the "Miscellanies" number or entry number is also indicated. For example, ("Misc." 241, 13:358) means "Miscellanies," no. 241 in volume 13 of the Yale edition, page 358. For complete information on the Yale series, see the list on pages 311–12.

Chronology of Edwards' Life and Writings

Compiled by Kenneth P. Minkema

This chronology of Edwards' writings is based on that established by Thomas A. Schafer, Wallace E. Anderson, and Wilson H. Kimnach, supplemented by information in volume introductions in *The Works of Jonathan Edwards*, by primary sources dating from Edwards' lifetime, and by secondary materials such as biographies. Attributed dates for literary productions indicate the earliest or approximate points at which Edwards probably started them. "Miscellanies" entries are listed in numerical groupings by year rather than chronologically; for more exact dating and order, readers should consult relevant volumes in the Yale edition. Entries not preceded by a month indicate that the event in question occurred sometime during the calendar year under which it is listed. Unless otherwise indicated, all verbs refer to Edwards.

1703	October 5: born at East Windsor, Connecticut
1710	January 9: Sarah Pierpont born at New Haven, Connecticut
1712	Awakening at East Windsor; builds prayer booth in swamp
1716	September: begins undergraduate studies at Connecticut Collegiate School, Wethersfield
1718	October: moves to New Haven to continue studies in newly built Yale College, but shortly returns to Wethersfield upon dissatisfaction with tutor Samuel Johnson
1719	June: returns to New Haven after Johnson's removal
	Writes "Of Insects"
1720	May: completes baccalaureate degree
	September: delivers Valedictory Oration; begins graduate studies at New Haven
1721	Summer: conversion experience at East Windsor
	Writes "Of the Rainbow," "Of Light Rays"
	Begins "Natural Philosophy," "Of Atoms," "Of Being," "Prejudices of the Imagination"
1722	May: completes graduate studies
	August: begins preaching to English Presbyterian congregation in New York City
	September: Yale College rector Timothy Cutler and two tutors convert to Church of England
	Begins "Resolutions," "Diary," "Catalogue of Books," and "Miscellanies"

1723	April: New York City pastorate ends, returns to East Windsor
	July–August: prepares Master's *Quaestio*
	September: delivers *Quaestio* at New Haven, receives M.A. degree; begins "The Mind"
	October: writes "Spider Letter," begins "Notes on the Apocalypse"
	November 11: agrees to settle as pastor of Bolton, Connecticut
	Writes "Apostrophe to Sarah Pierpont"
	"Miscellanies," nos. aa–94
1724	January: begins "Notes on Scripture"
	May 21: elected tutor at Yale College, leaves Bolton
	"Miscellanies," nos. 94–146
1725	May: begins "Beauty of the World"
	September-December: illness; convalesces at North Haven and East Windsor
	December: begins "Table to the Miscellanies," "Christ's Example"
	"Miscellanies," nos. 152–95
1726	Early summer: returns to New Haven
	August 29: asked to assist Solomon Stoddard by Northampton church
	"Miscellanies," nos. 196–237, 261–62, 267–74, 313–14
1727	February 15: ordained at Northampton as assistant pastor
	July 28: marries Sarah Pierpont
	"Miscellanies," nos. 238–55, 279–305, 315–17
1728	January: begins "Faith"
	August: begins "Images of Divine Things," "Signs of Godliness"
	"Miscellanies," nos. 256–60, 265–66, 275–78, 306–10, 318–84
1729	February 11: Solomon Stoddard dies; Edwards becomes senior pastor
	April–June: illness
	July: resumes preaching
	"Miscellanies," nos. 385–454
1730	January: begins "Discourse on the Trinity"
	October: first entries in "Blank Bible"
	"Miscellanies," nos. 455–87
1731	January: "Miscellanies" beginning at no. 488
	July 8: preaches Boston lecture, later published as *God Glorified in the Work of Redemption*
1732	"Miscellanies" in late 500s
1733	January: "Miscellanies," no. 612
	June: "Miscellanies," no. 625
1734	August: preaches *A Divine and Supernatural Light*, thereafter published
	November: "Miscellanies," no. 668
	December: Connecticut Valley revivals begin

1735	June 1: Joseph Hawley, Sr., commits suicide by slitting his throat; Connecticut Valley revival ends
1736	August: "Miscellanies," no. 698
	September 16–27: new meetinghouse raised
	November 6: completes short account of late revivals published as appendix to William Williams' *Duty and Interest of a People*
1737	March 13: Northampton meetinghouse gallery falls
	December 25: new meetinghouse dedicated
	Publishes *A Letter to the Author of the Pamphlet Called An Answer to the Hampshire Narrative* (coauthored with brother-in-law Samuel Hopkins of Springfield)
	A Faithful Narrative of the Surprising Work of God published in London
1738	April–October: preaches *Charity and Its Fruits* (published 1852)
	October: "Miscellanies," no. 756
	Publishes *Discourses on Various Important Subjects*
	Corrected edition of *Faithful Narrative* published in Boston
1739	February: "Miscellanies," no. 788
	March–August: preaches *History of the Work of Redemption* (published 1774)
	July 22: Abigail Bridgman excommunicated for drunkenness
	August: "Miscellanies," no. 807
	Winter: "Miscellanies," no. 832
1740	January: "Miscellanies," no. 841
	August: "Miscellanies," no. 847
	October 17–19: George Whitefield preaches in Northampton
	November: "Miscellanies," nos. 859–60
	December: writes "Personal Narrative"
1741	May: "Miscellanies," no. 862
	July 8: preaches *Sinners in the Hands of an Angry God* at Enfield, published shortly thereafter
	August–September: awakening peaks in Northampton
	August 24: Hannah Pomeroy excommunicated
	August–September: "Miscellanies," no. 874
	September 2: preaches funeral sermon for William Williams of Hatfield, published as *The Resort and Remedy of Those That Are Bereaved by the Death of an Eminent Minister*
	September: delivers *Distinguishing Marks of the Work of the Spirit of God* at Yale commencement, published shortly thereafter
	December–late March: "Miscellanies," no. 903
1742	January 19–February 4: Sarah Edwards experiences series of religious ecstasies; afterward undergoes treatment for "hysterical original" (uterine disorder)

	January 27: supply preacher Samuel Buel arrives at Northampton and renews awakening until after Edwards returns home from preaching journey in eastern Massachusetts
	March 16: covenant renewal at Northampton
	June: "Miscellanies," no. 991
	Fall–winter: writes *Some Thoughts Concerning the Present Revival of Religion in New England*
	Begins sermon series (apparently ending in 1743) eventually published as *Treatise Concerning Religious Affections*
1743	March: *Some Thoughts* published; Edwards leads council of ministers in New London to "reclaim" people affected by James Davenport
	June 8: preaches ordination sermon for Jonathan Judd in Southampton, published as *The Great Concern of a Watchman for Souls*
	June 12: Samuel Danks excommunicated for fornication
1744	March: "Bad Book" hearings begin
	June 3: "Bad Book" culprits Oliver Warner and Timothy and Simeon Root make public confession before church
	August 30: preaches ordination sermon for Robert Abercrombie at Pelham, published as *The True Excellency of a Minister of the Gospel*
	"Miscellanies," nos. 1067–69
1745	March: Cape Breton expedition
	June 17: Louisburg taken after forty-seven day siege
	Publishes *Copies of Two Letters Cited by The Reverend Mr. Clap* and *An Expostulary Letter from the Reverend Mr. Edwards*
1746	August 19: French and Indians take Fort Massachusetts; Edwards parsonage "forted in" and quartered with soldiers
	September 19: preaches ordination sermon of Samuel Buel at East Hampton, Long Island, published as *The Church's Marriage to Her Sons, and to Her God*
	Publishes *Treatise Concerning Religious Affections*
1747	May 28: David Brainerd arrives in Northampton
	June 9–25: Brainerd and daughter Jerusha journey to Boston
	October 9: Brainerd dies at Edwards parsonage
	October 12: preaches Brainerd's funeral sermon, published as *True Saints, When Absent From the Body, Are Present With the Lord*
	October: *An Humble Attempt to Promote Explicit Agreement and Visible Union of God's People in Extraordinary Prayer* published
	Autumn: begins work on Brainerd's *Life*

1748	February 14: daughter Jerusha dies
	June 26: preaches funeral sermon of John Stoddard at Northampton, published as *A Strong Rod Broken and Withered*
	August: Elisha Hawley excommunicated for fornication
	Summer: "Miscellanies," no. 1101
	December: completes *An Account of the Life of the Late Reverend Mr. David Brainerd*
1749	June 28: preaches ordination sermon of Job Strong at Portsmouth, New Hampshire, published as *Christ the Great Example of Gospel Ministers*
	August: *An Humble Inquiry into the Rules of the Word of God* published
	December 26: preliminary council meets to consider controversy between Edwards and Northampton church
	Winter: "Miscellanies," no. 1118
1750	February 7–8: second council meets to consider controversy between Edwards and Northampton church
	June 19: final council meets to consider controversy between Edwards and Northampton church
	June 22: dismissed as pastor of Northampton
	July 2: preaches *Farewell Sermon* (published 1751)
	September: Joseph Bellamy's *True Religion Delineated* published, with preface by Edwards
	October: preaches in Stockbridge
1751	January–March: preaches in Stockbridge
	February 22: called to settle as minister of Stockbridge
	March: "Miscellanies," no. 1180
	May 16: council convened in Northampton to advise on forming a second church, with Edwards as pastor
	August 8: formally installed as pastor to English and Indian congregations at Stockbridge
1752	Summer: *Misrepresentations Corrected, and Truth Vindicated* published
	August: "Miscellanies," no. 1200
	September 28: at Newark, New Jersey, preaches *True Grace, Distinguished From the Experience of Devils* to Synod of New York and New Jersey (published 1753)
1753	April: completes first draft of *Freedom of the Will*
	"Miscellanies" beginning with no. 1227
1754	February: given sole charge (by chief donor, Isaac Hollis) of Indian schools at Stockbridge

March: Frustrated by abuses from Edwards' predecessors, nearly all the remaining Indians leave Stockbridge; "Miscellanies," no. 1277b

July: beginning of long period of ill health, lasting about a year, including "fits," "agues," and "scorbutic maladies"

Summer: Edwards parsonage fortified and quartered with soldiers for fear of Indian attacks

December: *Freedom of the Will* published

1755 February: completes *End for Which God Created the World*, reads it to Bellamy and Hopkins; *The Nature of True Virtue* probably completed thereafter (published 1765)

June: Crown Point expedition

August 28: fast after Braddock's defeat at Monongahela River

September 8: English victory at battle of Lake St. Sacrament

September 9: Battle of Lake George

1756 "Miscellanies" beginning with no. 1281

1757 May: completes *Original Sin*

September 24: son-in-law Rev. Aaron Burr, President of College of New Jersey, dies

September 29: trustees of College of New Jersey write to offer presidency

"Miscellanies" beginning with no. 1358

1758 January 4: council convened at Stockbridge releases Edwards from Stockbridge post

February 16: assumes office as president of College of New Jersey

February 23: inoculated against smallpox

March 22: dies of complications from inoculation

October 2: Sarah Pierpont Edwards dies of dysentery in Philadelphia

Original Sin published

One

Jonathan Edwards: A Theological Life

Kenneth P. Minkema

New England and the Young Edwards

The world into which Jonathan Edwards was born, on Oct. 5, 1703, was one steeped in theological history and controversy. His family had been part of the Puritan migration from England to escape religious persecution and to establish a "Bible Commonwealth" that would fulfill the promise of the Reformation. The son and grandson of pastors, and related to some of the most influential church leaders of New England—Mathers, Hookers, and Stoddards—Edwards inherited the Calvinist orthodoxy of New England, its grandeur and its tensions. Within this orthodoxy, nation, province, town, church, and individual were joined in a network of interlocking covenants and obligations that bound the fabric of society. Theology served to justify God's ways to humankind, to prescribe proper channels for human inquiry and redemption, and to define the nature of human interaction. Even more, nature was imbued with religious meaning. Seemingly mundane natural phenomena and human events were seen as "illustrative providences" that contained supernatural messages of reward, punishment, and warning.

Chief among this society for interpreting God's word and the meaning of events was the clergy, and this was the class into which Edwards was born. Timothy Edwards, Jonathan's father, had been the pastor of East Windsor for more than sixty years by the time he died, only a couple of months before his only son. Under the direction of his father, mother, and sisters, Jonathan acquired the necessary knowledge for a young gentleman bound for college and the ministry. Reason and learning went hand in hand with the heart and "affections." He sat under his father's preaching week after week, witnessing his father's trials with his congregation as well as his triumphs. The most happy times of all were "awakenings," times when the Spirit of God moved among the church to convict and convert a number of souls. Also famous for the "stirs" in his church was Edwards' grandfather, Solomon Stoddard, of Northampton, Massachusetts. During his pastorate, no less than five "harvests" occurred, making Stoddard one of the most respected ministers in New England, and possibly the most powerful outside of Boston. Timothy was also renowned in Connecticut as a revivalist. It was during one of these "seasons" in his father's church, when Jonathan was about ten years old, that he built a "prayer booth" in the swamp behind his house. Edwards' earliest extant letter dates from a few years later; fittingly, the letter is an awakening report, a genre he would make his own.

But theology cannot remain static. Forces from within and outside of New England forced the theology of the founding Puritans to change dramatically. The revocation of the Massachusetts Bay charter at the end of the seventeenth century ended the practice of limiting the franchise and office-holding to full church members, effectively unseating the Puritan theocracy. Such political changes had deep religious implications. For a quarter-century or more, the nature of the New England Way was under stress, because—despite innovations such as revival preaching—fewer and fewer of the descendants of the founders were joining the churches. As a result, the Congregationalists were slowly losing their monopoly on religious and political culture. Measures to ease membership requirements, such as the Half-Way Covenant of 1662, entailed a reexamination not just of ecclesiastical practices but also of how conversion occurred and how the very nature of covenant itself was defined.

The tensions between church and society were played out in Edwards' closest role models, his father and his grandfather. Although both defended the prerogatives of the ministry, Timothy did so (albeit not without complaining) within the context of the autonomous local congregation, while Stoddard sought a Presbyterian-like hierarchy that could coerce conformity and obedience from above. And while both were famed revivalists, each had different notions of conversion and admission to the church: Timothy put less emphasis on the order and nature of the steps to conversion—the traditional "morphology" that Puritan theologians had outlined—but was strict about admitting people into covenant, requiring a lengthy conversion narrative by applicants and careful scrutiny by minister and congregation. Stoddard, on the other hand, abided strictly by the steps to salvation but slackened the obstacles to membership, even arguing that the Lord's Supper was a converting ordinance, a means of grace.

The young Edwards himself reflected these tensions and shifts. He tells us in his *Personal Narrative* that as a boy he questioned the central doctrines of his Calvinist heritage. In particular, he resented the doctrines of God's sovereignty (that everything was absolutely dependent on divine will for continuance) and God's eternal decrees (that everything divinely preordained must come to pass). Also, in his diary he noted that the stages of his spiritual life did not match what the "old divines," including his grandfather, taught. He pledged to solve the discrepancy through study and self-examination. The task of understanding the human heart—including his own—would take him a lifetime.

Larger shifts in Puritan thought and society, felt so palpably on the personal level by individuals such as Edwards, were related as well to new modes of thought making their way across the Atlantic. In the wake of the divisive and violent reign of the Puritans in England, the cultural and intellectual climate favored tolerance, reason, and latitude. Inexorably, and despite the efforts of the most talented of New Englanders, such as Increase and Cotton Mather, colonial religion and society grudgingly deferred to the dictates of the mother country.

College Years and Early Preaching

Growing diversity of opinion on theological topics—from the nature of God and the Trinity to the terms of salvation to the nature of the church—reflected this new climate and were on the rise as Edwards matriculated at the Wethersfield branch of the fledgling Connecticut Collegiate School in 1716. When the students were able to take up residence in the new Yale College building on the New Haven green three years later, so attuned was Edwards to the potentially corrupt influences of heterodoxy that, upon meeting tutor Samuel Johnson (later an Anglican missionary), he promptly returned to Wethersfield. Only after Johnson was dismissed did Edwards go back to New Haven.

Everything from physics to psychology was undergoing reappraisal too. The discoveries of Locke, Newton, and Berkeley presented a new world and a new order to Edwards' fertile mind. Here, however, were ideas that could be accommodated to Protestant orthodox thought, and Edwards energetically set about doing so. Newton's universal laws confirmed to Edwards the wisdom and benevolence of the Creator; Locke's psychology, how God communicated to "perceiving being"; and Berkeley's philosophy, the immanence of God in all reality.

Edwards finished his undergraduate work in 1720 and then returned for graduate studies. This was an especially fruitful time for him, both intellectually and spiritually. Reading voraciously in the college library, he wrote copiously and innovatively on cosmology, being, natural philosophy, light, optics, atoms, and the nature of the mind. He outlined a treatise on a history of the mental world and compiled a stupendous list of subjects on which to write—from the world as "one vast spheroid" to gravity to comets. He commented on Locke's theories, selectively adapting his epistemology but questioning him on other issues, such as the nature of identity and of the will. During this period Edwards developed the concept that all reality is an idea in the mind of God, even that "space is

God," and that spirit, rather than matter, is true substance. This idealism—the notion that God upholds reality from moment to moment—became a signature feature of his thought. Eventually, out of this idealism would arise an aesthetic perception of the "excellency," or beauty, of God and holy living.

If his idealism was an answer to philosophical currents flowing from Europe, it was also an indication that he was embracing divine sovereignty and Calvinist notions of God and humankind. In the summer of 1721, he experienced what he called, using Lockean terminology, a "new sense" of God's glory while reading certain passages of Scripture. He thirsted for more. Then, while home during a break from studies, he had what he later described as a pivotal religious experience. After talking with his father about his "discoveries," Edwards walked abroad in the pasture, and, looking around and at the sky, he perceived the simultaneous, paradoxical "majestic meekness" and "awful sweetness" of God.

This experience at once changed his focus and prepared him for ministry. In the summer of 1722, he went to preach to a small group of English Presbyterians in New York City for a period of about eight months. Here he began his "Miscellanies," his private notebooks, with meditations on "holiness" that were keenly personal in nature. Indeed, much of his preaching to this intimate band of Christians reflected the personal contours of his budding spirituality, encouraged by the familylike atmosphere that the group provided. It was with sorrow that he had to leave, but other duties called.

East Windsor, New Haven, and Northampton

His New York City sojourn over, Edwards returned to East Windsor in April 1723. After some travel, he settled down to compose his Master's *Quaestio*, the final requirement for his graduate degree. Through the summer he worked on it and, at the great day in September, delivered it in New Haven before the assembled college community and colony dignitaries. Here, for the first time in public, he took on the forces of heterodoxy. He defended the proposition that sinners are saved through faith in the sacrifice of Christ alone. This was a standard enough Reformed tenet, but in the context in which it was delivered, Edwards' words were fraught with meaning.

When Edwards had finished his undergraduate work, he had been chosen to give the valedictory address. In his oration, he had praised in flowery terms the rector Timothy Cutler, the tutors, and the trustees. He, and many in the audience, would come to regret the trust and praise they had lavished on the college's leader. For at commencement exercises in 1722,

Cutler, the tutors, and several area ministers revealed their conversion to the Church of England. Thus, when Edwards and his fellow graduates mounted the platform a year later, everyone paid close attention to them in order to detect any lingering heterodoxy. Edwards' defense of justification by faith alone and his criticism of any who would make a "new law" did not disappoint. From this beginning, he faced the challenge presented by new theological opinions coming from abroad and from within New England.

While Jonathan had his eyes on a brave new world, his father was intent on bringing him back home, or as near to it as possible. Timothy had been in contact with the newly formed church at Bolton, Connecticut, not far from East Windsor, to interest them in his promising son. Through 1723, he apparently continued to cultivate the relationship, because by November Jonathan had signed on as pastor. Before going there, however, he had some free time, which he used for writing. Besides beginning a commentary on the Book of Revelation, he revisited earlier notes on insects and wrote them up in October as a letter to Massachusetts judge Paul Dudley, a member of the Royal Society. Timothy Edwards was a friend and correspondent of Dudley, who had communicated some of Timothy's botanical observations to London for publication in the Society's famous *Transactions*. At his father's urging, Jonathan addressed his "Spider Letter" to Dudley in the hopes that the good judge would deem that worthy of publication as well. He did not. However, Edwards would later on make famous rhetorical use of spiders in his sermons.

Bolton was able to keep Edwards only until the spring of 1724, when Yale again beckoned, this time with an offer to serve as a tutor. As Edwards noted in his "Diary," this began a spiritual slump, caused by the endless concerns and diversions of his post, that lasted for about three years. But if the life of the spirit did not fare well, the life of the mind thrived. With the college library to rummage and academic classes to teach, Edwards built on his reading and study. Always physically frail, however, he succumbed in late 1725 to exhaustion and spent three months recovering under his mother's care. As soon as he was able, he was back at his studies, adding to the "Miscellanies" and beginning other notebooks.

Then, in August 1726, he was asked to assist his grandfather, the venerable Stoddard, at the prestigious church in Northampton. From here on, milestones came fast. In February he was ordained and in July married Sarah Pierpont of New Haven, whom he had met as a student. Now a pastor, Edwards' attentions shifted from the meditative and abstract to the practical. He now had to deliver sermons at an increasing rate, including the full round of regular sermons (two each sabbath) as well as occasional sermons for sacraments, fast days, and political and military events. Also, his private writings shifted to more pastoral topics, such as faith and signs of godliness. He even started to scrutinize his grandfather's views on the church, sainthood, conversion, and the sacraments with increasing dissatisfaction, committing these reservations to the "Miscellanies" and to other notes.

While learning the exigencies of the parish round, Edwards also kept his vision on the wider world and the "fashionable schemes of divinity" that were everywhere gaining strength. By 1731, he was ready to enter the larger fray. Invited to preach a lecture in Boston in August of that year, Edwards delivered *God Glorified in the Work of Redemption*, his first published work. Here, in the spirit of his Master's disquisition, he skewered any positions that sought to establish a different relation between God and humanity beside that outlined in the Bible (as he interpreted it). God was sovereign in his disposal of everything, especially the plan of redemption, which was God's greatest work, the be-all and end-all of creation itself. Humanity, meanwhile, was absolutely dependent on God for everything, even, as Edwards had privately formulated, for existence from moment to moment. Nothing human beings did could merit favor, much less salvation. Sinners, he could now assert with a certainty based on personal experience, were utterly reliant on the sovereignty and decrees of God. Furthermore, it was to God's glory that this relationship of sovereignty and dependency, of depravity and redemption, was established.

Pastor of a large, prominent church, and with his theological stance firmly in place, Edwards now looked to take his doctrines and preaching a step further. He sought to emulate his father and grandfather by sparking a revival. It would not take long.

The Connecticut Valley Revivals, 1734–1735

In August 1733, Edwards preached a sermon in Northampton that would be published the following year as *A Divine and Supernatural Light*. His second printed writing, *A Divine Light* set forth the scripturality and rationality of God's indwelling presence in the hearts of believers. This inner light renovated the entire psychic constitution, or "affections," of the individual. Asserting doctrines like these, Edwards saw a "softening" among his congregation, especially young people, toward the end of 1733.

What seemed to have a special effect on his congregation—at least according to Edwards—was a lecture on justification in which he reached back to his Master's *Quaestio* to construct a detailed defense and analysis of the doctrine of *sola gratia*. That Edwards should preach in 1734 on this doctrine was polemical as well as hortatory, for in this year the threat of foreign ideological invasion in the form of Arminianism had, to Edwards' way of thinking, become a reality right in Hampshire County. William Rand of Sunderland was preaching an Arminian take on works and salvation, and Robert Breck, who also was rumored to be infected by this humanistic theology, was seeking ordination in Springfield. While neither *Justification by Faith Alone* nor the Hampshire Association's campaign succeeded in thwarting Breck's ordination, it had the desired emotional effect. By mid-1734, Edwards was overseeing a blossoming revival, the first major one in Northampton since Stoddard's heyday.

Edwards encapsulated the Connecticut Valley awakenings that were sparked by the justification discourse in *A Faithful Narrative of a Surprising Work of God*, which went through several iterations, each one longer than the previous. This account, which was eventually translated into several languages, became a manual for revivalists in the Anglo-American world and beyond. It also catapulted Edwards into the international limelight as a leading evangelical, as a scientist of revivalism, and as an expert on conversion psychology. Throughout the rest of his career, revivalists seeking to make a name for themselves would emulate Edwards' *Faithful Narrative*—right down to the title—and he would be consulted on a number of awakening-related issues.

After an all-too-brief period of piety, blissful social accord, and rapturous church singing—even the men sang in three-part harmony—the revivals came to an abrupt halt. First, a man named Thomas Stebbins, who was apparently mentally unstable, tried to slit his throat. Then, in June 1735, Edwards' uncle Joseph Hawley, in a fit of melancholy over his eternal state, followed Stebbins' lead but, tragically, was successful in taking his life. Edwards' emphatic plea for conversion just a few months before in *Pressing into the Kingdom*, " 'tis NOW, at this day; NOW is the accepted time, even while it is called today!" had become the devil-inspired parody, "Cut your own throat, now is good opportunity: *now*, NOW!" Edwards is often unjustly portrayed as driving Hawley to suicide. Hawley apparently suffered from chronic depression, and for his part, Edwards was deeply affected by his uncle's desperate act, so much so that from that time forward he set melancholy aside as a special category in his writings on the conversion process.

Edwards' response to Hawley's death, as well as more generally to the "backsliding" of his congregation into their pre-revival viciousness and impiety, prompted him to rethink his approach. Certainly the cooling affections of the hundreds he had let into full membership played a part in this reappraisal too. Added to this was the ridicule Edwards was facing both at home and in neighboring towns. Edwards, quite frankly, came to realize that his inexperience and his people's enthusiasm had misled both him and them. *A Faithful Narrative* was still hugely popular, which pleased its author. But it had also become an embarrassment to Edwards, who feared comparison of the real Northampton with the one he had created in the minds of readers. In the months and years following the Connecticut Valley stir, he preached and wrote in a remedial vein, seeking to restore balance to his views on the true marks of conversion, in effect to qualify *A Divine and Supernatural Light* by reinstating other important dimensions of religious experience. In sermons, in notebooks such as the "Miscellanies" and "Signs of Godliness," and in memoranda such as "Directions for Judging of Persons' Experiences," he moved away from an emphasis on the affections alone and toward an emphasis on perseverance and enduring Christian behavior. Sanctification was now to become as important for Edwards as justification had been earlier.

Through the late 1730s, Edwards alternately browbeat his congregation, comparing their present "dullness" to their engagedness during the awakening, and pursued the doctrine of true Christian practice in some of the most ambitious and extended sermons and discourses of his career. In late 1737 and early 1738, he delivered a nineteen-sermon series on Matthew 25, the parable of the wise and foolish virgins. Here he pointed up the similarities and differences between true and false saints, and how many in Northampton were evangelical hypocrites with empty lamps. To demonstrate the content of Christian living here on earth and in its final state in heaven, he spent the rest of 1738 preaching a series on 1 Corinthians in twenty-one installments, later published as *Charity and Its Fruits*. Not content with this, beginning in early 1739 he spent no less than thirty preaching occasions laying out the cosmic narrative of salvation, sermons later collected as *A History of the Work of Redemption*. Here he sketched the histories of heaven, hell, and earth, and God's unfailing covenantal arrangement with the church through all time, culminating in the establishment of the church's period of peace during the millennium.

The Great Awakening

One of the central features of *A History of the Work of Redemption* was the argument that human history was propelled by periodic revivals. If Edwards had been handed a hard lesson after the high times of 1734 and 1735, his faith in the necessity and efficacy of revival was not shaken, and he anticipated the day when the next awakening, possibly the prelude to the millennium, would come. He had good reason to believe it was not far off. Already in late 1739 he had heard of the efforts of the English itinerant George Whitefield and of the Wesley brothers and relayed news of awakenings abroad. In his sermons and through his correspondence, Edwards sought to rekindle the flames of revival locally and to learn of similar events from across the globe. In early 1740 he preached a lengthy series on Hebrews 12 that extended the millennialistic tone established in the *History of Redemption* discourse by portraying the company of true Christians coming to Mount Zion, the heavenly Jerusalem. Reaching out to the young people, who had spearheaded the Connecticut Valley movement, Edwards exhorted them to live pious lives and to avoid the temptations offered by competing secular sites such as the tavern and nightly "frolics." Meanwhile, he sent letters to individuals highly placed in the transatlantic evangelical network, through which he collected news and became a regular correspondent with religious leaders in the colonies and in England and Scotland.

Whitefield himself became one of Edwards' correspondents and acquaintances. When Edwards invited the Grand Itinerant to preach in Northampton on his journey through New England, Whitefield accepted. In October 1740, he preached to packed, weeping auditories who were carried away by his dramatic style. And then he departed, leaving the settled pastor to pick up the pieces. As in the aftermath of the previous awakening, Edwards turned to a parable. This time he picked the parable of the sower in Matthew 13, warning listeners who had been impressed by Whitefield's eloquence that sudden conversions, like seeds planted on hard or thorny ground, can flourish temporarily but then die quickly. In the sermon *Sinners in Zion*, which picked up on the Hebrews sermon from earlier in the year, Edwards, seeking to direct the secure and the newly awakened, severely excoriated his congregation, declaring, "*You* are the sinners in Zion!" In another, more famous sermon on sinners, *Sinners in the Hands of an Angry God*, Edwards set forth a world in which humankind have nothing to rely on, nothing in their own power to keep them from a dismal fate, but the power of God. To make his point clear, he depicted sinners held over the pit of hell by God much as one would hold a "loathsome" spider.

Clearly, Edwards was trying to channel the energy of the awakening in ways he had not before. He knew he ran the risk of a less intense, less prolonged stir, but the experience of the earlier revival had taught him that it was more important to insure the experiences of the few who were true subjects of the new birth than to multiply communicants inadvisedly. But despite Edwards' caveats, conversions, "high transports," and other intense religious experiences continued among the congregation through 1741, and he was encouraged, so much so that his hope for the millennium grew to its greatest height. On fast days in 1741 he called on his congregation to pray for millennial glory and described "seasons of ingathering" as sure signs of its prelude. "Miscellanies" entries from this period are peppered with chiliastic information and speculations. In *Some Thoughts Concerning the Revivals*, written in 1742, Edwards for the first and only time publicly dared to hope that the millennium would begin in New England. And, through his network of correspondents, he would become involved in the Concert of Prayer, quarterly days of supplication for the ushering in of the "glorious times," in support of which he would publish his *Humble Attempt to Promote Explicit Prayer*.

Still, Edwards was ever on the alert to stand against new forms of religious thought and practice. For all of his idealistic hopes for the "great and general awakening" of the 1740s, he was a cautious observer. When engaging the colonial leadership, he had to be, for the ministry and magistracy had split over whether the revivals were an authentic work of the Spirit, or the product of human imagination, or, worse, a delusion of the Devil. As a politician of revival, if we may call him that, Edwards came out against many of the things to which antirevivalist Old Lights objected, including Separatism, claims to revelation, lay preaching, and female exhorters. We know, too, that he opposed some of Whitefield's central teachings, such as spiritual "impulses" and assurance of salvation. Furthermore, Edwards' 1741 Yale commencement lecture, *Distinguishing Marks of a Work of the Spirit of God*, delineating true and false signs of grace, was meant to placate the college faculty upset by student separatism and censoriousness. Here, in *Some Thoughts*, and in *Religious Affections*, Edwards was standing in judgment of the conversion phenomena his times had witnessed.

But in these major revival treatises and elsewhere, Edwards' careful analysis and his moderate position served another end. He was advocating that, ultimately, though intermingled with corruptions, the revivals were the real thing. By providing models of piety, first in the persons of Abigail Hutchinson and Phoebe Bartlett in *Faithful Narrative*, then Sarah Pierpont Edwards in *Some Thoughts*, and then David Brainerd in his *Life*, as well as by scrupulously separating false and true signs of grace, Edwards empowered clergy and laity alike to examine their experiences and to model their behavior accordingly. Significantly, the lesson learned back in 1734–35 had stuck. The twelfth, final, and most developed positive sign of true grace in *Religious Affections* famously states that "Gracious and holy affections have their exercise and fruit in Christian practice."

Qualifications

Through the 1740s, continuing his campaign against heterodoxy, Edwards worked on a number of fronts toward a defense of Christianity and the Bible against critiques by Deists and others. One of the goals of the *History of the Work of Redemption* was to show, through prophecies, the verity of Christian revealed religion. Edwards had been stockpiling observations along these lines in scriptural commentaries, such as his "Notes on Scripture" and "Interleaved Bible," and in the "Miscellanies," under rubrics such as "Christian Religion." But in the 1740s he produced lengthy compositions on the prophetic tradition that demonstrated the necessity of revelation and the accuracy of the Bible. One ambitious project, "The Harmony of the Old and New Testaments," was to show, through comparison, the similarity of spirit, genius, and teachings between the two revelations. Elsewhere, he took on the messianic prophetic tradition in three massive entries in the "Miscellanies." Nos. 1067 and 1068 assembled "Prophecies of the Messiah" in the Old Testament and showed their fulfillment in the New, while 1069 dealt with biblical types of the Messiah. In "Traditions of the Heathen," a series of entries compiled through the decade, Edwards defended Christian faith and doctrines by pointing to similar teachings in ancient pagan writers, evidence he amassed from a number of sources. For Edwards, these similarities argued a common revelation to humankind in the distant past that had become corrupted with "human additions" through time but that had been kept alive in Judaism and restored with the coming of Christ.

Edwards was able to accomplish all of this writing during a relative lull following the subsidence of the revival. He was even able to begin work on a long-projected study on freedom of the will, aimed against Arminians. But then, starting in late 1748, he and his church were taken up with a prolonged dispute over the qualifications for admission to the church. Even before coming to Northampton, Edwards had been uncomfortable about Stoddard's views of the church and his procedure for admitting communicants, but for the sake of peace he had kept his qualms to himself. The revivals only heightened his uneasiness about who could get into covenant. After an extensive search of Scripture, he came to the conclusion that requirements had to be stricter.

The noncommittal form developed by Stoddard—and used by Edwards for more than two decades—no longer satisfied Edwards' conviction that a profession had to be an expression of a sincere belief in the workings of grace and a desire to live a Christian life. His aim was to establish a purer church that was, as much as possible, the domain of real saints and that kept out hypocrites. His early writings, especially his "Miscellanies," showed a tension between the notions of a "visible" versus an "invisible" church and a concern for how to achieve a proper balance of real saints and a "mixed multitude." Furthermore, the awakenings had shown him the dangers that fanaticism, censoriousness, schisms, and claims to higher revelations posed to the churches. Ironically, Edwards found that his "new" views on qualifications were most popular among Separatists and "Strict Congregationalists." This unanticipated sympathy—which Edwards' opponents used to bolster their accusations of heresy—may help explain why he so consistently criticized Separatists, antinomians, and other "enthusiasts" in regular sermons, ordination sermons, and published treatises. Ironically, Edwards came to be identified with the very religious extremism that he had opposed since his college years.

Whatever ecclesiastical questions Edwards was trying to resolve, for many in his congregation he had gone too far. His views threatened their status as church members and the baptismal qualifications of their children. On top of other differences that had arisen during the 1740s—for example, over his salary, the necessity of renewing the church covenant, and the notorious "Bad Book" affair, in which young men ridiculed young women with knowledge obtained from midwives' manuals—Edwards' effort to change church admission policies was the last straw. After a bitter and protracted dispute, Edwards was dismissed on June 22, 1750. A week later he delivered his famous *Farewell Sermon* that anticipated the day when he and his former congregation would have to meet before the judgment seat of God to give account of themselves. However, dismissal did not spell the end of Edwards' involvement in the debate over church membership. The controversy would engage him for the next couple of years, as he answered an extended criticism of his *Humble Inquiry* with a polemical riposte, *Misrepresentations Corrected, and Truth Vindicated*. But by that time, he was in a very different position.

Stockbridge

The Indian mission at Stockbridge had been founded back in the 1730s. Northampton leaders, such as Colonel John Stoddard, had been instrumental in establishing it, and Edwards too had participated. Edwards himself had shown keen interest in spreading the gospel to the Indians—and in "civilizing" them into English allies. His efforts to raise funds for the mission from his congregants, his nurturing of missionaries-to-be, such as Elihu Spencer and Gideon Hawley, and, most importantly, his publication of *The Life of David Brainerd*, which presented to the world the selfless model of a missionary martyr, are ample proof. After being deprived of the Northampton pulpit, Edwards trolled for a new pastorate, preaching in small towns in the Berkshires and receiving invitations to take churches in Virginia and even Scotland.

But he had his eye on the Stockbridge post. The first missionary, John Sargeant, had died in 1749, leaving a congregation of over two hundred Mahicans and a small group of English settlers (about twelve families).

Through 1749, Edwards wrote to Boston church leaders about the necessity for a successor, in effect setting himself up for consideration once the dismissal that he was almost sure would come had occurred. Through late 1750 and early 1751, Edwards commuted back and forth between Stockbridge and Northampton, preaching to the Indians and English. He was finally installed in the summer of 1751 and set to work.

He had no lack of things to do. Stockbridge was no sylvan retreat where he could finally sit back and compose the theological treatises he had envisioned for years. Although he managed to produce some of the most significant of his works during this period, he did so while dealing with a broad range of complex and divisive issues and individuals. One problem was stopping the English from exploiting the Indians by taking their lands and disenfranchising them in town meetings. Related to this was the challenge of keeping the Indians at the mission in the face of the abuse and neglect they suffered. Another challenge was wresting control of the Indian boys' and girls' schools from the hands of his own relatives, who were personally benefiting from the funds meant to support the schools and from labor provided by the students who were supposed to be attending them. Also, disapproving members of the oversight boards tried at every turn to have Edwards removed. And still another concern was the threat of attack by the French and their Indian allies, particularly with the beginning of the Seven Years' War in 1754. At one point, Edwards' own house was "forted in" and quartered by militia because of the fear of enemy attacks.

Somehow, Edwards persevered through all of these trials. He obtained sole charge of the mission from its chief benefactor in England. But the cost of his personal victory was great for the mission. By 1754, many of the Indians had left, the schools were almost nonexistent, and Edwards had succeeded in making a great number of enemies.

With all of these distractions and responsibilities, it is all the more remarkable that Edwards was nonetheless able, during a space of about five years, to write some of the most important theological and ethical disquisitions in the history of American thought, not to mention Christian thought as a whole. He had been compiling notes and drafting pieces of *Freedom of the Will* off and on since the late 1720s, which helped him, when he finally was able to write, produce a draft of it in just three months. By early 1755, he had also written at least one of the two dissertations that form the basis of his ethical thought: *The End for Which God Created the World*, which he read to his colleagues Samuel Hopkins and Joseph Bellamy, and *The Nature of True Virtue*. These pieces were composed during a year-long illness including "fits" and "agues" that left Edwards weakened and even thinner than normal. Nonetheless, by early 1757 he had completed yet another treatise, *Original Sin*, which would not be published till after he was dead. *Original Sin* had its inception in 1748, when Edwards received John Taylor's treatise on the subject from his Scottish correspondent John Erskine. Taylor continued to concern Edwards, who in his *Farewell Sermon* warned the people of Northampton not to fall prey to Taylor's comfortable assertions about human nature. Here, Edwards forged a synthesis of opposing schools of thought on the doctrine of imputation, introducing his views on identity and his idealistic conception of continuous creation to describe the "constitutional" unity of humankind with its progenitor, Adam.

These writings, not to mention the extensive notes made in his private manuscripts, range across the broad spectrum of topics that are described in the essays in this volume. But they do share certain qualities that bear mentioning here. Most of all, they are polemical in nature. Each treatise is aimed at a particular person or persons who represented a certain mode of thought to which Edwards objected. In this sense, they are a culmination of Edwards' efforts, begun in his *Quaestio* and *God Glorified*, to reverse the changing tide of theology. *Freedom of the Will* was a vestige of his old campaign against the Arminians, begun all those years ago on the New Haven green in 1723. The subsequent productions, however, were aimed at proponents of "humanitarian" philosophies who sought to remove God from the moral and salvific landscape. In this way, the ethical concerns hark back to his earliest writings.

Another thing to note about the Stockbridge treatises is that—for all of their reputation and influence—they were of secondary interest to Edwards, who was pursuing larger projects. Following the death of the Reverend Aaron Burr, president of the College of New Jersey, in September 1757, the college trustees pitched upon Edwards as the successor. The following month, Edwards wrote a letter describing his current and future interests in detail. One of the "great works" he planned to produce was his *Harmony of the Old and New Testaments*, begun a decade before, which would take in the voluminous materials on messianic prophecies and typology. Still another was *A History of the Work of Redemption*. From his college days Edwards had outlined a summa defending the rationality of the main doctrines of Christianity. By the late 1730s, however, the traditional systematic format gave way to an "entire new method": a narrative that would incorporate cosmology, natural philosophy, doctrine, anthropology, and scriptural exegesis in a grand historical account of heaven, earth, and hell. His lengthy series on Isaiah 51:8, preached in 1739, would form the nucleus, but since then he had scoured his writings, keying pieces for inclusion, adding material in his "Miscellanies," and constructing a series of notebooks devoted to the topic.

It was left to his devotees to publish the History Discourse, for Edwards would never finish it. A council in January 1758 freed him from his Stockbridge responsibilities, and he accepted the Princeton post. He went on ahead, set up housekeeping, preached in the chapel, and began to meet with students. However, smallpox was in the vicinity. Among the many who had fallen ill was Edwards' oldest son, Timothy, preparing to matriculate at the college. The trustees recommended that Edwards take an inoculation. Though inoculation was still a controversial—and risky—procedure at the time, Edwards, a man of science at the beginning and the last, set an example by submitting to it. Unfortunately, the serum was corrupted. After a promising initial reaction, Edwards sank into a secondary fever, characterized by severe swelling of the throat. Expressing resignation to the will of God, he died on March 22, 1758.

Edwards had begun his career amidst changing theological currents. He spent his career dealing with those currents, sometimes conforming to them, often drawing from them for his own purposes but also constructing a considerable critique of them. Ultimately, his defense of the Calvinist version of Christianity, featuring innovative and forceful arguments, may have failed. But in mounting his defense, he left behind a legacy that, as the essays in this volume testify, is still felt to this day.

Suggested Further Readings

Conforti, Joseph A. *Jonathan Edwards, Religious Tradition, and American Culture*. Chapel Hill: University of North Carolina Press, 1995.

Kimnach, Wilson H., Kenneth P. Minkema, and Douglas A. Sweeney, eds. *The Sermons of Jonathan Edwards: A Reader*. New Haven: Yale University Press, 1999.

Lesser, M. X. *Jonathan Edwards*. Boston: Twayne Publishers, 1988.

Marsden, George M. *Jonathan Edwards: An Eighteenth-Century Life*. New Haven: Yale University Press, 2003.

Miller, Perry. *Jonathan Edwards*. New York: William Sloane Associates, 1949.

Murray, Iain H. *Jonathan Edwards: A New Biography*. Carlisle, Pa.: Banner of Truth, 1987.

Smith, John E., Harry S. Stout, and Kenneth P. Minkema, eds. *A Jonathan Edwards Reader*. New Haven: Yale University Press, 1995.

Tracey, Patricia J. *Jonathan Edwards, Pastor: Religion and Society in Eighteenth-Century Northampton*. New York: Hill & Wang, 1980.

Winslow, Ola E. *Jonathan Edwards, 1703-1758: A Biography*. New York: Macmillan Publishing, 1940.

Two

Edwards' Intellectual Background

Peter J. Thuesen

THE PAST FIFTY YEARS of resurgent interest in Jonathan Edwards have often seen him caught between the opposing worlds of the secular academy and the evangelical Protestant subculture. On the one side, the late Harvard historian Perry Miller, whose celebrated 1949 intellectual biography rehabilitated Edwards for a secular academic audience, highlighted his precocious mastery of Enlightenment philosophy and likened him to a "master of relativity" speaking to "a convention of Newtonians who had not yet heard of Einstein." Miller insisted that Edwards' seeming traditionalism could not always be taken at face value; his writings were "almost a hoax, not to be read but to be seen through." Consequently, Miller took little interest in Edwards' straightforward engagement with the Bible and regarded his heavily scriptural *History of the Work of Redemption* as scarcely better than a "story book for fundamentalists." Miller's attitude left the field wide open for an evangelical rejoinder, and several decades later, Iain Murray, a founding trustee of the Banner of Truth Trust, an Edinburgh publisher dedicated to the recovery of Puritan literature, produced a more popular biography of Edwards in which he criticized the "anti-supernatural animus" of Miller (a reputed atheist) and other secular interpreters. Unlike Miller, who repeatedly emphasized Edwards' refashioning of Lockean empiricism, Murray barely mentioned Locke and insisted that philosophy was "peripheral" to Edwards' thought, which he judged first and foremost as religious. Thus emerged two conflicting portraits of "America's theologian": Miller's preternaturally modern Edwards, whose appropriation of empirical psychology led him to articulate human self-destructiveness with a force that anticipated Freud or later twentieth-century prophets like Reinhold Niebuhr; and Murray's unswervingly traditional Edwards, whose warm, revivalistic piety and defense of Christian orthodoxy against the Enlightenment made him the perennial hero of a transatlantic evangelical tradition.[1]

These divergent interpretations may say as much about Miller and Murray as about Edwards himself; yet taken together, they accurately reflect the conflicting worldviews that profoundly influenced Edwards' intellectual biography. All his life, Edwards was torn between Puritan traditionalism, with its roots in the premodern heritage of Western Christian thought, and Enlightenment rationalism, with its critical assumptions that would eventuate in modern skepticism. These opposing forces did not overcome him: to his dying day he remained an eclectic thinker who resisted unambiguous identification with either traditional or modern forms of thought. As such, he mirrored the intellectual ambiguity—the fertile in-betweenness—of the culture of British America in the first half of the eighteenth century. In this essay, I shall trace some of the competing influences on Edwards as a thinker and show how his intellectual development was intimately related to a burgeoning transatlantic culture of print.

Edwards' Early Education

As Wilson Kimnach has noted, the two earliest and most important influences on Edwards as a thinker were the Bible and the preaching of his father, Timothy Edwards, which provided the idiom and rhetorical conventions for much of his later writing (10:4). The Bible's influence, in particular, should not be underestimated: Miller's Edwards, who seems to prefer Locke to Scripture, is a misrepresentation. In his posthumously published "Personal Narrative," Edwards attested that throughout his life he had "the greatest delight in the holy Scriptures, of any book whatsoever" (16:797), and his exegetical writings reveal that in many respects, he inherited the essentially premodern scripturalism of his Puritan forebears. Edwards also imbibed the Puritan heritage of his father's parsonage in East Windsor, Connecticut; the family's books included works by American divines such as Samuel Willard, Increase and Cotton Mather, and Edwards' own grandfather Solomon Stoddard.[2]

As the only son in a family with ten daughters, Edwards was expected to continue in the line of Congregational clergy, and thus his parents geared his home education toward his being admitted to college and training for a ministerial vocation. Candidates for admission to the Collegiate School (later renamed Yale) had to be conversant in Latin, and by age seven, Edwards was already learning this language from his father and older sisters. Timothy also gave his children writing assignments, and probably instruction in elementary arithmetic. Little else is known about Edwards' early education beyond what may be inferred about the family atmosphere, which, despite its conventional piety, also presented young Jonathan with the possibility of departing from tradition. His grandfather Stoddard, whom he would eventually succeed as pastor in Northampton, had run afoul of Boston traditionalists like Increase Mather for liberalizing strict standards of admission to the Lord's Supper while also arguing for greater clerical authority. Timothy Edwards, in advocating his father-in-law's system, encountered significant resistance from his congregation, and conversations over this protracted conflict would have been frequent at home during Jonathan's childhood.³

In 1716 the twelve-year-old Edwards entered Yale College, which was then torn by a controversy over its permanent location. Edwards spent his first three years with the faction temporarily settled at Wethersfield (ten miles from his home at East Windsor), which was led by his cousin Elisha Williams. Logic was the first subject in the Yale curriculum, and the Harvard-trained Williams, as Norman Fiering has shown, was an exponent of the Port-Royal logic of Antoine Arnauld and Pierre Nicole, authors of *La Logique, ou L'art de penser* (1662), which rejected Aristotelian categories, or what Williams called "rote names of arbitrary signification." This influential text of Cartesian logic, in English translation, was still being consulted in Edwards' senior year, and a copy with his signature survives in Yale's Beinecke Library (16:33). Behind Arnauld and Nicole stood a longer tradition of logic, beginning with the sixteenth-century French humanist Petrus Ramus, and also including the more obscure Dutch Calvinists Franco Burgersdijck and Adrianus Heereboord, who all formed part of Edwards' broad inheritance from Puritanism. Yet in the wake of Descartes, this tradition was now differentiating itself from the Aristotelianism of the medieval past and moving away, as Fiering notes, "from preoccupation with forms of reasoning for their own sake and more toward the problem of how useful knowledge and factual truth could be attained." Along with modernization in the field of logic came new paradigms in other fields, and some of these changes would be felt at the fledgling Yale College.⁴

Unfortunately, no direct evidence of the overall curriculum at Wethersfield survives, but records of Harvard's regimen, along with other documents, testify to Edwards' likely course of study. In addition to studying logic, he continued to refine his Latin and Greek, and also took up Hebrew. Rhetoric was another essential subject, probably covered through William Dugard's *Rhetorices Elementa* (1648). In the fields of metaphysics and ethics, the Cambridge Platonist Henry More was then the standard, along with Heereboord and possibly others. More (1614–87), according to Fiering, was probably the most influential philosopher in America during Edwards' college days. More's *Enchiridion Ethicum* (1667) and *Enchiridion Metaphysicum* (1671) were often summarized in Harvard student notebooks, though the widespread use of his works in New England was ironic given his rejection of Calvinist orthodoxy in favor of a more benevolent view of both God and humans. Meanwhile, in natural philosophy (or science), Edwards possibly studied Jacques Rohault's Cartesian physics in the 1697 Latin translation (with Newtonian annotations) by Samuel Clarke. A letter from Edwards to his father reveals that the favored geometry text at Yale was by the German Calvinist Johann Heinrich Alsted (16:33). Alsted was famous in Puritan circles as the author of the four-volume folio set *Scientiarum Omnium Encyclopaediae* (1630), which modestly attempted to summarize all realms of human learning. Edwards' letter also indicates that he studied the astronomy of Pierre Gassendi, a seventeenth-century French scientist who advocated Epicurean philosophy.[5]

Finally, there was divinity. Yale students, like their Harvard counterparts, participated in regular disputations on the principal loci. Early American Puritans had typically studied Calvinism as refracted through William Ames's *Medulla Sacrae Theologiae* (1627; English translation, *The Marrow of Sacred Divinity*, 1642), and Edwards undoubtedly was exposed to this text. (The Yale Library owns a copy used by his college roommate and cousin Elisha Mix.) Ames was eventually superseded, at Harvard at least, by the *Compendium Theologiae Christianae* (1626; English translation, *The Abridgment of Christian Divinitie*, 1650) of the Swiss Calvinist Johannes Wollebius. Another widely circulating Continental systematic theology was Peter van Mastricht's *Theoretico-Practica Theologia* (1699). Regardless of whether Edwards encountered his work at Yale, Mastricht would later loom large for him as a theological source.[6]

The New Books at Yale

In the meantime, however, weighty tomes of Reformed dogmatics were about to be pushed aside at Yale for more controversial fare. Founded in 1701, Yale was a school of rather provincial resources until the gift of a major book collection brought the college into full contact with the polite "republic of letters" of the European Enlightenment. As recent scholarship has shown, this republic of letters was an informal network of learned individuals who eschewed the dogmatism of the medieval and Reformation eras and instead adopted a moderate, latitudinarian, worldly sensibility. Members of this imagined community, in theory at least, ignored distinctions of nationality and religion and willingly assisted each other in cultivating an ecumenical spirit of dispassionate inquiry.[7] In England, this new attitude of polite learning was associated especially with John Locke, but its proponents also included the Cambridge Platonists Ralph Cudworth and Henry More, the Anglican bishop Edward Stillingfleet and archbishop of Canterbury John Tillotson, the essayists Joseph Addison and Sir Richard Steele, and the philosophers Samuel Clarke and Anthony Ashley Cooper, third earl of Shaftesbury.[8] These and other figures, writing between the late seventeenth and early eighteenth centuries, espoused a version of Christianity that emphasized morality and reason over strict doctrinal formulations. By the early eighteenth century, this "polite" style was so pervasive in the Church of England that the once-triumphant Calvinism of the Puritan revolution had virtually disappeared as an effective force in English life.[9]

But latitudinarian and liberal ideas—though well-worn in England by the early eighteenth century—were still a relative novelty in Connecticut during Edwards' early years at Yale until Jeremiah Dummer, London agent for the Massachusetts and Connecticut colonies, gave the college more than eight hundred books covering every major branch of learning. Though the books were donated in 1714, they were not accessible until Edwards' senior year, by which time the college had been consolidated in New Haven. Edwards had further opportunity to use the new library during his years as a master's degree candidate (1720–22) and a tutor (1724–26). Indeed, Edwards and the other tutors received an extra stipend for sorting the books, which Dummer had collected from individual donors, many of them prominent figures, including Richard Steele and Isaac Newton, who contributed some of their own works. Not only did the gift introduce Yale students to the thought of Locke but it contained a generous sampling of such polite figures as Clarke, More, Shaftesbury, Stillingfleet, and Tillotson. The collection also included works by Daniel Defoe, a 1710 edition of Pierre Bayle's four-volume *Historical and Critical Dictionary* (a compendium of philosophy), and even an English translation of the Qur'an.[10]

Though many of the authors represented in the collection were already known, especially among the Boston elites, the Dummer gift caused an unanticipated scandal at Yale. This controversy forms an important part of Edwards' intellectual milieu, for it highlights the tension between traditional and Enlightenment ideas that would continue to define his career. By themselves, of course, the volumes posed no threat to Congregational orthodoxy, but as Edmund S. Morgan once wryly observed about colonial Yale, the "trouble with books is that people *will* read them." Rumors about the nature of the Dummer gift soon spread beyond New Haven, such that one New Jersey pastor, whose son was a Yale student, wrote to Cotton Mather in 1722 that he was "frighted" by reports of "Arminian Books . . . cryed up in Yale Colledge for Eloquence & Learning."[11] The danger of the Dummer books was made starkly apparent later that year when Yale rector Timothy Cutler, tutor Samuel Johnson, and five local ministers declared their Congregational ordinations invalid and announced their intention to seek Episcopal reordination. This defection to Anglicanism, as one historian has noted, had an effect similar to that which might have been produced in the twentieth century if the entire Yale football team had suddenly joined the Communist Party. The *Boston News-Letter* reported that Yale College, which had been "set up . . . according to Scripture Rule, Free of Humane Traditions and Impositions . . . is now become Corrupt." The aging Increase Mather, holding forth at Boston's Old North Church, bewailed the "Connecticut Apostacie," and within a year, the shock of creeping infidelity contributed largely to his death, according to his son Cotton and the poet Edward Taylor, who opined that "Cutler's Cutlary gave th'killing Stob."[12]

The major reason cited by most observers—and the apostates themselves—for the Episcopal defection was the influence of the Dummer collection, with its substantial number of Arminian, latitudinarian, and other heretical titles. Cutler and his co-conspirators had been meeting regularly in his home to discuss these works, and out of these meetings came their dramatic apostasy, carefully timed for Yale's 1722 commencement day. The Yale trustees, convened by Connecticut governor Gurdon Saltonstall, immediately dismissed Cutler and voted to require of future rectors and tutors evidence of "opposition to Armenian [*sic*] & prelatical Corruptions." Meanwhile Dummer himself bristled at the "slander" that his books had been the source of all the trouble, insisting that "there never was an Eminent Dissenter . . . whose works are not in that Collection."[13]

Dummer's disclaimer aside, the appeal of the "New Learning" was such that his books were left uncensored in the Yale library, where they proved a feast for the young tutor Jonathan Edwards, who had never before had access to such a large and up-to-date library. And just as the Yale trustees decried the influence of fashionable new Anglican texts but left the Dummer collection intact, Edwards himself, throughout his subsequent career, seemed torn between two philosophical worlds: the tradition of Protestant scholasticism and the new republic of Enlightenment letters. The latter's siren song was especially powerful during his Yale tutorship when, in a memorandum to himself about writing style, he noted favorably the genre of philosophical dialogue employed by the third earl of Shaftesbury. In the same memorandum, Edwards revealed his ambition to make a name for himself in the European republic of letters: "Before I venture to publish in London, to make some experiment in my own country; to play at small games first, that I may gain some experience in writing" (10:184–85). Edwards' writing style was further influenced, as Wilson Kimnach has shown, by another polite figure in the Dummer collection, the Cambridge Platonist John Smith (10:6–9). Smith's rhetoric about "spiritual sensation" and other means of attaining divine knowledge later figured into Edwards' *Treatise Concerning Religious Affections* (2:65–66).

John Locke—Edwards' "Master-Spirit"?

Yet the Enlightenment figure most often associated with Edwards is John Locke. The long unquestioned assumption of his early intellectual debt to Locke originated with Samuel Hopkins' 1765 biography, which claimed that Edwards first read Locke's *Essay Concerning Human Understanding* (1690) in his second year of college, at age thirteen. According to Hopkins, Edwards later recalled devouring Locke like "the most greedy miser in gathering up handfuls of silver and gold from some new discovered treasure." Perry Miller accepted Hopkins' claim that Edwards read Locke at Wethersfield. As Miller put it, the youthful Edwards "grasped in a flash" that Locke was the "master-spirit of the age, and that the *Essay* made everything then being offered at Harvard or Yale as philosophy, psychology, and rhetoric so obsolete that it could no longer be taken seriously." Edwards' encounter with Locke's *Essay* thus became the "central and decisive event" of his intellectual development.[14]

More recently, scholars have discredited the assumption that Edwards read Locke at Wethersfield and have suggested that he first encountered him as a graduate student, after the Dummer gift had brought the *Essay* to New Haven. Moreover, Wallace Anderson, Norman Fiering, and others have argued that Edwards was more of a rationalist than a Lockean empiricist, contrary to Miller's judgment that Edwards' thought could be summed up as "Puritanism recast in the idiom of empirical psychology." To be sure, there was some truth in Miller's assertion, for Edwards' *Freedom of the Will* draws on Locke in rejecting the traditional psychology dividing the human being into various distinct faculties (1:47–65), and Edwards seems to draw on Locke's empiricism in other places, such as the *Religious Affections*, where the "new spiritual sense" (2:271) has Lockean overtones. Yet, as Fiering asserts, "Edwards' mind was profoundly antithetical to Locke's on most matters of importance." Locke distrusted metaphysical speculation and endeavored to show in his *Essay* the limits of human understanding. Edwards remained more traditionally speculative, though the extent of his speculation remains a matter of debate, with some scholars pointing to his apparent commitment to occasionalism (the idea that God, as the sole cause, continuously recreates the existing world), and others explaining his view of divine causation in terms of God's continual upholding of finite laws and habits.[15] The young Edwards also espoused an un-Lockean immaterialism in which "God is as it were the only substance" (6:398; cf. "Misc." 177, 13:327) and in which existence was entirely dependent on divine perception—a claim that, as Thomas Schafer has suggested, seemed almost to reduce the universe to God looking at himself in a mirror (13:49).[16]

Fiering sees a clearer affinity between Edwards and the Cambridge Platonists, and also the French Cartesian philosopher Nicolas Malebranche (1638–1715). Though there is no conclusive evidence that Edwards read it, an English translation of Malebranche's *Recherche de la Vérité* (1674) was in the Dummer collection, and Malebranche's ideas had also circulated in America, thanks to his English disciple John Norris, whose 1704 opus, *An Essay towards the Theory of the Ideal or Intelligible World* (which was highly critical of Locke), was among the Dummer books. Edwards shared with the Cambridge Platonists, Malebranche, and Norris an almost mystical conception of existence and causation that ultimately focused all attention on God. Malebranche, in particular, may have been a source for Edwards' occasionalism and may even have influenced his ideas on motion, though at first glance these seem more clearly indebted to Newton, whom Miller highlighted as a major influence on Edwards. As Fiering has pointed out, Malebranche foreshadowed Newton in conceiving of the spiritual universe as analogous to the gravitational motion of corporeal bodies.[17]

Yet in the end, the ongoing debate about the primary intellectual influence on Edwards, or who served as his "master-spirit," must be settled by the conclusion of William Sparkes Morris that Edwards' affinities as a thinker were fundamentally eclectic. In his 688-page, posthumously published dissertation, *The Young Jonathan Edwards*, Morris details not only the eclecticism of Yale College during Edwards' day but also his lifelong tendency to seek wisdom from any quarter. If Edwards was "Protestant in his convictions and direction," Morris writes, he was "genuinely Catholic in his sympathies and understanding." It is no accident, Morris continues, that the record of Edwards' reading "included much more in it than the names of John Locke and Isaac Newton, or Thomas Shepard and Richard Sibbes."[18] Put differently, the tension in Edwards between traditional and Enlightenment forms of thought—though omnipresent and at times even stark—never devolved into a simple "either/or" proposition. The complex of ideas in Edwards on virtually any question of philosophy or theology defies a clear-cut genealogy.

Edwards' Book Lists

Nowhere is the complexity of Edwards' intellectual interests clearer than in that portion of his manuscript remains dealing directly with reading and books. In the first study of the subject, Thomas H. Johnson, writing in 1931, surveyed Edwards' reading interests as revealed in his "Catalogue," a document that Edwards biographer Ola Winslow deemed "in many ways the most interesting of all his manuscript remains."[19]

A forty-five-page notebook containing some 720 entries and spanning Edwards' entire career, the "Catalogue" is a list of books he had either read or hoped to read.[20] (Some of the entries are crossed out, perhaps indicating that Edwards actually obtained these books, though the meaning of the strikethroughs is not certain.) Johnson surveyed the range of books mentioned in this list, comparing it with actual quotations and citations of authors in Edwards' major treatises. He concluded that though Edwards read more widely than most of his contemporaries, he remained essentially provincial in temper.

In the seventy years since Johnson's study, however, another significant manuscript discovery has augmented our understanding of Edwards' reading. Edwards' "Account Book," besides recording mundane financial transactions and describing the distinctive markings of his cattle, contains references to over a hundred different books that he had lent to friends and parishioners.[21] Unlike the "Catalogue," which lists many books that Edwards probably never acquired, the "Account Book" holds added historical significance because it records books that were actually circulating, especially among Edwards and his ministerial colleagues. Book transactions among Edwards and other clergy are also recorded in the minutes of the ministerial association of Hampshire County, Massachusetts, which convened twice a year during Edwards' pastorate of the First Congregational Church in Northampton.[22] Taken as a body, the "Catalogue," the "Account Book," and the Hampshire Association records reveal a detailed picture not only of Edwards' own bibliographic universe but also of book circulation patterns in the Connecticut River valley during the first half of the eighteenth century.

On one level, these records of Edwards' reading interests seem to indicate that he was still, as Johnson put it, "tightly bound by theological dogma"—still operating within a Puritan frame of reference in which the sixteenth-century "sola scriptura" was the principal bibliographical criterion. Indeed, the young Edwards' first entry in the "Catalogue"—simply "Bible"—has an almost talismanic quality, testifying to his obeisance to the Puritan principle that Scripture must be the judge of all things. Not surprisingly, we also find at the outset of the "Catalogue" a healthy dose of Old and New World Puritan works by Thomas Shepard, John Owen, Cotton Mather, and others. Moreover, the document contains references throughout to devotional, exegetical, homiletical, and polemical works by Nonconformist divines.

American and European Calvinists are equally abundant in the "Account Book," which reveals that Edwards owned a copy of Mastricht's *Theoretico-Practica Theologia* and lent it several times to fellow ministers. Cotton Mather, in his instruction manual for new ministers, *Manuductio ad Ministerium* (1726), had deemed Mastricht second only to Scripture as a "Store-house to which you may resort continually," and Edwards heeded Mather's book recommendations, citing them no fewer than ten times in the "Catalogue."[23] Later, in a letter to Joseph Bellamy, Edwards strongly recommended Mastricht, calling his work better than "any other book in the world, excepting the Bible" on matters of divinity (16:217). He also recommended the Genevan Calvinist Francis Turretin, whose *Institutio Theologiae Elencticae* (1685) he owned and lent to friends.

Yet at the same time, we find in the manuscript sources abundant evidence of Edwards' interest in the new polite culture of reading. The ninth entry in the "Catalogue" is a reference to Steele and Addison's *Guardian*, which the "Account Book" confirms that Edwards owned and lent out on several occasions. Similarly, Edwards and his friends eagerly perused Steele's *Ladies Library*, a compendium of polite literature by various authors; Edwards lent out this three-volume collection eight times—more than any other work listed in the "Account Book." Edwards also made frequent use of periodicals such as *The Present State of the Republick of Letters* and the *London Magazine*, which reported extensively on the polite European world of print. The last page of every issue of the *London Magazine* included a "Catalogue" of new books; Edwards cites these book notices in his own "Catalogue" at least sixteen times, and refers with equal frequency to book listings in the *Republick of Letters*.[24] Moreover, Edwards' fellow clergy in western Massachusetts shared these aspirations to polite reading. After the Hampshire Association ministers began acquiring books for their common use, for example, they commissioned Edwards in 1738 "to find for the L[ibrary the] Last Vol. of the Republick of Letters."[25]

Many of Edwards' theological book interests also tended toward the polite and latitudinarian. As early as the tenth entry of the "Catalogue," we find a reference to the "B[isho]p of Bangor," that is, the eighteenth-century Anglican Benjamin Hoadly, whose latitudinarian pragmatism incensed Nonconformists when he argued that they should submit to episcopal reordination as a matter of expediency and church order.[26] The "Account Book" also reveals that Edwards circulated among his fellow clergy a variety of Anglicans of "Arminian" or other suspect persuasion, including Locke, who belongs in this "Arminian" company even though his theology is often overshadowed by his work as a philosopher; Thomas Sherlock, the bishop of London and a prominent high-churchman; William Warburton, bishop of Gloucester, who was famed for his arrogance in controversies with dissenters; and Samuel Clarke, whose Arian tendencies were well known. Fiering has judged Clarke's *Discourse Concerning the Unchangeable Obligations of Natural Religion* (1706) an important influence on Edwards' ethics, and the "Account Book" shows that he twice lent it to friends. Edwards and his colleagues also circulated, perhaps unwittingly, the latitudinarian writings of Archbishop Tillotson, who was among the anonymous authors of the *Ladies Library*.[27]

Thus, even as the revivalist George Whitefield was complaining after a visit to Harvard that "Tillotson and Clarke are read instead of Shepard, Stoddard, and suchlike evangelical writers," Edwards and his colleagues in western Massachusetts were exchanging Tillotson, Clarke, and other fashionable divines, as the "Account Book" reveals.[28] To be sure, the reading of such figures need not imply endorsement; indeed, Edwards himself, when engaging in theological debate, often turned to the likes of Tillotson or Clarke for statements of "the other side of the question," as he put it in 1738 in *Discourses on Various Important Subjects* (19:155). But even an ideological antagonist can retain a certain seductiveness. In a letter late in his career, Edwards mentioned having read the philosopher David Hume and remarked: "I am glad of an opportunity to read such corrupt books; especially when written by men of considerable genius; that I may have an idea of the notions that prevail in our nation" (16:679).

Such comments again reveal an Edwards caught between two worlds. In the end, though, what can be said about the relative proportions of "polite" versus "impolite" books in his working library? As we have seen, the "Account Book" provides a rough index of works that mattered to Edwards and his acquaintances. Of the approximately seventy-seven strictly theological works mentioned in the document, two in seven are "polite" (Anglican, latitudinarian, or Enlightenment) volumes, while the rest may be classified broadly as Nonconformist or Reformed. (A theological work fitting into neither of these categories is an English translation of select sermons by Martin Luther.) Books standing in the Puritan lineage therefore predominate, though the smaller number of "polite" titles in his purely theological reading must be seen alongside his frequent use of more wide-ranging works such as Steele's *Ladies Library* and *Guardian*. He also frequently lent out Daniel Defoe's *Family-Instructor* (1715) and *Religious Courtship* (1722), as well as Samuel Richardson's phenomenally popular novels *Pamela* (1740) and *Clarissa* (1748). Richardson was a favorite of other members of Edwards' family, including his wife, Sarah, and his daughter Esther Edwards Burr.[29]

To be sure, the category of "politeness," as it has been employed in recent historiography of the book, is only useful to a point. Edwards once lent to a ministerial colleague the *Morning-Exercise Against Popery* (1675), a compilation of twenty-five sermons by eminent seventeenth-century divines. Sermons and treatises attacking the Church of Rome were standard fare among virtually all English Protestants; "polite" anti-Catholicism therefore transcended the usual divide between conservative Calvinists and liberal Anglicans. And then there is the curious case of the book Edwards read most frequently: the Bible. In the print culture of eighteenth-century London, which Edwards regarded so fondly, was the Bible polite reading? John Locke had employed the Bible in an eminently polite way in seeking to prove the "reasonableness" of Christianity. But just as the deist Anthony Collins once quipped that nobody doubted the existence of God until Samuel Clarke sought to prove it, nobody doubted the politeness of Scripture until Locke and others sought to vindicate it.[30] The "impolite" Bible of a fully critical age—a book regarded as tainted with multiple redactions and even outright historical falsehoods—was just around the corner. Edwards profoundly feared such a critical assault on scriptural truth, even as he continued to feed his insatiable appetite for the latest in polite reading.

Edwards and Critical History

Indeed, the emerging critical works on Scripture, and on religion in general, dominated much of Edwards' later reading, as is clear in his manuscript "Miscellanies" as well as in the treatises and sermons he published in his lifetime. These materials, in addition to the "Catalogue" and the "Account Book," are essential indicators of the intellectual influences on Edwards, though as any scholar who has ever studied his manuscripts knows, modern standards of attribution and citation do not apply. Where the source of Edwards' references is clear, his conflicted attitude toward Enlightenment thinkers is often apparent. For example, in "Justification by Faith Alone" (published in *Discourses on Various Important Subjects*), he offers lengthy supporting quotations from Locke's biblical exegesis in *The Reasonableness of Christianity* (1695). He adds a disclaimer, however, noting that "nobody will think [Locke] to be a likely person to be blinded by prejudice in favor of the doctrine [of justification] we are maintaining" (19:189). This remark suggests Edwards' unspoken fear that Locke, while useful on an ad hoc basis, represented a larger trend toward replacing traditional doctrines with new standards of reasonableness. Taken to its logical conclusion, the Age of Reason resulted in deism—and this more radical skepticism increasingly occupied Edwards as a reader in his later career.

Gerald McDermott has calculated that of the 1,412 entries in Edwards' "Miscellanies," fully 25 percent relate directly or indirectly to the deist challenge. Especially in his later years, Edwards became familiar with most of the major English deists, including Herbert of Cherbury, Charles Blount, Matthew Tindal, John Toland, Thomas Woolston, Anthony Collins, and Thomas Morgan. Many of these he encountered secondhand through compilations such as Philip Skelton's *Deism Revealed* (1748), a text Edwards copied from at considerable length in

"Miscellanies" number 1350. Edwards also used John Leland's *View of the Principal Deistical Writers* (1754) and recommended to Joseph Bellamy the two-volume response to Tindal published by Leland in 1733 (16:700–701). Edwards had direct exposure to works by a few deists, including the freethinking journeyman Thomas Chubb, author of *A Collection of Tracts* (1730), who serves as a convenient foil in Edwards' *Freedom of the Will* (1754). Chubb's work was also among those that Edwards lent to friends.

Closely related to deism, the emerging critical scholarship on the Bible loomed large for Edwards as both a threat and an intellectual stimulus. As Stephen Stein has observed, it is no accident that the biblical book most commented on by Edwards in his "Notes on Scripture" is Genesis, for the Mosaic authorship of the Pentateuch and the accuracy of biblical chronology were highly contested issues at the time (15:14). Scholars are only now beginning to appreciate the intensity of Edwards' interest in such questions—and his desire to defend scriptural truth against its detractors. Edwards' own exegetical approach, as Stein notes, remained heavily indebted to the Protestant commentarial tradition represented by such figures as Matthew Poole and Matthew Henry. Edwards cited Poole's five-volume *Synopsis Criticorum* (1669–76) and Henry's six-volume *Exposition of the Old and New Testaments* (1708–10) repeatedly in his "Blank Bible" and was influenced by their theological perspectives, including their zealous anti-Catholicism (15:6–7). Yet Edwards also read extensively in other sources that introduced him to the contentious debates about biblical chronology, geography, and history; these texts included Edward Wells' *Historical Geography of the Old Testament* (1711), Humphrey Prideaux's *Old and New Testaments Connected in the History of the Jews* (1718), and Arthur Bedford's *Scripture Chronology Demonstrated by Astronomical Calculations* (1730).

A good example of Edwards' later critical interests is "Miscellanies," no. 1060 (written circa 1742–43), a long entry in which he quotes extensively from Jeremiah Jones' three-volume *New and Full Method of Settling the Canonical Authority of the New Testament* (1727), a text that ranged widely in early Christian noncanonical gospels and other writings (20:396–427). Edwards himself had planned to write a major work dealing with the canon, "The Harmony of the Old and New Testament," a major portion of which (on the Bible's messianic prophecies and their fulfillment) survives as "Miscellanies," nos. 1067–68. His wide engagement with issues of critical biblical scholarship has led Robert E. Brown to dub his exegetical approach a "hybrid traditionalism," reflecting in certain respects his accommodations to the new learning.[31]

The later Edwards also developed a keen interest in comparative religion, as Gerald McDermott has shown. In this quest, he copied extracts from several seventeenth-century writers, including the Dutch theologian Hugo Grotius and the English Nonconformist Theophilus Gale, to support the claim that the ancient "heathens"—that is, the philosophers of classical antiquity—articulated in their works the germ of Christian doctrines such as the Trinity (20:11–17). Edwards pursued this strategy in "Miscellanies," no. 1359, a lengthy entry which consists of fifty-five manuscript pages of quotations from *The True Intellectual System of the Universe* (1678) by the Cambridge Platonist Ralph Cudworth, whose own work was mainly a series of extracts from Greco-Roman philosophers (23:640–713). Meanwhile, Edwards was less charitable toward, but no less interested in, other world traditions. In the last decade of his life, he relied heavily on the German Reformed theologian Johann Friedrich Stapfer's five-volume *Institutiones Theologiae Polemicae* (1743–47) to draw a negative picture of Islam.[32]

Conclusion

Perry Miller regarded Edwards' tendency in his later notebooks to copy long extracts as evidence that his "inspiration was tiring," but recent interpreters such as Amy Plantinga Pauw have suggested instead that it reveals Edwards in an intellectually vital "acquisitive mode, industriously gathering food for theological consumption" (20:11).[33] Throughout his career, as we have seen, Edwards endeavored to stay abreast of the latest developments in many fields of inquiry. Early in the "Catalogue," in a note probably written during his Yale tutorship, he listed several categories of "Books to be enquired for," including the "best Geography," "the best Exposition of the Apoca[lypse]," "the best General Ecclesiastical history," as well as those "which are the most usefull & necessary of the Fathers," "the best historical dictionary of the Nature of Bayle's dictionary," and "the best that treats of the Cabbalistical learning of the Jews." Three decades later, in the last year of his life, Edwards was still pursuing the latest developments, this time in the field of revival, through an exchange of books with the Scottish evangelicals John Erskine and John Gillies. In 1757 Edwards lent his copy of Gillies' two-volume *Historical Collections* (1754), which reported on the transatlantic course of the revivals, to Samuel Hopkins. The volumes, inscribed to Edwards by Gillies himself, remain in the Yale library as a testament to Edwards' immersion in the eighteenth-century culture of print.[34]

Indeed, Edwards' intellectual world, for all its implicit debt to the Reformation and even to medieval scholasticism, was largely a contemporary one. Citations of Calvin and other sixteenth-century figures are few and far between in his work. The Enlightenment—its promise and its peril—was Edwards' reference point, and had he lived to complete his anticipated "body of divinity in an entire new method" (16:272), we can assume that he would have continued his lifelong pattern of borrowing and creatively refashioning ideas from his immense storehouse of self-acquired knowledge.

Notes

1. Perry Miller, *Jonathan Edwards* (1949; reprint, Amherst: University of Massachusetts Press, 1981), pp. 51, 63, 183, and introduction by Donald Weber, p. xxi; Iain H. Murray, *Jonathan Edwards: A New Biography* (Edinburgh: Banner of Truth Trust, 1987), pp. xx, xxix.

2. See the 1719 inventory in Kenneth P. Minkema, "The Edwardses: A Ministerial Family in Eighteenth-Century New England" (Ph.D. diss., University of Connecticut, 1988), pp. 645–53.

3. Patricia J. Tracy, *Jonathan Edwards, Pastor: Religion and Society in Eighteenth-Century Northampton* (New York: Hill and Wang, 1980), pp. 52–57.

4. Norman Fiering, *Jonathan Edwards' Moral Thought and Its British Context* (Chapel Hill: University of North Carolina Press, 1981), pp. 26, 38; on Ramus, see Perry Miller, *The New England Mind: The Seventeenth Century* (Cambridge, Mass.: Belknap Press, Harvard University Press, 1939), pp. 116–53, 493–501; on Burgersdijck, see William S. Morris, "The Genius of Jonathan Edwards," in *Reinterpretation in American Church History*, ed. Jerald C. Brauer (Chicago: University of Chicago Press, 1968), pp. 29–65.

5. On the Harvard curriculum in Edwards' day, see Wallace E. Anderson's introduction (6:11–13); and Fiering, *Jonathan Edwards' Moral Thought*, pp. 31–32. On More, see Fiering, *Jonathan Edwards' Moral Thought*, pp. 16, 21, 207–8, and on Alsted, see Miller, *New England Mind*, pp. 102–3.

6. On commonly used Puritan texts of divinity, see Miller, *New England Mind*, pp. 96–97.

7. Anne Goldgar, *Impolite Learning: Conduct and Community in the Republic of Letters, 1680–1750* (New Haven: Yale University Press, 1995), pp. 2–3, 6–7, 20. See also David D. Hall, "Learned Culture in the Eighteenth Century," in *A History of the Book in America*, vol. 1, *The Colonial Book in the Atlantic World*, ed. Hugh Amory and David D. Hall (Cambridge: Cambridge University Press, 2000), pp. 416–17.

8. All of these figures, according to David Lundberg and Henry F. May, are part of the "First Enlightenment" that prefigured the later deism of Anthony Collins, Matthew Tindal, John Toland, and others; see Lundberg and May, "The Enlightened Reader in America," *American Quarterly* 28 (1976): 262–93, esp. pp. 265, 273–76.

9. G. R. Cragg, *From Puritanism to the Age of Reason: A Study of Changes in Religious Thought within the Church of England, 1660–1700* (Cambridge: Cambridge University Press, 1950), p. 30. Compare Horton Davies' similar observation about post-Restoration Anglican liturgical controversies, in which the Puritans

were "utterly routed." Horton Davies, *Worship and Theology in England*, vol. 2, *From Andrewes to Baxter and Fox, 1603–1690* (1975; reprint, Grand Rapids: Eerdmans, 1996), pp. 391–92.

10. Anne Stokely Pratt, "The Books Sent from England by Jeremiah Dummer to Yale College," and Louise May Bryant and Mary Patterson, "The List of Books Sent by Jeremiah Dummer," in *Papers in Honor of Andrew Keogh* (New Haven: Yale University Library, 1938), pp. 7–44, 423–53; Ola Elizabeth Winslow, *Jonathan Edwards, 1703–1758: A Biography* (New York: Macmillan, 1941), p. 92. See also Fiering, *Jonathan Edwards' Moral Thought*, pp. 22–23; and Richard Warch, *School of the Prophets: Yale College, 1701–1740* (New Haven: Yale University Press, 1973), pp. 60–66.

11. The Reverend Joseph Morgan to Cotton Mather, 28 May 1722, in Franklin Bowditch Dexter, *Documentary History of Yale University, Under the Original Charter of the Collegiate School of Connecticut, 1701–1745* (New Haven: Yale University Press, 1916), p. 225. For Edmund S. Morgan's observation on the controversy at Yale, see his lecture "The Trouble with Books," published in *Michigan Alumnus Quarterly Review* 65 (1959): 185–96, quotation on p. 186.

12. Increase Mather mentioned in Samuel Sewall, *The Diary of Samuel Sewall, 1674–1729*, vol. 2 (New York: Farrar, Straus, and Giroux, 1973), p. 995; on his death, see Kenneth Silverman, *The Life and Times of Cotton Mather* (New York: Columbia University Press, 1985), pp. 364–69. *Boston News-Letter* quotation from no. 976 (8–15 October 1722). The quip about the Communist Party is from Henry F. May, *The Enlightenment in America* (New York: Oxford University Press, 1976), p. 77.

13. Jeremiah Dummer to the Reverend Timothy Woodbridge, 3 June 1723, in Dexter, *Documentary History*, p. 241; on the vote of the Yale trustees, see Dexter, *Documentary History*, p. 233. On Cutler, his colleagues, and their engagement with the Dummer books, see Warch, *School of the Prophets*, pp. 104–9; see also Joseph Ellis, *The New England Mind in Transition: Samuel Johnson of Connecticut, 1696–1772* (New Haven: Yale University Press, 1973), pp. 55–81.

14. Miller, *Jonathan Edwards*, pp. 51–53; Samuel Hopkins, *The Life and Character of the Late Reverend Mr. Jonathan Edwards* (Boston, 1765), reprinted in *Jonathan Edwards: A Profile*, ed. David Levin (New York: Hill and Wang, 1969), pp. 5–6.

15. Some passages seem to support an occasionalist ontology (see 6:241–42 and 13:288). For the view that the mature Edwards was a full-fledged occasionalist, see Norman Fiering, "The Rationalist Foundations of Jonathan Edwards' Metaphysics," in *Jonathan Edwards and the American Experience*, ed. Nathan O. Hatch and Harry S. Stout (New York: Oxford University Press, 1988), p. 81, and Oliver D. Crisp, "How 'Occasional' was Edwards's Occasionalism?" in *Jonathan Edwards: Philosophical Theologian*, ed. Paul Helm and Oliver D. Crisp (Aldershot: Ashgate, 2003), pp. 61–77. For an opposing view, see Sang Hyun Lee, *The Philosophical Theology of Jonathan Edwards*, rev. ed. (Princeton: Princeton University Press, 2000), especially p. 107.

16. It is important to remember that the debate over Locke's influence is complicated by debates over influences on Locke himself, whose empiricism included

lingering rationalist assumptions. On doubts about a Lockean Edwards, see Fiering, *Jonathan Edwards' Moral Thought*, pp. 35–40; and Fiering, "Rationalist Foundations," pp. 73–101. See also Anderson's introduction to Edwards' scientific and philosophical writings (6:17, 26), and Wallace Anderson, "Immaterialism in Jonathan Edwards' Early Philosophical Notes," *Journal of the History of Ideas* 25, no. 2 (1964): 181–200. For a defense of Locke's influence on Edwards, see John E. Smith, *Jonathan Edwards: Puritan, Preacher, Philosopher* (Notre Dame: University of Notre Dame Press, 1992), pp. 14–28. For a comparison of Locke and the Cambridge Platonists as influences on Edwards, see Lee, *Philosophical Theology of Jonathan Edwards*, pp. 117–25.

17. Fiering, *Jonathan Edwards' Moral Thought*, pp. 40–47, 79; and "Rationalist Foundations," p. 92.

18. William Sparkes Morris, *The Young Jonathan Edwards: A Reconstruction* (Brooklyn, N.Y.: Carlson Publishing, 1991), pp. 219–20. See also Fiering, *Jonathan Edwards' Moral Thought*, p. 38.

19. Thomas H. Johnson, "Jonathan Edwards' Background of Reading," *Publications of the Colonial Society of Massachusetts* 28 (Transactions, 1930–33): 193–222; Winslow, *Jonathan Edwards*, p. 120.

20. MS in Beinecke Rare Book and Manuscript Library, Yale University. The notebook contains forty-three numbered pages, along with a loose leaf listing books on both sides.

21. MS of seventy-four pages in the Beinecke Library at Yale. A critical edition of the "Catalogue" and the "Account Book" is forthcoming in *The Works of Jonathan Edwards* (New Haven: Yale University Press, 1957–).

22. Hampshire Association of Ministers Records, 1731–47, Forbes Library, Northampton, Mass.

23. Cotton Mather, *Manuductio ad Ministerium: Directions for a Candidate of the Ministry*, Facsimile Text Society, no. 42, ed. Thomas J. Holmes and Kenneth B. Murdock (New York: Columbia University Press, 1938), p. 85.

24. On Edwards' interest in these and similar publications, see Fiering, *Jonathan Edwards' Moral Thought*, pp. 17–19; cf. Fiering's earlier article, "The Transatlantic Republic of Letters: A Note on the Circulation of Learned Periodicals to Early Eighteenth-Century America," *William and Mary Quarterly* 33 (1976): 642–60.

25. Minutes of meeting at Longmeadow, Mass., 18 April 1738, Hampshire Association of Ministers Records, 1731–47, Forbes Library, Northampton, Mass.

26. Ronald N. Stromberg, *Religious Liberalism in Eighteenth-Century England* (London: Oxford University Press, 1954), pp. 89–92, 132; and Warch, *School of the Prophets*, pp. 105–7.

27. On the inclusion of Tillotson in this work, see Fiering, *Jonathan Edwards' Moral Thought*, pp. 18–19. Edwards also quoted directly from Tillotson in various places, including "Justification by Faith Alone," in *Discourses on Various Important Subjects* (19:155). On Clarke and Edwards, see Fiering, *Jonathan Edwards' Moral Thought*, pp. 87–94, 277–78 n. 40.

28. Quoted in Murray, *Jonathan Edwards*, p. 212; see also Amy Plantinga Pauw's introduction to "Miscellanies," nos. 833–1152 (20:12).

29. See the various references to Richardson in *The Journal of Esther Edwards Burr, 1754–1757*, ed. Carol F. Karlsen and Laurie Crumpacker (New Haven: Yale University Press, 1984).
30. The comment by Collins is mentioned in Stromberg, *Religious Liberalism*, p. 10.
31. Robert E. Brown, *Jonathan Edwards and the Bible* (Bloomington: Indiana University Press, 2002), p. xvii; on the "Harmony" project, see Kenneth P. Minkema, "The Other Unfinished 'Great Work': Jonathan Edwards, Messianic Prophecy, and 'The Harmony of the Old and New Testament,' " in *Jonathan Edwards's Writings: Text, Context, Interpretation*, ed. Stephen J. Stein (Bloomington: Indiana University Press, 1996), pp. 52–65.
32. Gerald R. McDermott, *Jonathan Edwards Confronts the Gods: Christian Theology, Enlightenment Religion, and Non-Christian Faiths* (New York: Oxford University Press, 2000), pp. 166–75.
33. Miller quotation from introduction to Jonathan Edwards, *Images or Shadows of Divine Things*, ed. Perry Miller (New Haven: Yale University Press, 1948), p. 41.
34. Edwards frequently obtained books through Erskine; see his last letter to Erskine (16:718–24). On the construction of a transatlantic revival tradition (including the role of the *Historical Collections* of Gillies), see Frank Lambert, *Inventing the "Great Awakening"* (Princeton: Princeton University Press, 1999).

Suggested Further Readings

Anderson, Wallace E. "Immaterialism in Jonathan Edwards' Early Philosophical Notes." *Journal of the History of Ideas* 25.2 (1964): 181–200.
Brown, Robert E. *Jonathan Edwards and the Bible*. Bloomington: Indiana University Press, 2002.
Fiering, Norman. *Jonathan Edwards' Moral Thought and Its British Context*. Chapel Hill: University of North Carolina Press, 1981.
———. "The Rationalist Foundations of Jonathan Edwards' Metaphysics." In *Jonathan Edwards and the American Experience*, ed. Nathan O. Hatch and Harry S. Stout. New York: Oxford University Press, 1988.
Johnson, Thomas H. "Jonathan Edwards' Background of Reading." *Publications of the Colonial Society of Massachusetts* 28 (Transactions, 1930–33): 193–222.
McDermott, Gerald R. *Jonathan Edwards Confronts the Gods: Christian Theology, Enlightenment Religion, and Non-Christian Faiths*. New York: Oxford University Press, 2000.
Miller, Perry. *Jonathan Edwards*. 1949. Reprint, Amherst: University of Massachusetts Press, 1981.
Morris, William Sparkes. *The Young Jonathan Edwards: A Reconstruction*. Brooklyn, N.Y.: Carlson Publishing, 1991.
Smith, John E. *Jonathan Edwards: Puritan, Preacher, Philosopher*. Notre Dame, Ind.: University of Notre Dame Press, 1992.

Three

Being and Consent

Richard R. Niebuhr

JONATHAN EDWARDS IS as complex a person as we could hope or fear to encounter in the chronicles of American culture. One of the difficult tasks of historians of colonial culture is to clarify Edwards in the setting of his milieu, while an equally difficult task of the philosophical theologian is to make Edwards' ideas intelligible to the interested present-day reader. Certainly, historians and theologians need each other's insights in addressing Edwards. This essay is of the philosophical, theological kind and so depends heavily on the achievements of social and intellectual historians. It is chiefly concerned, however, with certain philosophical and theological ideas Edwards set out in his works, from the 1720s to his death in 1758. The emphasis here is on Jonathan Edwards' earlier writings, though some of the references appearing below are to works published posthumously.

In the first entry of the manuscript Jonathan Edwards named "The Mind"—evidently begun in 1723–24[1]—he wrote several propositions that in my view have come to stand for or symbolically represent a theme that runs through *much*—though not through *all*—of what we now have from their author's hand. These propositions appear in two groups.

To begin to explain my view, I reproduce these two sets of propositions in the order in which Edwards offers them, and add the forewarning that I believe a plausible and adequate interpretation of either one of them requires a similarly plausible and adequate interpretation of the other, even though a fair amount of dense material separates them.

The first set reads as follows:

> For being, if we examine narrowly, is nothing else but proportion. When one being is inconsistent with another being, then being is contradicted. (6:336)

The second set is this:

> One alone, without reference to any more, cannot be excellent; for in such a case there can be no manner of relation no way. . . . But in a being that is absolutely without any plurality there cannot be excellency. (6:337)

The issue occupying Edwards in these relatively late paragraphs of "The Mind" [1] resembles the query of ancient philosophers, whether reality is fundamentally of one "stuff" or "substance" or of more than one. He had started to lay down the first principles for settling that question in the somewhat earlier writings "Of Being" and "Of Atoms." In the former, Edwards exclaimed: "[I]t is really impossible . . . that anything should be, and nothing know it. Then you'll say, if it be so, it is because nothing has any existence anywhere else but in consciousness. No, certainly nowhere else, but in either created or uncreated consciousness" (6:204). A little further along Edwards continues: "Certainly, [the universe] exists nowhere but in the divine mind" (6:206).[2] This passage in "Of Being"—evidently written in the summer of 1723 (6:203 n. 5)[3]—exhibits the author's cast of thought as an objective idealism.[4] Immediately thereafter, he stipulates in Corollary 1, "It follows from hence, that those beings which have knowledge and consciousness are the only proper and real and substantial beings, inasmuch as the being of other things is only by these" (6:206). Corollary 1, then, establishes that in Edwards' early thought "real and substantial beings" are effectively defined as the operations of *knowing* and *being conscious*.

"Of Atoms" is complementary to "Of Being" and in composition is roughly contemporaneous with the first part of "Of Being" (1720/21) (6:186).[5] In "Of Atoms" Edwards argues that of the primary properties commonly attributed to material bodies and their constituent atoms "solidity" or resistance to annihilation is the foremost. It is likely that he had in mind Henry More, who conceived of material bodies as being made of infinitesimally small, indivisible parts. (More's word for indivisible is "indiscerpible.") Edwards shows, at least to his own satisfaction, in Corollaries 8 through 11 of proposition 2 that atoms and bodies constituted of atoms owe their resistance to annihilation not to any underlying material substance but to the immediate exercise of God's power, "acting in particular manner in those parts of space where he thinks fit." "[S]peaking strictly," he continues, "there is no proper substance but God himself (we speak at present with respect to bodies only)" (6:215). The triumphant conclusion to Corollary 11 is: "How truly, then, is he said to be *ens Pentium*" (ibid.). God is the being of beings.

When we take "Of Being" and "Of Atoms" together, we have a rudimentary metaphysics. We have learned that the term "substance" is applicable only to beings that are conscious and know. God is the being of beings and the only being that exists through itself. If we should use scholastic terms, then we would say that the essence and existence of the being of beings are one. Other proper and real beings exist solely in dependence on God; they are composite entities. Material "bodies," bodies that are not conscious and do not know, bodies having such primary properties as solidity, extension, figure, and so forth, "inhere"—if they can be said to inhere at all—in the actions of God in ways and places such as God deems fit. Hence, we see why Edwards became accustomed to using the language of shadows when speaking of bodies. Natural phenomena are, accordingly, not substantial; they are the shadows of being.

At this juncture, having briefly surveyed two early writings antecedent to "The Mind" [1], namely, "Of Being" and "Of Atoms," we shall do well to remember two points that have already come before us which will later receive further elaboration and/or modification at Edwards' hand. The first has to do with Jonathan Edwards' characterization of "proper and real and substantial being" as having knowledge and consciousness. Knowledge is knowledge of something, and hence it is a species of relation. More remains to be said about this. Consciousness is the mind's awareness of itself, awareness of the operations that constitute it. As Edwards puts this in "The Mind" [16], "Consciousness is the mind's perceiving what is in itself—its ideas, actions, passions, and everything that is there perceivable. It is a sort of feeling within itself. The mind feels when it thinks, so it feels when it desires, feels when it loves, feels itself hate, etc." (6:345). These operations of the mind imply that mind or proper being is plural in some sense; the mind's operations—the operations that *are* the mind—are active relations, transpiring within the mind or between the mind and ideas of objects external to it. Moreover, such operations bring about consequences. In "The Mind" [45],[6] Edwards summarizes what he has already said about excellency and adds to it. When we speak of spirits, he reiterates, excellency signifies consent of being to being, that is, consent of mind to mind, and such consent is love, the highest form of consent. Dissent of mind (and will) to being is a kind of deformity. Thereupon he goes on to say, as it were in passing, that consent in a "high degree" of being to being brings about the consequence that such consenting being becomes "bigger" (6:363).[7] The language here is rough, but with effort we can decipher the meaning: the operation of consenting, when directed to an appropriate object, viz., another consenting being, changes and enhances consenting beings. I venture to put the meaning in this way: the act of being consenting to being is a complex *event* in which "plurality" is present and, indeed, is indispensable. Plurality is present but no pluralism, in the traditional philosophical sense of that term.

The second point to keep before ourselves at this juncture is that despite Edwards' habit of using shadow language when referring to natural phenomena, his interest in phenomena is intense. The intensity derives in part from Edwards' conviction that the mind is moved by an appetite for knowledge. "When the mind beholds a very uncommon object, there is the pleasure of a new perception." He calls this appetite the passion of admiration (6:367). Moreover, he is careful to advise that his idealism, which holds that the material universe exists in God's mind, does not abrogate the legitimacy and importance of natural philosophy. "We would not . . . be understood to deny that things are where they seem to be. For [our] principles . . . do not infer that. Nor will it be found that they at all make void natural philosophy. . . . For to find out the reasons of things in natural philosophy is only to find out the proportion of God's acting" (6:353).

Edwards' enthusiasm for Isaac Newton's discoveries in optics and his captivation with other natural phenomena fostered in him the passion of admiration on which we have already seen him comment in "The Mind." No amount of cogitation on abstract metaphysical principles displaces it. Such writings as "Of Insects" and his later "Spider Letter"[8]—"spiders sailing in the air . . . doubtless with abundance of pleasure"—or "Of the Rainbow" (1722), or "Of Light" (1721), or "The Beauty of the World" (1725–26), as well as his many other notes in "Natural Philosophy," directly attest to such a trait of his intellect. Hence, although Edwards routinely refers to nature's particulars as "shadows" of spiritual things, he acknowledges that these "shadows" surpass "the art of man" (6:305). Edwards' "shadows" are iridescent. In this natural world, there are, he writes, "beauties that are more palpable and explicable, and there are hidden and secret beauties. . . . Thus we find ourselves pleased in beholding the color of the violets, but we know not what secret regularity or harmony it is that creates that pleasure in our minds. These hidden beauties are commonly by far the greatest, because the more complex a beauty is, the more hidden is it" (6:306). Like Calvin before him, Edwards celebrated the artistry displayed in the great fabric of nature; but while for Calvin these works of divine artifice have become "mute teachers" in our decaying consciousness, for Edwards they remain still sensible and eloquent, though yet mysterious. In "Images of Divine Things," Edwards rhapsodizes that "[if] we look on these shadows of divine things as the voice of God. . . . we may, as it were, have God speaking to us. Wherever we are, and whatever we are about, we may see divine things excellently represented and held forth" (11:74).

In the opening sentences of "The Mind" [1], Edwards poses the question, What is this excellency with which we are more concerned than with anything else? In the pages that follow he appears to be occupied above all else with the hidden and secret beauties, which—owing to their great complexity and to our inattention—routinely escape our notice. Wallace E. Anderson's characterization of Edwards' thinking as a "phenomenalistic idealism" (6:112) is especially appropriate to the observations Edwards sets out in that entry. "We would know why," Edwards writes, "proportion is more excellent than disproportion; that is, why proportion is pleasant to the mind and disproportion unpleasant" (6:332). The inquiry he pursues from this point on is indeed an inquiry into esthetics, as Roland Delattre has taught us all. But in my view the embracing term *excellency* carries valency not only in aesthetics but also in morality and anthropology; and since these matters cannot be treated separately, these opening sentences strongly suggest inquiry into metaphysics or ontology as well.

In "The Mind" we find Edwards absorbed with the nature of harmony, symmetry, and proportion and with the reasons why perceiving beings respond to the apprehension of these qualities with pleasure or displeasure. Perforce, then, he must occupy himself with specific phenomena and with the experiences of pleasure (or its opposite) that arise when two or more things, whether they be geometrical figures such as parallel lines, circles of equal diameters, or equilateral triangles, come within the scope of our attention. This is a very important point in the early paragraphs of "The Mind" [1]. Here, where Edwards attends especially to constructed figures as instances of equality or "simple beauty," he is ever concerned with perceptions or ideas of pairs or triads or with multiples of other constructed kinds. The knowledge afforded in perception is, then, of a "relative" kind, as John Locke wrote in his *Essay Concerning Human Understanding*, wherein he argues, "knowledge . . . seems to me to be nothing but the perception of the connexion or agreement, or disagreement and repugnancy, of any of our ideas. In this alone it consists."[9] In his definition of truth Edwards at first echoes this statement by Locke, but shortly thereafter he modifies it to bring it into conformity with his idealism. Thus, while in entry 6 of "The Mind" he writes that "[truth] is the perception of the relations there are between ideas. . . . It is ideas, or what is in the mind alone, that can be the object of the mind," in entry 10 he corrects himself and states, "Truth, in the general, may be defined after the most strict and metaphysical manner: the 'consistency and agreement of our ideas with the ideas of God'" (6:340, 341f.). There are empirical and metaphysical reasons motivating these and kindred assertions Edwards makes. As we broach them, we enter into Edwards' thoughts about "complex beauty" or proportion and various matters immediately associated with them.

The first of these reasons appears in the form of his conviction that perception is the primary organ of our knowledge or ideas. "All sorts of ideas of things," Edwards writes, "are but the repetitions of those very things over again—as well the ideas of colors, figures, solidity, tastes, and smells, as the ideas of thought and mental acts" (6:383). Moreover, he is convinced that perceptions of "agreement" between two or more ideas of phenomena are indubitably constituent in our experience. The same would also necessarily hold true of perceptions of disagreement. And what is more—what is of inestimable importance to our understanding of Edwards—he affirms that perceptions of agreement bring *pleasure* to the perceiver. *Agreement among perceptual ideas elicits a sense of agreeableness in an intelligent percipient.* The experience of *pleasure* on the occasion of a perception of agreement between two or more phenomena supplies a new relation—perhaps we may say a new dimension—to the event of apprehending agreement among phenomena. To be sure, at this point in "The Mind," Edwards does *not* put this insight into so many words. Nonetheless, it is a clear implication of what he does explicitly write, namely, "Disagreement or contrariety to being is evidently an approach to nothing, or a degree of nothing . . . and the greatest and only evil; and entity is the greatest and only good" (6:335). Without perception of this order, perceptions of relation, which involve pleasure or pain, our cognitive experience would be barren.

It is especially to living things in nature that Edwards appeals, as he expands upon our perceptions of relations that are agreeable to perceiving beings and that evoke in them pleasure; so it is that he mentions the beauty of the shape of flowers, of the body of man, of animals, of trees, and so forth. In these instances he is especially attentive to the sheer complexity of the relations that appear in these natural phenomena—harmonious complexities that infinitely exceed those that his earlier geometrical figures exhibited. In effect, at this juncture Edwards has entered the domain of the senses, in which proportions express themselves not only in quantity and number but also in intensity. Plainly, it is the sheer abundance of living things that lifts our minds to the apprehension that we experience ourselves as dwelling in the midst of splendor. It is this realization, of which Edwards gives us an account in his "Personal Narrative," that enables him to exclaim, "For being, if we examine narrowly, is nothing but proportion."

In puzzling over the possibly opaque statement I have just repeated, we may help ourselves if we notice that even at this early moment Edwards uses the noun *being* to signify a particular being or entity, as well as being in general, and sometimes both at the same time. Here, I believe, he has in mind *being in general*, so that the sentence may be read as follows: "For being in general, if we examine narrowly, is nothing else but proportion." This reading commends itself particularly if we also take note of a statement Edwards makes in this vicinity, almost as in passing, that "Particular disproportions sometimes greatly add to the general beauty and must necessarily be, in order to a more universal proportion" (6:335). Although our author does not expand on this seemingly casual comment, I have long been persuaded that it represents an insight which became ever more significant for Edwards. And we shall see how that is so, when we briefly consider certain tenets that are utterly central to his treatise on virtue. But even here, it serves to caution us that when we bring a priori concepts of beauty to bear, as we contemplate this or that view of things, we run the risk of judging some object of our perception as a "deformity," when a little humble patience would enable us to discern that the existence of this displeasing deformity may be indispensable to the widening of our intellectual view upon a greater and more intense harmony than our unassisted imaginations could ever open to us.

Resuming his meditative course, Edwards goes on to say, "Spiritual harmonies are of vastly larger extent, i.e., the proportions are vastly oftener redoubled and respect more beings and require a vastly larger view to comprehend them. The reason why equality [of ratios] thus pleases the mind, and inequality is unpleasing, is because disproportion . . . is contrary to being" (6:336). If we take "being" and "being in general" as equivalent terms, then we have the reading: *Disproportion is contrary to being in general*. But as we have already noticed, "Particular disproportions sometimes greatly add to the general beauty and must necessarily be, in order to a more universal proportion." Edwards must hold to both of these positions.[10] And all of the reasoning he has carried out thus far finds its culmination in the second set of propositions quoted at the outset of this essay. There we found Edwards saying: "One alone, without reference to any more, cannot be excellent; for in such a case, there can be no manner of relation no way." He then continued with these words: "But in a being that is absolutely without any plurality there cannot be excellency." However, the last clause of this passage remains to be added now, viz., "for there can be no such thing as consent or agreement."[11] One alone cannot be excellent because there can be no room for being in general. Edwards then adds immediately, "One of the highest excellencies is love" (6:337). Apart from being in general, there can be no agreement, no consent, no love.

With Edwards' invocation of love as one the highest excellencies, we turn briefly to his exceptional, posthumously published treatise, *The Nature of True Virtue*. Though we cannot dwell on this treatise, there are several features to be noticed that are illuminated by his early manuscript "The Mind," and these same features reflect additional light upon that early manuscript.

I begin, of course, with Edwards' definition of true virtue. Virtue, he writes "is the beauty [excellency] of those qualities and acts of the mind that are of a moral nature, i.e., such as are attended with . . . worthiness or blame" (8:539). Virtue pertains to disposition and will, to what Edwards calls the "heart." But not all virtue is true virtue, because there are differences between dispositions and acts directed merely to particular "objects" and dispositions and acts having being in general as their "object." Dispositions and acts having being in general as their object are beautiful in a general way, and as such may include particular objects. But dispositions and acts having only particular objects are without the character of general beauty. The first of these kinds of virtue operates only in a "private sphere" (8:540). This distinction is critical to the whole of *The Nature of True Virtue*. Edwards' definition of true virtue is, then, "*benevolence to being in general*. It is consent, propensity and union of heart to being in general, which is immediately exercised in a general good will" (ibid.). True virtue is love toward being in general.

For the purpose I have in mind, I shall proceed now to an important distinction Edwards makes with respect to virtuous love. He distinguishes between "love of benevolence" and "love of complacence." Love of benevolence is . . . that propensity of heart to any being, which causes it to incline to its well-being, or disposes it to desire and take pleasure in its *happiness*" (8:542, emphasis added). Love of complacence, on the other hand, "presupposes beauty" in its object. Love of complacence "delights" in its object (8:543). These two loves are distinct, but they ought not to be considered apart from one another. Benevolence centers in the good and happiness of the being which it unites itself to. Love of complacence differs in this sense, that the agent of this love experiences enjoyment or delight as it loves the beauty of its object. The force of the distinction between these two loves is that benevolence has *being in general* for its object; while love of complacence has *beauty* in the beloved for its object. Now, we may well ask what this distinction amounts to. The significance of the distinction appears when Edwards observes that if we say true virtue lies in the love of moral beauty, then we are saying no more than that virtue loves virtue, and this would be nothing but a tautology. Or else, to say as much would be to say that the moral beauty to which the love of complacence is directed may be no more than a repetition of the lover's own beauty. Therefore, Edwards insists that the first object of a virtuous benevolence is being simply considered or, what amounts to the same thing, being in general. This stipulation guards against a parochial idea of virtuous love. Being in general must always be the first ground of virtuous love. Only when the virtuous mind strives ever to take into view being in general—and being in general can never be exhausted or comprehended entirely—may it then enjoy the delight of the love of complacence. *The Nature of True Virtue* thus opens to us a quest to which there can never be an end. True virtue must always be open to the possibility of greater and greater plurality. William James once wrote that a system, to be a system at all, must be a closed system. Edwards, it seems to me, could not agree. Being in general is an open system.

Notes

1. See Wallace E. Anderson's discussion of the dating of "The Mind" (6:326). Anderson accepts Thomas Schafer's finding that Jonathan Edwards began writing the "The Mind" [1] as entry number 78 in the long series of observations he entitled "Miscellanies"; however, Edwards crossed out the text of this entry and commenced anew his discussion of the topic "excellency" in "The Mind" [1]. This significant change occurred before the end of 1723. See also Anderson's "Editor's Introduction" (6:29f.). Thomas Schafer provides an abundance of invaluable information about the chronology of Edwards' writings in his introduction to "Miscellanies," nos. a–500 (13:1–109). See his chronological tables of entries in *"Miscellanies"* (especially table 2, 13:91–109; cf. 13:243 n. 8).

2. I make no attempt to reproduce Jonathan Edwards' circuitous line of argument here.

3. Jonathan Edwards wrote "Of Being" in stages. The quoted words here belong to the second stage.

4. Henry More, a leading Cambridge Platonist whom Jonathan Edwards read, is one source of his idealism. Jonathan Edwards repeats More's contention that since space cannot be thought away or removed from the mind, it is God. See the third paragraph in "Of Being." This position derives from More's disagreement with Descartes, who maintained that spirit is not extended, while material bodies are.

5. See Schafer's introduction, table 2 (13:91f.).

6. Schafer dates "The Mind" [45] to 1725–26. See table 2 (13:91f.). Hence, little time has elapsed between the composition of [1] and [45].

7. "The Mind" [45] (6:362–66). In section 5 of [45] the pertinent sentences read: "This [dissenting from being] is disagreeable to being, for perceiving being only is properly being. Still more disagreeable is a dissent from a very excellent being (or, as we have explained, to a being that consents in a high degree to being, because such a being by such a consent becomes bigger), and a dissenting from such a being includes also a dissenting from what he consents with, which is other beings or being in general" (6:363).

8. Anderson dates these to 1719/20 and 1723 (6:150).

9. *An Essay Concerning Human Understanding*, ed. A. S. Pringle-Pattison (Oxford: Oxford University Press, 1924), book 6, chapter 1, p. 255. In section 5 of this chapter, p. 256f., Locke discusses the *relativity* of knowledge as the perception of agreement or disagreement.

10. He must hold to both because finite minds can apprehend actual ideas drawn from reflection, such as "being in general," but their apprehension is partial. Only God understands all things "by the actual and immediate presence of the idea of the thing understood." See "Miscellanies," no. 782 (18:475f.).

11. I have extended this quotation from "The Mind" [1] to emphasize the kind of plurality that is at stake for Edwards. In 1724, just after he began "The Mind," Edwards wrote "Miscellanies," 117 with the heading "Trinity." The entry concludes with an appendix, as it were, which reads: "Again, we have shown that

one alone cannot be excellent, inasmuch as in such case, there can be no consent. Therefore, if God is excellent, there must be a plurality in God; otherwise, there can be no consent in him" (13:284).

Suggested Further Readings

Anderson, Wallace E. "Editor's Introduction." *The Works of Jonathan Edwards*, 6, *Scientific and Philosophical Writings*. New Haven: Yale University Press, 1980.

Delattre, Roland A. *Beauty and Sensibility in the Thought of Jonathan Edwards: An Essay in Aesthetics and Theological Ethics*. New Haven: Yale University Press, 1968.

Lee, Sang Hyun. *The Philosophical Theology of Jonathan Edwards*. Princeton: Princeton University Press, 2000.

Four

The Trinity

Amy Plantinga Pauw

IT IS ONLY IN the last twenty-five years that the doctrine of the Trinity has received much attention in studies of Jonathan Edwards' theology. Before then the mainstream of his theological legacy followed other channels, into explorations of human will and virtue, morphologies of spiritual revival, and assertions of divine sovereignty. Meanwhile, the tremendous renewed interest in the doctrine of the Trinity in contemporary Western theology proceeded almost completely without reference to American theology before the twentieth century. There was a brief flurry of interest in Edwards' unpublished writings on the Trinity in the late nineteenth century, fed by rumors of their unorthodoxy (13:548–49).[1] But in general these writings have been more neglected than controverted. Fortunately, as more of Edwards' writings become widely available, his trinitarian reflection is beginning to claim a place both in wider theological discussion and in Edwards' own legacy.[2]

Within Edwards' theocentric universe, "God is the prime and original being, the first and last, and the pattern of all, and has the sum of all perfection" (6:363). The distinctively trinitarian pattern of God's perfection in Edwards' theology links two aspects of his thought that have often seemed disconnected and have been studied in isolation: his profound metaphysical musings and his zeal for the church and the Christian life. Ultimate reality for Edwards concerned the dynamics of union—eternally within God, between God and creatures, and among creatures themselves. The Trinity was the paradigm of this union, "the supreme harmony of all" ("Misc." 182, 13:329), and it provided a framework for pondering the diverse intellectual and pastoral puzzles Edwards confronted throughout his career, from the problems of substance metaphysics and deist assaults on Christian doctrine to God's end in creating the world and the outbreak of colonial revivals.

The basic outlines of Edwards' trinitarian thought were established when he was only twenty years old, in an entry in the notebooks he entitled "Miscellanies." There he asserted that "if God has an idea of himself, there is really a duplicity. . . . And if God loves himself and delights in himself, there is really a triplicity, three that cannot be confounded, each of which are the Deity substantially" ("Misc." 94, 13:262). Throughout his twenties, Edwards returned to the doctrine of the Trinity frequently, stockpiling scriptural evidence and exploring the connections between the eternal "triplicity" in God and root metaphysical notions such as relation, proportion, and excellency. These deep correlations between his metaphysics and his doctrine of the Trinity were thus in place before Edwards' major treatises were written. Even where the doctrine is not mentioned explicitly, his abundant use of terms like love, understanding, consent, and beauty in his later writings has a distinctively trinitarian cast to it.

The Trinity was also at the center of Edwards' mystical, affective faith. "God has appeared glorious to me on account of the Trinity," he declared in his *Personal Narrative*. "It has made me have exalting thoughts of God that he subsists in three persons; Father, Son, and Holy Ghost" (16:800). While he was still at Yale, Edwards ruminated in his notebooks, "I used to think sometimes with myself, if such doctrines as those of the Trinity and decrees are true, yet what need was there of revealing them in the gospel? what good do they do towards the advancing [of] holiness?" Answering his own question in a typically Puritan fashion, Edwards exclaimed, "I know by experience how useful these doctrines be. . . . for such doctrines as these are glorious inlets into the knowledge and view of the spiritual world, and the contemplation of supreme things; the knowledge of which I have experienced how much it contributes to the betterment of the heart" ("Misc." 181, 13:328). Edwards' trinitarian reflections join metaphysical profundity with an intensely practical concern for "the advancing of holiness." They are a splendid illustration of what Robert Jenson has referred to as "the native unity of speculation and adoration in his life."[3]

Two Trinitarian Models

In 1730 Edwards began work on a "Discourse on the Trinity," drawing on numerous "Miscellanies" entries he had already written on the topic.[4] After writing eight folio pages, he put the manuscript aside, picking it up a few years later to edit it and add several more pages. By the 1740s Edwards was treating this work as a source book, adding discrete entries from time to time and cannibalizing it for well-known sermons and treatises like *A Divine and Supernatural Light* and *Religious Affections*. Already in the earliest portion of "Discourse on the Trinity," Edwards signaled the two interrelated models that funded all his trinitarian reflections: God is like a mind that knows and loves itself, and God is like a society or family of three.

The first model came down to Edwards, however circuitously, from the Augustinian tradition. Cotton Mather, perhaps a proximate source for Edwards' appropriation of it, depicted the Father as "the Fountain of the Deity," the Son as "the Express Image of the Father's Person," and the Holy Spirit as "that wonderful Joy and Love, which God has in Himself by the Grateful Perception which the Father and Son Eternally have of one another."[5] In "Discourse on the Trinity" Edwards experimented with idealist transmutations of this trinitarian model:

> And if it were possible for a man by reflection perfectly to contemplate all that is in his own mind in an hour, as it is and at the same time that it is there, in its first and direct existence; if a man had a perfect reflex or contemplative idea of every thought at the same moment or moments that that thought was, and of every exercise at and during the same time that that exercise was, and so through a whole hour: a man would really be two. He would be indeed double; he would be twice at once: the idea he has of himself would be himself again. (21:116)

And because God's understanding is also by idea, and because the divine self-contemplation is perfect, "that idea which God hath of Himself is absolutely Himself" (21:116). "By this means the Godhead is really generated and repeated" (21:114). Having thus demonstrated to his satisfaction the "distinct subsistence or person" of the Son as the Father's idea, Edwards went on to show how

> the divine essence itself flows out and is as it were breathed forth in love and joy. So that the Godhead therein stands forth in yet another manner of subsistence, and there proceeds the third person in the Trinity, the Holy Spirit, viz. the Deity in act: for there is no other act but the act of the will. (21:121)

Though his use of this trinitarian model was fluid and often understated, the constellation of images referring to God's understanding, word, and idea, on the one hand, and to God's love, will, holiness, and beauty, on the other, was integral to Edwards' entire theology. From his fascination with typologies to his ponderings on true virtue and the course of the revivals, a dependence on this conceptuality can be observed, even where Edwards did not appeal to the Trinity explicitly.

In no. 94 of the "Miscellanies," Edwards had prefaced this doctrinal exploration with worrisome bravado: "I think that it is within the reach of naked reason to perceive certainly that there are three distinct in God" (13:257). However, in his reprise of the argument in the "Discourse," a much more Augustinian humility about the human capacity to know God emerges:

> But I don't pretend fully to explain how these things are, and I am sensible a hundred other objections may be made, and puzzling doubts and questions

raised, that I can't solve. I am far from pretending to explaining the Trinity so as to render it no longer a mystery. I think it to be the highest and deepest of all divine mysteries still, notwithstanding anything that I have said or conceived about it. (21:134)

It is perhaps a mark of the sincerity of Edwards' confession that, in his pervasive use of this model in his later writings, he largely abandoned the language of "reflex acts" of knowledge and will and evidenced little continuing interest in contemplating "the Deity in its direct existence" apart from the eternal presence of the Son and Spirit.

The second trinitarian model Edwards relied on was a social model, indebted perhaps to the twelfth-century Augustinian theologian Richard of St. Victor. Richard insisted that God, who is love, is necessarily a community of persons, since the perfection of any person is found in loving another person. A mere duality of persons would not suffice, because there would be no opportunity to communicate and share the delights of their mutual happiness. Therefore the Trinity must consist of three persons, united by perfect confluence of love and purpose. In "Discourse on the Trinity," Edwards closely echoed Richard's approach:

That in John, "God is love" [1 John 4:8, 16], shows that there are more persons than one in the Deity: for it shows love to be essential and necessary to the Deity, so that his nature consists in it; and this supposes that there is an eternal and necessary object, because all love respects another, that is, the beloved. (21:113–14)

Corresponding to this social conception of God's triune nature, Edwards affirmed "the equality of the persons among themselves, and that they are every way equal in the society or family of the three. They are equal in honor besides the honor which is common to 'em all, viz. that they are all God; each has his peculiar honor in the society or family" (21:135). Edwards' homiletical focus on the work of Jesus Christ and his deep concern for nurturing Christian community fueled his use of the Victorine model for the Trinity.

The step from the biblical language of Father and Son to calling the Godhead a family or society may seem like a small one. In fact, within the Reformed theological framework, it was a large one, and rarely ventured. God is never referred to in the Bible as a family or society, and Reformed emphasis on the primacy of Scripture and the oneness of God, combined with theological convictions about human sinfulness and a corresponding distrust of human analogies for God, made overtly social metaphors like these unusual, and even daring. Yet throughout his writings Edwards showed his willingness to use these metaphors and expressed concern for the equality of the trinitarian persons in this divine "society."

In particular, he worried that the honor traditionally accorded to the Holy Spirit was "not equal in any sense to the Father and the Son's" (21:191), a problem Edwards himself was not able to solve within the confines of the Victorine model.

Edwards' use of different trinitarian models reflects the richness and tensions of his broadly Augustinian theological inheritance. Portraying the Trinity both as the overflowing of God's eternal wisdom and love and as a society of three persons required modulating between different theological conceptualities. The first trinitarian model accents the Father's primordial effusiveness, in which the Son and Holy Spirit become, in the idiom of Sang Hyun Lee's dispositional ontology, the "repetition or communication of the Father's eternal actuality."[6] The second model accents the equality and interdependence of the triune persons. Edwards' modulations between these models were not always harmonious. Furthermore, his appeals to each model were uneven. Despite his foregrounding of the Son as the perfect idea of the Father in "Discourse on the Trinity," Edwards' larger corpus of writings reveals that the Son's role as Idea or Wisdom was not as central to his theological reflections as the Spirit's role as Love. Conversely, the role of the Holy Spirit was often slighted in his portrayal of the Godhead as a society of three persons. As a bridge between these two trinitarian models, Edwards (again following Augustine) often depicted the Holy Spirit as the mutual love of the Father and the Son.

Edwards gave no hint that he was troubled by the dissonances among these models for the Trinity. That he refused to choose a single model is an indication of the diverse polemical and pastoral situations in which he forged his trinitarian reflections, as well as his high tolerance for theological tension. More profoundly, Edwards' trinitarian multivalence reveals that he appealed to different models of the Trinity not as conflicting blueprints of the inner life of the Godhead but as complementary linguistic resources for narrating God's saving work. Like Augustine before him, Edwards employed a variety of mutually correcting trinitarian vocabularies in the service of a creative theological exploration of God's work of redemption. According to Edwards' basic soteriological story line,

> God having from eternity from his infinite goodness designed to communicate himself to creatures . . . [chose] to unite himself to a created nature, and to become one of the creatures, and to gather together in one all elect creatures in that creature he assumed into a personal union with himself, and to manifest to them and maintain intercourse with them through him. ("Misc." 744, 18:389)

Edwards found contrasting trinitarian models indispensable for articulating how that union between God and creatures takes place and reaches perfection. The power and versatility of Edwards's reflections on the Trinity are best seen in the intricate connections he wove between the perfect consent of God's immanent being and God's creative, saving, and sanctifying work.

Apologetic Strategies

However, Edwards lived in a time when the doctrine of the Trinity had come under fierce attack by a small but influential number of Christians who saw it as an irrational encumbrance to faith, rather than a glorious mystery. Starting at the end of the seventeenth century, intermittent battles had been raging in England over the doctrine of the Trinity. As Edwards noted in his "Miscellanies" notebooks in the early 1720s, "There has been much cry of late against saying one word, particularly about the Trinity, but what the Scripture has said; judging it impossible but that if we did, we should err in a thing so much above us" ("Misc." 94, 13:256). Edwards was probably alluding to the extended furor over the 1712 publication of *The Scripture-Doctrine of the Trinity*, by Anglican bishop Samuel Clarke. After a diligent search, Clarke professed to find no definite biblical statement to support creedal orthodoxy that the Son was of one divine substance with the Father. Clarke's advice to treat the trinitarian question as a nonessential of the faith, on which Christians could reach their own conclusions, proved a crushing blow for orthodoxy. Conrad Wright has described Clarke's *Scripture-Doctrine of the Trinity* as "a pervasive influence, spreading anti-Trinitarianism in the Church of England and dissenting circles alike for two generations after its publication."[7]

New England was not impervious to English antitrinitarian currents, although the main disagreement between theological liberals and conservatives in the first half of the eighteenth century concerned human, not divine, nature. Edwards expended much of his pastoral energy in combatting Arminianism, a view that he thought derogated from God's glory by denying humanity's "absolute and universal dependence on God" for salvation (17:212). However, Arminian tendencies in New England, at least among the seekers of a more "reasonable" faith, proved to be harbingers of antitrinitarianism. Edwards explicitly linked the two in his first published work, *God Glorified in Man's Dependence* (1731), in which he argued that Arminian views on human nature deny "our dependence on each person in the Trinity for all our good," by attempting to "exalt man into the place of either Father, Son, or Holy Ghost" (17:201, 212). In the sermon's doxological rhetoric, Calvinist anthropology and trinitarian orthodoxy perfectly coincide: "There is an absolute dependence of the creature on every one for all: all is *of* the Father, all *through* the Son, and all *in* the Holy Ghost. Thus God appears in the work of redemption, as all in all" (17:212).

At the end of Edwards' life, explicit attacks on trinitarian doctrine arose in New England. Jonathan Mayhew scandalized the Massachusetts clergy by boldly declaring that "my Bible saith not . . . that there is any other true God, besides '[Jesus'] Father and our Father, his God and our God.' "[8] New Englanders who defended trinitarian orthodoxy were likewise troubled by Thomas Emlyn's *Humble Inquiry into the Scripture-account of Jesus Christ* (Boston, 1756), with its preface challenging theologians to refute a subordinationist view of Jesus. In a 1757 letter to Professor Wigglesworth at Harvard, Edwards expressed his uneasiness after reading a book by Mayhew "wherein he ridicules the doctrine of the Trinity," and, in response to Emlyn's book, sounded "the call of God that some one should appear in open defense of this doctrine" (16:698–99).

Edwards himself appeared in open defense of the doctrine of the Trinity throughout his life. Like other orthodox Christians during the English Enlightenment, he thought it appropriate to counter attacks on the reasonableness of the doctrine of the Trinity with reasonable arguments. As early as 1724, Edwards planned to write a treatise entitled "A Rational Account of the Principles and Main Doctrines of the Christian Religion," with the aim of showing that "the present fashionable divinity is wrong" ("Misc." 832, 18:546). In an outline to this projected work, Edwards reminded himself "[t]o explain the doctrine of the Trinity before I begin to treat of the work of redemption" (6:396). While he eventually abandoned his plans to write this treatise, Edwards never gave up his conviction that belief in the Trinity was reasonable and continued to propose a variety of arguments on its behalf.

As his perception of the deist threat to Christian belief escalated in the last two decades of his life, Edwards brought a new theological urgency to defending the doctrine's reasonableness. To those who found it unbiblical, Edwards countered with extended demonstrations that an eternal threefold distinction in God was "agreeable to the tenor of the whole New Testament" (21:134). Even in the Old Testament, "[t]he very frequent joining of the word *Elohim*, a word in the plural number, with the word *Jehovah*, a word in the singular number" struck Edwards as "a significant indication of the union of several divine persons in one Essence" ("Misc." 1105, 20:487). To more radical critics of Christian orthodoxy, disdainful of biblical revelation and enamored with the wisdom of "the ancient heathen," Edwards argued that even "[t]he heathen philosophers speak of the Son of God as Wisdom or Idea or Logos, and of the Holy Spirit as Love" ("Misc." 955, 20:227). In Edwards' view, their foreshadowings of trinitarian doctrine were so remarkable that they must have had "some degree of INSPIRATION of the Spirit of God which led 'em to say such wonderful things concerning the Trinity" ("Misc." 1162, 23:84).[9]

Even in his youthful brashness about the powers of unaided reason, Edward's explicit reliance on Scripture for his exposition of the Trinity reflected the conviction that divine revelation was "exceeding needful" for correct theological understanding. Without God's declaration to humanity concerning "what manner of being he is," human reason is helpless. "For though reason may be sufficient to confirm such a declaration after it is given, and see its consistence, harmony and rationality in many respects, yet reason may be utterly insufficient first to discover these things" ("Misc." 1338, 23:348). At times Edwards conceded that the frailty of human reason renders even confirmation of the "consistence, harmony and rationality" of divine revelation difficult. Elsewhere in his "Miscellanies" notebooks, he cited the case of a thirteen-year-old boy who refused to believe that a two-inch cube was eight times as big as a one-inch cube, noting that "it was a much more difficult mystery to him than the Trinity ordinarily is to men." "[W]hy should we not suppose," Edwards demanded, "that there may be some things that are true, that may be as much above our understandings and as difficult to them, as this truth was to this boy" ("Misc." 652, 18:192–93). "The doctrines of the Trinity, incarnation, etc." are "so above human comprehension" that even when divinely revealed they remain "difficult to be received by the judgment or belief" ("Misc." 839, 20:54–55). Edwards thus found deist Matthew Tindal's insistence that "reason is the judge whether there be any revelation" to be a most "unreasonable way of arguing" ("Misc." 1340, 23:359).

In his trinitarian thought Edwards joined in the larger theological tumult of his day, an era torn between a desire for a "reasonable Christianity" and the comforts of a rich, finally ineffable tradition. Many of his particular philosophical, biblical, and historical arguments for the doctrine of the Trinity appear quaint or even outlandish today. But what Michael McClymond has referred to as Edwards' "implicit apology,"[10] his stunning ability to incorporate diverse philosophical, ethical, and pastoral interests into his theological reflections, remains compelling. Edwards' confident assumption that the Trinity is in fact at the center of Christian faith and his multifaceted articulation of the beauty and excellency of the triune God retain a deep spiritual and theological resonance.

Divine Beauty and Excellency

As the sum of ontological and moral perfection, the Trinity was at the heart of Edwards' perception of beauty and excellency. "[O]ne alone cannot be excellent," Edwards wrote, "inasmuch as, in such case, there can be no consent. Therefore, if God is excellent, there must be a plurality in God; otherwise, there can be no consent in him" ("Misc." 117, 13:284). Abandoning metaphysical visions of God's solitary perfection, Edwards depicted divine excellency as relations of harmonious consent within an irreducible plurality. "It appears that there must be more than a unity in infinite and eternal essence, otherwise the goodness of God can have no perfect exercise" ("Misc." 96, 13:263). God's relations with creatures do not allow for this perfect exercise, because "that which infinitely and perfectly agrees is the very same essence, for if it be different it don't infinitely consent" ("Misc." 117, 13:283). Divine excellency requires that God's eternal identity be an identity in otherness.

This understanding of divine excellency made Edwards dissatisfied with the version of the Augustinian model that posited the Holy Spirit as God's "infinite love to himself." "That which is often called self-love is exceedingly improperly called love" (6:337), he declared. True consent and thus true excellency within the Godhead required *reciprocal* love and delight. Edwards frequently resolved this problem by following Augustine in portraying the Holy Spirit as the bond of love between the Father and Son. In *Charity and Its Fruits*, for example, he portrayed the Holy Spirit as the mutual love of the Father and Son for each other, so that "the Son of God is not only the infinite object of love, but he is also an infinite subject of it. He is not only the infinite object of the Father's love, but he also infinitely loves the Father" (8:373). As noted earlier, this habitual modification of the Augustinian model provided a bridge to the emphasis on social union in the Victorine model of the Trinity. God is not "one alone," but subsists in a perichoretic unity of love and consent.

Edwards most commonly portrayed this plurality within the Godhead in interpersonal terms. As he noted in a sermon on Acts 20:28, "the eternal, infinite happiness of the Divine Being seems to be social, consisting in the infinitely blessed union and society of the persons of the Trinity, so that they are happy in one another."[11] Though Edwards was aware of a long theological tradition of affirming true distinctions in the Godhead via the notion of "real relations,"[12] he rarely appealed to it. Instead, he expressed confidence regarding the appropriateness of the term *person* to signify trinitarian distinctions:

> though the word "person" be rarely used in the Scriptures, yet I believe that we have no word in the English language that does so naturally represent what the Scripture reveals of the distinction of the eternal three—Father, Son and Holy Ghost—as to say they are one God but three persons. (21:181)

Edwards firmly rejected the tritheism of "three distinct Gods, friends one to another" ("Misc." 539, 18:84). Yet he was willing to break with traditional construals of divine unity and affirm "distinct personal agents" within the eternal society of the Trinity (21:181). In his deeply relational understanding of God, God does not make a decision to come into relation but from eternity exists as perfect loving communion.

All creaturely excellency echoes the consent-within-complexity of the Trinity. The eros of human desire for union with the other is not a mark of creaturely deficiency or a carnal distraction from the business of religion: desire for society and communion "cannot be because of our imperfection, but because we are made in the image of God; for the more perfect any creature is, the more strong this inclination" ("Misc." 96, 13:264). In Edwards' extended reflections on true sainthood—beginning with *A Faithful Narrative, Distinguishing Marks*, and *Some Thoughts on the Revival* and culminating in *Religious Affections* and *The Nature of True Virtue*—there is a consistent emphasis on the work of the Holy Spirit as creating capacity and desire for loving union with God and with fellow creatures. Conversion, justification, sanctification, and glorification for Edwards had their roots in the eternal consent and excellency of the Trinity. When the disposition to acts of love and delight in God is infused in human persons by the indwelling of the Holy Spirit, they are enabled to partake of God's own "excellence and beauty; that is, of holiness, which consists in love" (6:364).

Beauty as well was irreducibly relational for Edwards. Anything that is beautiful exhibits consent and agreement, and so must be "distinguished into a plurality some way or other" (6:337). Physical beauty, while delightful, is an image and shadow of "true, spiritual original beauty, . . . consisting in being's consent to being, or the union of minds or spiritual beings in a mutual propensity and affection of heart" (8:564). Thus, the aesthetic dimensions of Edwards' theology derived from the more basic category of loving consent, because "all the primary and original beauty or excellence that is among minds is love" (6:362). While creatures are beautiful "in loving others, in loving God, and in the communications of his Spirit" " 'tis peculiar to God that he has beauty within himself" (6:365). The perfect consent within the Trinity is the reason "God is God, and distinguished from all other beings, and exalted above 'em, chiefly by his divine beauty" (2:298).

The Triune Work of Redemption

The work of redemption formed the centerpiece of Edwards' reflections on God's relation to the created world, and the beauty of the Trinity was more in evidence in this complex divine work than anywhere else. Ordained from eternity, the work of redemption "may be looked upon as the great end and drift of all God's works and dispensations from the beginning. All other works of providence may be looked upon as *appendages* to this great work, or *things* which God does to subserve that grand design" ("Misc." 702, 18:284). While punishment of sins and the eternal rejection of some sinners were integral parts of Edwards' theology, he was clear that judgment is God's "strange work," executed "for the sake of something else," not for its own sake ("Misc." 1081, 20: 464–65). The dominant themes of grace and union in Edwards' trinitarian reflections reveal a profound asymmetry in his understanding of God's relations with creatures. At the headwater of his theology is the identification of divine glory with the communication of God's overflowing love beyond the boundaries of the Godhead. Edwards' vivid defense of hell's torments does not deserve the preeminence it has often been accorded in accounts of his work. The work of redemption was so much "the great end" of the divine economy that even "the world itself seems to have been created in order to it" (9:118).

This work concerns "not only what Christ the mediator has done, but also what the Father and the Holy Ghost have done as united or confederated in this design of redeeming sinful men" (9:117–18). In fact, the work of redemption makes clear why "it was requisite that the doctrine of the Trinity itself should be revealed to us": "that by a discovery of the concern of the several divine persons, in the great affair of our salvation, we might the better understand and see how all our dependence in this affair is on God, and our sufficiency all in him, and not in ourselves" (19:239–40). The work of redemption reveals the depth and ultimate triumph of God's desire that the creation participate in the beauty and excellency of the Trinity.

Edwards used two idioms to describe how the work of redemption graciously extends God's internal consent to the creation. The idioms of emanation and covenant correspond to Edwards' two trinitarian models. The model of God's eternal wisdom and love accommodated the imagery of emanation and remanation. "There is an infinite fullness of all possible good in God, a fullness of every perfection, of all excellency and beauty, and of infinite happiness" (8:432–33). This fullness distinguishes God from everything creaturely. "God is a communicative being" ("Misc." 332, 13:410), however, and therefore the perfections of the Trinity do not remain within the Godhead but flow out toward creatures. The eternal trinitarian processions of wisdom and love within God find fitting external expression in God's communication of wisdom and love to creatures. The Logos as "God's perfect understanding of himself" and the Holy Ghost as "the love, the joy, the excellence, the holiness of God" ("Misc." 331, 13:409–10) correspond in the work of redemption to "Christ's being in the creature in the name, idea or knowledge of God being in them, and the Holy Spirit's being in them in the love of God's being in them" ("Misc." 1084, 20:467). God's perfect knowledge and love emanate beyond the inner life of the Godhead through the indwelling of Christ and the Holy Spirit in the hearts and minds of believers. This human knowledge and love of God remanates in joy and praise to God, and God's being is glorified and enlarged. But the accent for Edwards was always on God's gracious superabundance: "the main end of his shining forth is not that he may have his rays reflected back to himself, but that the rays may go forth" ("Misc." 448, 13:496).

Despite the beautiful symmetry this scheme achieved between the immanent perfections of the Godhead and their external expressions, the economic role it ascribed to the Son did not adequately reflect the risk and costliness of God's engagement with humanity in the work of redemption. The notion of Christ as the indwelling idea or knowledge of God could suggest that redemption was a bloodless process of spiritual enlightenment. The heart of Edwards' preaching suggested otherwise: in a world marked by sin and death, God's desire to incorporate human creatures into the divine life required a fierce struggle against all that stands in the way of this intimate union. The social model, in its depiction of the Son as a distinct personal agent, capable of entering human history as a helpless infant and atoning for human sin on the cross, was more helpful to Edwards in portraying the Christological heart of the work of redemption. What saints receive in union with Christ through the power of the Spirit is not wisdom and love in general but the grace that conforms them to the trustful wisdom and gratuitous love embodied in Christ's own life. The intrinsic self-giving character of the Trinity was communicated to human sinners in the particular self-giving of the incarnate Son.

However, the Son's extraordinary self-giving posed trinitarian problems of its own. Human assurance of salvation demanded that there be a deep coherence between God's eternal being and the temporal work of redemption. Orthodoxy required that this coherence not be obtained at the expense of a subordination of the Son and Spirit that prevented them from being properly "worshiped and glorified together" with the Father. Edwards needed another bridge between God's immanent fullness and economic outworkings that would play out his basic themes of relation and dynamism in an explicitly social way. He found this bridge in the Reformed notion of an eternal covenant of redemption made between the Father and the Son on behalf of human sinners. *Covenant* became the other primary idiom in which Edwards described the great work of redemption.

"Miscellanies," no. 1062, originally published by Egbert Smyth under the title *Observations Concerning the Scripture of Œconomy of the Trinity and Covenant of Redemption*,[13] is an extended exposition of "that agreement which the persons of the Trinity came into from eternity as it were by mutual consultation and covenant" (20:323). In this carefully written entry, Edwards argued that "there is dependence without inferiority" (20:430) in both the Godhead's eternal being and redemptive work. Edwards perceived a complex harmony between the internal, loving consent of the Trinity and the order of acting agreed upon by the divine persons for the work of redemption. Redemption according to the covenant idiom is a matter of intimate social union, and God's grand design in this work is to expand the immanent "divine family" so that the perfect consent between the Father and Son embraces the redeemed as well. As Edwards declared at the end of his famous sermon *The Excellency of Christ*,

> Christ has brought it to pass, that those that the Father has given him, should be brought into the household of God; that he, and his Father, and his people, should be as it were one society, one family; that the church should be as it were admitted into the society of the blessed Trinity. (19:594)

The idiom of emanation and remanation captured beautifully the redemptive role of the Holy Spirit as "an infinite fountain of divine glory and sweetness" (16:801). Likewise, the idiom of covenant was crucial to Edwards' portrayal of the work of Christ. Together, they illustrate how the Trinity is both the source and pattern for all of God's works *ad extra*.

The "supreme harmony" of the Trinity becomes even more explicit in Edwards' portrayals of the eschatological culmination of the work of redemption. In the millennium, that "future promised glorious day of the church's prosperity" (5:481) on earth, the gifts of the Spirit would be poured out as never before. In this superabundance of love, the Father and Son will "be most eminently glorified on earth," and the "glorious beauty" of the saints will echo the beauty of the society of the Trinity: "all the world [shall then be] as one church, one orderly, regular, beautiful society, one body, all the members in beautiful proportion" (9:484). But the millennium, however glorious, was only God's penultimate gift to the church—the enduring blessedness of saints would occur in heaven. Heaven is glorious because it is the dwelling place of the persons of the Trinity: there the Father and Son "are united in infinitely dear and incomprehensible mutual love," and the Holy Spirit, who is "the spirit of divine love," flows forth to all heaven's inhabitants (8:369):

> in heaven this fountain of love, the eternal three in one, is set open without any obstacle to hinder access to it. There this glorious God is manifested and shines forth in full glory, in beams of love; there the fountain overflows in streams and rivers of love and delight, enough for all to drink at, and to swim in, yea, so as to overflow the world as it were with a deluge of love. (8:370)

God and Christ join with the saints and angels to form a society overflowing with mutual love and joy. In heaven the redemptive work of the Trinity achieves a dynamic and unhindered fullness.

The heavenly love of the saints for each other and for God is safe from diminution, but it is not a static perfection. "How happy is that love," Edwards declared,

> in which there is an eternal progress in all these things; wherein new beauties are continually discovered, and more and more loveliness, and in which we shall forever increase in beauty ourselves, where we shall be made capable of finding out and giving, and shall receive, more and more endearing expressions of love forever. ("Misc." 198, 13:337)

Heaven, in Edwards' theological scheme, is "a progressive state" (8:706), a place where the pilgrim's progress in loving union with God and the company of saints will continue eternally. In heaven saints can look forward to an unending expansion of their knowledge and love of God, as their capacities are stretched by what they receive. The source and archetype for this heavenly dynamism is God's own eternal disposition toward self-knowledge and self-love. As the heavenly saints reflect back knowledge and love of God, the inner triune being of God is repeated and the divine beauty itself is enlarged. This heavenly reciprocity between divine glory and the saints' happiness will never cease, because the glory God deserves is infinite, and the capacity of the saints to perceive this glory and praise God for it is ever increasing.

In the soaring rhetoric of a sermon on the Christian journey toward God, Edwards compared God's glorious perfection to the most "pleasant accommodations" of earthly life: "These are but shadows; but God is the substance. These are but scattered beams; but God is the sun. These are but streams; but God is the fountain. These are but drops; but God is the ocean" (11:13–14; 17:437–38). Nowhere is the superabundant fullness and beauty of God more visible in Edwards' theology than in his reflections on the Trinity.

Notes

1. See also Richard D. Pierce, "A Suppressed Edwards Manuscript on the Trinity," *Crane Review* 1 (Winter 1959): 66–80.

2. This chapter is based on my larger study of Edwards' trinitarianism, *The Supreme Harmony of All: The Trinitarian Theology of Jonathan Edwards* (Grand Rapids: Eerdmans, 2002).

3. Robert W. Jenson, *America's Theologian: A Recommendation of Jonathan Edwards* (New York: Oxford University Press, 1988), p. 22.

4. See the numerous entries under "Trinity" in Edwards' table to the "Miscellanies" (13:149). The "Discourse" was published in 1903 by George P. Fisher as "An Unpublished Essay of Edwards on the Trinity." A fuller and more accurate form is available in volume 21 of the Yale edition.

5. *Blessed Unions* (Boston, 1692), pp. 47–48.

6. Sang Hyun Lee, *The Philosophical Theology of Jonathan Edwards*, expanded ed. (Princeton: Princeton University Press, 2000), p. 189.

7. Conrad Wright, *Beginnings of Unitarianism in America* (Boston: Beacon Press, 1966), p. 201.

8. *Sermons upon the Following Subjects, Viz. On Hearing the Word* (Boston, 1755), p. 269.

9. Here Edwards was appealing to a long Christian tradition of *prisca theologia*, or ancient theology. See Gerald R. McDermott, *Jonathan Edwards Confronts the Gods: Christian Theology, Enlightenment Religion, and Non-Christian Faiths* (New York: Oxford University Press, 2000).

10. Michael J. McClymond, *Encounters with God: An Approach to the Theology of Jonathan Edwards* (New York: Oxford University Press, 1998), p. 101.

11. Richard A. Bailey and Gregory A. Wills, eds., *The Salvation of Souls: Nine Previously Unpublished Sermons on the Call of Ministry and the Gospel by Jonathan Edwards* (Wheaton, Ill.: Crossway Books, 2002), p. 157.

12. See, for example, Edwards' claim that "personal relations are not the divine essence" (21:146).

13. New York, 1880 (20:429–43).

Suggested Further Readings

Danaher, William J., Jr. *The Trinitarian Ethics of Jonathan Edwards*. Louisville: Westminster John Knox Press, 2004.

Edwards, Jonathan. *The Works of Jonathan Edwards*, vol. 21, *Writings on the Trinity, Grace, and Faith*. Ed. Sang Hyun Lee. New Haven: Yale University Press, 2002.

Jenson, Robert W. *America's Theologian: A Recommendation of Jonathan Edwards*. New York: Oxford University Press, 1988.

Lee, Sang Hyun. "Jonathan Edwards' Dispositional Conception of the Trinity: A Resource for Contemporary Reformed Theology." In *Toward the Future of Reformed Theology: Tasks, Topics, Traditions*, ed. David Willis and Michael Welker, pp. 444–55. Grand Rapids: Eerdmans, 1999.

Pauw, Amy Plantinga, *The Supreme Harmony of All: The Trinitarian Theology of Jonathan Edwards*. Grand Rapids: Eerdmans, 2002.

Five

God's Relation to the World

Sang Hyun Lee

ONE OF THE MOST remarkable aspects of Edwards' thought is his understanding of the God-world-relation. According to Edwards, God is not only perfect within himself but capable of being increased or self-enlarged through the world. The essential nature of God's being is an eternal disposition as well as an actuality, at once fully actual and also continuously tending to further actualizations and thus to further self-enlargement. This dynamic view of the divine being leads, in Edwards' thought, to a view of the creation of the world as God's repetition outside of himself, in time and space, of his prior actuality. The created world, then, is the framework in and through which God adds to God's own being. In other words, what God does in time and history, through some human beings and through nature, is a part of God's own life. In short, Edwards brought an element of becoming into God's being without compromising God's prior actuality, and thereby made it in principle possible for the creatures in the realm of becoming to participate in the life of God himself. In short, what God does in the world matters to God. In this sense, the world matters and is important to God. This essay will briefly elaborate on these points.

Dispositional Ontology and the Reality of the World

Edwards' interpreters so often stress his view of the omnipresence of God's direct causal involvement in the world that the nature of the reality of the created world is not sufficiently noticed. We must, therefore, begin with a brief discussion of Edwards' dispositional reconception of the nature of reality. Edwards saw reality not in terms of substances and forms, as had been done for so many centuries, but rather as a network of lawlike habits and dispositions. What made this fundamental metaphysical reformulation possible for Edwards was his realist, as opposed to nominalist, idea of habits and dispositions. For him, a habit or disposition has a mode of reality apart from its manifestations in actual actions and events. A habit, is an abiding principle, is also lawlike for Edwards, in that it actively and prescriptively governs the occurrence and character of actual events. "All habits," writes Edwards, "[are] a law that God has fixed, that such actions upon such occasions should be exerted" ("Misc." 241, 13:358). When there is a habit or disposition, it functions like a prescriptive law that certain events will, not only may, occur whenever certain circumstances prevail. Habits and dispositions, in short, are ontologically real and causally active lawlike powers.[1]

Redefining Aristotelian metaphysics, Edwards declares, in a remarkable sentence in "Subjects to Be Handled in the Treatise on the Mind," "it is the laws that constitute all permanent being in created things, both corporeal and spiritual" (6:391). In "Of Atoms," Edwards stated that "all body is nothing but what immediately results from the exercise of divine power in such a particular manner" (6:215). An actual entity, in other words, is God's immediate activity occuring in line with "a particular manner," and this "particular manner" refers to habitlike law that God has previously established. Without God's immediate activity, nothing can exist. But the divinely established and now abiding laws also "govern" the way God acts in time and space ("Misc." 1263, 23:201–12). To put the matter differently, a habit is a law that is triggered into exertion only when certain conditions are met. The primary condition is God's immediate activity of causing existence; without this divine action, no habit or law could be exercised and bring about actual existence or an actual event.[2]

In his early notes to "Natural Philosophy," Edwards wrote that "the universe is created out of nothing every moment" (6:241). This statement has led many scholars to characterize Edwards' view of God's relation to the world as "occasionalism," the view that the universe is newly created moment by moment.[3] But Edwards' early remark is overshadowed by his lifelong belief that God establishes the laws according to which he would cause "resistance," and once established these laws are abided by God's continuously immediate action of resistance. Edwards' view, therefore, is not a simple occasionalism, according to which the world is created ex nihilo every moment. The habitlike laws constitute the relative and yet abiding reality and structure of the world as distinguished from God and are observed by God in his actions in the world. Habits and laws are active and causal powers. Since human beings and physical entities, according to Edwards, are essentially dispositions and habits, human beings and the rest of the natural world have a reality distinguishable from God and are in principle capable of actively participating in what God does in the world. So Edwards can write: "God has made intelligent creatures capable of being concerned in these effects, as being the willing, active subjects, or means, and so they are capable of actively promoting God's glory" ("Misc." 1218, 23:53). Non-sentient physical entities participate in God's life in time and space through the converted sentient beings' perception of them as the images of God's beauty.[4]

God as Disposition and Actuality: The Trinity

For Edwards, the ground of God's creation of the world and continuing activity in the world is rooted in the nature of God's own internal being. And Edwards articulates God's own being in terms of the doctrine of the Trinity. Edwards makes a new beginning in the development of the doctrine of God in the West by reconceiving God's being as essentially a disposition rather than a substance. "It is [God's] essence to incline to communicate himself" ("Misc." 107, 13:277–78). This "disposition to communicate Himself" is what "we must conceive of as being originally in God as a perfection of His nature" (8:433–34). Edwards then resolves this communicative disposition into God's disposition effectually to exert himself ("Misc." 1218, 23:53). In other words, God's disposition to operate as God is the essence of the divine being; God is dispositional. And since God, for Edwards, is also true beauty and a knowing and loving being, God is the eternal disposition to know and love true beauty.

Edwards follows the tradition by affirming that God is fully actual. Edwards points out that God "is an eternal, adequate and infinite exercise of perfect goodness that is completely equal to such an inclination in perfection" ("Misc." 104, 13:272). This eternal and infinite exercise of the divine disposition to know and love true beauty is articulated through Edwards' doctrine of the immanent Trinity.

Edwards articulates the doctrine of the Trinity using both the logic of dispositional ontology and also John Locke's psychology of the self—namely, the self, the self's reflexive idea of the self, and the self's love of the reflexive idea. The three distinctions in God, says Edwards, are "God, the idea of God, and delight in God" ("Misc." 94, 13:262). The first subsistence of the divine being, or the Father, is then God in his first true actuality. As Edwards states, "The Father is the Deity subsisting in the prime, unoriginated & and most absolute manner, or the deity in its direct existence" (21:131). In other words, the Father is the first true and full exercise of the divine dispositional essence to know and love true beauty, and, therefore, the first actuality of God is truly knowing and loving true beauty. The Father is, thus, the first "instance" of God in full actuality or "direct existence." But the divine disposition remains a disposition even after its full exercise. In the Father, therefore, actuality coincides with disposition.⁵

God as the Father, therefore, is a disposition to communicate himself, just as he is an eternally perfect actuality. God as the Father is disposed to further exercise, and this exercise brings about a repetition of what God already is. This is so because God is primordially actual. So the Son, "God's idea of himself" (21:120) is the intellectual exercise of the Father as actuality-disposition or the Father's reflexive knowing of himself. Thus the second Person is "generated." This eternal generation of the Son is not the actualization of God as God, because the Father already is God in full actuality (21:114–120). The Son's generation as the Father's exercise of his dispositional essence can only be the intellectual repetition or communication of what the Father already is. Thus, in the Son "the deity is truly and properly repeated by God's thus having an idea of himself . . . [and] by this means the Godhead is really generated and repeated" (21:114). And like the Father, the Son is the eternal disposition to communicate himself as well as a full actuality as the intellectual repetition of the Father. "The Son is the adequate communication of the Father's goodness, and the express image of him. But yet the Son also has an inclination to communicate himself" ("Misc." 104, 13:272). The Son is different from the Father in that the Father is "un-originated" as the first exercise of the divine disposition, while the Son is "generated" by the Father, in that He is the repetition of the Father. The Son in his full deity is, like the Father, both actuality and disposition to communicate further.

The Father's dispositional essence and the Son's dispositional essence are now exercised affectionally as "the Father and the Son infinitely lov[e] and [delight] in each other" ("Misc." 94, 21:260). In this way the Father's and the Son's prior actuality is affectionally repeated, and the Third Person "proceeds" from the Father and the Son. And like the Father and the Son, the Holy Spirit is the full actuality of God's affectional repetition of his prior actuality and the disposition to love further.

In short, God in his intra-Trinitarian life is at once fully actual qua God and also essentially disposed to communicate himself. Within the Trinity, God as the eternal disposition to know and love true beauty is exercised and also repeated in a way that is "an eternal, adequate and infinite exercise" of the divine dispositional essence ("Misc." 104, 13:272). Unlike the God of contemporary process theology, God for Edwards is fully self-actualized as God as well as eternally disposed to further self-communication. In this dynamic reconception of the immanent Trinity, Edwards lays the foundation for a doctrine of God's creation and activity in the world through which God's already-actual being is further increased and enlarged and thus is genuinely affected.

God's End in Creation

Edwards uses his idea of the divine being as essentially dispositional and the ad intra/ad extra distinction to explain God's creation of the world. God is fully actual ad intra, but also remains essentially a disposition to communicate himself. Now this divine disposition "delights in all kinds of its exercises" ("Misc." 553, 18:97)—that is, ad extra, or outside of himself, as well as ad intra. So the "same disposition" that inclines him to delight in his glory [ad intra]" now seeks to be exercised ad extra (8:452). Now, a disposition is the law that a certain event will occur when certain occasions arise, and the divine disposition is that God will feel delight as delightful occasions, such as God's idea of himself in God ad intra, arise. But outside of God there is nothing that can function as an occasion for the exercise of the divine disposition. This is the point where we realize that the divine disposition, according to Edwards, is in some ways radically different from the finite and created dispositions. The divine disposition is sovereign and absolutely self-sufficient; it can bring into being the occasions for its own exercise. God's disposition "will make occasion for the communication" ("Misc." 445, 13:494). So the creatures "are made that God may have in them occasions to fulfill His pleasure in manifesting and communicating himself" ("Misc" 48, 13:496).

How can a perfectly actualized God aim at any goal? Edwards says that God can only seek the highest good, and the highest good is none other than God himself as true beauty. But then God himself ad intra is already fully actualized. There is nothing for God to actualize or achieve in order for God to be God. The only possible answer is that in creating the world God aims at himself, "existing ad extra" (8:527). "His own glory was the ultimate, Himself his end—that is himself communicated" ("Misc." 247, 13:361). The aim is not God's prior actuality as God; that is eternally accomplished ad intra. What can be aimed at is God's prior actuality existing ad extra or an "increase, repetition or multiplication" ad extra—that is, in time and space—of the divine actuality ad intra (8:433). Intelligent beings are created so that through their acts of knowing and loving true beauty, God's internal Trinitarian knowing and loving may be repeated in time and space. The physical universe, of which humanity is a sentient part, is also created to repeat God's glory as the "images or shadows" of the divine things, although their actualization as the physical repetition of God's infinite glory happens only through the converted human being's acts of knowing and loving the physical universe as images of God's beauty.

According to Edwards, the end of making creatures happy is subordinate to the end of repeating God's own glory in time and space. By this subordination Edwards does not wish to in any way belittle the dignity of the creatures. According to Edwards, "an ultimate end is that which the agent seeks in what he does for its own sake . . . [something] which he values upon its own account" (8:405). In this sense, God's end of glorifying himself and giving creatures being and happiness are both ultimate ends. God delights in the creation for its own sake and on its own account, and thus it is of value to him. But Edwards says there are different kinds of ultimate ends. A "chief or highest end" is "an end that is most valued; and therefore most sought after by the agent in what he does" (8:407). Now, "to be an end more valued than another end is not exactly the same thing as to be an end valued ultimately, or for its own sake." Thus, "two different ends may be both ultimate ends, and yet not be chief ends. They may be both valued for their own sake . . . and yet one valued more highly and sought more than another" (8:407). Edwards also puts the matter in another way. Between two ultimate ends, one is "an *original*, independent ultimate end and the other *consequential* and dependent" (8:412–13). Edwards concludes that God's repetition of himself ad extra is his chief, highest, and original ultimate end in creating the world, while making creatures happy, though also an ultimate end, is implied by, and comprehended in, the other. Edwards' perspective is thus thoroughly theocentric. Yet he wants to preserve the dignity of the creatures and the ultimate significance of their happiness. The latter end is to be understood strictly within the larger framework of God's chief end of glorifying himself, although the creatures do possess a dependent and yet ultimate meaning as a reality distinguishable from God.

The process of God's self-repetition in time, according to Edwards, takes an infinite amount of time, since God's internal actuality and its internal repetition is infinitely perfect. The repetition of the infinite fullness of God ad extra will take an "eternal duration, with all the infinity of its progress and infinite increase of nearness and union to God." Indeed, "the time will never come when it can be said it has already arrived at this infinite height" (8:534). The world will everlastingly continue to repeat in a spatio-temporal way the infinite glory of god. But the world will never become God. The God/world distinction is never abolished.

It is important to note here that in his discussion of God's creation of the world Edwards freely mixes emanationist and teleological language. God's creation of the world, Edwards says, is a "flowing forth," a "diffusion" of God's internal fullness as well as an act in which God "aims at" a goal and "seeks" to achieve an end. Edwards' emanationistic language can give the impression of a Neoplatonic influence, but whatever Neoplatonic elements there may be in Edwards' thought, his view of creation certainly is not Neoplatonic emanationism, a concept of creation as a nonpurposive "overflowing." Nor is he simply using language carelessly. He speaks as he does because he sees the creation as both a purposive act and an ontological self-enlargement. The exercise of the divine disposition in God's creative act is an ontological increase of God's fullness because the exercise of a disposition brings a real possibility to actuality, thereby increasing the degree of actuality. In this sense, God's creation of the world is an ontologically productive extension of his own prior actuality—thus Edwards' emanationist language. But at the same time, the exercise of the divine disposition is a teleological movement, because what the disposition is disposed to is the aim that the disposition's exercise brings about. Actuality is aimed at by the disposition's exercise. On this point, Edwards' reconception of the divine creativity must be distinguished clearly from that of Plotinus, for whom the category of necessary emanation excludes any room for teleology. For Edwards, God's emanation of himself is a purposive activity. The marriage in Edwards of the emanationist and teleological languages is made possible by the logic of his dispositional reconception of the divine being.

The Meaning of Temporality for God's Own Life

If the same disposition that is exercised fully in God ad intra, "the original property of [God's] nature," is exercised in God's creation of the world, the world then brings about "more" of God's actuality, although God does not need such an increase to be God (8:435). In asserting this consequence of his dynamic reconception of the divine being, Edwards is also anxious to reaffirm the historic Christian doctrine of the perfection of God. Especially in regard to God's aseity or self-sufficiency (the belief that God is and does what he is and does completely out of his own resources, without depending upon any other being), Edwards is resolute in refusing to make any compromises. Whenever Edwards denies that God cannot be added to, he has in mind an addition to God that comes from the creature's own power. Edwards states that "nothing that is from the creature adds to or alters God's happiness, as though it were changeable either by increase or diminution" (8:448). The latter half of this statement does give the impression that Edwards might be denying in principle the possibility of any increase of God's being. But at the end of the paragraph, he makes his point clear: "[God's joy] can't be added to or diminished by the power or will of any creature; nor is in the least dependent on anything mutable or contingent" (8:448).

So the sovereign self-sufficiency and independence of God is uncompromisingly affirmed. But when it comes to classical theism's doctrine of God's immutability in the Aristotelian sense, the tradition cannot contain or restrain Edwards' dynamic reconception of the deity any longer. As long as the divine self-sufficiency is not questioned, Edwards forcefully asserts that God indeed can be "added to" and that God takes "proper delight" in what God does in time and history. Edwards writes:

> God's joy is dependent on nothing besides his own act, which he exerts with an absolute and independent power. And yet, in some sense it can be truly said that God has the more delight and pleasure for the holiness and happiness of his creatures: because God would be less happy, if he was less good, or if he had not that perfection of nature which consists in a propensity of nature to diffuse of his own fullness. (8:447)

Given that God did not create the world grudgingly but out of his delight in self-communication, and given that God's creation was an intentional and purposive act, Edwards finds no reason why God should not be seen as taking proper delight in the fulfillment of his will and thus having his being and happiness increased. Edwards writes:

> If the last end which he seeks in the creation of the world, be truly a thing grateful to him (as certainly it is if it be truly his end and truly the object of his will), then it is what he takes a real delight and pleasure in. . . . It may therefore be proper here to observe that let what will be God's last end, *that* he must have a real and proper pleasure in: whatever be the proper object of his will, he is gratified in.

Edwards explains further:

> But we have reason to suppose that God's works in creating and governing the world are properly the fruits of his will, as of his understanding. And if there be any such thing at all as what we mean by *acts of will* in God, then he is not indifferent whether his will be fulfilled or not. And if he is not indifferent, then he is truly gratified and pleased in the fulfillment of his will: or which is the same thing, he has a pleasure in it. And if he has a real pleasure in attaining his end, the attainment of it belongs to his happiness. (8:449)

And if God's real pleasure in the attainment of his will in creating the world "belongs to his happiness," then God is really "happier" and is thereby "enlarged" and "increased" by his self-communication ad extra. So God's self-sufficiency, in Edwards' way of thinking, does not preclude "addition to" God's actuality. Edwards in fact repudiates explicitly the view that God's self-sufficiency and immutability would prevent God's taking real delight in what he does through creation.

> Many have wrong notions of God's happiness, as resulting from his absolute self-sufficiency, independence, and immutability. Though it be true that God's glory and happiness are in and of himself, are infinite and can't be added to, unchangeable for the whole and every part of which he is perfectly independent

of the creature; yet it don't hence follow, nor is it true, that God has no real and proper delight, pleasure or happiness, in any of his acts or communications relative to the creature. (8:445–46)

The Aristotelian picture of God as the Unmoved Mover, incapable of being affected in any way, is clearly left behind by Edwards through his dynamic conception of God creating the world on purpose and because he is who he is.

In the dissertation *Concerning the End for Which God Created the World*, Edwards makes a comment on the eternal nature of God's knowledge which at first gives the impression of not fitting well with his position on God's self-enlargement through his activity in time. Edwards' concern here is that God's taking a real and proper delight in what happens in time is not inconsistent with the traditional concept of God as eternal.

> Nor does anything that has been advanced in the least suppose or infer that it does, or is it in the least inconsistent with the eternity, and most absolute immutability of God's pleasure and happiness. For though these communications of God, these exercises, operations, effects and expressions of his glorious perfections, which God rejoices in, are in time; yet his joy in them is without beginning or change. They were always equally present in the divine mind. He beheld them with equal clearness, certainty and fullness in every respect, as he doth now. They were always equally present, as with him there is no variableness or succession. He ever beheld and enjoyed them perfectly in his own independent and immutable power and will. And his view of, and joy in, them is eternally, absolutely perfect, unchangeable and independent. (8:448)

Eternity in the sense of timelessness certainly has to be asserted in the case of the Father's act of knowing himself and loving himself. In other words, there was no time when God did not know and love himself. There was no time when the Son had not been begotten of the Father, and the Holy Spirit had not proceeded from the Father and the Son. God's knowledge and love of himself are truly timeless and without succession. But in the above paragraph Edwards is talking about God's knowledge of the world in time, which involves succession and duration. The question is, Is Edwards asserting here that God knows events in time in a timeless fashion, without any duration or succession whatsoever? If so, then temporal events would not be known by God as temporal (that is, as involving duration and succession) and thus would not be ultimately meaningful to God. But Edwards, as we have seen, insists that God takes a real and proper delight in certain events as they occur in time. We should here consider Edwards' discussion of what God had in view as the ultimate end of creation. Edwards writes, "In this view, those elect creatures which must be looked upon as the end of all rest of the creation, considered with respect to the whole of *their eternal duration*, and as such made God's end, must be viewed as being, as it were, one with God" (8:443). In regard to the same point, Edwards also writes, "the creature's good was viewed in this manner when God made the world for it, viz. with respect to the whole of *the eternal duration* of it, and the *eternally progressive* union and communion with himself" (8:459). Such statements as these suggest that in God's view of events in time, duration and progressive succession are somehow included in what God knows. Thus, we may surmise that, for Edwards, God timelessly knows events in time in their succession and progress. This would make sense in analogy with the human experience of knowing now without succession and in a simultaneous instant two events that occurred in succession in the past.[6] For Edwards, then, God timelessly knows time in succession (i.e., temporality as temporality). Time as such matters to God when God himself acts in time to enlarge his own actuality.

The Importance of Temporality in Edwards' Thought

To summarize: for Edwards, although God does not need temporality for his internal actuality and perfection, God needs or uses the world in space and time to exercise his dispositional essence outside of his own internal being. What God does in time and space makes time and space important to God himself. In other words, it is not that the created world in space and time as such increases the divine being; it is rather what God himself does in and through the world in time and space that affects the divine being by adding to it. In this specified sense, nevertheless, the world in space and time really matters to God's own life. The point we are highlighting in this essay, however, is that it is *time as such* and *space as such* that is indispensable in God's own activity of enlarging himself *ad extra*, although not all space and time, not space and time as separated from God's self-expanding, communicating activity, is indispensable to God.

Edwards and Plotinus both spoke of the world as overflowing from the fullness of God. But for Plotinus, the overflowing is neither teleological nor ontologically incremental to God's own life in any sense. In such a perspective, the temporal world is not of any meaning or importance to God himself, who remains eternally and absolutely unaffected by anything. We can safely say that Edwards clearly left behind him the old classical theism's Aristotelian concept of God as the Unmoved Mover, who is absolutely impassible and unaffected by what happens in the world of space and time. Further, whatever Neoplatonic influences there may be in

Edwards' thought, Edwards' dynamic new thinking on the God-world relation certainly does not reflect them.

This new thinking of Edwards on the God-world relation cannot but have a profound impact upon his theology as a whole, manifested in a heightened attention to the place of space and time in God's scheme of things. In this essay we can only mention, without elaboration, some of those areas in Edwards' thought where temporality and spatiality are taken with a particular seriousness. For example, in Edwards' theological epistemology, the act of knowing and loving the transcendent beauty of God is not conceived of in any way as an act of leaving behind the temporal and spatial world. The new "sensible knowledge" that the Holy Spirit makes possible is not some new information separate from the human words in Scripture but rather a new apprehension of what already was in Scripture. Finite, creaturely ideas, including concrete ideas of the physical universe, are all necessary "stuff" in and through which the transcendent is experienced and known. For God to extend his intratriune knowing and loving, he must repeat them in time and space. Edwards is not a "mystic," if the term denotes one who contends that true knowledge of ultimate reality involves a departure from the sensible and mundane.

Edwards' emphasis upon Christian practice as the most important "sign" of the veracity of a person's conversion is well known. Edwards' understanding of regeneration as the indwelling of the Holy Spirit, creating a new disposition in the regenerate, of course implies an emphasis upon the actual practice of the regenerate. Given appropriate occasions, a disposition will necessarily be exercised in the form of a certain type of behaviors. Christian practice necessarily follows regeneration. But the deeper reason, I suggest, for Edwards' strong emphasis upon Christian practice has to be found in God's end of creation—namely, repeating God's intra-Trinitarian acts in time and space. The actual holy deeds of a converted person in this temporal and spatial world are what are required for God's own end of creation, so God delights "properly in the devotions, graces and good works of the saints" ("Misc." 107(b), 13:278). There cannot be a more profound grounding for Christian ethics.

Finally, we should mention Edwards' eschatology, to indicate the heightened importance of temporality and spatiality in his thought. According to him, the world will end on the day when God's work of redeeming the elect is completed. On that day the world as we know it will cease. But history will not be finished. What has to be repeated in time and space is the fullness of God's being, which is infinite and will, therefore, take an infinite duration of time. So "there never will come the moment, when it can be said, that now this infinitely valuable good has been actually bestowed" (8:536). On the "last day," Christ as bridegroom and the church as bride will be reunited and will marry before the Father. But this wedding day will be "an everlasting wedding day," and their enjoyment of the Father's glory will continue into eternity. In other words, history will continue in the newly inaugurated "new heaven and new earth." And the increase and repetition of God's glory in time and history will go on "throughout the never ending ages of eternity" (9:508–9).

In the new heaven and the new earth, the saints will see the beauty of God with their bodily eyes mainly as manifested in Christ Jesus. The saints above "see" the beauty of God, "most of all mediate ways, in the man Christ Jesus" ("Misc." 137, 13:296). And the beauty of God in the physical universe will be more intense in heaven than on earth, appearing "chiefly on the bodies of the man Christ Jesus and of the saints" ("Misc." 182, 13:328). Edwards, unlike some medieval theologians, held that the beatific vision is mediated by the incarnate Jesus Christ. The temporality and humanity of Jesus Christ continue in heaven, since God's work of repeating his glory in time and space continues there.

Paul Ramsey, in "Heaven Is a Progressive State," astutely observed that, for Edwards, the Christ's mediatorial role as the incarnate Son of God continues in heaven. Ramsey calls this "the eternity of the incarnation" in Edwards' eschatology. Ramsey concludes that "In the entire history of Christian theology, there is no more dynamic understanding of the relation of God to his creatures than that of Jonathan Edwards" (8:720, 716). I would only add that Edwards' "dynamic understanding" of God's relation to the world went even further than Ramsey might have thought: God in that relation is enlarged and increased, thereby making what happens by God's grace in time and history a participation even in God's own life.

Notes

1. For a fuller discussion of Edwards' concept of habit or disposition and of his dispositional ontology, see my *The Philosophical Theology of Jonathan Edwards*, expanded edition (Princeton: Princeton University Press, 2000), pp. 34–114.

2. In the set of early notes called "Of Atoms," Edwards asserted that the "resistance" (or existence) of an entity (thus, by implication, an event or action) is the result of the immediate activity of God, which abides by the previously established laws of nature (6:214–15).

3. See, for example, Norman Fiering, *Jonathan Edwards' Moral Thought and Its British Context* (Chapel Hill: University of North Carolina Press, 1981), pp. 279–80, 307–8.

4. Lee, *Philosophical Theology*, pp. 89–94.

5. Ibid., p. 188.

6. I am indebted to Robert W. Jenson for suggesting the interpretation offered here.

Suggested Further Readings

Lee, Sang Hyun. *The Philosophical Theology of Jonathan Edwards*. Princeton: Princeton University Press, 2000.
McClymond, Michael J. *Encounters with God: An Approach to the Theology of Jonathan Edwards*. New York: Oxford University Press, 1998.
Pauw, Amy Plantinga. *The Supreme Harmony of All: The Trinitarian Theology of Jonathan Edwards*. Grand Rapids: Eerdmans, 2002.
Wilson-Kastner, Patricia. "God's Infinity and His Relationship to Creation in the Theologies of Gregory of Nyssa and Jonathan Edwards." *Foundations* 21 (October–December 1978): 305–21.
Zakai, Avihu. *Jonathan Edwards' Philosophy of History*. Princeton: Princeton University Press, 2003.

Six

Christology

Robert W. Jenson

JONATHAN EDWARDS' Christology is one of the more astonishing, and even eccentric, aspects of his thought. There is no doubt that he intended to be thoroughly orthodox in the matter, but he arrived at orthodoxy—if he did—on anything but usual paths.

The orthodox limits for christological reflection and speculation were, of course, set by the fifth-century Council of Chalcedon. The stories of the council and of its particular appropriation in the Western church are often told, and I will not here retell them in any detail.[1] The bishops at Chalcedon accomplished much, but insofar as their teaching is taken as a systematic construction—and was in some measure intended to be one—there is a hole in the middle of it.

The Gospels' narrative about Christ, the Chalcedonian fathers said, can be intelligible and true only if he is truly both God and man, which they conceptualized by saying that he has two "natures": the divine nature, which the Son shares with the Father and the Spirit, and human nature, which the man Jesus shares with us. In the incarnate Son, both natures are constitutive, yet they retain their integrity: neither do the two mix to produce a third something, nor is either attenuated to accomodate the other. So far—in this language—so good.

But how then are these "natures" one Christ?[2] They are one, said Chalcedon, in that there is in Christ only one "hypostasis." What, however, is a "hypostasis?"

The term was taken from the trinitarian theology that had been developed in the previous generation and denotes the Father or the Son or the Spirit each in his distinction from the others. Thus the Son, who is but one God with the Father, is nevertheless another hypostasis than the Father,[3] etc.; God is "one divine nature in three hypostases." But in Chalcedon's *christological* use of this language, the relation of plurality and unity is reversed: here there is one hypostasis with two natures. Moreover, there is an assymetry of import. The plural hypostases in God—Father, Son, and Spirit—do not individuate the divine nature, which would result in three gods; thus, the one hypostasis of Christ does not make him an individual god. But this same hypostasis of Christ does individuate him as one among the multitude of other human individuals. Clearly, for use in Christology the notion of hypostasis demanded some strenuous new thinking, but the fathers of Chalcedon did not provide it.[4]

The parties whose mutual suspicions led to the council in the first place were the "Alexandrians,"[5] concerned first about the oneness of Christ, and the "Antiochenes," concerned first about the abiding distinction between God and creature even in him. The council's failure to develop the notion of "hypostasis" left the field open for each to continue on its previous way, at least within systematic theology. Chalcedon fulfilled its strictly dogmatic function: the errors of which each party suspected the other were condemned,[6] so that some limits were set to their divergence. But the council gave little conceptual guidance for further reflection.

Subsequent Western theology has typically begun with concern for the integrity of the *natures*;[7] its recurring problem has then been to give a plausible account of the one acting and suffering Christ of the Gospels. How can two natures—or two under any category of this metaphysical type—make one protagonist of a historical narrative? Arguably, a fully satisfactory answer has never been given. The first remarkable thing about Edwards' christological reflections is that they must be understood against this history of struggle—we could not have done without this excursus—but themselves proceed almost entirely undeterred by reference to it, and in particular pay no attention to the strictures of Edwards' Western tradition.

Edwards' Christology can be conveniently discussed under four headings: the concern that drove it, the metaphysical convictions that constrain it, the way of talking about Christ that it aims at, and the conceptual means to that end. Finally, I will ask, "So what?"

The Soteriological Concern

The concern that drives Edwards' christological constructions is soteriological—as of course, in one way or another, it is for most theologians. Our salvation, according to Edwards,[8] is effected in "closing" with Christ, in his cleaving to us and our cleaving to him. But if this mutual closing is to *save*—as Edwards understands salvation—then it must be that in closing with the man Christ we close with God himself and that in Christ's closing with us God himself closes with us; and all our propositions about Christ must elucidate this good news. Thus Edwards' Christology is inseparable from, or indeed is an immediate implication of, his doctrine of atonement, which explicates God's closing with us, and of justification by faith, which explicates our closing with God. And here I must again look back into the tradition.

Even a brief acquaintance with Edwards' texts will discover that very little is left in his thinking of Protestantism's standard Anselmian understanding of atonement or of the coordinated doctrine of justification as imputation "in the court of heaven," though he can use the language of both. We will consider justification by faith first.

Edwards was, of course, firmly committed to the Reformation doctrine itself, but his answer to the question, *Why* does faith justify? little resembles the Melanchthonian answer which is commonly taken for normative Protestant doctrine: that God, moved by Christ's death, "reckons" his righteousness to our account—an imputation *in foro coeli*, "in the court of heaven." Edwards' answer is more like a reinvention of Martin Luther's own and different answer, in *Christian Liberty* and in the 1533 commentary on Galatians.

Luther—at least in these writings—taught that faith justifies because faith is hearing Christ speak in his church, and just as such is an opening of the soul for Christ to enter and rule. Luther adopts imagery for this union from patristic and monastic theology: it is a "marriage of Christ and the soul." In this new unit there is a "blessed exchange" of moral qualities: the soul becomes righteous with Christ's righteousness, and Christ becomes "the chief of sinners." And it is this new unit, Christ-and-the-believer, which is the object of God's judgment.

Luther's actual doctrine is thus more or the less the opposite of that which is popularly attributed to him. We are justified by faith in Christ because Christ and the one who believes are, without further ado, one moral agent, in whom Christ's divine righteousness necessarily "swallows up" the believers' mere created sin.[9] When God judges the believer righteous, he is in the first instance registering a fact, of the moral status of Christ-and-the-believer, not manipulating the books.[10]

Turning to Edwards, we see that already his way of putting the question about justification sets him on this same doctrinal path. What is it about faith, he asks, that "renders it a meet and suitable thing, in the sight of God, that the believer, rather than others, should have [Christ's righteousness] assigned to them?" (19:153).

Edwards' doctrine is indeed a doctrine of imputation[11]—in the citation, "assigning"—but the imputing is not itself the act of justifying grace. For the imputation is not gratuitous; it must be "meet and suitable," enabled by some fact about the believer in distinction from the unbeliever. Nor is it the Crucifixion itself that renders the imputation meet; the Crucifixion belongs to Christ's righteousness but does not enable its imputation to us. It is what Protestant scholasticism called "the mystical union," the mutual indwelling of Christ and the soul,[12] that makes the imputation "meet." Thus the imputation recognizes a fact, that Christ and the believer are a single moral unit, so that Christ's righteousness is the actual character of the believer's moral existence.[13]

Such union is possible because persons are not, according to Edwards, impermeably bounded entities, certainly not for God. I will be quoting mostly chestnuts of Edwards scholarship, and here is one: "What insight I have of the nature of minds, I am convinced that there is no guessing what kind of union and mixtion, by consciousness or otherwise, there may be between them" (3:304). And indeed, not just a moral agent but anything at all is, and is what it is, solely in God's regard of it.

Thus God in a very abstract sense *could* simply choose to regard Christ and the soul as one moral agent, and that would be that: they would in reality be one object of moral judgment. But, of course, even to speculate about such an arbitrary act by God is not Edwardsean, since according to Edwards God is God precisely because everything he is and does is perfectly harmonious with everything else he is and does. In order, therefore, that God's regarding Christ and the believer as one subject of righteousness not be arbitrary but meet and fitting, God ordains that something "real in the union between Christ and his people" must legitimate the imputation: "God sees it fit, that in order to a union's being established between two . . . persons, so as that they should be looked upon as one, there should be a mutual act of both, that each should receive the other" (19:152–54). Faith is the believer's act of reception.

But *whom* do I thus, from my side, "receive?" In a more Melanchthonian doctrine, it might be sufficient that I close with Christ "according," as the slogan has had it in so many connections, "to his human nature." But if my sharing Christ's righteousness is indeed to make meet and fitting the giving of all that Edwards understands by salvation—that believers be "in a sort admitted into that society of three persons in the Godhead" (18:110), and not as aliens but as "partakers of [the Son's] relation to the Father" (5:5–6, 19:593), so that in eternity "the good that is in the creature comes forever nearer and nearer to an identity with that which is in God" (19:419f.) the final result of the closure is what the Fathers called "deification"—then the matter presents itself differently. Then, as in Luther, the righteousness with which I close in closing with Christ must be God's own righteousness. Then the one with whom I am, by closing with Christ, one moral subject must simply be God the Son himself, with no restrictions "according to his humanity."

We turn now to Christ's side of the relation. On Edwards' understanding of the relation, a similarly drastic "closing" must occur from Christ's side. Christ, as we will see, so closes with us, that what he thereby does and suffers God the Son does and suffers, and indeed God the Father with him.

Christ's act of union with us is analyzed, in Edwards' systematics, by the doctrine of atonement. Atonement—that is, the overcoming of estrangement between God and us—happens in that Jesus—again the language appears—is so united to us that we "may justly be looked upon as the same." In my earlier general study of Edwards' theology, I provided "a crude statement" of Edwards' atonement doctrine: "the atonement worked by Jesus' life and death is achieved by such a community of him and us that if the Father loves the Son he must love us also."[14]

But there is "no other way of different spirits being thus united but by love"; and the union is total only if the love is total, that is, self-giving unto death ("Misc." 547, 18:93; 867, 20:108). And nothing less than total union will do in our case, that of creatures who define our lives precisely as resistance to union with God[15] and will certainly use any opening of difference to escape.

So now from this side: *Who* thus loves unto death, in order to close with us? The man Jesus. But would that by itself reconcile us with God? Again, in an Anselmian-Melanchthonian scheme, it might suffice.[16] But within Edwards' thinking, *Jesus*' perfect at-one-ment with us can perfectly reconcile us to *God* because and only because God is Jesus. Within Edwards' scheme, we can only be reconciled to God if the love between the Father and the Son, which is the very being of God, becomes inseparable from love for us, a love that is unto death.

The outcome of all this for Christology is plain. We may indulge no "if"s, "and"s, or "on the other hand"s in asserting that God the Son is Jesus and Jesus is God the Son, that the protagonist of the Gospels is a single subject of actions and sufferings, divine and human—whatever that does to our usual prejudices about what deity consists in.

The Metaphysical Vision

To avoid repetitive explanations later, I must here describe, very quickly and apodictically, for readers who may be coming to Edwards for the first time, Edwards' metaphysics, his general construal of reality.[17] That I must omit his arguments and present only sloganlike statements of a few resulting positions may result in caricature of this powerful and subtle thinker, and readers should be aware of this. Those who wish more may turn to other essays in this volume, or to the works just referenced.

The root of all Edwards' thinking was a sudden vision of God as the beautiful harmony of Father, Son, and Spirit. But we will begin our exposition at the other, epistemological end.

Here Edwards begins by attacking the distinction, becoming standard in his time, between "external" reality and our "internal" percepts of it.

John Locke had laid it down that external objects, themselves unperceived,[18] *cause* the "ideas" in our minds. This, said Edwards, is mythology. On Locke's own grounds, he argued, we have no basis on which to posit the existence of those "substances" out there; Lockean confidence in their reality is a leap of faith, and of idolatrous faith, since it populates the material world with godlets, sovereign causes of our experience.

According to Edwards, we perceive what we perceive, and that is an end of the matter. This does not mean that he supposed there are only our ideas of things, for the "only" again presupposes the very distinction he denies. He does not deny the reality of animal bodies or planets or trees and houses, only the picture of the world as a large container for "material substances" and for minds, as smaller containers, of "ideas."[19] Or we may say: Edwards wanted to abolish mechanism, the construal of reality through a metaphor of the machine.

The objectivity of what we perceive, and of our own presence to one another, is funded not by a sovereign reality of material substances but by the reality of God. God is indeed other than each of us; *his* idea of a piece of matter, or of one person as other than another, is its "substantiality"—if, as Edwards says, "we must needs use that word." What finally exists is a universal community of "spirits": the mind that God is, the minds he creates by communicating with them, and the intersubjectivity of created minds, the material universe, also a posit of and in the divine mind.

For Edwards, the supreme good is therefore the value pertaining to spiritual community, that is, harmony, and that is, beauty. God is the harmony of Father, Son, and Spirit; angels and humans are the harmonious chorus of created spirits doubling the divine harmony; and the material universe, as the intersubjectivity of created spirits, is an image and images of the encompassing spiritual harmony. A founding moment in Edwards' thinking was his reading of Newton, who presented a universe ruled by laws of harmony—to every action there is an equal and opposite reaction, etcetera—the very universe appropriate to Edwards' vision of God and humanity.

This encompassing construal of reality provided the conceptual framework within which Edwards worked out his Christology. Just so, of course, it constrained the conceptual moves he could make: the reality of God and humanity in Christ will be construed always in terms of personal communion.

The Christological Cross-Predications

It has been apparent from the beginning of the gospel's mission: the gospel requires us to say things about Christ and God that deeply offend the inherited theology of our culture,[20] whose concept of God has been as much formed by the vision of the great Greek thinkers as by Scripture[21]— an observation which is in no way intended to denigrate the benefit Christian theology has in general has derived from converse with "the Greeks." There could hardly be a more primal statement of the gospel than "Jesus saves." Yet this proposition offends the religious common sense of our culture, since it has for its subject the name of a human individual, and of him predicates an act which seems the very paradigm of what only God can do. It is nearly as primal in Christian discourse to say, the other way around, that "God the Son died on the cross." This proposition has God for its subject and says that he was mortal, that is, by our culture's understanding, presumptively not God. Our culture's inherited religious common sense has thus at all times objected to such statements: they blur the difference between God and not-God, indeed violate the rules the Christians themselves set at Chalcedon.

The theological tradition has labeled this character of believing discourse the "communication of natures" and/or "communication of attributes":[22] faith cross-predicates doings or characteristics ontologically appropriate to Jesus as a man to God the Son and doings or characteristics ontologically appropriate to God the Son to the man Jesus. Thus, for example, Christians do and must say things like "God has a mother," or, the other way around, "The Lord Jesus ruled the universe from his Cross." In terms of "attributes," Christians say things like, "The flesh of Christ is life-giving" or "God the Son suffered." Yet, although the theological tradition has acknowledged the truth and necessity of such propositions, it has also been alarmed by them, and has tried to limit their contexts of applicability and the range of what could be taken to follow from them. In the West, the restrictive devices have been particularly sophisticated and severe.

Jonathan Edwards simply discarded all such worries. In my earlier— now very much "earlier"—book about Edwards, I assembled a catalogue of his uninhibited cross-predications[23] and will here simply select a few choice items from it. Edwards makes it the chief "distinguishing mark" of the "one and only Jehovah" that he *creates*; then he says that "the man, Christ Jesus . . . , a creature," is the one who "created all things." So bluntly does he mean this that he acknowledges a problem it makes for him, that Jesus seems to have created himself ("Misc." 958, 20:234). It is the "ordinary operation and care" of the specific "creature" Jesus is, to uphold and govern the universe.[24] The miracles in the Gospels are "divine works" that "the man Christ Jesus" did "in his own name and of his own will as the God of nature."[25] As for eschatology, it will be the beam of Christ's *bodily* glory "shining on the dead that shall raise them" (17:202ff.).

The tradition has been especially nervous about "communications" in the other direction, attributing human characters to God the Son. Thus "God has a mother"[26] and "One of the Trinity died for us," which attribute to God the Son the two defining events of mortal humanity, birth and death,[27] eventually even became dogma, but only after conflicts that split the church, and subsequent theology has often submitted the second—and sometimes, among Protestants, the first also—to "the death of a thousand qualifications." Even Edwards is less fulsome here, but one often and justly cited *Spitzensatz* illumines, in my judgment, all his writing: God's love as it is merely in the divine nature, "is not a passion, is not such love as we feel, but by the Incarnation [God] is really become passionate to his own, so that he loves them such a sort of love as we have to him, or to those we most dearly love" ("Misc." z, 13:176).[28] That God, as incarnate, is *passionate* in the very way we are passionate is the heart of what theology has rarely dared say about him; Edwards just goes ahead and does it.

I will close this section with a longer citation, from the "Exposition on the Apocalypse." Commenting on the passage the "Lamb slain from the foundation of the world," Edwards finds four senses in which this is true. "1. He was the person typified, by the slaying of lambs from the beginning of the world. 2. He was slain in the decree, and according to the eternal agreement between the Father and him. 3. The efficacy of his death reached to the very first of mankind. 4. He was slain mystically in his members" (5:111). Who here is the "he?" One is first inclined to say, "Jesus," the man on the cross. But then we note that the *eternal* decree that the Cross occur is an agreement between the Father and "him." If then we say that "he" is the eternal Son, this Son becomes the one slain on the Cross. The passage simply does not sort out the "two natures," and precisely that makes it work.

The Conceptual Means

How is the man Jesus thus one with the Logos? In an early draft, Edwards surmises that "the union of the divine with the human nature of Christ" is "by the Spirit of the Logos dwelling in him after a peculiar manner and without measure," since "[p]erhaps there is no other way of God's dwelling in a creature but by his Spirit" ("Misc." 487, 13:528). On its face, and carried out to what it seems to imply, this proposition would yield a Christology in which two ontically antecedent entities, God the Logos and this "creature," were united by a special indwelling of the Spirit in the second. This would be an extreme,[29] and lamentably unsophisticated, instance of the way Western theology starts with the two natures. It might even exemplify the heresy of which the Alexandrians suspected the Antiochenes, an understanding of Christ as only quantitatively different from other Spirit-filled persons, prophets, martyrs, etcetera.

In a later and more developed draft, however, the triune and divine-human relationships are very differently ordered[30]—and indeed the only reason for adducing the earlier note is by way of contrast. In the later draft, the work of the Spirit remains central but has a different role. There are, Edwards here says, two aspects of Christ's union with the Logos. The first, with which we are in this connection concerned, is that the man Christ is united to the Logos because God "loveth him as his own Son; this man hath communion with the Logos in the love which the Father hath to him as his only begotten Son. Now the love of God is the Holy Spirit" ("Misc." 487, 13:529).

Here it is the relation of the *Father* to the man Jesus—not first the relation of the Logos—in which this man is God's Son or Logos. Edwards depends on classical trinitarianism, in which the Spirit is the bonding love between the Father and the Son, and just so "the love of God." What the Spirit does in the Incarnation is to give himself, as the love of the Father for the Son, to be the love of the Father for the man Jesus, thus making this man and God the Son equivalently the one object of the Father's love, the one term of the relation of the Father to "his only begotten Son." Whatever then "communion with" the Logos may mean—and that we are about to find out—it is constituted in the Father loving Jesus as the beloved Son.

By this move, Edwards has recovered—or at least come very close to recovering—the most ancient postbiblical construal of how Christ is the Son or Logos. Until perhaps A.D. 180, Christ's oneness with the Son was not thought of as constituted in a relation of Christ to "the" Son, but rather as constituted in his relation to the Father; "I and the Father are one," said John's Christ-the-Logos, not "I and the Logos are one." God in this construal is paternally related to someone: that someone is Jesus, and *just so* Jesus is God's Son.

Initially, the concept of "the" metaphysical Son or "the" Logos was introduced to explicate Christ's sonship or revealership. But then, starting with "the Apologists" in the second half of the second century, the construct usurped the place of the one whose status it was intended to explicate,[31] and it came to be thought that Christ is Son in that he has a certain relation to "the" Son.[32] It will be apparent that I think this an unfortunate development; Edwards' effective elision of it, without access to critical knowledge of the history, is a remarkable christological insight.

We come then to the second aspect of the union. The man Jesus is united with the Logos by a "communion of understanding and . . . of will, inclination, spirit or temper . . . such that there is the same consciousness.

Thus the man Christ Jesus was conscious of the glory and blessedness the Logos had in the knowledge and enjoyment of the Father before the world was, as *remembering* [emphasis added] of it" ("Misc." 487, 13:529–530).

That the man Jesus is one consciousness with the Logos, so that he even *remembers* the eternal life of the Logos, is of course a difficult proposition, especially for readers of the Synoptic Gospels, but Edwards has no systematic choice but to affirm it. For in his metaphysics, two memories with different contents would be two persons,[33] at least insofar that closing with the one would not necessarily be fully closing with the other. We must note that Edwards here teeters on the brink of formal heresy.[34] There are, according to the succession of christological councils after Chalcedon, *two* wills and *two* energies ("spirit or temper") in Christ. Edwards does not, to be sure, directly deny this, but he lumps together will, understanding, spirit, etcetera as "consciousness," and then asserts that the Logos and Christ are "the *same* consciousness."

The *brink* of heresy is, however, often the best place to be. And if Edwards' proposition about Jesus' consciousness is difficult, it is perhaps no more difficult than those put forward in the tradition. How indeed are we to rhyme what the Gospel narratives say about Jesus' knowledge with what they say about his ignorance? Is it a coherent proposition to say that Christ entertained two separate—and at points evidently incompatible—stores of knowledge? Could Christ have succumbed in Gethsemane, obeyed "what I will" instead of "what you will," and fled? If we say he could not have because he is God the Son, that spoils the Gethsemane story; if we say he could have, that spoils the narrative drive of the total story told by the Gospels, which is throughout carried by a sense of divine inevitability. Attempts to deal with such questions have not been the most glorious moments in the history of theology.[35] Great thinkers have found themselves driven to such puerilities as the speculation that Christ in Gethsemane was only acting out human struggle with God's will, as an example to us.

Finally, how are two spirits that are the identical consciousness in fact *two* of anything? If this is a problem for Edwards' christological thinking, at least he has the right problem.[36] Christology's fundamental and unproblematic datum must be the single protagonist of the Gospels, who does and suffers divine and human things, defined as divine and human, moreover, by the total biblical story about God with humans. Conceptualizing the duality is second-level reflection, which is indeed demanded by features of the gospel narrative, but which must not make the narrative's unity itself into a problem.

So what are there actually two of, for Edwards? The answer, I think, is not far to seek, if we do not isolate Edwards' christological remarks from the rest of his thought. All reality is for Edwards a community of "spirits," posited by and within the divine spirit. The divine spirit is himself a community of spirits, of Father, Son, and Spirit. I propose that one *can* understand Edwards so: the incarnate Son is two in that he belongs to both communities, the human community and the divine community, without mitigating their difference from each other.

Indeed, wherein is the Spirit really needed in Edwards' scheme? We have seen that Edwards does not, when he analyzes more fully, mean that two antecedent persons, the Logos and Christ, are brought into communion by the Spirit. Let me therefore suggest a different possible reading of Edwards at this point: the Spirit is the bond of Christ's unicity precisely in that he, *as himself one person*, maintains the person of Christ in two distinct personal relations, on the one hand to the Father and on the other to humanity, the terms of which relations are just so united.

To see how this is plausible Christology and perhaps a plausible reading of Edwards, we must consider the Spirit's role in the life of the Trinity. The Father and the Son are not eternally two *only* because the Father "begets" the Son and the Son is "begotten." For in the thinking and piety of most religions such an emanation of one divine entity from another regularly eventuates in the emanated one's being drawn back into undifferentiated unity with its source. In the triunity of the Christian God, this does not happen: the Father and the Son are eternally two, because a third, the Spirit, maintains a *relation between* them, the supremely personal—as Edwards notes—relation of love.

Just so, I suggest, the Spirit maintains the identity between God and man in Christ as a *personal* unity, which is nevertheless not the unity of two persons who would otherwise obtain. In Edwards' whole thinking, it is finally, I suggest, the personal relation, and so distinction, between God and other spirits within the one great community of spirits that the Spirit's christological act maintains.

So What?

However readers may judge some of my suggested interpretations, such as those in the last two paragraphs, I claim that the kind of Christology adumbrated by Edwards' description of the two aspects of Christ's union with the Logos, and active in his way with the *communicatio idiomatum*, is the kind urgently demanded by the church's present historical situation.

Whether we label our present situation "postmodern" or "late modern" makes little difference. Either way, the insight evoked is that Western modernity has run out its string and is stuck fast at its end. Modernity was constituted by faith in the universality of secularized reason, of reason resting on its own foundation of indubitable truth.[37] We have lost that faith but found no other; thus, our politics and culture live by unfaith itself, by active "suspicion" of their own bases. The terror in this situation has, for present purposes, two aspects.

First: If there is no universal reason, there is no way for different persons and communities to reason together. Society and polity must become in fact what liberal thought posited in theory, an arena for the contest of parties committed to incommensurable notions of truth. What liberalism did not predict, though perhaps it should have been obvious, was that the contest would inevitably become struggle, often enough armed.

Second: "Deconstruction" has become the great slogan of the universities and official culture. What is to be deconstructed is the human person: a person, were there any, would be constituted in the coherent meaning of a life, that is, of a certain temporal sequence of events. But if there is no eternal truth, there are no such meanings and therefore no persons. The notion that there are persons and that I am one is, we are told, an illusion, which may be unavoidable but must over and over be exposed for what it is.

It is noteworthy that Edwards predicted much of this,[38] as the inevitable outcome of the developments he deplored. We do not, I think, know whether he intentionally shaped his Christology to combat looming nihilism, but the correlation in fact obtains, in respect of both threats just noted.

First: We cannot live without truth, and truth that was not truth for everyone would of course be truth for no one. But where is universal truth to be found? In the collapse of modernity, a Christian insight may again be comprehensible: universal truth is constituted and found precisely as some particular. Christianity's claim for the universality of the single person who is its truth, however "triumphalist" or "hegemonic," can and must now be made without qualifications: Jesus of Nazareth, this first-century Jew and none other, is the one and only universal Reason. Only Edwards' drastic kind of discourse about the Christ, who just *is* both the Logos and the man Jesus, the creature who creates the universe, can have any moral or political bite in late modernity.

Second: Jesus the Logos is particular *as* a person in communion. Just therefore we can be sure that persons and community are not illusions. In order not to undercut this good news, Christology must eschew all ways of speaking that presuppose the priority of impersonal being to persons: the supposition, for example, of a human "nature" that is itself impersonal, "shared" by actual humans.

Pagan antiquity knew there were persons, but regarded these as a subclass of "beings"; the ancient church's trinitarianism effectively reversed this order.[39] In this theology, the Father, the Son, and the Spirit are persons first, and only so is there the being God. In late modernity, we must take up this line of conceptual revision anew, specifically for Christology. Edwards' christological language of "spirits" and their various communions can be a splendid model. Abstract talk of Christ principles, "ultimate being" variously "imagined," and the like was always wrong, and in late modernity must be socially and morally destructive.

Notes

1. For my own longer retelling, see Robert W. Jenson, *Systematic Theology* (New York: Oxford University Press, 1997–99), 2:90–114.
2. Which of course, the fathers of Chalcedon definitely wanted to assert. The first, narrative part of their decrees positively harps on "one and the same."
3. How this works is another story and too long for telling here.
4. And probably could not.
5. In the usual historians' shorthand.
6. The Alexandrians denounced the Antiochenes for allegedly teaching that Christ was in fact two persons, in close cooperation; the Antiochenes denounced the Alexandrians for allegedly mixing God and a creature into some third thing. All present at Chalcedon swore off both departures.
7. And so has continued, though not by design, the generally Antiochene line.
8. For the general interpretation of Edwards that will appear in the following, I must inevitably refer to Robert W. Jenson, *America's Theologian: A Recommendation of Jonathan Edwards* (New York: Oxford University Press, 1988).
9. For all this at greater length, with citations, see Jenson, *Systematic Theology*, 2:293–301.
10. It may be useful to insert here a long footnote, with a more conceptual account of Luther's teaching, also for comparison. In the writings named, Luther holds that faith justifies because (1) faith consists in hearkening to the actually spoken word of the gospel, (2) this word has God's own righteousness as its matter, and (3) the human soul and words are so ontologically mutual that the soul becomes what it hearkens to. The third point is Luther's deliberate switch on a key bit of Aristotle's epistemology. Aristotle observed that there is nothing to consciousness but the things of which we are conscious and a sheer potential to receive such contents. It follows that the actively conscious soul just *is* what it knows. For Aristotle himself, seeing was the paradigm of apperception: thus the soul becomes what it beholds. For Luther, the paradigm of apperception is hearing: thus the soul becomes what is addressed to it. If, then, the word to which one hearkens is the gospel, one is, merely in that being-addressed, shaped to the content of the gospel, to God's own righteousness, antecedently to any righteous works done by the soul so shaped. This analysis in place, Luther can then move to the more dramatic and familiar language: since the content of the gospel word is Christ's life, death, and resurrection, and since the speaker of this word is finally Christ present in his church, union with the word is just so union with Christ.

11. To the following, Jenson, *America's Theologian*, pp. 53–64.

12. Protestant scholasticism preserved this doctrine from Luther but shunted it to the side of the question about justification.

13. Ibid., pp. 60–62.

14. Jenson, *Edwards*, p. 126.

15. Ibid. See also "Miscellanies," no. gg.

16. And when you work out all the dialectics of medieval and Protestant-scholastic doctrine, had to.

17. Instead of scattered references to support so compact a summary as follows, I will refer to a general presentation, Sang Hyun Lee, *The Philosophical Theology of Jonathan Edwards*, 2d ed. (Princeton: Princeton University Press, 2000); see also Jenson, *America's Theologian*, pp. 23–49.

18. As Edwards points out, Locke's "primary qualities," those that can be turned into geometry, which are supposed to characterize the substances themselves, are the very ones we do *not* immediately perceive.

19. Edwards is certainly correct, by the way, in this denial. The misbegotten metaphor he attacked continues to hex our epistemology, despite its now blatant unsuitability to the actual results of the sciences it was supposed to frame.

20. The earliest fathers reveled in devising offending paradoxes: "Immortality died," "the Invisible is seen," etcetera.

21. We need not here speculate about whether this would be so in any religious history at all.

22. *communicatio idiomatum*.

23. Jenson, *America's Theologian*, pp. 117–19.

24. Ibid., p. 791.

25. Ibid., p. 117.

26. Usually, of course, put in the form that became controversial, "Mary is the mother of God."

27. The association of wombs and tombs, and consequent identification of women with mortality, was one of the cultural features of pagan antiquity against which Christianity most offended.

28. The passion of *love* is of course the case where the refusal to attribute passions to God is most contrary to the bent of Christianity. Much of the greatness of the great Origen was that he overcame all his prejudices to assert that God loves us passionately. Origen had many followers in much of his theology, despite after-the-fact condemnation as a heretic—if only they had followed him in this!

29. And indeed heretical.

30. When I wrote *America's Theologian*, I had not fully worked through Christology on my own behalf and did not notice the importance of this shift.

31. A common occurrence in the history of ideas.

32. Jenson, *Systematic Theology*, 1:125–27.

33. Edwards should by rights extend this also to his vision of the life of saints in heaven. I know of no place where he does this.

34. If in one draft he was seemingly Nestorian, here he surely sounds like a monophysite.

35. Perhaps Maximus the Confessor, in the sixth century, registered the only real success, with conceptual moves whose underlying structure is much like that of Edwards. Jenson, *Systematic Theology*, pp. 134–137.

36. At least in the view of this author. The great historian Henry Chadwick once told me that an essay of mine reminded him of a sixth-century monophysite treatise; he did not, I think, mean it as a compliment, but I took it as one.

37. These truths could be empirical, as the "protocol sentences" of positivism, or supposedly self-evident to reason. The campaign against "foundationalism" thus coincides with postmodernist denials.

38. Jenson, *America's Theologian*, pp. 141–76.

39. To this, see everyone's current favorite on the subject, John Zizioulas, *Being as Communion* (Crestwood, N.Y.: St. Vladimir's Press, 1985).

Suggested Further Readings

Bush, Michael. "Jesus Christ in the Theology of Jonathan Edwards." Ph.D. diss., Princeton Theological Seminary, 2003.

Carse, James P. *Jonathan Edwards and the Visibility of God*. New York: C. Scribner's Sons, 1967.

Jenson, Robert W. *America's Theologian: A Recommendation of Jonathan Edwards*, Pp. 111–22. New York: Oxford University Press, 1988.

Williamson Joseph C. "The Excellency of Christ: A Study in the Christology of Jonathan Edwards." Ph.D. diss., Harvard University, 1968.

Seven

The Bible

Robert E. Brown

JONATHAN EDWARDS' biblical interpretation is the subject most neglected in the study of his writings and intellectual pursuits, and the subject most deserving of attention by scholars and admirers alike. All told, the material encompassing his biblical interpretation constitutes the large majority of his written corpus. Even his more properly theological and philosophical treatises rely heavily on the Bible for the substance of their arguments. Thus, how he integrated the beliefs and values represented in the pages of that text into his own perception of the world ought to be of great consequence to anyone attempting to understand his theology. It is a real irony and curiosity, then, that his biblical interpretation has received so little attention.

No doubt the chief reason for this state of affairs has been the relative lack of availability of his biblical commentary. There is good reason to believe that as his career was drawing to a close, Edwards was preparing to share his understanding of the Bible in published form. His death prevented this, and ensured that this aspect of his career would remain largely out of the public eye. To be sure, his earliest biographers recognized the importance of the Bible to Edwards. Samuel Hopkins, for example, asserted that despite his ambitious efforts to acquire every manner of knowledge, Edwards studied the Bible "more than all other books." He "cast much light upon many parts of the Bible, which has escaped other interpreters. And by which his great and painful attention to the Bible, and making it the only rule of his faith, are manifest."[1] Sereno Dwight, the editor of his works, observed that Edwards made it his "standing rule, to study every passage which he read, which presented the least difficulty to his own mind, or which he had known to be regarded as difficult by others, until such difficulty was satisfactorily removed." To this end, he "had already entered on a series of investigations, which if ultimately found correct, would effectuate most important changes in the opinions of the Christian world . . . perhaps no collection of Notes on the Scriptures, so entirely original, can be found."[2] Both Hopkins and Dwight overestimated the significance and originality of Edwards' biblical interpretation, but they were right on the mark as to his consuming preoccupation with it. None of his early admirers or adherents, however, made an effort to integrate his biblical commentary into their development of an Edwardsean theology. While Dwight did manage to include some of his biblical commentary (in heavily edited form) in his early nineteenth-century edition of Edwards' works, the full measure and scope of his expositions never reached a wider audience.

While lack of accessibility may explain in part why Edwards' biblical interpretation never experienced the kind of cultural appropriation that his theological treatises enjoyed, it fails to explain the relative absence of interest in these materials by contemporary scholars. As Stephen Stein has commented, "the Bible, one of the shaping forces in the theological development of Jonathan Edwards, has largely been ignored in the assessment of this colonial divine," and the "contemporary renaissance of interest in Edwards has hardly touched this dimension of his work."[3] To some degree this lack of attention is probably contextual: many of those who have had the liveliest interest in Edwards' thought, such as Perry Miller and H. Richard Niebuhr, have had a pressing social interest in the kinds of philosophical and moral questions that animate Edwards' treatises. And as Douglas Sweeney as argued, the desire by some to rehabilitate Edwards as a moral and religious arbiter for American culture more or less required that his biblicism be minimized or obscured. Yet it is also probably the case that Edwards' valuation of the Bible as divine revelation, as well as his "precritical" appropriation of it, are perspectives not widely shared among Edwards scholars and may therefore have impeded to the study of this material.[4] The difficulty in identifying any contribution that his commentary might make to modern biblical interpretation or to broader theological and ethical discussions has reduced its perceptible relevance to contemporary academic concerns. As a result, Edwards' interest in and reading of the Bible has often been dismissed as "medieval," "fundamentalist," "inaccessible," "pathetic," and even "tragic," thereby allowing it to be ignored.[5] It can only be hoped that with the appearance of critical editions of his major works of biblical commentary, this aspect of Edwards' thought will begin to receive the attention it deserves.

Edwards was a lifelong student of the Bible, and he left a repository of writings that testify to this fact. His sermons, of course, represent an important component of his biblical interpretation. They span the length of his professional career: roughly twelve hundred are still extant, representing perhaps 80 percent of what he produced (10:130). However, his private commentaries, from which many of his sermons are drawn, are also from the period and are the most important sources of his interpretive work. In late 1722, while a young pastor in New York City, he began what would come to be entitled his "Miscellanies," a collection of topical theological speculations that would in time number well over thirteen hundred entries. The "Miscellanies" contain some of his earliest expositions of biblical passages; more importantly, they contain the most significant treatments of his theological understanding of the Bible as divine revelation. About a year later he began his notes on the Apocalypse. A few months after this, in early 1724, the kind of biblical expositions that had appeared in the early "Miscellanies" were given their own notebook, the "Notes on Scripture."

Edwards continued to add new sets of commentary as his career progressed. In late 1728 he began the first of his typological notes, the *Images of Divine Things*.[6] In 1730 he began recording his scriptural observations in an interleaved Bible, the so-called "Blank Bible." This notebook, which he had received from his brother-in-law Benjamin Pierpont, is a bound volume of blank pages interspersed with small printed pages of the Bible, thus allowing space for commentary on the passages at hand. The "Blank Bible" served as an extension of, or sister-commentary to, the "Notes on Scripture."

In addition to these expository collections of notes, consideration must also be given to Edwards' formal theological treatises as important resources for studying his biblical interpretation. Of equal importance, his use of the Bible needs to be taken into account when assessing the structure and content of his theological dissertations. In almost all of his major treatises, Edwards operates as a self-consciously biblical thinker. For example, in each of the three major sections of *Original Sin* (1758), Edwards claims to be engaged in a largely expositional enterprise. Part 1 offers "evidences of original sin . . . as found by observation and experience, together with representations and testimonies of holy Scripture." Part 2 consists of "observations on particular parts of the Scriptures, which prove the doctrine of original sin." Part 3 considers "the evidence given us, relative to the doctrine of original sin, in what the Scriptures reveal concerning the redemption by Christ." In *Freedom of the Will* (1754), he dedicates a section to the biblical evidence for God's foreknowledge (pt. 2, sec. 11) and another to the exposition of the scriptural portrayal of Jesus' actions as both necessary and virtuous (pt. 3, sec. 2). His *Religious Affections* (1746) offers, in effect, one long exposition of Scripture; biblical references pepper it throughout.[7] The entire second half of *The End for Which God Created the World* (written in 1757, published in 1765) is devoted to "what is to be learned from the holy Scriptures concerning God's last end in the creation of the world." Only its companion piece, *The Nature of True Virtue*, lacks any overt attempt to develop an argument from scriptural evidences.

Such an integration of biblical references into his theological treatises ought to be expected from Edwards: it was, after all, the ground on which doctrine was contested in the eighteenth century. But it ought not for this reason be dismissed or overlooked as mere proof-texting. Rather, we need to examine more closely just how his biblical interpretation extended itself into his theoretical arguments, to consider the substantive contribution it made to the development of his thought. Recognition needs to be given to the fact that for Edwards, the content of the Bible served as a vital resource for his constructive theology, and not merely as a rhetorical referent. In the same way that contemporary theologians employ fiction, narrative, and other forms of literature in shaping the form and substance of their ideas, Edwards used biblical literature and narrative as a source of creative reflection, as an evocative influence. It was the "stuff" out of which his theology was made, without which it would have been inconceivable. More attention needs to be given, therefore, to the nuances in his use of scriptural texts in theological argument.

Finally, we must consider the two culminating but unfinished treatises in Edwards' body of work, the *History of the Work of Redemption* and the *Harmony of the Old and New Testament*. Edwards first preached the sermon series that represented the preliminary version of the *Work of Redemption* in 1739. Comprised of thirty preaching units, it took some six months to work through. Structured along the lines of the grand narrative of the Bible, it begins with creation, runs through the history of the people of Israel (including the intertestamental history) and the history of the church to his own era, and concludes with the final restoration of all things. The *Harmony of the Old and New Testament* is a 220-page notebook, begun around 1748, in which Edwards planned to treat some of the vexing issues surrounding the purported historical, moral, and doctrinal discrepancies between the sacred texts of the Jewish and Christian dispensations.[8] Edwards died before he was able to transform it into a prose treatise. In fact, Edwards' premature demise frustrated his intentions to offer these two treatises to a wider public. In his letter to the trustees of the college at Princeton (1757), he laid out his writing plans for the near future, and among several other unnamed projects, he identified these two as the crowning efforts of his career:

> I have in my mind and heart (which I long ago began, not with any view to publication) a great work, which I call *A History of the Work of Redemption*, a body of divinity in an entire new method, being thrown into the form of an history, considering the affair of Christian theology . . . I have also for my own profit and entertainment, done much towards another great work, which I call *The Harmony of the Old and New Testament* . . . In the course of this work, I find there will be occasion for an explanation of a very great part of the holy Scripture; which may, in such a view be explained in a method, which to me seems the most entertaining and profitable, best tending to lead the mind to a

view of the true spirit, design, life and soul of the Scriptures, as well as their proper use and improvement. (16:727–29)

These two works represent some of Edwards' most complex and creative work in biblical interpretation. In the *Work of Redemption* he planned to take the innovative step of shaping a comprehensive work of divinity along the lines of the narrative structure of the Bible, rather than employ the traditional topical method favored by Protestant scholastics.[9] The *Harmony* clearly would have served as the major venue for his interpretive conclusions, while providing the opportunity to consider the nature of the Bible itself. After drawing upon the Bible for decades in writing his systematic treatises, Edwards was ready to turn his attention to the difficult interpretive problems surrounding his primary theological resource.[10]

When we think about Edwards' biblical interpretation, it is useful to think in terms of three components: his understanding of the Bible as divine revelation (theological), his explanation of the Bible as a product of human culture (historical), and his exposition of the content of the Bible (exegetical).

Edwards, of course, received from his Reformed heritage a pronounced estimation of the authority and sanctity of the Bible and a rich tradition of ideas with which to articulate its divine origins. He shows a concern for explicating fundamental concepts such as the inspiration, necessity, sufficiency, and self-authenticating nature of Scripture, as well as for dealing with theoretical problems such as prophecy, infallibility, and illumination. For the most part, however, his discussion of the Bible's religious authority is not couched in terms of anti-Catholic polemics, nor is it treated in the perfunctory manner that might be found in a scholastic work of dogmatics.[11] Rather, the clear context for the development of his theological interpretation of the Bible is the pressing challenge represented by deism. The urgency with which Edwards addressed this concern resulted in a theological interpretation of the Bible that was vigorous, timely, and innovative.

The religious ethos of deism was represented in a demand for the authority of reason, and thus the autonomy of the individual, against the authority and teachings of the established church. This movement, which reached its zenith within the Anglican church from the late seventeenth to mid-eighteenth century, sought to construct a "rational" religion that was universally accessible and comprehensible at all times and in all places. This the deists saw as an alternative to the "revealed" religion of the church, which made claims to exclusivity and embraced seemingly irrational ideas by relegating them to the category of "mystery." The so-called "natural religion" of deism, it was proposed, was derived from a rational reflection about God and moral duty, as revealed in the workings of the natural world. Deism rejected the scandal of organized religion's exclusivity and particularity, and therefore rejected the need for any direct, special revelation from God to a specific ethnic or religious community. Natural religion meant that the Bible was no longer the only or the best means to true religion. Deists therefore dismissed it as an authentic, necessary, or sufficient means to religious truth: at best, it was redundant of natural religion; at worst, it represented a form of primitive superstition, deception, and intolerance.

Since the Bible provided the rationale for the political, social, and legal arrangement of European Christendom, critiquing its authenticity—pointing out its religious, moral, and historical shortcomings—became a major occupation among deist authors.[12] Deists and other skeptics were particularly keen to employ the results of the emerging field of biblical criticism in their attempts to undermine the Bible's social authority. Their popularization of the ideas of critics such as Thomas Hobbes, Benedict Spinoza, and Richard Simon helped to raise significant doubts about the historical and scientific reliability of the text—and a book without intellectual cogency was a book without religious authority. It was precisely this challenge to the Bible's divine origins—and thereby its authority and relevance—to which Edwards' theological reflections on the nature of the Bible were directed.

There are close to one hundred entries in the "Miscellanies" that address issues of biblical interpretation. A few dwell on the exposition of a particular passage; considerably more deal with critical historical problems. But most confront the problem of understanding the Bible as divine revelation (most often under the heading "Christian Religion"). Edwards is most concerned to demonstrate the "necessity" of divine revelation, since this was the point at issue with deists. His chief appeal is to the defectiveness of human religious and moral knowledge in the absence of the Bible. Nature alone "is not sufficient for the discovery of the religion of nature." " 'Tis therefore unreasonable to suppose that philosophy might supply the defect of revelation." Without a revelation from God, "there is no one doctrine of that which we call natural religion [but] would . . . forever be involved in darkness, doubts, endless disputes and dreadful confusion" ("Misc." 1337, 23:342–45). Even more importantly for Edwards, there are two positive reasons why revelation is necessary. First, it is in the nature of spiritual (intelligent) beings to communicate with one another: "God made spirits to have communion; and will he not have any communion with them himself, although they are made for this very end?" ("Misc." 204, 13:339). Furthermore, human beings are most in need of a revelation of God's acts of providence (redemption), not his acts of creation (natural religion). And the redemptive acts of God's providence in history are not available to mere rational reflection: "we may strongly argue that the Scriptures are the word of God because they alone inform what God is about or what he aims at in these works that he is doing in the world" (9:522).[13]

Perhaps the most distinctive element in Edwards' effort to demonstrate the divine nature of the Bible, however, lies in the application of his aesthetic understanding of the divine-human relationship. His theory of the "spiritual sense" or "sense of the heart" as the means of perceiving the divine beauty or excellence is perhaps the most studied aspect of Edwards' thought, and with good reason. It forms the core of his analysis of nearly all aspects of the Christian religion, from emotion to ethics to the nature of the universe. Not surprisingly, then, this aesthetic theory also played a crucial role in his understanding of the Bible as divine speech.[14] As the preeminent form of God's communication to humanity, the Bible possesses all of the aesthetic qualities that emanate from God's being: beauty, excellence, harmony, proportionality, etcetera. It does not just speak of these qualities, or communicate information about them through ideas; rather, it literally possesses them. In the same manner that the timbre of a human voice betrays the identity of its owner, so God's identity—the beauty and excellence of God's being—is revealed through his voice, impressed onto the pages of Scripture. "So there is that wondrous universal harmony and consent and concurrence in the aim and drift . . . such stamps everywhere of exalted and divine wisdom, majesty and holiness in matter, manner, contexture and aim; that the evidence is the same that the Scriptures are the word and work of a divine mind" ("Misc." 333, 13:410).

Edwards was most concerned to use his notion of the sense of the heart to distinguish the supernatural perceptions and experiences of God on the part of those who have been truly converted from those of "natural men" (and women). Conversion was not just a change of mind but a reconstitution of the soul and its affections. It should come as no surprise, then, that the divine characteristics of the Bible, its excellence and majesty, should require a renewed capacity of perception in order to be appreciated. If this text has a spiritual quality impressed upon it, then a spiritual capacity is requisite to perceive it and appreciate its fullness—an affective state whereby one embraces what the Bible relates as a personal good; that is, a new "sense of the heart." Like corresponds to like: "There is that disposition of the mind, that . . . sweetly corresponds and harmonizes with the expressions of God's word . . . as one instrument of music answers of itself to another in harmony and accord" ("Misc." 126, 13:290).

Edwards thus understood the Bible to be a book of divine origin, with a unique content and set of aesthetic qualities that required special interpretive considerations. Its true meaning and significance were not arrived at by mere cognition but required an affective apprehension as well, one that gave the (illumined) reader a moral conviction of its certainty, truth, and majesty. It was by calling attention to this uniqueness that he hoped to undermine the claims of deists, who proposed that true religion could be fashioned without any special, direct communication from God. But Edwards was also confronted by the very human qualities of the Bible, namely, those features that resulted from the historical context in which it was written. The emergence of critical historical thought in the eighteenth century found immediate application in the discipline of biblical interpretation, and increasingly pointed to the disparities between the conceptual worlds of ancient and modern culture. As much as any issue in biblical interpretation, Edwards devoted his energies to resolving the myriad critical problems attending the Christian revelation.

His interest in critical historical thought is evident from the earliest moments of his career and became increasingly concerted over time. His "Catalogue of Reading," in which he kept a list of books which he had read or wanted to read, contains numerous titles pertaining to biblical interpretation, including commentaries, encyclopedias, geographies, chronologies, histories of the ancient Near East and other parts of the world, and evidentialist apologetics.[15] One of the earliest entries in this booklet, for example, is Pierre Bayle's *Historical and Critical Dictionary*. Historical concerns also crop up in the early strata of his biblical notebooks. One finds in his apocalyptic materials, for example, that he is quite concerned to anchor highly symbolic descriptions of Christian eschatology in mundane time and space (appealing to works such as Nathaniel Lardner's *Credibility of the Gospel History* and Arthur Bedford's *Scripture Chronology*). Some of the earliest entries in the "Notes on Scripture" attempt to reconcile biblical history with geography, secular history, and natural science. In both the "Notes on Scripture" and the "Blank Bible," entries on critical interpretation are increasingly common in the 1740s and 1750s. The "Miscellanies" too contain their share of this material, with entries on such issues as the reliability of biblical geography ("Misc." 202, 13:338–39), the confirmation of the Old Testament by other ancient histories ("Misc." 1015, 1020, 20:347–48, 351–53), and the historical accuracy of the gospel accounts ("Misc." 276, 13:376).

Two essays from these notebooks deserve special notice. Entry 416 of the "Notes on Scripture," "Whether the Pentateuch was written by Moses," shows Edwards' engagement with the preeminent critical issue of his day, the authorship of the first five books of the Bible. Written in the early 1740s, and the longest entry in the "Notes," number 416 possesses the analytical depth and literary refinement of a proper treatise.

It is perhaps his most significant attempt at a rigorously historical analysis. It was almost certainly one of those projects alluded to in his letter to the Princeton trustees as a work bound for publication, for in the early 1750s he began a new notebook on this topic (one that reached 131 pages in length) intended to revise and expand upon it (15:423–69). The second entry of note is "Miscellanies," no. 1060, "Concerning the Canon of the New Testament" (20:396–427). Exceeded in length only by two other entries, it addresses in great detail the historical development of the canon and the different recensions of the New Testament corpus.[16] While lacking the literary refinement of his essay on the Pentateuch, it nonetheless represents a major exploration of this critical problem. Its scope indicates that he may have also considered it as a potential treatise; at the very least, this material would have found its way into works like the *Harmony of the Old and New Testament*.

His final two "great works," the *Work of Redemption* and the *Harmony*, are themselves especially taken up with critical interpretive issues. The original (1739) series of redemption sermons is filled with references to a variety of critical problems, such as canonicity, inspiration, and prophecy. The thirteenth sermon, for example, is almost wholly diverted to the problem of the historical authenticity of the Bible and answers the accusations of the deists that at best it represented a defective vehicle of knowledge, at worst an intentional fraud. "To object against a book's being divine merely because it is historical is a silly objection, just as if that could not be the word of God that gives us an account of what is past" (9:432). The three revision notebooks of the *Work of Redemption* (c. 1755) reveal an even more pronounced interest in critical historical problems. The *Harmony*, of course, would have been the major repository of his treatment of critical issues. Judging by the vast number of entries in the "Miscellanies," "Notes on Scripture," and "Blank Bible," this last great work would have been his most ambitious effort to integrate these diverse interests in biblical interpretation.

Despite his consuming interest in such interpretive problems, Edwards himself was not a critic, in the sense of being skeptical about the Bible's historical or religious integrity, or in the sense of employing a thoroughgoing historical analysis in his resolution of interpretive problems. Rather, Edwards was interested in critical issues primarily because of the conceptual and apologetic difficulties they posed for the traditional understanding of the Bible as a form of divine revelation. This should hardly come as a surprise, however, since it was the polemical use of critical scholarship on the part of ideological critics such as the deists that was of primary concern to him. Edwards immersed himself in modern criticism principally to head off its potentially destructive implications for the Bible's authority. And among thinking persons in the eighteenth century, historical (and scientific) reliability had become the sine qua non for intellectual respectability. This meant that Edwards was committed at all costs to harmonizing his interpretation of the Bible with modern knowledge, whether history, philosophy, astronomy, physics, geography, or medicine.

One should not draw the conclusion, however, that Edwards' biblical interpretation was not "modern" in the truest and most contextually appropriate sense of the term. As his notes in "Natural Philosophy" and other writings, such as the famous "Spider Letter," indicate, he was completely enamored with the modern intellectual enterprise and accepted its claims to produce real knowledge about the world.[17] In many cases this meant that he had to adjust his interpretation of the Bible. This is most clearly illustrated, perhaps, in his attempts to adjust biblical cosmology and eschatology to Newtonian astronomy and physics.[18] He was unwilling to accept the notion, however, that the ancient biblical authors' representation of the world could not be brought into conformity with modern history and science. Thus, his energies were in large measure devoted to reconciling these two increasingly divergent sources of information. But such an approach to interpretive problems does not make Edwards exceptional, or anachronistic, for his era. In fact, it makes him typical. Like the majority of intellectuals of his day, Edwards retained a great confidence in the ultimate coherence of all knowledge, and hence of the Bible's coherence with modern knowledge.

All of these factors raise the issue of how best to categorize his interpretive strategy. If Edwards is not "critical" in the fullest contemporary sense of the word, is he then a "precritical" interpreter? In terms of his methodological and theoretical assumptions, such a conclusion is probably difficult to sustain. That is, like everyone else in the eighteenth century, including the most radical critics of the Bible, Edwards accepted the legitimacy of the modern canons of historical investigation and writing and employed them in his interpretive conclusions. Everyone agreed on the criteria that made for reliable history, and nearly everyone, including Edwards, agreed that the Bible should be subjected to these criteria when assessing its historical authenticity. What distinguished them was whether they thought the Bible met modern historical demands for descriptive precision, a question that remained open to speculation in the eighteenth century.

Furthermore, Edwards' immersion in critical interpretation meant that his own conclusions were no longer innocent of its influence. Even after rejecting those ideas he deemed too radical or injurious to orthodox theology, he was forced to adapt his own interpretation in significant ways in response to them. His interpretive consciousness was thus subject to many of the historicizing influences of critical thought. In fact, Edwards openly welcomed the work of critical scholars: in many instances he expressed esteem for figures like Jean Alphonse Turretin for the judiciousness of their critical views. He certainly considered himself to be part of the republic of critical learning. It is probably more accurate and more useful, then, to think of Edwards' biblical interpretation as some kind of composite of traditional and critical views. As Stephen Stein has noted, Edwards lived in a transitional age, and so it should come as no surprise that his views embrace elements of both approaches. Eighteenth-century interpretation is best characterized as a spectrum of critical and historical views, from conservative to radical, on which Edwards clearly occupies the more conservative end. As such he is representative of the period and can be placed alongside early modern critics such as Johann Bengel and John Lightfoot.[19]

The third component of Edwards' biblical interpretation, exegesis, is clearly the largest, encompassing the bulk of his commentary notebooks as well as his sermons. In an essay of this nature it is simply impossible to do justice to its breadth and complexity.[20] The most notable aspect of his exposition of biblical texts is undoubtedly his typology (and its christological orientation). Everything in the Bible, even the seemingly most mundane or inobvious, was for Edwards a template for considering the redemptive work of Jesus. For example, when considering priestly regulations for conducting New Moon festivals (Numbers 10.10), he observes: "The change of the moon at her conjunction with the sun seems to be a type of three things . . . of the resurrection of the church from the dead by virtue of her union with Christ . . . of the conversion of every believing soul . . . [and] of the state and administration of the church at the coming of Christ" (15:290). Here a passing reference in the text about a religious holy day becomes pregnant with Christian meaning. While such an approach might seem foreign to the sensibilities of the modern reader, its use in Christian interpretation is ancient and widespread. And for Edwards it was a means to a creative and rich practice of exposition.[21]

Edwards' typology is wide-ranging, extending beyond its traditional use as a means for understanding how the Old Testament foreshadows the New, and how the New Testament fulfills the Old. Even New Testament passages themselves can have a typological significance imbedded in them. And of course, Edwards was not content to relegate typology to the pages of scripture. Human history, the natural world, indeed all of reality, was imbued with typological significance. Edwards saw the purpose of all space and time as redemptive in nature; every created thing and every event in human history was potentially inscribed with the message of redemption and ordered so as to promote that end. Thus, in his hands, biblical typology became the means for "reading" the world outside of the pages of Scripture as well.

Typology was not his only interpretive principle, however. As was common to Protestant interpreters, Edwards was also interested in the literal or historical-grammatical sense of biblical passages. His sensitivity to this mode developed out of his interaction with critical thought. Biblical criticism focused attention on the historical context in which the Bible was written—the identity of its authors, date of composition, original languages, etcetera. Thus, what the original author intended to say, and how such language and descriptions could be rendered into contemporary vocabulary, were of utmost importance to early modern interpreters. Edwards devoted considerable effort attempting to delineate the "plain sense" of the texts, both as a way to ground them in the real world (of science and history) and as a way to elucidate their true theological implications. For this project he had access to a number of encyclopedias, biblical dictionaries, and historical commentaries, such as those of Augustin Calmet and John Locke.

Since Edwards' biblical interpretation has been so neglected, the needs and opportunities for research are wide-ranging and immediate. No grand synthetic treatment exists, and with the exception of my *Jonathan Edwards and the Bible* and Stephen Stein's introductions to volumes 5 and 15 of the Yale edition, no monographic work exists either. Perhaps the greatest need is in the area of exegesis. The immense amount of material in the "Notes on Scripture," the "Blank Bible," and the sermons has hardly been tapped. His expositions of the Bible in the sermons need to be correlated with the notebook commentaries ("Miscellanies," "Notes," "Blank Bible"). How did they inform each other? Did his public discourse differ from his private reflections? How did his interpretation change over time? What were the major thematic emphases? What interpretive strategies (e.g., typology) did he employ? Did he gravitate toward a particular constellation of texts, and if so, why? Which books in the Bible did he find most useful? Which did he omit or ignore?

Attention also needs to be given to the role his biblical interpretation played in the way he structured his theological treatises. As discussed above, many of them contain entire sections devoted to biblical exposition. More often than not, these have been simply overlooked by scholars interested in his theology or philosophy, but this certainly has been to the detriment of the overall integrity of Edwards' thought. Since he did not think of the Bible as incidental to the development of his arguments, we should not make the mistake of treating them as if they were. To what extent would closer attention to his use of specific texts illuminate his theological development? Did his appeal to certain biblical passages in *Original Sin*, for example, give a distinctive cast to his views? Does the second half of the *End for Which God Created the World* reveal important clues to his understanding of the purposefulness of the universe?

What role did the religious experiences of biblical characters have in shaping his understanding of the revivals and of the religious affections? Did they substantively shape his psychology of religious experience? How did he use the Bible both as a stimulus for revival and as a means of checking what he perceived to be its aberrations? Is there a relationship between the narrative rhythms of the Bible and Edwards' own narrative works, such as the *History of the Work of Redemption*, his accounts of individual and communal revival, and his sermons? Why did Edwards self-consciously choose to structure his systematic treatment of divinity, the *Work of Redemption*, according to the biblical narration of history, and how did this affect his understanding of the nature and practice of theology as a learned and pastoral enterprise?

Above all, there is a need for studies that integrate his biblical interpretation within his formal theological program, and for studies that place his thought within the wider context of eighteenth-century intellectual and social history. We know pretty well which authors he was reading, but we know substantially less about how they influenced his thinking, about what larger social and political considerations were at stake, or about where he fits in the broader world of early modern biblical interpretation. We need to reconstruct the interpretive world in which Edwards lived, in order to understand more fully how the Bible functioned as a creative stimulus for his theology.

Notes

1. Samuel Hopkins, *The Life and Character of Jonathan Edwards* (Northampton, Mass.: S. E. Butler, 1804), p. 88.

2. Sereno Dwight, "The Life of President Edwards," in *The Works of President Edwards*, ed. Sereno Dwight, vol. 1 (New York: G. & C. & H. Carvill, 1830), pp. 57, 108.

3. Stephen J. Stein, "The Quest for the Spiritual Sense: The Biblical Hermeneutics of Jonathan Edwards," *Harvard Theological Review* 70.1–2 (1977): 99.

4. Sweeney has suggested that it is precisely Edwards' biblical supernaturalism that has discouraged many contemporary scholars from taking his commentary seriously; see his " 'Longing for More and More of It'?: the Strange Career of Jonathan Edwards' Exegetical Exertions" (paper presented at the conference on "Edwards the Theologian," April 10–12, 2003, Princeton Theological Seminary, Princeton, N. J., used with permission).

5. See Perry Miller, *Jonathan Edwards* (New York: Sloane Associates, 1949), pp. 307–30; Peter Gay, *A Loss of Mastery: Puritan Historians in Colonial America* (Berkeley: University of California Press, 1966), pp. 88–117; and Bruce Kuklick, "An Edwards for the Millennium," *Journal of Religion and American Culture* 11.1 (2001): 114–17.

6. This was followed up c. 1745–46 with a second, shorter set of notes entitled "Types." In addition, Edwards has an extensive disquisition, the "Types of the Messiah," written at about the same time, as no. 1069 of the "Miscellanies."

7. The same can be said of its literary predecessors, *The Distinguishing Marks of a Work of the Spirit of God* (1741) and *Some Thoughts Concerning the Present Revival of Religion* (1742).

8. The title that appears on the notebook itself is "The Harmony of the Genius, Spirit, Doctrines and Rules of the Old Testament and the New." In subsequent letters he refers to it simply as "The Harmony of the Old and New Testament."

9. For a fuller discussion of his intentions, see my *Jonathan Edwards and the Bible* (Bloomington: Indiana University Press, 2002), pp. 164–83.

10. In addition to the works of Edwards already mentioned, there are a number of other important manuscripts that the student of his biblical interpretation will want to be aware of. These include his "Notebook on the Pentateuch," three notebooks on the "History of the Work of Redemption," the "Book of Controversies," the "Rough Notes on the Truth of the Christian Religion," the "Subjects of Enquiry," a letter cover to Eleazar Wheelock (with notes on the Mosaic history), the "Extracts Out of the Bishop of London's Third Pastoral Letter" (c. 1732), his "Catalogue of Reading," and the "Account Book." All of these are deposited at the Beinecke Rare Book Library at Yale University. The "Catalogue" and "Account Book" will be published in the final volume of the Yale series, *The Works of Jonathan Edwards*. Yale is also expected to make the others available over time in an electronic or digital format.

11. He does have several rather measured entries on the question of the authority of the patristic authors, vis-à-vis the Bible as the sole "rule of faith." See, for example, "Miscellanies," nos. 72, 166, 535, and 828.

12. See, for example, J.A.I. Champion, *The Pillars of Priestcraft Shaken: The Church of England and Its Enemies, 1660–1730* (Cambridge: Cambridge University Press, 1992).

13. Sermon 30 contains a long exposition of the Bible's unique role in the revelation of God's providence. See also, for example, "Miscellanies," nos. 514, 752, and 760.

14. See Stein, "The Quest for the Spiritual Sense: The Biblical Hermeneutics of Jonathan Edwards," *Harvard Theological Review* 70.1–2 (1977): 99–113.

15. This notebook was begun in 1722; the last entries were made in 1757. Roughly one-third of the nearly seven hundred titles in the "Catalogue" bear upon critical issues of biblical interpretation.

16. These two longer entries, "Miscellanies," nos. 1067–68, "Prophecies of the Messiah," and "Miscellanies," no. 1069, "Types of the Messiah," are similarly concerned with problematic issues in early modern biblical interpretation.

17. See *The Works of Jonathan Edwards*, 6, *Scientific and Philosophical Writings*, ed. Wallace E. Anderson (New Haven: Yale University Press, 1980). For a fuller discussion of this phenomenon, see my *Edwards and the Bible*, pp. 183–94.

18. See Stephen J. Stein, "Editor's Introduction," *The Works of Jonathan Edwards*, 15, *Notes on Scripture*, ed. Stephen J. Stein (New Haven: Yale University Press, 1998), pp. 12–21; also Brown, *Edwards and the Bible*, pp. 89–99.

19. For a fuller discussion of Edwards' exegetical thought, as well as his influences, see Stein, "Editor's Introduction," pp. 1–46.

20. At least one scholar has seen in Edwards' typology intimations of contemporary language theory; see Stephen H. Daniel, *The Philosophy of Jonathan Edwards: A Study in Divine Semiotics* (Bloomington: Indiana University Press, 1994).

21. For treatments of Edwards' typological hermeneutic, see the essay by Janice Knight in this volume, and Conrad Cherry, "Symbols of Spiritual Truth: Jonathan Edwards as Biblical Interpreter," *Interpretation* 39 (1985): 263–71; Mason I. Lowance, Jr., " 'Images or Shadows of Divine Things' in the Thought of Jonathan Edwards," in *Typology and Early American Literature*, ed. Sacvan Bercovitch (Amherst: University of Massachusetts Press, 1972), pp. 209–48.

Suggested Further Readings

Brown, Robert E. "Edwards, Locke, and the Bible." *Journal of Religion* 79.3 (1999): 361–84.

———. *Jonathan Edwards and the Bible*. Bloomington: Indiana University Press, 2002.

Chamberlain, Ava. "Brides of Christ and Signs of Grace: Edwards' Sermon Series on the Parable of the Wise and Foolish Virgins." In *Jonathan Edwards' Writings: Text, Context, Interpretation*, ed. Stephen J. Stein, pp. 3–18. Bloomington: Indiana University Press, 1996.

Cherry, Conrad. "Symbols of Spiritual Truth: Jonathan Edwards as Biblical Interpreter." *Interpretation* 39 (1985): 263–71.

Gerstner, John H. "Jonathan Edwards and the Bible." *Tenth: An Evangelical Quarterly* 9 (1979): 2–71.

———. *The Rational Biblical Theology of Jonathan Edwards*. Powhatan, Va.: Berea Publications, 1991.

Hatch, Nathan O., and Mark A. Noll, eds. *The Bible in America: Essays in Cultural History*. New York: Oxford University Press, 1982.

Logan, Samuel T., Jr. "The Hermeneutics of Jonathan Edwards." *Westminster Theological Journal* 43 (1980): 79–96.

Lowance, Mason I., Jr. " 'Images or Shadows of Divine Things' in the Thought of Jonathan Edwards." In *Typology and Early American Literature*, ed. Sacvan Bercovitch, pp. 209–48. Amherst: University of Massachusetts Press, 1972.

Minkema, Kenneth P. "The Other Unfinished 'Great Work': Jonathan Edwards, Messianic Prophecy, and the 'Harmony of the Old and New Testament.' " In *Jonathan Edwards' Writings: Text, Context, Interpretation*, ed. Stephen J. Stein, pp. 52–65. Bloomington: Indiana University Press, 1996.

Noll, Mark A. "Review Essay: the Bible in America." *Journal of Biblical Literature* 106.3 (1987): 493–506.

Stein, Stephen J. "America's Bibles: Canon, Commentary, and Community." *Church History* 64 (1995): 169–84.

———. "Jonathan Edwards and the Rainbow: Biblical Exegesis and Poetic Imagination." *New England Quarterly* 47.3 (1974): 440–56.

———. "'Like Apples of Gold in Pictures of Silver': The Portrait of Wisdom in Jonathan Edwards' Commentary on the Book of Proverbs." *Church History* 54 (1985): 324–37.

———. "Providence and the Apocalypse in the Early Writings of Jonathan Edwards." *Early American Literature* 13 (1978–79): 250–67.

———. "The Quest for the Spiritual Sense: the Biblical Hermeneutics of Jonathan Edwards." *Harvard Theological Review* 70.1–2 (1977): 99–113.

———. "The Spirit and the Word: Jonathan Edwards and Scriptural Exegesis." In *Jonathan Edwards and the American Experience*, ed. Nathan O. Hatch and Harry S. Stout, pp. 18–130. New York: Oxford University Press, 1988.

Eight

Religious Affections and the "Sense of the Heart"

John E. Smith

EDWARDS' MOST comprehensive treatment of the affections is found in his *Treatise Concerning Religious Affections* of 1746, but he had much to say about affections and "heart religion" in other writings, such as his "Miscellanies" and sermons. In the *Treatise* Edwards had a twofold purpose. He sought first to show that affections are a great part of true religion and then to offer signs for appraising them ("test the spirits"), because he did not believe that all religious affections are genuinely from God. Both aims must be understood in terms of these revivals—a series of powerful expressions of anxiety and concern about God, the soul, faith, and redemption, the most important of which came to be known as the Great Awakening. From the outset, Edwards insisted that religious faith is more than a purely "notional" understanding of doctrine; it is more truly a love of God that kindles in believers the affections of joy, hope, trust, and peace and bestows upon them what he called "the sense of the heart." His second aim was to test religious experiences by means of what he called the "signs" of gracious affections to be found throughout the Bible, but especially in St. Paul's account of the life in Christ in his letters to the ancient Christian churches. In so doing Edwards hoped to confound the opponents of "heart religion"—most of whom supposed that it meant wild displays of emotion, visionary experiences, shrieking and moaning, and claims to know immediately the meaning of scriptural passages—by showing that these have no validity as signs for judging genuine religion. To achieve his two aims, he set forth his original conception of religious affections—his name for the biblical "fruits of the Spirit"—followed by a description of the signs, twelve in number, whereby they are to be tested.

To understand what Edwards meant by affections, one should begin with his distinction between affections and passions. Passions are inclinations that overpower the individual so that "it is less in its own command," whereas affections are *active* responses by a person to another person or to an object that are evoked by an *idea* or *understanding* of the nature of what affects us (2:98).

Edwards laid great stress on the difference between, as he called it, a person's having "a merely notional understanding" of a thing and that person's "being in some way inclined" toward it. We can know that an object is round or small and thus have a notional understanding that is neutral, involving no preference. To be "inclined"—the term is drawn from the image of a scale that is not in balance—however, is a choice to accept or reject, to like or dislike (2:96–97). Unlike passions, affections are "[the] more vigorous and sensible exercises" of inclination, which are accompanied by understanding.

In saying, as he often does, that affections are "the actings of inclination and will," Edwards is trying to determine the relation between inclination and will, and in so doing to bring out the two sides of inclination. One must remember that, for Edwards, will is a complex affair; it means choice and judgment primarily and overt action only secondarily. In every choice the soul likes or dislikes, and when these inclinations are "vigorous" and "lively," they correspond to love and hatred. Affections are the *lively* inclinations which reveal the fundamental intent and direction of the heart. "Affections," he says, "are not essentially distinct from the will," but neither are they identical with it. His point can be put succinctly as follows: "will" is *inclination expressed in action*, and "heart" is *inclination expressed in the mind*. Edwards made these distinctions in order to preserve the integrity of the self against division into separate "faculties" (2:97–98). The will, for example, does not will; the person as a whole wills, and we call the person's capacity to do so by the name "will." But there is, in fact, no separate entity or faculty that corresponds to this word.

Following the biblical picture of true religion, Edwards claims that love is primary among the affections and that it has a double role. On the one hand, holy love is "the essence of all true religion," and on the other, it is "one of the affections... and the fountain of all the affections." Love is the *first* fruit of the Spirit, establishing a person's basic relation to God—the "sealing of the Spirit," as it was called—and it is also the source of the other affections: faith, hope, peace, joy, zeal. Edwards shows what the love of God—"unmixed"—means by contrasting it with the rejection of God symbolized in the Bible by "hardness of heart" or the "heart of stone" (2:109–14). The hard of heart, says Edwards, lacks holy love to God, and if the rejection of God is the opposite of true religion, holy love to God must be its very nature.

Here, as in many other places, one must bear in mind that Edwards' aim is to show that true religion consists largely in holy affections, what he sometimes calls "heart" or "experimental" religion. It is important to note that this conception of true religion was not accepted by everyone in Edwards' time. There were those who laid greater stress on acceptance of doctrine than on personal experience and others, like Charles Chauncy, who strongly attacked the revivals, calling them mere "commotions," and insisted on a "more decorous" form of piety.[1] As a result, Edwards found himself in an unenviable position; on the one hand, he was committed to defending the importance of gracious affections, but, on the other, he had to admit that there are false affections, and that one must find criteria for distinguishing these from the true ones. We shall return to this problem later; in the meantime, much more remains to be said about Edwards' unique understanding of the affections—especially what he calls the "sense of the heart"—and the individual affections themselves as they are described in his list of the Twelve Signs.

To understand what Edwards means by the sense of the heart, it is necessary to be clear about his conception of affections. First, one must put aside the longstanding belief that "emotion" and "reason," the "heart" and the "head," are totally at odds with each other. The two elements can be *distinguished*, as he shows, but they need not be *opposed*. Setting them against each other clouded the disputes about the revivals in Edward's day and has continued to confuse many readers ever since. The reason is clear: Edwards' basic insight about the affections is that they consist in a *unity* of an idea and a felt response; to *oppose* these two features to each other simply prevents us from comprehending what he is trying to say from the outset. By idea he means an understanding of the true nature and excellence of the object of our inclination; the felt response is the affection that is "raised" in us in conjunction with that understanding. A good example is found in the affection of holy love to God. Love to God is not a mere "feeling" descending on us from the blue but the affection that arises in the mind when we understand the true being and excellence of God—the divine holiness, beauty, and harmony. For Edwards, it is impossible for anyone to have a proper understanding of that excellence without also experiencing the gracious affection that goes by the name of holy love. Neither the understanding nor the affection can stand alone; one may "know" about God's true beauty in the sense of having a "notional" understanding" gained from reading the Bible without having a "sense" of that beauty. Likewise, one may claim to love God, but for Edwards that love is not genuine unless it has been evoked by a proper understanding of God's true nature. Behind Edwards' whole outlook stands a thought that he learned early in his reading of John Locke's *Essay Concerning Human Understanding*, and he illustrated it with the same example many times over: a person may know that honey is sweet, but no one can know what "sweet" means until they *taste* the honey (2:272).

Since Edwards speaks of the "sense" of the heart, it has been supposed by some that he intended to add to the standard five senses a sixth to be called by that name. This supposition is not only erroneous but misleading as well, since the sense of the heart is obviously not a sense connected, like the others, to a particular organ. Students of the Bible know that there the "heart" is the symbol for the spiritual center of the person in relation to God. Edwards takes that for granted as the basis for developing the quite original conception which he called the sense of the heart. Nothing like it is to be found in the thought of Edwards' contemporaries. Drawing from the Bible, the insights of the Cambridge Platonists, and the empirical philosophy of John Locke, Edwards appealed in the end to his own experience (as we know from his *Personal Narrative*) in arriving at the idea of affections and the sense of the heart. The importance he attached to these notions can be seen in the sustained effort he put forth in presenting them and in defending them against misunderstanding.

The idea of a new sense, a new attitude, as regards the things of religion found novel and powerful expression as early as Edwards' August sermon of 1733, *A Divine and Supernatural Light* (17:408–26). His fully developed conception of that sense and attitude appears in the description of spiritual understanding—the Fourth Sign of gracious affections in the treatise of 1746. In addition, there is Edwards' entry in the "Miscellanies," no. 782 (c. 1745; 18:452), where he sets forth the basic conceptions, which he had learned from the philosophy of John Locke, that lie behind the sense of the heart. There are differences of expression and emphasis among these writings; at times it is the spiritual light that stands out, and at others it is either the sense of the heart or the conviction of saving faith that commands attention. But one and the same message runs throughout: there is a spiritual light consisting in "a true sense of the divine excellency of the things revealed in the word of God, and a conviction of the truth and reality of them thence arising" (17:413).

In *A Divine and Supernatural Light*, Edwards places himself squarely in the tradition of understanding through illumination—"In thy light shall we see light"—begun by Augustine and carried on by Anselm, the Victorines, and Bonaventura. But he added a new dimension: understanding is now something more than a speculative "dry light," because it includes a first-person experience, a direct "sense of" what is to be understood—God, sin, repentance—in a truly religious life. In presenting his new conception of the divine light, Edwards made effective use of a negative method which he used in other writings. Here he begins with a clear statement of what the light is *not*, followed by an equally definitive statement of what it *is*. These negatives are extremely important; they invariably point to those confusions and extravagances in the religious revivals which Edwards rejected as perversions of heart religion.

Accordingly, the divine light is *not* the convictions that "natural men" have of their sin; these are no more than the Spirit acting *upon* the mind of the "natural man"—common grace—while in special grace the Spirit acts *in* the mind of the saint. For Edwards it is the crucial difference between *assisting* natural principles and *infusing* new principles (2:206–7; cf. "Misc."147, 13:300). The divine light is *not* any lively impression of the imagination, since such impressions may be caused by the devil transformed into an angel of light. Unlike Coleridge, who celebrated the role of imagination in religion, Edwards was skeptical of the imagination and often described it as wayward and deceptive (2:210–11).[2] The divine light is *not* the suggestion of new truths or propositions not contained in the Word; the light reveals no new doctrine, but gives instead a "due apprehension" of what is already taught in the Word. Here Edwards flatly rejects what was known in Reformed tradition as "enthusiasm" (literally, "being filled with the god"), or the claim by those now living to have special insight into the meaning of passages in Scripture or to possess the inspiration given *only* to prophets and apostles in accordance with Scripture. Finally, the divine light is *not* every affecting view that individuals may have of the things of religion, since the Bible tells of graceless and evil people who were greatly affected by the sufferings of Christ but who did not believe in them and did not understand their place in the history of redemption. By means of these negatives, Edwards prepares the way for making clear what the divine light *is*. Stated briefly, the divine light is a true *sense* of the divine excellency—expressed in majesty, beauty, and truth—of the things revealed in the Word and the *conviction* of their truth and reality that arises from that sense (2:291f.). There is, he says, beyond the glory that is in nature, a divine and superior glory to be found in God, Christ, and the work of redemption. The spiritually enlightened see that glory. They go beyond mere belief in what they see, because they have a *sense* of it that surpasses notions and speculations; they have the sense of the heart. But we must bear in mind that what is here called by that name is also the divine *light*; both sides go together, even if Edwards sometimes stresses one to the neglect of the other. The best account of the synthesis of heart and light occurs later, in the Fourth Sign of the *Affections*, where Edwards explains the meaning of a spiritual understanding (2:272–80). The basic difference, nevertheless, between having an opinion about a thing and having a "sense of" that thing remains. An opinion may be based on reading or on the word of another, but a sense can come only from personal experience, or what William James would later call "acquaintance."

The most important feature of the divine light, which Edwards now calls "sanctified reason," is that it gives rise to a conviction of the truth and reality of what is contained in the Word. This conviction is brought about in part by removing existing prejudices against the truth of divine things and thus assisting reason by making it more open to arguments showing their truth. The emphasis Edwards placed on a sense of beauty as a mark of divinity is especially evident at this point. The new sense, he says, makes the notions more lively, engages the attention with the greatest clarity, fixity, and intensity, so that the mind dwells with *delight* on the excellency of the divine objects revealed in the Bible. This excellency, he insists, is so superlative that it goes beyond everything human—"what men are inventors of"—and for those who see it, the conviction of truth follows. As Edwards puts it, the enlightened *believe* the Word to be divine because "they *see* the divinity in it." Conviction, for Edwards, is the true saving faith chiefly because *conviction* transcends that *verbal assent* to the authority of the Word which is all that natural human beings are capable of giving (2:293–98).

The new sense, Edwards claims, is immediately given by God and is not attainable by natural means. In explaining this claim, he shows that he learned the Enlightenment lesson about autonomy. The divine light, Edwards says, does not set a person's natural faculties aside, as if he were a star or a stone; on the contrary, they are the primary subject of the light, and God, in letting the light into the soul, "deals with man according to his nature" as a rational being. Outward means must be taken into account, because the Spirit is said to work through the human faculties (2:206), but Edwards' main concern—as indeed it was in *Freedom of the Will*—is to show that these means, or so-called "secondary causes," are not to be thought of as operating by *their own power* and independently of God. His aim is to refute one of the main contentions of the Deists, which was that the laws of nature hold sway on their own without the need of divine power. The Deists were given to saying that God, after establishing the cosmic laws Newton later discovered, could abscond, so to speak, and the universe would keep on running of its own accord.

Much has been said, including what Edwards himself has written, about his indebtedness to John Locke's *Essay Concerning Human Understanding*, a work he studied with great enthusiasm as an undergraduate at Yale. Locke, it will be recalled, tells us at the beginning of the essay, in an "Epistle to the Reader," that his analysis of the nature and limitations of human understanding was prompted by a lengthy but futile philosophical discussion about religion that took place between him and several friends.[3] Since the company failed to come to any agreement in the matter, Locke decided that a new approach must be tried. Instead of meeting such issues head-on, he proposed, we should first examine our understanding in order to determine whether it is capable of dealing with issues of that sort. Thus Locke began an inquiry into the basis of knowledge—what knowledge is and what we can or cannot know; later called *epistemology*, or the theory of knowledge, it has engaged thinkers from Hume and Berkeley in Edwards' time to those of the present. However, as Perry Miller has pointed out,[4] Edwards, moved by his own religious insights and interests, bypassed this entire epistemological discussion and turned directly to Locke's analysis of the mind, because there he found ideas admirably suited to describing what he would later call religious "affections" and the sense of the heart.

Edwards had great respect for Locke and was a close reader of his writings; hence, we can follow his presentation of Locke's ideas with an assurance that he is interpreting them with care. As a prelude to this entire discussion it is necessary to bear in mind that Locke was resolutely opposed to the long-standing belief in the existence of innate ideas, insisting instead that all ideas originate in *experience*. Edwards, we may be sure, was well aware of the importance of this basic contention. Locke maintains in book 3 of the Essay, "Of Words," that all of our ideas have their *originals* either in sensible experience or in reflection.[5] The former have to do with the deliverances of our senses and the latter with an awareness of the exercises of our minds. Referring to the chief function of words, Locke points out that in thinking, conversing, and reading we use them as signs or substitutes for ideas, so that we think of the word without actually calling up the idea that it stands for. This substitution, Locke holds, is used especially with two kinds of subjects of thought; one is general things—kinds, sorts, or what he called "mixed modes"—and the other is what we know only by reflection—things of a spiritual nature, the ideas, acts, and exercises of the mind.[6] These ideas, the ideas known only by reflection, were paramount for Edwards because he saw how, through them, he could express the true nature of religious affections and at the same time confirm the authenticity of heart religion. The key for Edwards is that there is no actual idea of the acts and exercises of the mind but what consists in the *actual existence* of the same things in our own minds. Hence, he claims, to have an actual idea of any pleasure or delight—objects of inclination and will—there *must be excited in the mind a degree of that delight* ("Misc." 782, 18:455). Then, as if to clarify the point by contrast, Edwards continues by noting that for the most part we think, reason, and argue about a thing by means of signs or some identifying feature of the thing *without* having a clear or adequate idea of the thing itself beyond the words that denote it. Concretely, this means that we can *think* through words about, for example, the affection of humility without actually *experiencing* humility or being humble. It is interesting to note that, although Edwards knew well the power of words and could also write words of great power, he believes that our need to use signs is a great human limitation and source of error. The difference, he says, between human and divine understanding is that we are forced to use signs while God has the actual, unmediated ideas in his mind ("Misc." 782, 18:455–58).

It is characteristic of Edwards to highlight an important idea not by repeating it but by putting it under a new heading so as to expand its meaning. Thus, in pursuing the matter of signs and actual ideas, he adds that there are two ways of thinking about spiritual or mental things; in one way we do not directly view the things themselves in their ideas, but only indirectly through signs. He calls this "a mere cogitation without apprehension." The second way is "apprehension," wherein the mind has a direct ideal view of the thing thought of. Direct apprehension, in turn, is said to be either of things pertaining to the faculty of understanding or of things pertaining to the will. For Edwards, the former is figuratively called the "head" and the latter the "heart." Here it is important to bear in mind that, while he *distinguishes* the two, he does not *oppose* them to each other. To do so would run counter to his oft-repeated claim that the understanding and the sense of the heart are intertwined. As he expresses it in explaining the meaning of a "spiritual understanding" in the *Affections* treatise, "Holy affections are not heat without light; but evermore arise from some information of the understanding, some instruction that the mind receives, some light or actual knowledge" (2:266).

Nevertheless, in "Miscellanies," no. 782, he tends to stress the element of *sense*, which in turn involves will. Will here means not so much action as inclination, since it is said to encompass the pleasing and the displeasing, the agreeable and the disagreeable, beauty and deformity, pleasure and pain. An ideal view of this sort is called a sense, something that only the regenerate can have since it can come only from God and cannot be attained by natural men. Edwards sums up by saying that there is the understanding of the head, called *speculation*, and the understanding which consists in the *sense of the heart*. The latter has to do with all the ideal apprehensions of dignity, greatness, awesome majesty, meekness, value, and importance which, for him, constitute a *sensible* knowledge that goes far beyond any notional understanding. This means that no one can have an ideal sense of, for example, God's displeasure without having an ideal apprehension of the being of God, of God's greatness and the greatness of his power. Here Edwards joins company with Kierkegaard and William James in insisting that feeling and sense make up the more profound level in human experience, because they are more intimately connected with the being of the person—the heart—than conceptual knowledge is ("Misc." 787, 459f.).

The sense of the heart yields fruits of its own. The ideal apprehension and sensible knowledge of the things of religion lead to that conviction of their truth given only by the special and immediate influence of the Spirit of God. This work, Edwards says, goes beyond the assisting of natural principles—the common work of the Spirit—and requires an infusion of something supernatural. The saints alone enjoy the special power of the

Spirit from which springs the conviction of the truth and reality of God, Christ, and the Word. For Edwards, that conviction *is* the same as saving faith (2:303).

The foregoing distinction between common and special grace is one that runs throughout Edwards' thought. The *Affections treatise*, for example, is meant to show the influence of the special activity of the Spirit in the Awakenings, while *Some Thoughts* traces the effects of common grace in the same revivals. Edwards was very much aware of the need to relate these two activities of the Spirit—corresponding to the domains of nature and grace—in a way that does justice to both, but especially to the former. He was not always successful in explaining how we move from the *assistance* of natural principles (common grace) to the *infusion* of something supernatural (special grace). One of his best efforts in this direction is found in *True Virtue* where he gives an admirable account of the importance of common morality as compared with the holy love of the Christian life.[7] He claims that the former, although based on natural principles alone, is not only of great value but has such close affinities with true virtue that the one is often mistaken for the other. Accordingly, Edwards ends his discussion of the sense of the heart in "*Miscellanies*," no. 782, by calling attention to how the common work of the Spirit contributes by assisting human faculties to an ideal apprehension of the "natural things of religion" and by assisting natural reason to acknowledge the cogency of arguments for the grand design of redemption. He even allows that the sort of ideal apprehension of the things of religion attainable by natural human beings can lead to "some degree of the conviction of the truth of divine things" that goes beyond a merely notional understanding ("Misc." 782, 18:463f.). The underlying issue, however, of the relation between nature and grace runs through the entire fabric of Edwards' theology and is too complex to be pursued further here.

Edwards' most considered statement about the affections as such is found in his *Religious Affections* of 1746. In that work he also treats the special subject of the relations between the affections, the understanding, and the sense of the heart under the heading of "spiritual understanding" which he calls the Fourth Sign in his list of the signs of gracious affections. It was noted earlier that in the *Affections* Edwards aimed, first, to show that the affections or fruits of the Spirit are the substance of true religion, and, secondly, to offer signs or marks whereby genuine religious affections can be distinguished from false and counterfeit feelings and states of mind. In fulfillment of the second aim, he set forth a set of twelve signs or criteria that serve to identify those affections that come from the special work of the Holy Spirit. These signs encompass the whole of the Christian life and range from the holy love to God that is the foundation of all the signs to holy practice, the sign to which Edwards devotes more space than to any other.

To grasp the full meaning of these signs, one must bear in mind that he repeatedly set them in contrast to those experiences associated with the popular revivals which he regarded as inauthentic—fainting, moaning, having visions, claiming to know the "inner meaning" of biblical passages—and hence no work of the Spirit. In explaining the meaning of a spiritual understanding, for example, Edwards begins by insisting that gracious affections arise only from the mind's being *enlightened* to apprehend divine things. He goes on to claim that a person may be affected with a lively idea of some shape or pleasant form, a shining light or outward appearance—experiences of the sort frequently cited in the religious revivals—but that by themselves these are empty since there is no instruction in them and the person is not made more knowing about God. For Edwards, however, true affections do not arise from any common form of enlightenment, such as being deeply struck by discoveries in mathematics and natural philosophy or acquiring new knowledge even of religious matters. It is a spiritual understanding that he has in mind, an apprehension not possible for the natural man but peculiar to the saints alone, as in the verse from 1 Corinthians 2:14, "the natural man receiveth not the things of the Spirit of God." The immediate object of this understanding is, as Edwards stresses again and again, the supreme beauty and excellency, including moral beauty, of the nature of divine things as they are in themselves. This means that the *love* of divine things at the basis of true religion is the spiritual knowledge or apprehension of the *loveliness* of divine things. We cannot emphasize too much the significance Edwards attaches to *beauty, loveliness, harmony* in the proper apprehension of God, Christ, the Word—"the things of religion"—and the experience of delight in their spiritual beauty. Failure to appreciate this important feature of Edwards' thought is a result of the deeply rooted misconception in America that "Puritanism" rejected all that is connected with beauty—art, harmony, delight in the senses—and concentrated instead on an austere and unbending morality. Edwards does not fit that pattern in the least. One has only to consult the many biblical passages he cited in support of his position to see how seriously he took the repeated emphasis on "relishing," "smelling," "tasting" in relation to spiritual knowledge. "The savor of his knowledge" (2 Cor. 2:14); "thou savorest not the things that be of God" (Matt. 16:23); "ye have tasted that the Lord is gracious" (1 Pet. 2:2–3)—these are just a few of the countless biblical texts stressing the sensory face of spiritual apprehension that fill the pages of the *Affections* and other writings. Edwards, in short, knew well the profound meaning expressed in "the beauty of holiness," a phrase that at once reminds us of the powerful affinity that the aesthetic and the religious have for each other.

To understand Edwards' mature view of how the affections, the sense of the heart, and a spiritual understanding are brought together in one unity, there is no better statement than the following:

> From what has been said, therefore, we come necessarily to this conclusion, concerning that wherein spiritual understanding consists; viz. that it consists in a sense of the heart, of the supreme beauty and sweetness or moral perfection of divine things, together with all that discerning and knowledge of the things of religion, that depends upon and flows from such a sense. . . . Spiritual understanding consists primarily in a sense of heart of that spiritual beauty. (2:272)

No one can understand the depth of Edwards' conviction about religious affections and heart religion without taking into account the fact that he had to contend with opponents on two sides at once. He was quite literally caught between two fires in his attempt to defend, on the one hand, the importance of the affections and, on the other, his insistence on testing their genuineness. The opponents of heart religion who, like Charles Chauncy, identified it with all the errors and excesses of the popular revivals did not appreciate Edwards' intelligent account of the affections, although they did not object to his proposal to test their authenticity. Those who sympathized with heart religion welcomed his support but were not particularly pleased with his insistence on "testing the spirits," since they were inclined to believe that religious fervor authenticates itself and needs no signs to distinguish the false from the true. Fortunately, Edwards went ahead despite these obstacles and produced the *Affections*, a unique synthesis of religion, psychology, and theology.

Notes

1. Cf. Charles Chauncy, *Seasonable Thoughts on the State of Religion in New England* (Boston: Rogers & Fowle, 1743).

2. Edwards uses the term "imagination" narrowly to refer to the mind's power to have ideas of things of "external or outward nature . . . when those things are not present" (2:210–11). For an interpretation of Edwards' conception of mental activity as similar to Coleridge's theory of the imagination, see Sang Hyun Lee, *The Philosophical Theology of Jonathan Edwards* (Princeton: Princeton University Press, 2000), 115–69.

3. John Locke, *An Essay concerning Human Understanding*, ed. Peter H. Nidditch (New York: Oxford University Press, 1975), p. 7.

4. Perry Miller, *Jonathan Edwards* (Cleveland: William Sloane Associates, 1949), p. 65.

5. Locke, *Essay*, bk. 3, ch. 1, secs. 1–5, pp. 402–4.

6. Ibid., pp. 403–4.
7. See "Christian Virtue and Common Morality," in this volume.

Suggested Further Readings

Cherry, Conrad. *The Theology of Jonathan Edwards: A Reappraisal*, pp. 12–88. Bloomington: Indiana University Press, 1996.

Delattre, Roland A. *Beauty and Sensibility in the Thought of Jonathan Edwards: An Essay in Aesthetics and Theological Ethics*. New Haven: Yale University Press, 1968.

Kuklick, Bruce. *Churchmen and Philosophers from Jonathan Edwards to John Dewey*, pp. 15–42. New Haven: Yale University Press, 1985.

Lee, Sang Hyun. *The Philosophical Theology of Jonathan Edwards*, pp. 115–69. Princeton: Princeton University Press, 2000.

Miller, Perry. *Jonathan Edwards*. New York: William Sloane Associates, 1949.

Smith, John E. *Jonathan Edwards: Puritan, Preacher, Philosopher*. London: Geoffrey Chapman, 1992.

Nine

Freedom of the Will

Allen C. Guelzo

THE EXACT NATURE of the human will is, like the nature of human consciousness, a question so subjective and so interior that no one is ever likely to arrive at a satisfactory judgment about how it functions or even what it is—which may be the best proof that philosophy is not a science, and the best evidence that those social sciences which try to measure, quantify, and control aspects of human consciousness are not sciences either. Still, there is no denying that we are aware of a power or an impulse within us which translates thought into action, or at least responds to perceptions of threat or opportunity. So even if we have difficulty in defining the will, most of us can acknowledge that there is something like that at work as part of human consciousness.

What may be easier than defining this will is ascertaining whether it is free. At the same time that we are conscious of possessing a will, we are also conscious that this power, except in cases of mental illness, is not random. It is, after all, *our* will that we subjectively sense at work. So we might be able to say that, simply by virtue of its being a process that originates within ourselves, willing is free—free from external constraint, free because it belongs to us and not to someone else, free because nothing we sense subjectively seems to intervene between a desire for something and our reaching outward to satisfy that desire. Unless, of course, another desire intervenes—at which point we immediately realize that the transition from desiring to willing is not quite so simple as we thought. And as soon as we have recognized that, we are likely to acknowledge the operation of our wills is affected by our habits, our temperament, and our exterior circumstances. We might desire A, only to find out that B is equally attractive: which desire does the will obey? If the will "obeys" desires, is it still *free*? If it does not, it might be *free*, but then it will be unpredictable—something which the bulk of experience testifies against—or perhaps influenced by factors outside our consciousness, in which case our will seems hardly to belong to us anymore and can't be considered *free* after all. At this moment, we will recollect that we never actually defined what we meant by *free*, either, so that we are unsure, not only of how the will is working, but of what we mean by a *free* will. But unsure or not, we cannot avoid these problems, because knowing whether the will is free is involved in a series of practical and unavoidable questions:

How do we hold people accountable for their actions if their wills are not free?

How can people be considered politically free within a polity if they do not possess freedom of will?

How is it possible to understand the relationship of cause and effect if the human will has the power to rise above causality and act freely? (And if it cannot . . . return to the first question).

How can there be a God (or at least a God worthy of the name) unless he controls all events? But if he does, how can human choices be free? If he only controls some events, does he really control any? In either case, what incentive is there for obedience, prayers, petitions, and worship?

If a God does not control all events, who (or what) does? If there is no such control, are all events (including the operation of the human will) random? If they are, what's the point of doing anything at all?

Jonathan Edwards turned to the problem of the will in the 1740s with many of these questions in mind. Behind him was a long tradition of scholastic reasoning on the subject which he read as an undergraduate at Yale, plus the legacy of the Calvinist theology which had entered like iron into his soul. Around him was a bewildering new world of philosophical inquiry, defined by the scientific revolution of the seventeenth century and its Enlightenment popularizers, that opened up entirely new and uncomfortable trains of reasoning both for and against free will. Liberty was the byword of the Enlightenment—liberty from the shackles of the scholastic past, liberty from the dominance of theology, liberty from inherited, unearned, and unnatural status—and free will would become its moral corollary. Edwards would not be the only Calvinist, or theologian, or moralist, or American, to take on the subject, but he would become the most famous to challenge the inroads of a fashionable free-willism in the New England churches he loved and served. He would devote his single most sustained piece of philosophical and theological inquiry to it in *Freedom of the Will* (1754), where he would bend his energies to two tasks: undermining the notion that the human will possesses some sort of unique autonomy, or "self-determination," and showing that a universe in which all events have been determined by God is not inconsistent with human liberty or moral accountability.

It is hard to date exactly when questions about free will emerged as an independent discussion of their own. Both Plato and Aristotle were aware that the movement from thinking to doing was neither direct nor simple (as in the so-called Medean paradox: *I see the good but do the evil*), and Aristotle in particular was conscious of the logical irreconcilability of an action and its possible alternatives. (There will either *be* a naval battle or there will *not* be a naval battle today, Aristotle pointed out; it can't be both, so it is *necessary* that there be either one or the other). Similarly, thinkers as far removed as the unnamed Hebrew author of Job, and the Roman Stoic Seneca understood that the power of divine providence posed a genuine difficulty to all who supposed that their actions originated solely in his own will. But the idea that the will was a sort of separate power, or faculty, of its own within the human psyche, and that it might possess a role (and a freedom) in human decision making quite apart from the other faculties, really originates with the Christian Augustine. "I knew I had a will [*voluntas*] as surely as I knew I had life in me," Augustine wrote in his autobiographical *Confessions*, and this *voluntas* had sufficient power, not only to stymy the decisions of the intellect, but to carry the person in an entirely different direction. "I was held fast, not in fetters clamped upon me by another, but by my own will, which had the strength of iron chains."[1] This realization accomplished two things: first, it identified love with the will, and made the synthesis of loving/willing/desiring the superior of simple reason; second, it encouraged submission to a completely sovereign God. This not only discovered order in human experience by referring it to a totalizing providential plan but also ended the sense of ennui and purposelessness which pervades the atmosphere of late antiquity in the West (something which showed up in spades in Augustine's great paean to God's direction and control over human history, the *Civitatis Dei*).

No one in western Christendom could entirely tear loose from the overwhelming influence of Augustine's insistence on God's ultimate control of human events. In fact, to suggest otherwise was to associate oneself with pagan unbelievers like Lucretius, whose doctrine of the spontaneous and uncaused "swerve" of matter seemed to put chance on the throne of the universe. Not even the Protestant Reformation challenged the consensus in western Christianity about divine sovereignty. John Calvin, who shared Augustine's healthy respect for the power of the will and the undependability of the intellect, also insisted that "the will of God is the cause of all things that happen in the world." As for the evil that is done in the world, "these very things are the right and just works of God."[2] Attempts by Protestants to step out from under the shadow of God's predestination, which the Dutch theologian Jacobus Arminius proposed in the early 1600s, were promptly and systematically slapped down by confessionalists and Puritans alike as a kind of theological lèse-majesté.

But even as Arminius was receiving his comeuppance at the Synod of Dordt in 1619, a revolution in European thought was already swelling toward an eruption. The new scientific method proposed by Francis Bacon, and the new scientific discoveries of Galileo and Newton, completely rewrote the idea of providence by substituting for the intelligent design of God the soulless and mechanical activity of physics. For the first time in the West, unbelief rather then devotion became identified with the denial of free will, and the activity of the will became merely the last act in a rigid chain of physical causes. "Voluntary actions," wrote Thomas Hobbes, "have all of them necessary causes, and are therefore necessitated," but by material substances, not God.[3]

This set off an unseemly panic among the theologians, who regrouped throughout the eighteenth century around a defense of free will, reasoning that if people really do possess a power of choosing freely, then not everything is controlled by material cause-and-effect, and some room is left in the universe for genuine and responsible activity by both God and his creatures. Jonathan Edwards, who had graduated from Yale in 1720, hoped that Puritan New England would be spared the plague of "Arminianism." He knew from his own youthful experience what it was like to be "full of objections against the doctrine of God's sovereignty," and he also knew what it was like, once he had been genuinely converted, to receive "quite another kind of sense of God's sovereignty than I had then," so that it became "my delight to approach God, and adore him as a Sovereign God, and ask sovereign mercy of him" (16:791–92, 799).

But the blandishments of the new Arminianism crept in under the barred gate even of New England Puritanism. Unsettled New England divines like Boston's Charles Chauncy concluded that "Men . . . can't be *religious* but with the *free Consent of their Wills*; and this can be gain'd in no Way but that of *Reason* and *Persuasion*."[4] Edwards had just become pastor of a small congregation in New York when Yale was rocked by the "Great Apostasy"—the defection of seven of the Yale staff, including the rector, to the Church of England and the new "Arminianism." In May 1724, Edwards was recalled to Yale as a tutor to fill the vacuum caused by the "Arminian" scandal. But the "Arminian" influence proved exceedingly difficult to root out. Edwards' health broke under the strain, and it must have been with great relief that he received the call of the church in Northampton, Massachusetts (where his grandfather Solomon Stoddard was the senior pastor), to become the pastoral assistant in 1727, and then, after Stoddard's death in 1729, called again as senior pastor.

For the next twenty years, all explicit discussion of "Arminianism" disappears from Edwards' writings, but he remained vigilant against the possibility of its appearance. In the fall of 1734, a "great noise" went up in western Massachusetts "about Arminianism, which seemed to appear with a very threatening aspect upon the interest of religion here" (3:148,

16:50). The pastor of the church at Sunderland, William Rand, had been rumored to be preaching "new notions as to the doctrine of justification," and Robert Breck, the new pastor of the church in Springfield, was hailed before the regional ministerial association on suspicion of "Arminianism." But Edwards' response as pastor in Northampton was to begin preaching, not on predestination, but on justification. The results were two remarkable rekindlings of religious fervor in Northampton and western Massachusetts, first in 1734–35 and then again in the wake of the New England tour of the intinerant Anglican maverick, George Whitefield, in 1740–41. Edwards seized on these revivals as good reasons "for Arminians to change their principles" and "relinquish their scheme," since so much of the testimony of the spiritually awakened in Northampton had rounded on "the doctrine of God's absolute sovereignty with regard to the salvation of sinners" (3:168, 503). But in the public letter he wrote about the revivals for Thomas Prince's *Christian History* in 1743 (3:544–57), it was the "very lamentable decay of religious affections" and not Arminianism which was Edwards' principal concern to oppose.

It was only after the revivals had cooled and Edwards became embroiled in controversy with his own congregation over the terms of admission to communion that his attention began to turn to the project of writing a book against the Arminians. He had been "engaged in studies on the Arminian controversies and preparing to write something upon them" as early as 1747, and as he told the Scots Presbyterian John Erskine in 1752, his intention from the first was "to write something upon . . . free will and moral agency" (16:491). Just how far his thinking had gone appears in January 1750, when Edwards, having received a question about free will from his former pupil Joseph Bellamy, wrote a reply which contains the core of the argument he would later put into fuller form in 1754 (16:318, 491).

The communion controversy, which ended in Edwards' dismissal from Northampton in 1750, interrupted this "design of writing against Arminianism." It also convinced Edwards that Arminianism had somehow been the real issue behind the contention over communion, thus adding the fuel of personal humiliation to the fire of doctrinal conflict. In his *Farewell Sermon*, Edwards warned the restless Northamptonites that "Arminianism, and doctrines of like tendency" were "creeping into almost all parts of the land."[5] In 1751 he was called as pastor and missionary to the mixed Indian and white congregation at Stockbridge operated by the Society for the Propagation of the Gospel in New England, but he continued to fight the communion battle over his shoulder. In the letter to the Northampton church that he appended to *Misrepresentations*

Corrected and Truth Vindicated in 1752, Edwards declared that "it was evident, that Arminianism, and other loose notions in religion" had begun "to get some footing among you" (16:484). He told the Scots Presbyterian John Erskine just after the dismissal that he had discovered the leaders of the movement against him "falling in in some essential things with Arminians," while "four or five" of the ministerial council called to approve the dismissal "have heretofore had the reputation of Arminians" (16:353, 312).

There is, consequently, nothing surprising in finding that Edwards had no sooner completed the elaborate self-defense of his position on communion in *Misrepresentations Corrected* than he was once more at work "writing something on the Arminian controversy," especially on "the nature of that freedom of moral agents, which makes them the proper subjects of moral government, moral precepts, counsels, calls, motives, persuasions, promises and threatenings, praise and blame, rewards and punishments . . . endeavoring also to bring the late, great objections and outcries against the Calvinistic divinity, from these topics, to the test of the strictest reasoning" (16:491). He must have worked with tremendous speed and concentration, since the first draft was "almost finished" in only seven months, and in mid-April 1753, he forwarded "proposals for printing by subscription something I have been writing" to Thomas Foxcroft, a ministerial colleague in Boston who had agreed to act as his go-between with the printer, Samuel Kneeland (16:593–94).

His patience was short. All during the summer and winter of 1753, Edwards had to cope with bouts of illness and political in-fighting while managing the Stockbridge mission. He insisted to Foxcroft that the manuscript be printed "in the best character" Kneeland possessed, and when Foxcroft failed to keep him updated about the manuscript's prospects, Edwards wrote querulously to him, wanting "to know very much what is become of it" (16:619). In March 1754, Foxcroft finally sent a description of the printing for Edwards to approve. But Edwards disliked "such a small page as you mention, less than a psalter." He wanted "good white paper and the printer's best types," and he could not resist sending Foxcroft a last-minute insertion and a correction (16:625).

The book was finally published in October 1754, under the title *A Careful and Strict Enquiry into the Modern Prevailing Notions of that Freedom of Will, which is supposed to be essential to Moral Agency, Vertue and Vice, Reward and Punishment, Praise and Blame.* (For practical purposes, it would thereafter be known simply as *Freedom of the Will*, or more simply as "Edwards on the Will"). Once the finished volume was in hand, Edwards was still unhappy with it. He composed a list of errata for Kneeland and informed Foxcroft that Kneeland "binds the books poorly. The covers are so apt to warp that they will warp as they lie upon the table" (16:655). Of the 298 subscribers (including booksellers) who paid to receive copies of *Freedom of the Will*, only seven were from Northampton.

Edwards was not interested in writing a comprehensive, dispassionate survey of the entire problem of free will. What he really wanted to do was much more specific, and that was to destroy Arminianism as a viable option and justify Calvinistic theism as the only way to understand the sovereignty of God. Both the critique of Arminianism and the model he offers for understanding the justice of Calvinism are philosophically ingenious—his destruction of Arminianism is just as destructive when applied to almost any other version of libertarianism—and he certainly believed that he was dealing with a question which went straight to the root of larger problems in human self-identity and self-understanding. "The knowledge of ourselves consists chiefly in right apprehensions concerning those two chief faculties of our nature, the understanding and will," Edwards wrote in the preface to *Freedom of the Will* (1:133). But his task in *Freedom of the Will* is primarily apologetic and ethical rather than philosophical. He wants people not to have a satisfying romp through the garden of ideas but to become Calvinists.

The book divides into four "parts" and a conclusion. From the very opening of the first "part," Edwards moves at once to seize the high ground by offering a definition of the will which, if accepted by the unwary reader, will function like the hook in a fish's mouth. "The will (without any metaphysical refining) is plainly, that by which the mind chooses anything"; the will is, in fact, "the same as an act of choosing or choice" (1:137). In other words, Edwards describes the will as something which is analytically identical with the mental action of choosing, so that the will does not exist as a separate mental department, capable of checking, resisting, or amending what the intellect settles upon as its choice. "In every act, or going forth of the will, there is some preponderation of the mind, or inclination, one way rather than another" (1:140). Detach the will from those "preponderations," and you would get absolutely nothing, rather than independent action. Where there is no choosing in the intellect, there is no willing.

This shifts the real attention away from the will itself and onto the intimate connection of the intellect and the will. As Edwards puts it, let a *motive* appeal in any sort of way to the intellect, so that the *motive* appears as "the greatest apparent good" at that moment, and the will must move into action at once to apprehend that "good."[6] Hence, Edwards can say that any "motive, which, as it stands in the view of the mind, is the strongest, that determines the will" (1:140). Or, to put it more starkly, one may as well say "that the will always is as the greatest apparent good is" (1:142). The will, for Edwards, looks more like a highly fluid process than a stand-alone faculty, less like a review board and more like the terminal point of an electric current in which a *motive* triggers the assent of the intellect, and the will shifts into play. And his use of the term *motive* makes it clear that what the mind saw as "good" was not always the product of logic, reason, or deliberation.

This definition of the will gives it so little room for action that one might justifiably complain that Edwards has made willing *necessary*—which was the trump card Arminians in particular and free-willers in general liked to play, since *necessity* conjured up in the eighteenth-century mind images of orreries, mechanical animals, and other machines, forcing and grinding their helpless components into soulless patterns of activity. That, Edwards admitted, was indeed one way of using the word, and implies "some supposed opposition made to the existence of the thing spoken of, which is overcome, or proves in vain to hinder or alter it" (1:149). Transferred to his definition of the will, it would make matters look as if his *motives* dragged the kicking and screaming will into conformity with their demands. But that was not the only possible meaning of *necessity*, Edwards pointed out. There is such a thing as *natural necessity*, where people are compelled to will contrary to their intellect; but there is also a *philosophical necessity*, which "is really nothing else than the full and fixed connection between the things signified by the subject and predicate of a proposition, which affirms something to be true" (1:152). This is the kind of connection which is expressed, for instance, by a geometric theorem, or the description of a historical fact, or anything that enjoys "a connection with something that is necessary in its own nature, or something that already is, or has been; so that the one being supposed, the other certainly follows" (1:153–54). In this version of necessity, there is no kicking, no screaming, no felt sense of force, but rather the logical and harmonious process of moving from one logically connected proposition to another.

What Edwards is waiting to introduce is a subset of *philosophical necessity* that he designates *moral necessity*, and that describes the same sense of unresisting "connection and consequence," only this time arising "from such *moral causes*, as the strength of inclination, of motives, and the connection which there is in many cases between these, and such certain volitions and actions" (1:156). So, while we can deplore the intrusion of *natural necessity* into the operation of the will with the same energy as the Arminians, we can also insist on the perfect legitimacy of *moral necessity*, because moral necessity never involves "some supposable voluntary opposition or endeavor" (1:159). In fact, we can deploy the same distinction, not just between kinds of *necessity*, but between kinds of necessity's opposite, which is *ability*. We possess *natural ability* when we have the literal physical ability to carry out our volitions; *moral ability* describes the possession of the moral wherewithal to carry them out, since one might be in full possession of all the natural ability to perform an action but lack the moral ability, due to the power of depraved habits and inclinations, to raise a finger. "A woman of great honor and chastity may have a moral inability to prostitute herself to her slave," Edwards offered by way of example, while "a moral inability to love wickedness in general, may render a man unable to take complacence in wicked persons or things" (1:160). Although both situations employed the Arminian bogey-words *necessity* and *inability*, in neither case was anyone being forced, or deprived of freedom of action.

As Edwards closed the first "part" of Freedom of the Will, he had maneuvered the terminology in such a way as to disarm the Arminians even before the battle was joined. The will was not an independent faculty which possessed a liberty of its own ("That which has the power of volition or choice is the man or the soul, not the power for volition itself" [1:163]). And freedom for the will meant, not the power of the will to choose for itself, but "that power and opportunity for one to do and conduct as he will, or according to his choice." It mattered nothing to Edwards how the whole process was started—including if it originated in divine decree. If there was natural ability available, "and nothing in the way to hinder his pursuing and executing his will," then he was as perfectly free as anyone could desire (1:164).

It was now time, in the second "part," for Edwards to turn the weapons he had seized on the epistemologically confused Arminians, and to that end he began knocking over one Arminian objection to divine predestination after another. Did the Arminians believe that the will is an independent faculty which forms its own volitions? If this will decides on Z, then there had to be a prior act of will *in* the will to make that decision which we may call Y. But the same process by which Y called Z into action was also required to get Y moving as well, thus requiring yet another act of will, which we may call X, to cause Y; and thus to infinite regress. Or if infinite regress was not enough of a demonstration of Arminian folly, a demonstration of Arminian logical incoherence would work too. "If the will determines itself, then either the will is active in determining its volitions, or it is not," Edwards reasoned. "If it be active in it, then the determination is an act of the will; and so there is one act of the will determining another. But if the will is not active in the determination, then how does it exercise any liberty in it?" (1:176).

Perhaps one could simply say that the will operates without causes, but Edwards was only waiting to point out that uncaused volitions were pretty much the same thing as chaos—and did the Arminians really want to suggest that we lived in a universe of chaos? "If we begin to maintain, that things may come into existence, and begin to be, which heretofore have not been, of themselves, without any cause; all our . . . evidence of the being of God, is cut off at one blow" (1:182–83). In that case, pure, raw chance would rule our affairs, and chance's rule would be no less absolute than that of God. On the other hand, if the Arminian should hastily propose that the will is determined by the intellect, then what has the Arminian said which differs from Edwards' Calvinism? "If it determines them by an act of the understanding, or some other power, then *the will* don't determine *itself*; and so the self-determining power of the will is given up" (1:191). In the last ditch, one could do as Dr. Johnson did ("We know our will is free and there's an end on't") and appeal to the felt experience of choosing in spite of the intellect or a motive or a cause as a demonstration of the will's freedom. But Edwards would have none of it. Such an experience was illusory. It might be possible "for the understanding to act in indifference, yet to be sure the will never does; because the will's beginning to act as if the very same as its beginning to choose or prefer" (1:197). We can fool ourselves into believing that the will can do something in spite of what the intellect says, but that will be true only if the intellect is viewing the situation "remotely and generally." When you actually come to "the last step," the very next thing to be determined "is not what my mind is absolutely indifferent about" (1:202).

Edwards played cat-and-mouse like this with Arminianism all through the second "part" of *Freedom of the Will*. But even Edwards had the sense that he was shredding tissue paper rather than attacking the real core of the Arminian persuasion, and that was the terror of mechanism and the fear that determinism would cooperate with mechanism in tearing away every ethical restraint from evil and every moral incentive to good by persuading people that their actions were simply what they had to be. So in the third "part," Edwards finally settled on the real question underlying the flight to free will: is the Arminian notion of free will and self-determination actually needed to ensure moral accountability, even if it is logically flawed? Is it really the case that "such kind of liberty" is "requisite to moral agency, virtue and vice, praise and blame, reward and punishment, etc." (1:277)?

Edwards replied with a mixture of theological and philosophical ripostes. God is good, Edwards asserted, and "not only virtuous, but a being in whom is all possible virtue," to the point where he cannot do evil. He is, in other words, "necessarily holy, and his will necessarily determined to that which is good" (1:278). Yet, no one, even Arminians, had ever expressed an anxiety that, because God's goodness is *necessary*, it was unworthy of praise or considered as anything less than perfectly holy. Why should ours, if it is under God's direction? Likewise, "it was impossible, that the acts of the will of the human soul of Christ should, in any instance, degree or circumstances, be other wise than holy"—yet, by Arminian logic, that made Christ merely a machine, and completely lacking in the freedom necessary to being a genuine moral actor (1:281). If necessity was good enough for Jesus Christ, why should those who, like the Arminians, claim to be his disciples, complain?

It was Edwards' delight to remind the Arminian that the purpose of moral law was not to create an environment where all were free to create their own alternatives but "to bind to one side," to train people's responses to avoid some actions and do others. Allow the Arminian definition of free will as "indifference" to stand and we would have to say that every law ever passed "destroys liberty; as it puts the will out of equilibrium." Wasn't it the most basic "end of commands . . . to turn the will one way" rather than another, and to cultivate a partiality for doing the good, not to encourage it to gallop off madly in all directions (1:304)? Ironically, any free-willer who actually cultivated such an "indifference" to having their will caused to do good was performing what any normal person would consider the diametric opposite of virtue. "In order to the virtuousness of an act," the Arminians must demand that "the heart . . . be indifferent in the time of performance of that act, and the more indifferent and cold the heart is with relation to the act which is performed, so much the better; because the act is performed with so much the greater liberty" (1:321). If this is what Arminians believed was the original moral position, then no society could entertain much hope for a moral future.

To say, then, that people possess a *moral inability* to do good because of their vicious habits or temperament gives them no excuse because somehow they could not cultivate an "indifference" to those habits or temperaments; to the contrary, a *moral inability*, "consisting in the strength of . . . evil inclination, is the very thing wherein . . . wickedness consists" (1:309). Whereas people possessed of moral ability to do good would normally be the object of praise—except by Arminians, who would criticize them for being machines. Better in this case to be a machine, Edwards drily remarked. "Machines are guided by an understanding cause, by the skillful hand of the workman or owner," whereas among Arminians, "the will of man is left to the guidance of nothing, but absolute blind contingence" (1:371).

If the third "part" of *Freedom of the Will* was devoted to showing how Arminian self-determination did nothing to promote the goal of moral accountability, the fourth and last "part" had to bear the burden of showing that Calvinism did. And to do that, Edwards needed to call on the most important of the terms he had defined in the first "part," *necessity*. In the Calvinist universe, where God determined all things, every human action was consequently *necessary*. The lexicon of eighteenth-century philosophy was primed to regard anything which was *necessary* as lacking in moral content, because there were no real alternatives possible. But Edwards argued that necessity is not the enemy of virtue. Even if virtuous acts proceed from an individual equipped by God with virtuous dispositions, that did not destroy the virtue of the act itself. People have the notion, Edwards complained, that necessity always means forcible restraint or armed compulsion. But he had demonstrated in the first "part" that this was a "vulgar sense" of the term, and that a "metaphysical sense" was "entirely diverse." And as soon as people thought one step above the "vulgar," they would see that "the glorified saints have not their freedom at all diminished, in any respect; and that God himself has the highest possible freedom . . . and are so, for that very reason, because they are most perfectly necessary."

If Arminians argued that Calvinism promoted fatalism, they were indulging in a *post hoc, propter hoc* fallacy, since there was no inherent tendency within Calvinism to produce fatalism. If Arminians argued that Calvinism made God the "author" of evil, Edwards replied that they had made a category error. God, according to Calvinism, was merely "the permitter, or not a hinderer of sin; and at the same time, a disposer of the state of events, in such a manner, for wise, holy and most excellent ends and purposes" (1:399). And if Arminians argued that Calvinism helped to produce atheism, Edwards had no difficulty—based on what had happened in Northampton—in replying that "their doctrine," not his, "excuses all evil inclinations, which men find to be natural; because in such inclinations, they are not self-determined." It was not among Calvinists but among Arminians that the anxiety to get right with the eighteenth-century haut monde was the more prevalent. Ever since Arminianism had become the fashion, "vice, profaneness, luxury and wickedness of all sorts, and contempt of religion, and of every kind of seriousness and strictness of conversation" have begun to "proportionably prevail" (1:468). As he wrote to John Erskine three years later,

> This doctrine of a self-determining will, as the ground of all moral good and evil, tends to prevent any proper exercise of faith in God and Christ, in the affair of our salvation, as it tends to prevent all dependence upon them. For, instead of this, it teaches a kind of absolute independence in all these things that are of chief importance in this affair; our righteousness, depending originally on our own acts, as self-determined. (16:721–22)

To use a modern classification, Edwards was a *compatibilist*: liberty and necessity are compatible with each other. But all the same, it was a compatibilism in which necessity clearly played the dominant role and liberty served to explain necessity's operations. Stubborn Arminians would complain, he realized, that any idea of necessity, no matter how cleverly phrased or deployed, still reduced people to the level of something like machines, and in the process, surrendered theism to the mechanism that Enlightenment unbelief at its worst now espoused.

Freedom of the Will made a greater impact at first in Scotland than in New England, where many of its readers, like James Dana of Wallingford, found the book simply incomprehensible. That opinion changed abruptly after 1765, when Edwards' pupil, Samuel Hopkins, published an attack on the New England church establishment, using Edwards' doctrine of natural and moral ability to decry compromises New England church leaders had made over the decades with the Puritan ideal of a holy, gathered church. *Freedom of the Will* became the touchstone of the antiestablishment New Divinity, and the entire free will argument became the great issue of New England theology for a century after Edwards' death. The book's celebrity eventually pushed it into the main currents of American philosophy before the Civil War, and even the Civil War's president, Abraham Lincoln, "always hoped to get at President Edwards on the Will."[7]

With the waning of the New England Theology in the later 1800s and the rise of pragmatism, "Edwards on the Will" dropped back into a philosophical limbo. Even sympathetic biographers, like Ola Elizabeth Winslow in 1940 and Perry Miller in 1949, found that *Freedom of the Will*'s hammerlock obsession with strangling Arminian free-willism fit poorly into the new narratives they constructed for Edwards' life and for American intellectual history as the story of an escape from "the trammels of inability." Winslow conceded that *Freedom of the Will* was "an amazing performance," in which Edwards' "dexterity in accomplishing what at times appear to be logical impossibilities is thrilling to watch." But in the end, Winslow concluded, that it was a "great polemic" rather than a "great book," and "paralyzed debate when debate needed most to be stimulated."[8] Miller, likewise, hailed *Freedom of the Will* as "beyond all peradventure . . . [Edwards'] most sustained intellectual achievement, the most powerful piece of sheer forensic argumentation in American literature." Even so, for Miller it seemed oddly out of place in a story where Edwards figured as a frontier Niebuhr, calling down judgment on protocapitalist cupidity. It was not, after all, "so rich or human a book" as Edwards' writings on revival, and his arguments seemed "like a battleship wasting broadsides on a flimsy target."[9]

Perhaps because of these discouragements, perhaps because of the difficulties of tackling so mammoth an eighteenth-century philosophical text, *Freedom of the Will* made only brief appearances in the central texts on Edwards' theology and ethics by Conrad Cherry, Clyde Holbrook, and Roland Delattre. The publication in 1957 of Paul Ramsay's edition of *Freedom of the Will* as the first volume of the Yale series of Edwards' works was a turning point in the interpretation of the text. (Arthur E. Murphy hailed it in a substantial and perceptive review essay in *Philosophical Review* as "an event of philosophical importance . . . not merely to early American but to contemporary philosophy.")[10] John E. Smith's chapter on *Freedom of the Will* in *Jonathan Edwards: Puritan, Preacher, Philosopher* (1992) offers one of the most extended rereadings of the book in recent times.

Freedom of the Will still suffers among Edwardsean interpreters in almost inverse proportion to its importance in the Edwardsean canon. On the other hand, the American philosophical climate has swung since World War II substantially back in the direction of various forms of determinism. As in Edwards' day, the most recent forms of determinism have been cast into the hardest and most mechanistic patterns, with analogies to computers and computation replacing the eighteenth century's admiration for orreries and machines, while the most ambitious theistic and philosophical resistance to the new mechanism has resorted to contingency and process theology (or "openness-of-God"). Perhaps a new relevance may yet be found in Edwards' greatest work.

Notes

1. Augustine, *Confessions*, 10.38, 13.9, ed. R. S. Pyne-Coffin (London: Penguin, 1961), pp. 247, 317.

2. Calvin, *Concerning the Eternal Predestination of God*, ed. J.K.S. Reid (London: James Clarke, 1961), p. 169.

3. Hobbes, *Leviathan*, ed. W. G. Pogson Smith (1909; Clarendon Press, 1967), p. 161.

4. Chauncy, *The Only Compulsion Proper to be Made Use of in the Affairs of Conscience and Religion* (Boston, 1739), p. 10.

5. JE, "A Farewell Sermon Preached at the First Precinct in Northampton, After the People's Public Rejection of Their Minister . . . on June 22, 1750," in *The Sermons of Jonathan Edwards: A Reader*, ed. W. H. Kimnach, K. Minkema, and D. Sweeney (New Haven: Yale University Press, 1999), p. 238.

6. Edwards was at pains to emphasize that this *motive* was something which was "the direct and immediate object" of perception, not "some object that the act of will has not an immediate, but only an indirect and remote aspect to" (1:143); he did not want *motive* mistaken for a distant idea we are deliberating on at some length, but the percept which was immediately in view at the moment of willing.

7. Noah Brooks, "Personal Recollections of Abraham Lincoln," in *Lincoln Observed: Civil War Dispatches of Noah Brooks*, ed. Michael Burlingame (Baltimore: John Hopkins University Press, 1998), p. 219.

8. Winslow, *Jonathan Edwards, 1703–1758* (New York: Macmillan, 1940), pp. 301–3.
9. Miller, *Jonathan Edwards* (New York: Sloane Associates, 1949), p. 251.
10. Murphy, "Jonathan Edwards on Free Will and Moral Agency," *Philosophical Review* 68 (1959): 181, 202.

Suggested Further Readings

Boller, Paul F. *Freedom and Fate in American Thought from Edwards to Dewey.* Dallas: Southern Methodist University Press, 1978.
Conforti, Joseph A. *Jonathan Edwards, Religious Tradition, and American Culture.* Chapel Hill: University of North Carolina Press, 1995.
Fiering, Norman. *Jonathan Edwards' Moral Thought and Its British Context.* Chapel Hill: University of North Carolina Press, 1981.
———. "Will and Intellect in the New England Mind." *William and Mary Quarterly* 29 (October 1972): 515–58.
Guelzo, Allen C. *"Edwards on the Will": A Century of American Theological Debate.* Middletown, Conn.: Wesleyan University Press, 1989.
———. "From Calvinist Metaphysics to Republican Theory: Jonathan Edwards and James Dana on Freedom of the Will." *Journal of the History of Ideas* 56 (July 1995).
———. "The Return of the Will: Jonathan Edwards and the Possibilities of Free Will." In *Edwards in Our Time: Jonathan Edwards and the Shaping of American Religion*, ed. Sang H. Lee and Allen C. Guelzo. Grand Rapids: Eerdmans Publishing, 1999.
Heimert, Alan. *Religion and the American Mind: From the Great Awakening to the Revolution.* Cambridge, Mass.: Harvard University Press, 1965.
Kuklick, Bruce. *Churchmen and Philosophers: From Jonathan Edwards to John Dewey.* New Haven: Yale University Press, 1985.
Pahl, Jon. *Paradox Lost: Free Will and Political Liberty in American Culture, 1630–1760.* Baltimore: Johns Hopkins University Press, 1992.

Ten

Grace and Justification by Faith Alone

Sang Hyun Lee

IN HIS DOCTRINE of redemption, Edwards' chief concerns are to reaffirm the Reformation and biblical assertion of the absolute sovereignty of God's grace in the salvation of the fallen creation and at the same time to emphasize the reality of the change that occurs in the regenerate. This dual goal, as I will attempt to show in this essay, must be understood in light of his central thesis that human redemption ultimately serves the purpose for which God created the world. I cannot undertake here a full exposition of Edwards' understanding of grace and justification, but will deal rather with two issues, that have been subject to some recent debate among Edwards scholars: (1) How, exactly, does the Holy Spirit operate in the regenerate, according to Edwards? and (2) Is the Pauline and Reformation doctrine of the justification of the ungodly compromised by his emphasis upon the grace as infused prior to the act of faith? We turn first to Edwards' understanding of the Holy Spirit as grace.

Grace and the Holy Spirit as a New Disposition

Edwards states unambiguously that saving grace "is no other than the Spirit of God itself dwelling and acting in the heart of a saint" (21:192). And Edwards asserted that the Holy Spirit's direct presence and operation in the regenerate is not incompatible with his effects being the voluntary acts of the regenerate person. This compatabilist view was premised on Edwards' contention that the Holy Spirit works as a new disposition or principle of action internal, not external, to the regenerate person's own self. Edwards' interest in seeing grace as a personal reality for the regenerate hung on the concept of the Holy Spirit as dwelling and acting in the regenerate as a new disposition.

While rejecting the idea that human beings could contribute to the attainment of grace, Edwards, like other Calvinists, strongly emphasized the visible and behavioral reality of the effects of grace in regenerate persons. For Edwards, however, the importance of the reality of salvation for the regenerate was accentuated by his own theological framework, in which the redemption of fallen creation was comprehended in the ultimate end of God's self-communication or self-repetition *ad extra* and was the consequence of the exercise of God's own dispositional essence. God's own activities of self-communication are involved in human redemption, and this self-communication has to happen within the fabric of time and space. It was a matter of special importance to Edwards, therefore, to maintain in his doctrine of grace the reality of human regeneration as well as the absolute primacy of God in that regeneration.

Now, the key question here is this: What is the exact meaning of Edwards' contention that the Holy Spirit, the third person of the Trinity himself, acts in the regenerate "as" and "after the manner of" a new disposition or principle of action? How do the supernatural and natural meet in the workings of grace? This question has a long and complex history in the development of Christian doctrine, and a brief overview of that history will be useful to our understanding of Edwards' unique perspective.

One of the basic themes in the development of the theology of grace in the West is the distinction between "uncreated grace" (*gratia increata*)—God's grace as the direct presence or action of the Holy Spirit—and "created grace" (*gratia creata*)—God's grace as the abiding effect of the Holy Spirit, which dwells in the saints as a new habit or disposition.[1] In the twelfth century, Peter Lombard identified the grace of charity with the direct presence of the Holy Spirit. Many theologians who followed Lombard, however, believed that grace had to be emphasized as an enduring transformation just as much as absolute sovereignty. The distinction between "uncreated grace" and "created grace" was introduced in the thirteenth century to resolve this issue.

Thomas Aquinas, in particular, was eager to emphasize grace as having a fixed and stable nature because he, following Aristotelian metaphysics, conceived of the supernatural operation of God as working in and through the natural order of things rather than as a violation of them. For Aquinas, human nature had three principles: the being of the soul and the faculties of reason and will. The nature of the human soul is directed to the natural end of the human being and, as a substance, is a completed form (*forma completiva*) that cannot be modified or redirected in any way. Now, for Aquinas, without the change or elevation of human nature to a supernatural level, supernatural virtues and actions are not possible. Thus, God gives the saints a supernatural form, or an "entitative habit" (*donum habituale*), on the level of being, as the "basis" for the supernatural virtues that he also infuses into the saints' faculties and powers. Referring to the ontological level, where grace has to function first, Aquinas writes,

"Grace reduces to the first kind of quality. However, it is not simply a virtue; rather it is a kind of habitual state which is presupposed by the infused virtues, as their origin and root."[2]

Aquinas' conception of "created grace," both on the ontological and the operational levels, is undoubtedly intended to articulate the real change that occurs in the actual being and powers of the regenerate person. What became controversial later was that "created grace" for Aquinas appeared to be a kind of semi-independent or intermediary principle that could be separated from "uncreated grace." Grace on the level of being, says Aquinas, is "a kind of habitual state" and the infused virtues "an intermediary" by which grace issues forth in virtuous acts. Such mediating principles between God and the transformed saint's virtuous acts are necessary for Aquinas because, as Robert P. Scharlemann explains, the self-moving nature of the human will would be annulled if the actions of God's grace were direct and extrinsic. "An external movement might conceivably be a movement by the Holy Ghost, but it would not be a movement of love unless it were also an act of the will, that is intrinsic and voluntary."[3] Thus, for Aquinas, an "intrinsic and voluntary" act of a virtuous nature does not occur without (1) a mediating virtue that facilitates the movement of the will or (2) the "habitual state" of grace in the nature of the person. In this way, Aquinas rejected the Lombardian conception of grace as the direct activity of the Holy Spirit, although for him the presence of "created grace" did not negate the Holy Spirit's continuing activity for the regenerate.[4]

Nevertheless, the prominent role played by "created grace" in the thought of Aquinas and the Scholastics in general was seen by the Reformers as a threat to the absolute sovereignty and gratuitous nature of God's grace. And in reaction to Luther's strong emphasis on grace as God's absolutely gratuitous act of acceptance of the sinner, the Council of Trent emphasized the reality of "created grace" even more by describing it as an "inherent" quality in the regenerate.[5]

We may ask whether Edwards had in mind something like "created grace," an intermediary or quality produced by the Holy Spirit. When he says that the Holy Spirit operates in the regenerate "as" and "after the manner of" a disposition or principle of action, is he thinking of "created grace" in the Thomistic sense?

There are times when Edwards gives the impression that his view is similar to that of Aquinas.[6] In an early miscellany Edwards writes, "But by those expressions concerning a holy life, we can understand nothing else but a disposition that would naturally exert itself in holy [living] upon occasion; so we say of the believing disposition" ("Misc." 27b, 13:214). Later, in the *Treatise on Grace*, Edwards says that "this saving grace in the soul is not only from the Spirit, but it also partakes of the nature of that Spirit that it is from." In a 1737 sermon on Matthew 25:1–12, Edwards says that saving grace is "not from nature but is wrought in the heart wholly by the Spirit of that which is supernatural, or above nature." And in *Charity and Its Fruits*, Edwards goes so far as to say that "this blessing of the saving grace of God is a quality inherent in the nature of him who is the subject of it" (21:180). But such descriptions of grace as these—which appear to describe grace as an intermediary principle or quality in the regenerate person that is produced by, and thus distinguishable from, the Holy Spirit—are far outnumbered in Edwards' writings by descriptions that identify saving grace as the Holy Spirit. So, for example, toward the end of the *Treatise on Grace*, Edwards more typically states that "there is no other principle of grace in the soul than the very Holy Ghost dwelling in the soul and acting there as a vital principle" (21:196).

Alternatively, Edwards describes how the Holy Spirit "becomes" a new disposition in the regenerate person. At one point in the *Treatise on Grace*, Edwards writes, "Hence the Spirit of God seems in Scripture to be spoken of as to become a quality of the persons in whom it resided, so that they are called spiritual persons; as when we say 'a virtuous man,' we speak of virtue as the quality of the man" (21:197). In *Religious Affections*, Edwards says that in the Scriptures the Holy Spirit is represented as being in the regenerate "so united to the faculties of the soul, that he becomes there a principle or spring of new nature and life" (2:200).

How are we to interpret Edwards' intention in using the term "become" to describe the presence of the Holy Spirit in the regenerate person? It should be noted, first of all, that Edwards does not use "become" very often, and it is certainly not the most common way he refers to the Holy Spirit's indwelling in the regenerate. Second, when Edwards uses the term, he does not appear to mean anything different from his more usual expressions, namely, "as" and "after the manner of." Only a few sentences after Edwards uses the term "become" in the *Treatise on Grace*, for example, he resorts to his more typical terminology to describe the way the Holy Spirit acts as a new disposition. Third, Edwards' use of the term is always in the context of emphasizing the reality of the Holy Spirit's presence and action in the regenerate, which for Edwards is so real that the Holy Spirit's acts are also the regenerate person's own voluntary deeds. In one place he states, for example, that the Holy Spirit is said to "become" a quality in regenerate persons "so that *they are called spiritual persons*" (21:197, my italics). In *Charity and Its Fruits*, Edwards also observes, "By his producing this effect the Spirit becomes an indwelling vital principle in the soul, and *the subject becomes a spiritual being*, denominated so from the Spirit of God which dwells in him and of whose nature he is a partaker" (8:158). In short, it appears probable that by "become" Edwards did not mean that the Holy Spirit "turned into" a human disposition or became "incarnate" in the regenerate person. His use of this term reflects his emphasis upon the personal reality of grace for the regenerate person rather than an intentional departure from his usual view that grace is "the very Holy Ghost dwelling in the soul and acting there as a vital principle."

Edwards also speaks of the Holy Spirit as "united" with the regenerate person. "Christ's love, that is, his Spirit, is actually united to the faculties of their souls. So it properly lives, acts and exerts its nature in the exercise of their faculties" (21:195). As was the case with the term "become," Edwards' use of the term "united" is an expression of his emphasis on the personal reality of the effects of the Holy Spirit. The Holy Spirit is so "united" with the powers of the regenerate person that his acts are also properly the regenerate person's own acts. But Edwards is equally emphatic in his contention that the effects in the regenerate one are the direct actions of the Holy Spirit himself.

The Holy Spirit, according to Edwards, neither "turns into" a disposition of the regenerate person nor produces an intermediary principle logically distinguishable from the Holy Spirit himself. Thus, the meaning of the idea of "union" is not entirely clear. We are therefore brought back to the question of how to interpret the meaning of Edwards' typical formulation, that the Holy Spirit operates "as" or "after the manner of" a new disposition in the regenerate. The answer may lie in a most ingenious concept set forth in "Miscellanies," no. 629, where Edwards argues that, in the case of saving grace, the Holy Spirit operates independent of the preestablished laws of nature. "For the actings of the Spirit of God in the heart are more arbitrary and are not tied to such and such means by such laws or rules, as shall particularly and precisely determine in a stated method every particular exercise and the degree of it; but *the Holy Spirit is given and infused into the hearts of men only under this general law, viz. that it shall remain there and put forth acts there after the manner of an abiding, natural, vital principle of action, or a seed remaining in us*" (18:157, my italics). In other words, the Holy Spirit acts "after the manner of" a principle of action in the regenerate person neither by becoming nor by producing a new principle of action; rather, the Holy Spirit remains and acts directly and immediately as the Holy Spirit, except in accordance with the divinely established general law that the Holy Spirit act "after the manner" of a human principle of action.

Having posited this general law, Edwards can maintain that the Holy Spirit acts directly in the regenerate person and at the same time assert that the Holy Spirit's acts are properly the regenerate person's own voluntary acts. While Edwards' compatabilist view of human freedom enabled him to maintain that the Holy Spirit's functioning as a new inward disposition is fully consistent with his effects being the regenerate person's own voluntary actions, Edwards' general law explains how the Holy Spirit is led to operate like a disposition in the regenerate. The Holy Spirit is "united" to the powers of the regenerate by acting in and through, not from outside, the natural powers of the regenerate.

Now general laws, to Edwards' way of thinking, are dispositional principles, like habits, which have an abiding reality apart from their exercise and are in some sense causal powers that govern the character of certain events and actions. If this is the case, then is the general law governing the manner of the Holy Spirit's operations in the regenerate a kind of intermediate principle that mediates or facilitates the operation of the Holy Spirit and the natural powers of the regenerate? Not really. If this general law mediates anything at all, it governs the manner in which the Holy Spirit will act in the human self. It does not mediate the Holy Spirit's *presence* in the regenerate person; rather, the Holy Spirit himself directly dwells or "subsists" in the regenerate person. There is nothing in the regenerate person that is produced by, or is similar to, the Holy Spirit and that mediates the Holy Spirit's presence.

Nor does the general law dictate *that the Holy Spirit act at all*. The Holy Spirit acts only because of the covenant of redemption made within the Trinity and in response to the incarnate Second Person of the Trinity as witnessed to in the Scriptures and encountered by the believing soul. Moreover, the general law has no bearing on the fact that when the Holy Spirit acts, he does so in *his own divine nature*. The general law that Edwards speaks about in "Miscellanies," no. 629, does not have anything to do with the *presence*, the *origination of action*, or the *content* of the Holy Spirit's operation in the regenerate; it only determines that the Holy Spirit should act "after the manner of" a natural principle of action when he does indeed act in the regenerate. Scholars like Conrad Cherry and Anri Morimoto are therefore correct in pointing out that for Edwards, the Holy Spirit is never "domesticated" or "given over" to human possession.[7]

Thus, Edwards' general law governing the manner of the Holy Spirit's operation in no way prescribes saving grace; the Holy Spirit alone is the source of grace and, even more, is that grace itself. Edwards' doctrine is neither simply that of Lombard nor that of Aquinas but rather a unique synthesis of the two—specifically, of Lombard's idea of grace as the Holy Spirit himself and the Thomistic emphasis upon grace as functioning in and through the natural powers of the regenerate. Yet Edwards' general law governing the Holy Spirit's operation has to be clearly distinguished from the Thomistic concept of "created grace" as a virtue that is produced by the Holy Spirit and that makes the believer's own free act of faith possible.

It is in this light that Edwards' language about the intimate "union" of the Holy Spirit with the regenerate has to be understood. In *Religious Affections*, Edwards writes that "the soul of a saint receives light from the Sun of righteousness, in such a manner, that its nature is changed, and it becomes properly a luminous thing. . . . Grace is compared to a seed implanted, that not only is in the ground, but has hold of it, has root there, and grows there, and is an abiding principle of life and nature there." Earlier in the same work, he speaks of the Holy Spirit as dwelling in the saints "as his proper lasting abode" (2:343, 200). According to Edwards' descriptions in these passages, the Holy Spirit's indwelling in the regenerate person is so intimate that he "grows there," like a seed, and makes the nature of that person "properly a luminous thing." This is not a Thomistic conception of created grace distinguishable from the Holy Spirit. The Holy Spirit's immediate and direct actions in and through the regenerate person are so accurately and thoroughly "after the manner of" a human principle of action that he can be said to be "implanted," to "grow," and to be within the regenerate person as in a "lasting abode." And this is so *not* because the Holy Spirit "turns into" or produces an intermediate principle of virtue residing in the soul but rather because the Holy Spirit's own direct action is strictly in accordance with the general law governing the manner of his action in the regenerate person. Thus Edwards can say toward the end of the *Treatise on Grace* that "if God should take away his Spirit out of the soul, all habits and acts of grace would of themselves cease as immediately as light ceases in a room when a candle is carried out" (21:196). In this way, and to the extent that it is logically possible to do so, Edwards retains saving grace as immediately the Holy Spirit's own direct action while at the same time asserting that the Holy Spirit functions as a new principle of action in the regenerate person.

Justification by Faith Alone

Justification by faith is the hallmark doctrine of the Protestant Reformation. Calvin declared it "the main hinge on which religion turns." Yet whether this doctrine is also "the main hinge" for Edwards' theology has been questioned. It is clear that Edwards followed the Reformation tradition and considered this doctrine important. His first public theological discourse outside of the pulpit was his Master's *Quaestio* of 1723, entitled *A Sinner Is Not Justified in the Sight of God Except Through the Righteousness of Christ Obtained by Faith*. Some of the key ideas and arguments Edwards uses in his later discussions of the subject were already present in this oration. *Justification by Faith Alone*, delivered in 1734 and published in 1738, is his most elaborate and sustained articulation of his position. There are also important discussions of the topic in the "Miscellanies" as well as in other writings, such as *Religious Affections* (2:455–560).

Edwards clearly wanted to be faithful to the Pauline and Reformation principle that sinners are accepted as righteous by God only through his free grace in Christ rather than through their own works of merit. But given Edwards' basic theological framework and its internal concerns, his own treatment of the justification doctrine could not be a mere reiteration of that of his Reformed predecessors. Edwards was facing the challenge of how to maintain both that justification is by faith alone and that there is in the believer a prior disposition or principle of holiness of which faith is the first exercise. The divine disposition in the regenerate person, of course, is the Holy Spirit himself, but the Spirit acts in the saint after the manner of the saint's own principle of action, so that the act of faith is properly the saint's own act. If this is the case, is faith not a virtuous act which should be rewarded?

Just as in the doctrine of grace, Edwards' utmost concern in his treatment of justification is to affirm both the totally undeserved character of human salvation and also the reality of regeneration. He starts both his 1723 *Quaestio* and *Justification by Faith Alone* by explaining that justification means not only being freed from the guilt of sin and its deserved punishment (negative righteousness) but also receiving the gift of righteousness that entitles the regenerate to a new life of holiness and eternal life (positive righteousness) (14:55–64). "We should take the word [justification] in such a sense, and understand it as the judges accepting a person as having both a negative, and positive righteousness belonging to him," writes Edwards (19:150). Corresponding to this twofold definition of the justification of the sinner is the dual character of Christ's work of atonement, which makes justification possible. Christ through his suffering "satisfied" the guilt of the sinners and through his "active obedience" earned them a "positive righteousness" and the reward of heaven. Christ's suffering on the cross was itself a propitiation for humanity's sins and "an act of obedience to the Father's commands." Thus, "by the blood of Christ we are not only redeemed from sin, but also redeemed unto God." Edwards concludes: "To be justified is to be approved of God as a proper subject of pardon, and a right to eternal life" (19:154).

What, then, is the unique role of faith in justification? In *Justification by Faith Alone*, Edwards begins his discussion of the role of faith by acknowledging that "faith itself is a virtue" as an exercise of the new disposition. He goes on to ask how justification by faith alone can be said to be grounded not in human moral qualifications but only in God's grace. This is the point where Edwards brings in the idea of union with Christ. It is not, Edwards writes, "on account of any excellency, or value that there is in faith, that it appears in the sight of God, a meet thing, that he that believes should have this benefit of Christ assigned to him, but purely from the relation faith has to the person in whom this benefit is to be had, or as it unites to that Mediator, in and by whom we are justified" (19:155).

What is the significance of this union with Christ? Union or relation with Christ is brought about by Christ's offer of redemption to the sinner and the sinner's active reception of that offer. Edwards explains that God "treats men as reasonable creatures, capable of act and choice," and thus "sees it fit, that in order to a union's being established between two intelligent, active beings or persons, so as that they should be looked upon as one, there should be the mutual act of both, that each should receive the other, as actively joining themselves one to another." Christ has already done his part in this "mutual act" of receiving each other; the sinner now has to do his or hers. "Now faith," Edwards declares, "I suppose to be this act." And it is because of this union with Christ through faith that "God looks on it meet that [the believer] should have Christ's merits belonging to him." "God does not give those that believe," Edwards continues, "an union *with*, or an interest *in* the Savior, in reward for faith, but only because faith is the soul's active uniting with Christ, or is itself the very act of unition, on their part" (19:157, 156, 158).

It is not the goodness of faith but the believer's relation or union with Christ that is the ground of sharing the benefits of Christ, and thereby of justification. But why, then, is the goodness of the act of faith not counted for what it is, and thereby as a contribution toward justification? This question arises regardless of whether we say that faith is identical with the union or that it brings about that union. In other words, faith as a good act either constitutes the union with Christ or helps bring it about. So why is the goodness of faith *as a good act* not considered a contributing factor in justification?

This is the point at which Edwards invokes his distinction between "moral fitness" and "natural fitness." A person has a "moral fitness for a state, when his moral excellency commends him to it" and "a natural fitness for a state when it appears meet and condecent that he should be in such a state or circumstances, only from the natural concord or agreeableness there is between such qualifications and such circumstances." He continues, "And 'tis on this latter account only that God looks on it as fit by a natural fitness, that he whose heart sincerely unites itself to Christ as his Savior, should be looked upon as united to that Savior, and so having an interest in him." There is a "natural agreement" and "congruity" between the believer's faith and the benefit of the union with Christ. It is only because of God's love of order" that God has a regard "to the beauty of that order that there is in uniting those things that have a natural agreement, and congruity, and unition of the one with the other" (19:159–60).

In his "Controversies" notebook, when writing on justification, Edwards delimits more carefully the function of faith and natural fitness in justification. Neither faith nor natural fitness itself (and, by implication, union with Christ) earns or deserves justification. Edwards insists that natural fitness is "not so properly a fitness of the subject to be in Christ as the fitness of God's act in looking on such an one as being in Christ" (21:339). But "God insists on a proper capacity to receive, so that there should be a natural agreement between the qualification and capacity of the subject and the benefit that he is to be the subject of" (21:369). Thus, faith is only "such a state or qualification of the subject that, things being ordered as they are in the redemption of Christ, gives opportunity for the Most High fitly to look on that subject as belonging to Christ, or being in him" (21:339). In the "Controversies" notebook, Edwards uses the term "natural suitableness" instead of "natural fitness" in an effort to make his meaning clear. "This is what is meant by the particle BY when we read of being justified by faith; i.e. this is the qualification wherein lies the immediate suitableness, according as infinite grace and wisdom has constituted things, of our coming to an union and interest in Christ and BY which we have that union and interest" (21:410). Faith does not justify as a work or righteousness. The moral qualification of faith has no bearing on the affairs of justification.[8]

Edwards' contention that faith has only a natural fitness for union with Christ and his benefits, however, does not resolve the question of why the goodness of the act of faith does not count toward justification. The distinction between moral and natural fitness does not help explain Edwards' main point that the phrase "justification by faith" does not mean justification by faith as meritorious. Faith, he writes, "arises from love or a holy disposition and relish of heart," and is a "true virtue" (21:446). If this is so, why is faith looked upon by God as possessing only natural fitness, not moral fitness, for salvation?

Edwards was aware of the ambiguity, and he directly confronts it by using the forensic paradigm for justification. With this approach, he attempted to affirm as clearly and firmly as possible the Pauline and Reformation doctrine of the justification of the ungodly.

In *Justification by Faith Alone*, Edwards provides a full articulation of the forensic conception of justification. He begins by establishing that the obligation humans have toward God is infinite. "Our obligation to love or honor any being is great in proportion to the greatness or excellency of that being, or his worthiness to be loved and honored." Since God is "infinitely excellent and lovely, our obligations to love him are therein infinitely great." "What the evil or iniquity of sin consists in," he earlier observed, "is the violating of an obligation . . . and therefore by how much the greater the obligation is that is violated, by so much the greater is the iniquity of the violation." It follows, then, that the sinner has an "infinite guilt," because the sinner's sin is "infinitely heinous" (19:161, 163).

Legally, acquittal for the sinner requires nothing less than an infinitely worthy obedience and righteousness. Arminians asked why the loving God would require of us something that we could not possibly fulfill. Would not God, out of his kindness, justify us, or at least begin to do so, on the basis of our sincere obedience? Edwards retorts by asking how Arminians can affirm the need for Christ's atoning work if they want to believe in a lenient God. What law do these "imperfections of our obedience" transgress? God, for Edwards, is a consistent God, whose laws do not change. What is required of the sinner, simply yet impossibly, is a "perfect righteousness." "An imperfect righteousness before a judge is no righteousness" (19:166, 189).

Just as the demand is categorical, so must be the remedy. In commenting on Calvin's view of the matter, Thomas Coates puts it succinctly: "To be regarded, or 'reputed,' as just in the eyes of God, a man must be perfect—not only 99 percent perfect, but 100 percent. Nothing less will do."[9] But fallen sinners cannot attain this perfection on their own. Hence, our need for Christ. As Edwards explains it, "The reason why we needed a person of infinite dignity to obey for us, was because of our infinite comparative meanness . . . we needed one, the worthiness of whose obedience, might be answerable to the unworthiness of our disobedience" (19:162).

Considered apart from Christ, the sinner's act of faith is worth nothing. There is a degree of holiness in the believer, inasmuch as faith is an exercise of the newly infused disposition. But such a holiness can only be finite, imperfect; it cannot make up for the sinner's infinite guilt. Even if God accepted an imperfect holiness in the sinner, there would still remain the sinner's infinite guilt. Edwards writes, "While God beholds the man as separate from Christ, he must behold him as he is in himself; and so his goodness can't be beheld by God, but as taken with his guilt and hatefulness, and as put in the scales with it; and being beheld so, his goodness is nothing; because there is a finite on the balance against an infinite, whose proportion to it is nothing" (19:164).

If the act of faith is the immediate operation of the Holy Spirit, the infinitely holy third person of the Trinity, would not the believer's act of faith carry an infinite weight? Edwards' answer is that saints possessing the Holy Spirit are given holiness "according to the measure and capacity of a creature"; the regenerate are not " 'Godded' with God" or " 'Christed' with Christ" (2:203). The Holy Spirit operates "after the manner of the principle of action" in the regenerate person, making the regenerate person's act of faith properly the person's own act. So the act of faith, *considered as the regenerate person's act*, falls infinitely short of what is required by God. All the holiness the sinner may have, Edwards claims, cannot compensate for the infinite odiousness of sin; "the person, on the whole, must be looked upon as without any moral value or amiableness, yea, on the contrary, as being infinitely odious" (21:370).

In his argument for the requirements for justification, and in his description of the justification that is bestowed upon the sinner, Edwards is reminiscent of Calvin. Pointing out the complete perfection required of the sinner by the absolute justice of God, Calvin writes that God's justice "is held of precious little value if it is not recognized as God's justice and so perfect that nothing can be admitted except what is in every part perfect, and nothing can be admitted except what is in every part whole and complete and undefiled by any corruption. Such was never found in man and never will be."[10] Calvin also observes the inadequacy of the act of faith in meeting such a categorical requirement. "For if faith justified of itself or through some intrinsic power, so to speak, as it is always weak and imperfect, it would effect this only in part: thus the righteousness that conferred a fragment of salvation upon us would be defective."[11] So, according to Calvin's and Edwards' forensic mathematics, a finite degree of holiness present in the sinner is "nothing" when such holiness is measured against the categorical requirement of infinite perfection. Justification of the sinner is possible only by the imputation of Christ's infinitely perfect righteousness.

In terms of Edwards' forensic articulation, there is no question that justification is of the ungodly. Justification justifies the unjustifiable. There is an internal coherence in Edwards' forensic restatement of the Reformation principle of salvation as unmerited. We are, however, still left with the question we raised earlier: What are we to make of the goodness of the act of faith, which exists in the believer before justification? Edwards clearly states in *Justification by Faith Alone* that "there is indeed something in man that is really and spiritually good, that is prior to justification" (19:164). In the "Controversies" notebook, he reaffirms the point by saying that a person is justified "on one act of faith, and so on the first holy act" or "in the very beginnings of the person's holiness, or as soon as ever his holiness is begun, in the very first point or first step of his holy course" (21:371). However, such holiness, Edwards insists, does not function as a merit for justification. He maintains that "such a state, does go before justification, yet the acceptance even of faith as any goodness or loveliness of the believer, follows justification: the goodness is on the forementioned account justly looked upon as nothing, until the man is justified" (19:164–65).

Edwards' position, in a nutshell, is this: there is in a believing sinner a holy disposition and its holy exercises, which are absolutely without merit for justification and so, from God's point of view, unacceptable as holiness. What we have here in Edwards is a reaffirmation of the Reformation doctrine of the justification of the ungodly, as well as an articulation of the ontological (dispositional) grounding in the sinner for Christian practice, which is considered holiness only after justification through God's unmerited grace alone. Edwards is in complete agreement with Calvin's view that justification and sanctification constitute a "double grace" through the union with Christ. Edwards would applaud Calvin's insistence that "Christ justifies no one whom he does not sanctify at the same time."[12] But he is adding something to Calvin's doctrine of "double grace," namely, an ontological (dispositional) foundation for sanctified life, without making such a foundation or its exercises in any way meritorious for justification. Edwards has, in effect, carefully expanded the Reformed doctrines of regeneration and sanctification.

It has been suggested that Edwards' view of faith as an exercise of the divinely infused disposition makes his justification doctrine practically Roman Catholic, similar to the teachings of Thomas Aquinas.[13] Such, however, is not the case, for two fundamental reasons. For one thing, the act of faith for Aquinas merits justification, while for Edwards it does not. Faith, according to Edwards, is the "condition" for justification, not by merit but rather by being an act of union with Christ that is naturally (but not morally) fitting for God's granting of justification. Although faith has a kind of fitness or congruity for justification, it does not earn or merit that justification. Edwards explicitly denies that faith has a "merit of congruity, or indeed any moral congruity at all" to either union with Christ or his benefits (19:159). Indeed, any holiness in the believer "is looked upon as nothing, until the man is justified."

For Aquinas, in contrast, the act of faith is morally meritorious and in a sense earns, or is rewarded with, justification. Aquinas does not articulate justification in a juridical paradigm but rather in terms of making the sinner actually just and functionally adequate to strive toward a supernatural end. All changes in human beings, according to Aquinas' scheme, are made possible by attaining appropriate "forms"—a "form" being what makes a thing or an act what it is. So the infusion of sanctifying grace as an entitative or ontological habit heals the sinner and also elevates him or her to a new level of being, with a new capacity to strive with free will toward a supernatural end. To enable this striving, God infuses the sinner with the virtues of faith, hope, and charity. Virtues are qualities that function as forms for the new actions of a sanctified person.

The virtue of faith, for Aquinas, prepares and enables a person for a free act of faith. There are four things that make up justification: "the infusion of grace, the movement of the free-will towards God by faith, the movement of the free-will away from sin, and the remission of sins."[14] In regard to merit, Aquinas states that "our acts are meritorious in so far as they issue from a free will that is moved by God through his grace.... Now to believe is an act of mind assenting to the divine truth by virtue of the command of the will as this is moved by God; in this way the act stands under the control of free will and is directed towards God. The act of faith is, therefore, meritorious."[15] In Aquinas' scheme, the sanctified person is duly prepared for the act of faith. When such a person has faith, he or she by definition merits what faith is aimed at, namely, justification. "This implies," as Robert P. Scharlemann has noted, "that in some sense man earns—merits—eternal life."[16] Granted that Aquinas and Edwards are working within their own distinctive metaphysical and theological frameworks, it still is true that for Aquinas faith is meritorious, while for Edwards it is not.

The second reason Edwards' justification doctrine must be distinguished from that of the Roman Catholic tradition in general, and that of Aquinas in particular, has to do with the concept of imputation. For Edwards, justification involves the imputation of both the negative and positive righteousness of Christ. Edwards explains that a person's "sins being removed by Christ's atonement, is not sufficient for his justification; for justifying a man . . . is not merely pronouncing him innocent or without guilt, but standing right, with regard to the rule he is under, and righteous unto life." Imputation is both "negative" and "positive": remission of sins and acceptance as righteous. Positive imputation continues for the regenerate person even after the initial justification. The value of the good works of Christians "is founded in, and derived from Christ's righteousness and worthiness" (19:190–91, 215).

For Aquinas, imputation does play a negative role in justification. He writes that it "proceeds from the Divine love, that sin is not imputed to a man by God." But the idea of a positive imputation of Christ's righteousness has no place in Aquinas' doctrine of justification. For him, justification is defined as an actual change, or what he calls "transmutation," from the state of injustice to justice, and this change naturally proceeds from the infusion of grace.[17] In this framework there is no need for God to count Christ's perfect righteousness as a sinner's own. A positive imputation of Christ's perfect righteousness is an idea that belongs to the forensic doctrine of justification. Thus, for Edwards, unlike Aquinas, justification involves the imputation of a righteousness the source of which is "outside us."[18] Persons are not justified by what is in them but rather by what Christ has earned for them.

Therefore, at the points most crucial for the Reformation doctrine of justification—specifically, justification as unmerited and the positive imputation of Christ's righteousness—Edwards is Protestant and Reformed. There is, for Edwards, a degree of holiness in the believer prior to justification. But such holiness in no way merits justification and can be looked at as holiness by God only by means of a positive imputation of Christ's perfect righteousness. Thus Edwards does not blur but rather clearly asserts the distinction between justification and sanctification.

In his justification doctrine, Edwards is clearly an heir of the Reformation. But here we must return to a point we alluded to earlier: while reaffirming the Reformation doctrine of justification, Edwards also saw grace as laying a foundation for Christian practice even before justification. This foundation, which is none other than the indwelling of the Holy Spirit, ready to function as a new disposition, in no way enables the believer to deserve or merit justification. The new disposition, however, lays the ontological and psychological ground for the sanctified life of the justified. How are we to explain this particular emphasis on the reality of the new life of the regenerate? How is this enlarged doctrine of regeneration and the strictly forensic doctrine of justification integrated by Edwards into a coherent perspective?

The answer lies in Edwards' larger theological view that God's end in creating the world is to communicate and repeat in time and space his internal glory, and that the redemption of the elect must be understood as an integral part of God's pursuit of this end. The indwelling of the Holy Spirit in the regenerate, the justification of the ungodly, and the Christian practice of the justified, in other words, have an end beyond the salvation of fallen humanity.

> The Scripture teaches that the way of justification that is appointed in the gospel covenant, is appointed, as it is, for that end, that free grace might be expressed and glorified; Rom. 4:16, "Therefore it is of faith, that it might be of grace." The exercising and magnifying the free grace of God in the gospel contrivance for the justification and salvation of sinners, is evidently the chief design of it; and this freedom and riches of grace of the gospel is everywhere spoken of in Scripture as the chief glory of it. (19:183)

The end of justification is that God's "free grace might be expressed and glorified." And the justification of sinners by faith and not by works—"the gospel contrivance"—is the "design" through which this end is achieved. So any doctrine contrary to the doctrine of justification by faith and not works "diminishes the glory of divine grace (which is the attribute God hath especially set himself to glorify in the works of redemption)" (19:240). Here Edwards is arguing for the validity of the doctrine of justification by grace through faith on the basis of God's own end, which such justification is to serve. Edwards' forensic doctrine of justification, therefore, is an integral part of his overall theological framework.

Edwards' emphasis on the ontological reality of the new life of the regenerate is also to be understood in the light of his conception of God's end in creation, which is to repeat his internal glory in mundane human life as well as through nature. God fulfills this end not by externally coercing human beings but rather by working in and through the human subject and human actions—that is, by the Holy Spirit's operation as a natural principle of action. The presence of a disposition to holiness in the believer even before justification thus prepares the justified person to actually live a Christian life. The Holy Spirit as a new disposition enables the believer to have faith in and to unite with Christ, and God justifies the sinner because of the natural fitness of union with Christ (brought about by faith) and justification. So Edwards can say that "what is real in the union between Christ and his people, is the foundation of what is legal" (19:158). "What is real" refers to the natural fitness of faith for justification, not some meritorious qualification. Through his conception of faith as having a natural fitness, Edwards was attempting, without making faith a meritorious act, to answer the Arminian charge that forensic justification is nothing more than a legal fiction. His soteriology must certainly be viewed in the context of the polemic against Arminianism. But Edwards' emphasis upon the reality of the new disposition in the believer cannot be understood apart from his overall theological vision that through human beings and their actions God wishes to repeat his own internal glory.

Notes

1. Cf. E. M. Burke, "Grace," in *New Catholic Encyclopedia* (New York: McGraw-Hill, 1972), pp. 658–72.

2. Thomas Aquinas, *Summa Theologica*, trans. Cornelius Ernst (New York: McGraw-Hill, 1972), Ia2ae, 110, 4, p. 121.

3. Robert P. Scharleman, *Thomas Aquinas and John Gerhard* (New Haven: Yale University Press, 1964), p. 131; cf. C. Moeller and G. Philips, *The Theology of Grace and the Ecumenical Movement* (London: A. R. Mowbray & Co., 1961), pp. 19–21.

4. Cf. Moeller and Philips, *Theology of Grace*, pp. 19–21.

5. Cf. Burke, "Grace," p. 668.

6. For the interpretation of Edwards' idea of infused disposition as "a close correlative" of Aquinas' notion of the "intermediary habit," see Anri Morimoto, *Jonathan Edwards and the Catholic Vision of Salvation* (University Park: Pennsylvania State University Press, 1995), esp. p. 46 (cf. "Misc." 27b, 13:214; 21:180; "Misc." 818, 18:529, n. 3; 8:157; 21:196).

7. Conrad Cherry, *The Theology of Jonathan Edwards: A Reappraisal* (Bloomington: Indiana University Press, 1990), p. 41; Morimoto, *Jonathan Edwards*, pp. 44, 46.

8. Samuel T. Logan, Jr., has argued that for Edwards faith and evangelical obedience are connected with justification as "non-causal conditions" while justification's sole "causal condition" is the grace of God. See "The Doctrine of Justification in the Theology of Jonathan Edwards," *Westminster Theological Journal* 46 (1984): 26–52.

9. Thomas Coates, "Calvin's Doctrine of Justification," *Concordia Theological Monthly* 34 (1963): 325.

10. Calvin, *Institutes*, III.xii.1.

11. Ibid., III.xii.7.

12. Ibid., III.xvi.1.

13. Thomas A. Schafer, "Jonathan Edwards and Justification by Faith," *Church History* 20 (1950): 61; Morimoto, *Jonathan Edwards*, p. 46; Gerald R. McDermott, *Jonathan Edwards Confronts the Gods: Christian Theology, Enlightenment Religion, and Non-Christian Faith* (New York: Oxford University Press, 2000), p. 136.

14. Thomas Aquinas, *Summa Theologica*, q. 113, a. 6.

15. Ibid., IIaIIae, q. 2,a. 9.

16. Scharlemann, *Thomas Aquinas and John Gerhard*, p. 188.

17. *Summa Theologica*, q. 113, art. 22, 1146, 1145.

18. The expression "outside us" is Martin Luther's. See *Luther's Works*, vol. 26, ed. Jaroslav Pelikan (St. Louis: Concordia Publishing House, 1963), pp. 233–34.

Suggested Further Readings

Cherry, Conrad. *The Theology of Jonathan Edwards: A Reappraisal*. Bloomington: Indiana University Press, 1990.

Logan, Samuel T., Jr. "The Doctrine of Justification in the Theology of Jonathan Edwards." *Westminster Theological Journal* 46 (1984): 26–42.

Morimoto, Anri. *Jonathan Edwards and the Catholic Vision of Salvation*. Unviersity Park: Pennsylvania State University Press, 1995.

Schafer, Thomas A. "Jonathan Edwards and Justification by Faith." *Church History* 20 (1951): 212–22.

———. "Solomon Stoddard and the Theology of Revival." In *A Miscellany of American Christianity: Essays in Honor of H. Shelton Smith*, ed. Stuart C. Henry, pp. 328–61. Durham, N.C.: Duke University Press, 1963.

Eleven

Christian Virtue and Common Morality

John E. Smith

EDWARDS' VIEWS concerning the nature of divine love or charity and his conception of a virtuous or holy life are expressed in three principal works: *Charity and its Fruits, Concerning the End for which God Created the World*, and *On the Nature of True Virtue* (the latter two published together as *Two Dissertations*).[1] *Charity* consists of fifteen sermons that Edwards preached in 1738 on 1 Corinthians 13, St. Paul's well-known discourse on Christian love, and was first published by Tryon Edwards in 1852 with the title that it still bears. The *Dissertations*, as Ramsey points out, were meant to be published together since the "end" for which God created the world must also be the "end" of a virtuous life.[2]

The first sermon in *Charity* is entitled "Love the Sum of All Virtue," and Edwards begins by saying that charity and Christian love are the same, but that in the New Testament "charity" is used in a much wider sense than what is meant by the term in ordinary discourse. The ordinary meaning includes thinking the best of people, putting a "good construction on their words or behavior," and sometimes the disposition to give to the poor. Edwards, however, regards these things as but a part or fruit of charity as a virtue. As a Christian virtue, charity signifies both love to human beings and love to God. Edwards focuses attention on St. Paul's recounting of the excellent things that one may have—the tongues of human beings and angels, the gift of prophecy and all knowledge, the faith to move mountains—or do—bestow all one's goods on the poor, offer one's body as a sacrifice—and his claim that all of these come to *nothing* without charity. He derives from Paul's words this doctrine: "All that virtue which is saving, and distinguishing of true Christians from others, is summed up in Christian or divine love" (8:131).

Edwards, as always, was an ontological thinker, which is also to say a theological thinker; he ever and again sought to trace things back to principles. In developing the meaning of divine love, Edwards began with the meaning of self-love. Not unmindful of the command to love God with all one's being and one's neighbor "as thyself"—a measure that has been the subject of extended discussion within Christianity over the centuries—Edwards sets out to consider the nature of self-love. His first distinction is between *selfishness*, which is objectionable because it is confined to a narrow and exclusive love of self as if it were the entire universe, and a universal love of self that expresses our human capacity to love our own happiness, which for Edwards is the same as having a will.

This distinction is so important for Edwards' conception of Christian virtue under the commandment to love God and neighbor that we must consider it at greater length. Edwards repeatedly insists that "a Christian spirit is not contrary to all self-love" (8:254), nor is Christianity opposed to a person's loving himself, for this equates with loving his own happiness:

> Christianity is not destructive of humanity. That a man should love his own happiness is necessary to his nature, as a faculty of will is; and it is impossible that it should be destroyed in any other way than by destroying his being. (8:254)

Selfishness, however, is contrary to a Christian spirit, and Edwards goes on to indicate what is meant by the "inordinate" self-love which is for him identical with selfishness. When a person is redeemed, says Edwards, it is not by a reduction of his love to his own happiness, "but only by regulating it with respect to its exercises and influence, and the objects to which it leads" (8:255). Here Edwards is choosing his words very carefully; the root meaning of "inordinate" is to be "unregulated" or "without measure." Self-love becomes inordinate in two respects; first, it may be of so great a degree that it surpasses love to others and in this way comes to have undue influence on the person; secondly, self-love can be "placed" in the wrong channel, as when the person sees his or her own happiness only "in things that are confined to himself," so that others are excluded. This, Edwards writes, "is the thing most directly intended by that self-love which the Scripture condemns" (8:257). The Christian spirit, to the contrary, seeks not only its own benefit but the benefit of others, and it also may require that we part with what we have for the good of others.

Edwards expresses in specifically theological terms the difference between the self-love that degenerates into selfishness and self-love as it exists under the principle of divine love: "The ruin which the Fall brought upon the soul of man consists very much in that he lost his nobler and more extensive principles, and fell wholly under the government of self-love" (8:252). Edwards sees the difference between the soul before the Fall and after in terms of expansion and contraction. When man was governed by divine love, his soul was "enlarged to a kind of comprehension of all his fellow creatures" (8:253) and was not limited by the bounds of the creation, but "dispersed itself abroad in that infinite ocean of good." After the transgression, "those nobler principles were immediately lost and all this excellent enlargedness of his soul was gone and he thenceforward shrunk into a little point, circumscribed and closely shut up within itself to the exclusion of others" (ibid.).

Edwards makes it quite clear that the love of our own happiness is not to be construed solely in terms of the narrow and limited self, but must include all that is "grateful" in objects other than the self, that is, the character in them to which our appropriate response is *gratitude*.[3] It is this apprehension of all that goes to make up human happiness that takes us beyond the narrow and confined self.

Edwards was concerned to show that the Christian spirit does not run counter to a proper self-love, because love of our own happiness is natural and hence there is nothing inherently wrong about it. He goes even further and says that having such love is the same as having a will, so that if self-love were set at naught we would have to deny the very characteristic that sets us apart from stones and stars. As Ramsey puts it, Edwards saw the universal love of our own happiness as what "makes the world go around" (8:16).

Universal self-love, however, although essential, does not suffice, since it must be combined with "another principle" that involves, as Edwards says, "uniting a person with another." Edwards' idea is that universal self-love does not of itself inform us of *what* and *whom* we are to love; love to particulars requires recourse to another principle. What this principle implies is that love of what delights us must include the happiness of another. The commandment to love is twofold—love of God and love of neighbor—and Edwards is trying to show how the two are related as *particular* loves and joys that stem from a universal self-love "compounded" by another principle. How, in short, do we come to see that love and praise to God is the happiness that self-love seeks and that the happiness of another person is included in our happiness?

As Ramsey has pointed out, Edwards answers these questions most clearly in an entry in the "Miscellanies," dealing with "compounded self-love", where it is said to "arise from the necessary nature of a perceiving and willing being, whereby he loves his own pleasure or delight; but not from this alone, but it supposes also another principle, that determines the exercise of this principle, and makes that to become its object which otherwise cannot: *a certain principle uniting this person with another*, that causes the good of another to be its good. The first arises simply from his own being, whereby that which agrees immediately and directly with his own being, is his good; the second arises also from *a principle uniting him to another being*, whereby the good of the other being does in a sort become his own" ("Misc." 530, 18:75, emphasis added). Love of neighbor stems from the love of God that is common to us, so that our self-love is now channeled in a *particular* direction that takes it far beyond the confines of a self-love that is exclusive.

It is important to understand that, for Edwards, knowledge of God in the understanding and love of God in the will or heart means our *participation in* God's knowledge of himself and our *partaking of* divine love. The ambiguity in "knowledge of God"—that it can mean either our knowledge of God or God's knowledge of himself—and the ambiguity in "love of God"—that it can mean either our love of God or God's own love—is thus overcome. That is, if there is any knowledge of God and love of God in any created being, that can mean only that this being participates in God's knowledge of himself or is infused by the divine love. The doctrine upon which Edwards bases this conclusion is that the *only* knowledge of God there is is God's knowledge of himself, which is communicated to us through the Word, and all love to God in the creatures is from "the love of God's being in them" ("Misc." 1084, 20:467).

The emphasis here on God as the only effective power in the world, the supreme cause that acknowledges no "secondary" causes among the creatures—a stance that led William Ellery Channing (1780–1842) to place Edwards among the pantheists (for whom the mystery is why there should be anything else but God)—has to be understood against the background of what we may call Edwards' grand strategy. According to that strategy, it is necessary to take seriously into account all that belongs to nature and to nature's God as part of God's total providential design, but at the same time to show that the natural falls short of grace. Accordingly, in his treatment of our moral nature, Edwards is concerned to recognize the validity of natural benevolence or concern for the good of others and not set it at nought, and yet he is also determined to show that it does not suffice. True virtue, the mark of "saving" operations, goes beyond the most remarkable accomplishments of the natural man. Edwards' ultimate concern is to depict the regenerate human being as the "new creation" in Christ of which Paul spoke so eloquently, the being who is filled with the knowledge and love of God and whose redemption was the end sought by God in creation. In pursuit of his goal, Edwards discusses at length, focusing on the thought of the British moral philosopher Francis Hutcheson (1694–1746),[4] the rationalist's idea of disinterested benevolence as the criterion for moral judgment. To anticipate the outcome, we may say that Edwards saw this criterion as only a calculation of pleasure against pain—something that nature can achieve on its own account—whereas true virtue is different in kind, because it has to do with another dimension or what Edwards called the "consent of beings to Being"—the philosophical counterpart of "love to God." Here, in the spirit of Edwards, we might add "disinterested benevolence" to Paul's list of gifts in 1 Corinthians 13—"though I have such benevolence to the highest degree and have not charity, I am nothing."

The parallel between what Edwards was doing in finding distinguishing marks of truly gracious affections in the appraisal of heart religion and what he is doing here in the delineation of true virtue is clear. In both cases he aimed to set forth what goes beyond the capacity of nature and the natural man and thus to delineate the new dimension represented in the work of the Spirit as the power of grace. Gracious affections stand beyond the "natural" affections of which all are capable, and true virtue, or divine love, stands beyond the disinterested benevolence that marks the ultimate achievement of the "natural man." It is important to notice, however, that in neither case was he concerned to discount entirely the "natural" component.

In speaking of the duty of a Christian to do good to others, Edwards sets forth three considerations to be taken into account: the good itself, to whom we should do it, and the manner in which we do it. The most excellent way, says Edwards, is to do good to the souls of others, by which he means instructing them in the things of religion, counseling and warning those who are lax, and even reproving those who fail in their duty. Above all is the setting of a good example; words, says Edwards, without an example "will not be very likely to take effect" (8:207). In addition to this spiritual help, Edwards cites the giving of goods to those in need, taking pains to promote the welfare of another, and the suffering that goes with the effort to lighten the burden of another.

To whom should we seek to do good? Edwards answers that in Scripture the "neighbor" is the proper object of our actions, and he goes on to point out that Jesus' parable of the Good Samaritan was his response to the lawyer who, "wishing to justify himself," asked, "And who is my neighbor?" Despite the enmity between Jews and Samaritans, the Samaritan came to the aid of the Jew who had fallen among thieves and thus treated him as a neighbor. For Edwards, this relationship is meant to be mutual, "equally predictable of both," and from this fact he drew three corollaries: that we should do good to both *good* and *bad* (although we "should more abound in beneficence . . . to them who are of the household of faith"); to both *friends* and *enemies*; and to the *thankful* and the *unthankful*—and all this because we would "imitate our Father which is in Heaven."

In what manner should we seek to do good? Edwards' answer, as he says, is expressed in one word: "freely." That is to say, kindness is the disposition to do good freely, and again from this disposition, Edwards draws three corollaries: we are not to do good for mercenary reasons, as if we were hired to do so or expected a reward; we must do good cheerfully and not grudgingly; and, finally, we must be open-hearted and open-handed, giving without stint.

"The main thing," Edwards writes, "in that love, which is the sum of the Christian spirit, is benevolence or good will to others" (8:212), and he calls that "love of benevolence" or "that disposition which a man has who desires or delights in the good of another." In characteristic fashion, Edwards ends this portion of the sermon with an emphasis on *practice*: "The proper evidence of wishing good to another is doing good to another" (8:213). It is ultimately in the deed that we find the presence of love.

Edwards, as we can see from the amount of space he devoted to the topic, was greatly concerned to show that Christian love is contrary to a selfish spirit, and in doing so he gives further insight into the manner in which we are to regard the neighbor. Edwards begins by focusing on what we are to understand by "loving our neighbor as ourselves." This second part of the Great Commandment, says Edwards, is contrary to selfishness because it requires us to look beyond ourselves, "to look on [our] neighbor as being, as it were, one with self, and not only to consider our own circumstances and necessities, but to consider the wants of our neighbors as we do our own . . . to make their case our own, and to do to them as we would that they should do to us" (8:265). At this point Edwards enters into what he himself calls a "digression"—from the main point, which is to show that love to neighbor is contrary to selfishness—that throws a great deal of light on his conception of the continuity, but also the difference, between the Old Testament and the Gospel. The duty to love others is not new; the same kind of love was required by the commandment of Moses, but it remains to be explained why Christ said, "A new commandment I give unto you."

It is new because, says Edwards, the "rule and motive" of the commandment is new; in the old view the rule and motive was love to ourselves and that we should love our neighbors as ourselves, but in the Gospel view the rule and motive is the love of Christ for us—"that ye love one another, as I have loved you" (John 15:12) (8:266). Edwards makes the comparison quite explicit: "That we should love one another as we love ourselves is Moses' commandment . . . that we should love one another as Christ love[d] us is Christ's commandment" (ibid.).

Edwards' "digression" at this point is no mere intrusion into his argument, but rather the establishing of a new vantage point for spelling out the fuller meaning of love of neighbor and for consolidating his thesis that it runs counter to a selfish spirit. Edwards cites four ways in which Christ's love for us was expressed. Christ set his love on those who were enemies to him, which is to say that he loved those who had no love for him. Christ's love, moreover, was such that "he was pleased in some respects to look upon us as himself . . . and united his heart to [us]" (8:266). In the beginning of the passage, Edwards speaks of "love to men" (8:267), but in the sequel the referent changes: "His elect were from all eternity dear to him, as the apple of his eye"—and it was specifically the elect whose concerns, interests, and guilt Christ looked upon as his own.

In describing the third expression of Christ's love, Edwards returns to "us" and says that he spent himself "for us" in forgoing his own ease, comfort, and honor and offering himself as a sacrifice to the justice of God. From this Edwards concludes that Christ loved us without any expectation of our loving him in return, and he makes the application at once: "our love to others will not depend on their love to us; but we shall do as Christ did to us, love them, though enemies" (8:267).

Edwards took such pains to show that love is opposed to selfishness because he was concerned to make a proper place for the self-love that is *not* inordinate but belongs essentially to human nature. Here, as in so many of his writings, Edwards' negatives are of the utmost importance and serve to make clear the true nature of something through vivid contrasts. The point, however, goes even deeper than contrasts and showing what love or affections are *not*; Edwards' great concern is to distinguish between two ideas, attitudes, motives which, while *similar* in some respects, are not the *same*, and to explain why people mistake one for the other. As we shall see, there is a most telling example of this concern in *True Virtue* (ch. 7), the title of which speaks for itself: "The reasons why those things that have been mentioned, which have not the essence of true virtue, have yet by many been mistaken for true virtue." Hence, Edwards' method, while it includes in this case showing what true virtue is *not*, also directs attention to what is *similar* in the negative case to true virtue, but is not identical with it, hence a source of confusion.[5]

We must, nevertheless, not lose sight, as indeed Edwards did not, of the positive and the true virtuous life, because his method of negatives was meant to make the genuine form of virtue stand out more clearly than it otherwise would. We see this very well when we consider the moral *progression* that Edwards envisages in the Christian life. As Ramsey has pointed out, there is a parallel between this progression that ends with the "concatenation" of the graces in the fullness of love, and the eschatological movement wherein that fulfillment is seen as the "end for which God created the world." Even in Edwards' earliest reflections about God, Being, the consent to Being, excellency, and the divine *gloria*, there is to be found a recurrent theme: God wants out of the depths of his love to have in the creation a being capable of *appreciating* the beauty—"excellency," in one of its several meanings—and the splendor of the divine *gloria* as it appears in the creation. It is in this sense that Edwards understood God's end in creation as the full manifestation of his own glorious nature. What better way to achieve this end than through the person of true virtue, whose life, imbued with grace and the divine Spirit, shines forth with the fullness of holy love and practice?

The title of the present essay, "Christian Virtue and Common Morality," is meant to indicate the two strands of human nature and conduct

(Ramsey calls them the "two sources of morality") in Edwards' thought. We may identify these two strands as common morality, based on natural principles, and specifically Christian morality, based on holy love and benevolence toward God. There is, in short, a morality of nature and a morality of grace, a distinction employed by Edwards throughout his many writings and in different contexts. In his appraisal of the Awakening, for example, he treated common grace in his treatise *Some Thoughts* and concluded that "on the whole and in general" the Awakening was truly a work of the divine Spirit. In *Religious Affections*, on the other hand, he was concerned exclusively with the signs of *gracious* affections which serve to distinguish the life of the saints and which go beyond anything that can be achieved by the "natural man."[6]

Thus far we have been dealing with Edwards' conception of Christian morality as rooted in charity and manifested in its fruits. We must now turn to his treatment of common morality and his pursuit of "the essence of true virtue." First, however, to avoid confusion, a word of caution about Edwards' procedure is in order.

In *Charity* and the *End in Creation*, Edwards was dealing with pure benevolence and the biblical understanding of the nature of Christian love as distinct from, but still related to, common morality based on natural principles. In *True Virtue*, which is intended to develop the chief features of common morality and also to point out the reasons why people mistake one for the other, Edwards *begins with* another account of the pure benevolence that characterizes Christian morality, and this may confuse the reader. The reason for this starting point, however, is quite clear; Edwards wants to set before us the conception of true virtue as a basis for comparison and for showing why common morality, even in its highest form, falls short of Christian charity.

In seeking to understand what Edwards meant by true virtue, we need to recall the importance he attached to beauty, harmony, and "fittingness" or excellence as marks of divinity.[7] Hence, Edwards begins the dissertation with these words:

> Whatever controversies and variety of opinion there are about the nature of virtue, yet all (excepting some skeptics who deny any real difference between virtue and vice) mean by it something *beautiful*, or rather some kind of *beauty* or excellency. (8:539)

He goes on to say that not all beauty can be called virtue, but only that beauty belonging to beings having perception and will. This characterization, however, is still too broad, because there is a beauty in speculation and the ideas of great thinkers, but, says Edwards, this is different from what is "commonly meant" by virtue. The distinguishing feature must be found in the beauty of those acts of the mind that are of a *moral* nature and entail praise or blame. These, in turn, refer to will and disposition, which Edwards sums up in the term "heart," so that when we ask for the meaning of true virtue, we must seek to determine what makes any habit or exercise of the heart "truly *beautiful*."

Edwards next distinguishes between a particular and a general beauty. The former is when something appears beautiful only within a limited sphere, as when a few notes in a tune are harmonious with each other but prove discordant in relation to the tune as a whole. General beauty, on the contrary, is beautiful "as it is in itself" and as connected with everything it has to do with. Edwards is working toward the definition of true virtue in terms of what he described in many writings as "the consent of beings to Being in general," or God. Using the term "benevolence" in the sense of "consent, propensity, and union of heart," Edwards can define true virtue as "benevolence" to Being in general, the exercise of a general good will. He is willing to admit that a person can be disposed to have benevolence to some particular being or a number of beings and that such a tendency can be good in some respects, but since such benevolence is not to Being in general, it is not of the nature of true virtue. Edwards is emphatic on the point; the central virtue of love must have as its direct and immediate object Being in general or, as he sometimes puts it, "the great system of universal existence." Consent to anything less is inadequate.

Edwards, moreover, is not content merely to assert his claim. He offers several quite subtle arguments aimed at showing that virtue cannot consist in any love to its object because of its beauty. Nor can we say that virtue consists in love to virtue, for that would be going around in a circle: we would be supposing that virtue is *both* the cause and effect of virtue. Using a form of the infinite regress argument that he had so often invoked in the *Freedom of the Will*, Edwards claims that if virtue consists in love to virtue, then what is loved is the love of virtue, and virtue becomes the love of the love of virtue and so on without end. The central point can be simply stated: since we are in search of the "first benevolence" or benevolence which "has none prior to it," this cannot consist in love to any particular beings on the basis of their virtue, their beauty, or their gratitude, because that love presupposes a benevolence *prior* to each of the three which is their cause. Edwards claims that "there is room for no other conclusion than that the primary object of virtuous love is Being, simply considered; . . . true virtue primarily consists . . . in a propensity and union of heart to . . . Being in general" (8:544). In short, love to Being in general is the ultimate ground of virtue; to suppose any other object to fill this role is to be involved in an infinite regress.

Yet, Edwards continues, we are not to suppose that there is no virtue in any love other than absolute benevolence, since we must consider the good of particular beings in the light of our love to Being. If the good of a particular being is not so consistent or if there is any being that is opposed to Being in general, our consent to Being as such will induce "the virtuous heart" to forsake that being. Thus Edwards is led to introduce what he calls a "secondary object" of virtuous benevolence. Pure benevolence in its first exercise is, as we have seen, consent to Being, but there is a secondary object of virtue which Edwards calls "benevolent being," or the presence of virtuous benevolence in its object. Hence, when we, under the influence of general benevolence, see another being possessing the "like general benevolence," our hearts are drawn to that person. We attach our hearts to him or her in the knowledge that he or she has the same love to Being that we have.

Edwards' idea is that our love to the other goes beyond the fact that the other exists, since he or she, in having love to Being in general, has their own being extended. We, in turn, motivated by that same love, "must of necessity have . . . the greater degree of benevolence to him, as it were out of gratitude to him for his love to general existence" (8:546–47). Our hearts are extended to the other, and we come to regard his or her interest as our own. Edwards, as we have seen many times, can follow up a complex and involuted expression of a basic idea with a quite simple summary; in this case, when the heart is united to Being in general, it looks upon a benevolent propensity to Being, "wherever he sees it," as the beauty and excellency of the being who has it. Stated even more directly, Edwards is moving from love of God to love of neighbor.

The importance Edwards attached to the idea that the secondary ground of virtuous love arises solely from pure benevolence to Being in general can be seen in his spelling out six further considerations concerning the secondary ground.[8] These points can be summarized briefly, since they are largely corollaries of his main thesis. First, anyone who has a love to Being in general must love that same temper in others. Second, true moral or spiritual beauty is the secondary ground of virtue, including both qualities and exercises of the mind and the overt actions proceeding from them. Third, virtuous principles and acts are themselves beautiful because they imply consent to and union with Being in general. Fourth, spiritual beauty, as a secondary ground, is the ground of both benevolence and complacence, but the former is the *primary* ground of the latter.[9] Fifth, whoever sees benevolence in two beings will value it more than in one alone, because it is more favorable to Being in general to have two beings to favor it than only one. Sixth, and most characteristic of Edwards' emphasis on the understanding heart, no one can relish the beauty of general benevolence "who has not that temper himself." The appreciation of that beauty in another reveals the true disposition of the heart.

We may now consider in summary fashion what Edwards took to be the main ingredients of common morality—secondary beauty, self-love, conscience, and kindly affections—as a prelude to his discussion of "the reasons why those things that have been mentioned [i.e., the ingredients just noted] which have not the essence of Virtue, have yet by many been mistaken for true Virtue."[10] Edwards begins by repeating what he has said about primary beauty as the consent, agreement and union of beings with Being in mental or spiritual existence. There is, however, a secondary or inferior beauty—"which is some image of this"—that is not confined to spiritual beings but is found in inanimate things: the mutual agreement of the sides of a square or a regular polygon, the agreement of the colors, figures, and distances between spots on a chessboard, the beauty of the figures on a piece of brocade. In all these cases, says Edwards, there is a mutual agreement in form, manner, quantity, and visible end or design which we express in such terms as regularity, order, uniformity, symmetry, proportion, and harmony. Such beauty is an image of the primary beauty and serves as an analogy for God's work in patterning inferior things in accordance with what is superior. In so doing, God presents this inferior beauty, especially to those of a truly virtuous temper, as a way of making them aware of the divine love and of enlivening their sense of spiritual beauty.

As always, Edwards is concerned to point out that it is not by "any reflection" upon the resemblance of secondary beauty to primary beauty that such things appear beautiful; "their sensation of pleasure, on a view of this secondary beauty, is immediately owing to the law God has established, or the instinct he has given" (8:567). Having the sensation of pleasure is the result of the cosmic harmony that endows us with the capacity to respond in just that way.

Edwards sees other virtues stemming from secondary beauty, such as *order in society* where all have appointed places and everyone keeps to his place; *wisdom* in the unifying of thoughts, ideas, and actions to one general purpose; *justice*, or the harmonious system in which those who do evil will suffer evil in proportion to the evil done.[11] In this connection, Edwards speaks approvingly of Wollaston's idea that all virtue can be resolved into an agreement of inclinations, volitions, and actions with *truth*.[12] Edwards interprets this in terms of justice between two beings, so that in our duties and virtues we are to express such affections and behave toward another in a way that "hath a natural agreement and proportion to what is in them, and what we receive from them" (8:570), and he claims that here there is the same conformity of affection and action to its ground "as that which is between a true proposition and the thing spoken of in it."

The point is an important one because it involves the idea that, in Wollaston's words, "A true proposition can be denied, or things may be denied to be what they are, by *deeds*, as well as by express words or another proposition."[13] Hence, there is a truth of actions no less than the more familiar truth of ideas. "Most of the duties incumbent on us," Edwards writes, "will be found to partake of the nature of justice" (8:569). In short, secondary beauty is a major source of the common morality that makes possible the order of civil society.

The second principle of common morality is self-love, which Edwards defines in *True Virtue* as a "man's love of his own happiness," except that there is an ambiguity in "his own" which requires clarification. A person's "own happiness," says Edwards, may be taken in a universal sense to include all the happiness or pleasure a person envisages—in which case self-love coincides with the general capacity of loving and hating—or it may mean the pleasure a person takes in a proper, private, and separate good. That a person has the general capacity to love or be pleased does not of itself explain why that love comes to be placed in any object, whether it be one's neighbor or Being in general. Edwards rejects, however, the view that our loving particular persons stems not from our love to happiness in general but from a love to our own happiness, because this would reverse cause and effect. Put more concretely, our happiness in the happiness of the beloved is not the *cause* of love to that person, but the other way around. Our love to the person is the cause of our delighting or being happy in his happiness.

As regards self-love in the sense of private interest, Edwards distinguishes between the pleasures and pains we have in participation with others—"by our hearts being united to them in affection"—and those that are originally our own and determined by inclinations implanted in us. If, says Edwards, we take self-love in the latter sense, love to others may really be one of its effects according to the laws of nature. To love those who are on our side and promote our interest is the natural consequence of self-love, and no other principle is required to bring about this effect. Having made this claim, however, Edwards, ever aware of counterclaims, takes note of those who say that some further principle is involved, especially in feelings of gratitude and anger, namely, a *moral sense*.[14]

Edwards denies "that the reason we are affected with gratitude and anger toward men, rather than things without life, is moral sense" (8:580), or a principle of benevolence to others and love to the public which is present by nature in all mankind. If this is so, why do we not have grateful affections for the good done by inanimate objects—the sun and rain bring forth fruits for our benefit—and affections of anger at the mildew and overflowing streams which destroy these fruits? Edwards, in short, sees no need for a moral sense, since he believes that gratitude and anger can be accounted for through self-love and, as he had previously said, through our apprehensions of secondary beauty in things pleasing to us or in things to which we are averse. "There are," he concludes, "no particular moral virtues whatever, but what . . . come to have some kind of approbation from self-love, without the influence of a truly virtuous principle."

The third principle or disposition in natural morality is conscience, which, like the other ingredients, is regarded by Edwards as arising from self-love. The root meaning of conscience, for Edwards, is a disposition to be uneasy in a consciousness of being *inconsistent* with ourselves. To do to another person what we should be angry with him for doing to us, is to disagree with ourselves and to "contradict ourselves." In order to connect conscience and self-love, Edwards proposes a sort of parallel with pure love to others. In pure benevolence to others there is, as Edwards has put it several times before, a *union* of heart with the other and an enlargement of mind to include the other as one with ourselves. Likewise, self-love implies an inclination to feel and act *as one* to ourselves, and when we are inconsistent and feel and act *as one* to ourselves, and when we are inconsistent and feel and act in opposition to ourselves, uneasiness is the result. Having made this parallel, however, Edwards feels compelled to interject a sharp distinction between natural and divine principles. Approving or disapproving of actions according to their agreement or disagreement with ourselves "is quite a different thing" from approving or disapproving of them because we consent to and are united with Being in general. The latter is a divine principle and the former a natural one.

No doubt one reason for this interjection is Edwards' concern to provide a basis for a subsequent discussion of certain similarities between common morality and true virtue which lead people to mistake one for the other. But there appears to be something else involved as well, namely, Edwards' interest in relating the two moralities to each other even when he regards them as quite distinct. The problem becomes particularly acute in the case of virtues, such as pity, gratitude, and justice, that appear in both moralities under the same names. It is best, however, to postpone further discussion of this point until we consider Edwards' explanation of how the two moralities can be confused, and continue instead with the analysis of conscience.

Matters of conscience, thinks Edwards, always involve relations to other people, the most basic of which is the capacity to put ourselves in their places. According to his conception of experience and of ideas, this capacity requires imagination and projection. Since Edwards holds that we have no ideas of any of our states—passions, affections, inclinations— except what we ourselves are conscious of, "the only knowledge we have of the inner life of other selves is by ascribing to them ideas we have of ourselves" (8:591 n. 5). Nor is this requirement confined to the experience of human selves; Edwards goes on to say that we could have no idea of what understanding or volition is in God if we had not experienced them in ourselves. Edwards believes that a person naturally, habitually, instantaneously, and insensibly substitutes himself in place of the other in all matters of conscience and "easily and quietly sees whether he being in his place should approve or condemn, be angry or pleased as he is" (8:592).

In summary, Edwards says that natural conscience consists of two things. The first is the disposition to approve or disapprove our moral treatment of others according as we are easy or uneasy in the consciousness of being consistent or inconsistent with ourselves. We have a disposition to approve our own conduct in relation to others when we are aware of treating them as we should expect to be treated by them if they were in our case and we in theirs. The same holds for disapproval.

Secondly, there is, Edwards claims, another component in natural conscience which makes its appearance when we ask: What is the foundation for the approving or disapproving from uneasiness about consistency and inconsistency with ourselves? His answer is that some other grounds are needed, and he finds them in the sense of *desert* (which he sometimes calls justice) or a natural proportion and harmony between malevolence and punishment, on the one hand, and loving and being loved, on the other. When a person's conscience, says Edwards, disapproves of the way he has treated his neighbor, he is in the first place aware that were he in his neighbor's position, he would resent such treatment from a sense of justice. Following on this awareness is the perception that he is not consistent with himself in doing what he would himself resent in that case. In short, approval and disapproval of conscience require desert and justice as a ground for determining the consistency or inconsistency of the self.

It is noteworthy that Edwards makes a point of asking in what respect the natural conscience "extends to true virtue." His response is that conscience does not "taste" of the primary beauty, or union of heart with Being in general, but it may approve of it "from that uniformity, equality and justice which there is in it, and the demerit which is seen in the contrary" (8:594). Thus, Edwards concludes, by natural conscience men "may see the justice . . . there is in yielding all to God, as we receive all from God" (8:592). Natural conscience will approve of true virtue and disapprove the want of it, "and yet without seeing the true beauty of it." In the end, conscience falls short of being the exercise of a virtuous principle of the heart, and yet Edwards insists that it belongs to God's design that conscience should approve and condemn the same things approved and condemned by a spiritual sense.

The fourth and final ingredient in common morality is what Edwards calls "instinctual kind affections" which "in some respects resemble virtue" (8:600). By "instinctual" he means dispositions determining through natural laws our affections and actions toward particular objects. The purpose of these instincts in the divine economy is said to be twofold; first, the preservation of humankind, and, second, the promotion of a comfortable subsistence in the world. Certain instincts, says Edwards, of a mental and social type are "kind affections" and have a "semblance" of benevolence in them. However, anticipating his claim in the next section, Edwards goes on to say, "Yet, none of them can be of the nature of true virtue." Edwards begins with the mutual love between parents and children, which, on his view, may be understood either as natural instinct or as based on self-love; he sees no issue involved and leaves the matter there. But instead of proceeding through his list of instinctual affections, Edwards offers two reasons why they do not qualify as true virtue. We are now familiar with the basis of his claim. These affections do not arise from a principle of virtue or the union of the heart with Being in general, and, since they do not stem from general benevolence, they "have no tendency to produce it." In other words, according to Edwards, there is no way to reach general benevolence starting with a limited or, as he sometimes puts it, a "private" affection limited merely to particular objects.

Edwards continues the discussion by citing affectionate relations between men and women—and expresses his agreement with Hutcheson and David Hume (1757–1838) that there is a foundation in nature for these affections and that they are different from sensitive pleasure because there is in them a mutual benevolence and complacence that are not naturally "connected with any sensitive desires" (8:604).[15] These affections, however, are limited to opposite sexes and thus stem from a particular instinct rather than from the principle of general benevolence, which tends to no limits.

Edwards next considers pity, normally exercised toward those in calamity and having a more universal scope than the relations between the sexes. Pity, however, may be malevolent while still limited in scope, so that if the calamity of the other goes beyond the ill will one intended toward him, the natural instinct of pity comes into play. What Edwards has in mind is the case where one says, "I admit that I wished his venture would fail, but not that his life should be altogether ruined." Even the malevolent one takes pity when he sees the excessive character of the result.

Although Edwards is fully aware of the important role played by the morality of natural principles in furthering human life and in enhancing its quality, he is at pains to explain why these virtues have been mistaken for true virtue and why the two can never be the same. Stated most abstractly, the crucial difference between natural principles and true virtue for Edwards is the difference between limited virtues and the unlimited character of consent to Being in general. Nevertheless, there must be some resemblances between the two if we are to account for the fact that people confuse them. There is, says Edwards, something of the "general nature of virtue" in the instinctive affections, something of the appearance of love.[16] The resemblance, however, can be misleading, and Edwards intersperses in his analysis of these affections four more reasons why they are mistaken for true virtue.

People, says Edwards, take private affections for true virtue because they leave the Divine Being out of the picture. In failing to conceive of God as a real existent, they limit their view to a small part of the cosmic system. They think of God as "a kind of shadowy, imaginary being" (8:611); while most admit that there is a God, "yet in their ordinary view of things, his being is not apt to come into the account, and to have the influence and effect of a real existence." The result is that we "limit our consideration [of the beauty of affections and actions] to only a small part of the created system" (ibid.).

Another reason why people are misled in their estimate of instinctive affections is that, on Edwards' view, there "is a true *negative* moral goodness in them" (8:613). By this he means the negation or absence of true moral evil. A being without the natural virtues would be evidence of a much greater moral evil. The exercise of natural conscience, for example, is an evidence of the absence of that higher degree of wickedness that leads to insensibility or stupidity of conscience.[17] Thus Edwards is fully cognizant of the important role played by instinctive affections and natural virtues, at the same time that he is engaged in showing why they must not be mistaken for true virtue. His recognition of the contribution made by the natural affections becomes clear when he shows concern over the fact that their power may be greatly *diminished* by pride and sensuality, the two cardinal vices strongly decried by Edwards in the *Charity* sermons. Since God has implanted natural principles for the well-being of humankind, their corruption can only mean the increase of evil in the world.

There is, says Edwards, yet another reason why natural principles are mistaken for true virtue, and that is because that have "in several ways" the same effect to which true virtue tends. Natural pity, gratitude, parental affections tend to the good of humankind, as does general benevolence. But then, Edwards continues, natural hunger and thirst also tend in the same direction, and "nobody will assert that these have the nature of true virtue" (8:616). Natural principles have the same effect as true virtue in that they tend to constrain vice and curtail wickedness. Pity delivers us from cruelty, and natural conscience restrains sin. In short, for Edwards the self-love involved in these virtues plays its part in the divine economy, but it is not of the nature of true virtue, being instead a source of the world's wickedness.

Edwards' final reason why the inferior affections are taken for true virtue reveals his concern for language; some of these virtues have the same *names* as truly virtuous affections. There is, for example, a virtuous *pity* or compassion, springing from holy benevolence, that would be sufficient to excite pity to someone in calamity, even if there were no instinct determining the mind. There is also a holy *gratitude* that arises not from self-love but from a disinterested benevolence to Being in general and differs from the justice based only on what Edwards has been calling secondary beauty.[18]

We may conclude this much-condensed account of Edwards' conception of true virtue and common morality with a suggestion that may serve to clarify the entire discussion. Students of the history of religion, and not only Western religion, are aware of the need to distinguish between religion and morality, between the fundamental faith in and relation to God—our *being*—and the obligations to others we have as moral beings—what we are to *do*. The distinction, but also the relation, between the two is admirably expressed in the first epistle of John: "If a man say, I love God, and hateth his brother, he is a liar" (1 John 4:20). The love of God defines the relation to the neighbor; in biblical religion, morality is based on religion. The distinction, moreover, is not merely analytical, because time and again a tension, if not an open antagonism, has manifested itself between the two within religious traditions. Religion sees the person for whom morality is enough as a "mere moralist," who fails to see the need of religious faith and grace; morality sees the religious person as one who depends on "supernatural" powers and takes what William James called "moral holidays," firm in the conviction that in God all evil is already overcome.[19] This picture is, of course, oversimplified, but it does serve to underline the problem.

According to this pattern, we could understand Edwards' account of true virtue as essentially defining the *religious* relationship, or, in his terms, the consent to and union of heart with Being in general (the holy love of God), and his account of the relations between persons as defining the *moral* dimension, or what affections we are to have and what actions we must perform. The two sources of morality could then be understood as, on the one hand, Christian principles and, on the other, natural principles stemming from reason and order both in ourselves and the world according to the divine economy. In this way some confusion can be avoided, since "true *virtue*" may seem to point to the *moral* dimension, whereas it is clear that, in using this expression, Edwards means the *religious* relationship to God, and its consequences.[20]

Notes

1. The reader should consult *The Works of Jonathan Edwards*, 8 *Ethical Writings*, ed. Paul Ramsey, (New Haven and London: Yale University Press, 1989). This is the first complete and critical edition of these writings and the volume also contains references to most of Edwards' other works, including the "Miscellanies," which illuminate the basic ethical writings. Ramsey's detailed introduction is invaluable for a proper understanding of Edwards' thought about these essential topics.

2. The reader should note that the second dissertation has been published alone under the title *The Nature of True Virtue*, ed. William K. Frankena (Ann Arbor: University of Michigan Press, 1960; reprint 1969).

3. Ramsey is very helpful on this point and shows that Edwards uses the term "grateful" in an older sense; for example, "his coming was very grateful unto the king," means that it was agreeable, pleasing, and welcome. The important point is that, for Edwards, there is something in the nature of the thing or situation that, when *perceived*, calls for the grateful response (see 8:13 n. 4).

4. Hutcheson's main works were *An Essay on the Nature and Conduct of the Passions and the Affections* (1728) and *An Inquiry into the Original of Our Ideas of Beauty and Virtue* (1725). Edwards made extensive use of both.

5. One is reminded here, of the crucial distinction between *homoousios*—the same—and *homoiousios*—the similar—which played so great a role in the discussions that resulted in the formulation of the Nicene Creed, and perhaps Edwards himself had these discussions in mind. The "orthodox" position was that the Son is of the *same* substance with the Father, while the "heterodox" position was that the Son is of a *similar* substance with the Father. It is curious how recondite matters often find their way into ordinary language; when we say "I do not see one iota of difference between X and Y," the meaning derives from the two Greek terms noted above. But, of course, the difference was in just that iota!

6. A fine illustration of the point is found in *Charity*, where Edwards asks his hearers to decide whether "you are essentially distinguished and different in your spirit from the *mere moralist*, or the heathen sage or philosopher," and whether you have "a spirit of special esteem for and delight in these virtues that do especially belong to the gospel" (8:89).

7. See Roland A. Delattre, *Beauty and Sensibility in the Thought of Jonathan Edwards* (New Haven and London: Yale University Press, 1968). Delattre's subtitle, "An Essay in Aesthetics and Theological Ethics" highlights the connection between beauty and virtue.

8. There are more details in Edwards' account than can be treated in a brief survey, but mention must be made of an important distinction that he presupposed throughout the Charity sermons between *benevolence* and *complacence*,

both of which are included in Christian love. Referring to love going out toward others, Edwards writes: "as it respects the good enjoyed or to be enjoyed *by* the beloved, it is called *love of benevolence*; and as it respects good to be enjoyed *in* the beloved, it is called *love of complacence*" (8:212–13). For the derivation of "complacence," including its numerous spellings and its basic meaning of "to be pleased in," see Eric Partridge, *Origins: A Short Etymological Dictionary of Modern English*, 2d ed. (1958; reprint New York: Macmillan/London: Routledge & Kegan Paul, 1959), p. 503, para. 9.

9. Edwards clearly regarded benevolence as superior to complacence, and hence it was important for him to insist that any enjoyment *in* the beloved be based on concern for the good enjoyed *by* the beloved.

10. This in fact is the title of ch. 7 in *True Virtue*.

11. Edwards is clearly reviving the ancient doctrine of the Greek philosophers according to which everyone and everything has a proper place (*topos*) in the cosmic order. When one is "out of place," this can only mean that one is in someone else's place, and this is unjust.

12. William Wollaston, *The Religion of Nature Delineated* (London, 1722).

13. See 8:570 n. 1.

14. Despite the fact that, as Ramsey correctly notes, Edwards never provided an extended discussion of the idea of a moral sense—an idea that figures prominently in the writings of eighteenth-century British moralists such as Francis Hutcheson—he introduced it in the discussion of self-love and returned to it again in connection with the next ingredient in common morality, conscience. The topic, however, is too involved to be treated here; the reader should see 8:689–705 and Norman Fiering, *Jonathan Edwards' Moral Thought and Its British Context* (Chapel Hill: University of North Carolina Press, 1981).

15. See 8:603 n. 9 and 604 n. 1 for relevant quotations from both Hutcheson and Hume.

16. It is important to notice that "appearance" here does not mean a contrast with reality, as when one says that a person only "appears to be honest, but is not really honest." The meaning in Edwards' text is that the resemblance in question is present and makes its appearance in fact.

17. Edwards frequently speaks of "stupidity" of conscience and opposes it to conscience that is well informed; this is a sign that he recognized the *scientia* in conscience—a knowledge of principles and norms. The familiar figure of conscience as a "voice" has done much to make it into an intuitive, infallible oracle that simply "tells" us what to do. For Edwards, on the contrary, conscience must *judge* what to do, on the basis of moral knowledge.

18. Edwards spells out at greater length the role played by language in the analysis of morality (see 8:619–27).

19. See n. 6 above.

20. Once again, we see the role played by language; in the tradition of Western moral philosophy, from Plato and Aristotle to the British moralists Edwards had read, the term "virtue" signified a basically *moral* category, but by adding the term "true" Edwards was bringing in the religious dimension.

Suggested Further Readings

Byrnes, Thomas A. "H. Richard Niebuhr's Reconstruction of Jonathan Edwards' Moral Theology." In *Annual of the Society of Christian Ethics*, ed. Alan B. Anderson, pp. 33–55. Washington, D.C.: Georgetown University Press, 1986.

Delattre, Roland A. *Beauty and Sensibility in the Thought of Jonathan Edwards: An Essay in Aesthetics and Theological Ethics*. New Haven: Yale University Press, 1968.

Fiering, Norman. *Jonathan Edwards' Moral Thought and Its British Context*. Chapel Hill: University of North Carolina Press, 1981.

Gustafson, James M. *Ethics from a Theocentric Perspective: Theology and Ethics* pp. 171–76. Chicago: University of Chicago Press, 1981.

McDermott, Gerald R. *One Holy and Happy Society: The Public Theology of Jonathan Edwards*. University Park: Pennsylvania State University Press, 1992.

Spohn, William. "Sovereign Beauty: Jonathan Edwards and the Nature of True Virtue." *Theological Ethics* 42 (September 1981): 393–421.

———. "Union and Consent to the Great Whole: Jonathan Edwards on True Virtue." In *Annual of the Society of Christian Ethics*, ed. Alan B. Anderson, pp. 19–32. Washington, D.C.: Georgetown University Press, 1986.

Twelve

The Church

Douglas A. Sweeney

DESPITE HIS LIFELONG labors in pastoral ministry, Edwards' doctrine of the church has gone largely unnoticed by scholars.[1] In fact, were it not for a little-known article written half a century ago by Thomas Schafer, and a small assortment of chapters and passages, now nearly forgotten, in other sources (see the appended bibliography), we would have no scholarship at all on Edwards' ecclesiology per se.[2]

Part of the reason for this neglect is that Edwards himself did not publish a book, or even a pamphlet, devoted solely to this topic. He published quite a bit on the theme of church membership during Northampton's "communion controversy," focusing closely on what he referred to as "the qualifications requisite to a complete standing and full communion in the visible Christian church" (12:166). Indeed, his *Ecclesiastical Writings* make up a large volume in the Yale edition of his works. But inasmuch as these writings deal narrowly with the issue of local church membership, they speak but indirectly to the nature of the Christian church at large. Consequently, one must glean widely throughout the entire Edwards corpus—paying special attention to manuscript sources—to see the full range of his ecclesiological views.

Further, the leading scholarly treatment of Northampton's communion controversy largely dismisses ecclesiology as insignificant to the dispute. In his introduction to Edwards' *Ecclesiastical Writings*, David Hall depicts this affair primarily in terms of local history and what he deems Edwards' failure to honor the "popular religion" of his region. "From start to finish," Hall writes, "the Northampton controversy unfolded within a relatively narrow range of terms and categories." Edwards could have defended his arguments in ecclesiological terms, but "we look in vain in the *Humble Inquiry* [his major treatise on church membership] for a statement of Edwards' broader vision of the church." To be sure, Hall admits, ecclesiology factored into Northampton's controversy as well, and "as a philosophical theologian," Edwards "transcended [his local] circumstances." But "the nature of the church was no narrowly religious or doctrinal matter"; it was "a many-sided issue that quickly became charged with politics." Hall concludes, then, that "the struggle in Northampton was rooted in circumstances peculiar to that town and church, to the revivals of the 1740s, and to the Congregational tradition as it had developed in New England." Moreover, he contends, Edwards' *Ecclesiastical Writings* "cannot but remind us that he was . . . a person of his time and place," and "no more so than in his understanding of the church and ministry" (12:85, 4, 1).³

Clearly, Hall is right to highlight the social and political dimensions of Northampton's communion controversy and to affirm that Edwards was, after all, a man of his time and place. But as we will see in the pages that follow, Edwards' view of the local church—including its social and cultural affairs—was rooted deeply in ecclesiological soil. Indeed, Edwards had much to say about the doctrine of the church, much that illuminates the communion dispute itself. When one inspects his ecclesiology, it becomes clear that, at least for Edwards, even this controversy pertained to more than the right to local church membership. It pertained to the classical Christian doctrine of the communion of the saints, and to the saints' relationship to the person of Christ.

Edwards developed several definitions of the church throughout his life, his statements increasing in specificity in the wake of Northampton's revivals. In the early 1720s, while Edwards was still in his late teens, he preached a sermon called "Living to Christ" (Phil. 1:21) in which he defined the church in simple terms as "the body of Christ, [the] mystical body of Christ" (10:566). In 1735, in the midst of a major revival that swept the Connecticut River Valley and that Edwards made famous throughout the West in his *Faithful Narrative* two years later, he preached that "the church is the whole company or society of those that are true and real saints," distinguishing such "true and real saints" from those who only appear to be saints and thus do not in fact belong to the mystical body of Jesus Christ (Eph. 5:25–27, F. 781, L. 2r).⁴ A year or two later, he wrote in his "Miscellanies" notebooks that "the church is Christ mystical," reverting to his original, less contentious definition ("Misc." 710, 18:336). But in May 1741, at the height of the Great Awakening, Edwards again became more specific with his spiritually charged parishioners, repeating "the church of Christ is the whole society of true saints"(Rev. 22: 16–17, F. 932, L. 3r). In April 1744, by which time Northampton's revivals had ended and its pastor had grown more worried than ever before about counterfeit piety, Edwards provided his most extensive definition of the church: "the church of Christ," he explained, "is that company of men that is by the grace of God effectually called out from this fallen, undone [world] and gathered together in one in Christ

Jesus, through him to worship God and have the peculiar enjoyment of him" (Col. 1:24, F. 791, L. 2r).

Despite the obvious variations in Edwards' attempts to define the church, and despite his desire to define it more strictly during periods of revival (more on this below), his definitions all took root in the same ecclesiological ground—ground that was cultivated for years by Edwards' Puritan predecessors concerned to promote "true religion" and to distinguish the "true church" from what they called the "visible church." After the manner of such precursors, Edwards' descriptions of the church shared in common a basic commitment to the metaphysical notion that the church *really is* the mystical body of Jesus Christ. As such, it includes within its (true) membership only those who are born again, who have died to sin and risen with Christ, who have been supernaturally ingrafted by the Spirit into Christ, who share a new life together in him and a common mission to embody the presence of Christ in the secular world. Or as Edwards once insisted to the people of Northampton, " 'Tis the relation and concern that the members of the church have with Christ that is the thing wherein above all things the essence of the church consists" (Col. 1:24, F. 791, L. 5r).

This sounds strange to modern ears. For as Thomas Schafer said long ago, "Edwards' conception of the Church is rooted in his ontology and cosmology. . . . Edwards has a high doctrine of the transcendent oneness of the Church in Christ, a unity buttressed by his theological and philosophical realism."[5] Consequently, his definitions of the nature of the church had more in common with each other than any has had with most modern views, few of which are so cosmological, ontological, metaphysical. Even in Edwards' day, moreover, his ecclesial views sounded strange to some—so strange, in fact, that they contributed to his dismissal from Northampton.

Basic to Edwards' understanding of the nature of the church was his belief that God has "elected" the church *in Christ* for God's own glory. In his *Dissertation Concerning the End for Which God Created the World* (8:400–536), Edwards contended at great length that God created the world primarily to glorify himself by communicating himself and his own glory *ad extra* (i.e., outside of himself, outside of the Godhead, or outside of the immanent Trinity).[6] God thereby extends himself and his glory in the theater of creation. We, in turn, reflect his glory back to him in love and worship. In his ecclesiological writings, Edwards developed this concept further, suggesting that God communicates with us primarily in the person of Christ (and by the power of the Holy Spirit), and that we reflect his glory back to him primarily in Christ as we participate by the Spirit in the life and glory of God the Son.[7]

Thus, for Edwards, it is the church, or those elected by God the Father to be united to his Son, who best represent God's intentions for the creation of the world—but only *insofar as* the church is united to the Son and part of the Godhead's glorification of *itself* in and through the world. In fact, for Edwards, the church and its members do not exist apart from Christ. They have been chosen by God for his Son, and will be bound to the Son forever. As Edwards noted in "Miscellanies," no. 1245, "the sum of [God's] purposes with respect to creatures, was to procure a spouse, or a mystical body, for his Son." Before the creation of the world, God chose to shower us with his love, much as a bridegroom showers love upon his bride. But God foreknew that we would rebel and refuse to respond to him in love, that we would fail to reflect his glory, and thus would require a way of salvation. And in keeping with his design to procure a bride for his only Son, God chose some from our fallen race to be reunited with him *through* the Son, not only selecting them individually but also electing them corporately—as a singular bride for Christ—so that, in Christ, a holy remnant would remain in the family of God and would participate in the extension of God's glory in the world. "We must suppose," then, argued Edwards, "that Christ, in some respect, is first in this affair [of election], and some way or other the ground of our being chosen, and God's election of him some way or other including and inferring the election of particular saints." In other words, "though many individual persons were chosen, yet they were chosen to receive God's infinite good and Christ's peculiar love in union, as one body, one spouse, all united in one head." Indeed, "in their very first election there is respect to their union in the body of Christ. They are first chosen to be in the intended body of Christ, to be members of his spouse" (23:177–81; cf. 8:459–60, 9:124–25; 13:272–74).

As a result, the very salvation of those God has chosen for his Son depends on their union with the Son, "the chief of elect men and head of the whole," according to Edwards ("Misc." 776, 18:426). They receive forgiveness for their sins and gain a right to justification only because they dwell in him, because for his sake God forgives them and reckons Christ's righteousness as their own (19:155–56, 220). As Edwards preached in a public lecture in Boston in 1739, "Jesus Christ is the Great Mediator and Head of union, in whom all elect creatures in heaven and earth are united to God and to one another" (1 Tim. 2:5, F. 800, L. 5r; cf. Eph. 1:10, F. 769, L. 3r).

Furthermore, as Edwards taught his Northampton congregation five years later, Christ dwells in union with his people in two ways: "there is a twofold union between Christ and the church: real and relative." The church's *real* union with its Lord "consists in some real tie or bond between them whereby they are united and really become one—and not only relatively." It may be compared, Edwards suggested, to the union "between branches and . . . stock," between "head and members," or even between "foundation and superstructure." The "communication" in this union, Edwards insisted, "is wholly from Christ." It "is not mutual," he explained, for while "the church lives by Christ's life . . . Christ don't properly live by the church." Nevertheless, this union involves not only a metaphorical joining of the "hearts" of Christ and the church but also a real union of "nature," which means that Christ and the church in some sense really do "live one in another." The *relative* union between Christ and the church, in Edwards' view, is based on the real one. It not only involves what Edwards referred to as an "affinity" between them but also bestows upon the church a privileged status in God's sight. Because the saints do "live" in Christ, they enjoy a special *relationship* to the Father. The Father adopts them as his children and treats them legally as his own. Christ and the church "are looked upon and accepted as one by God the Father acting as the supreme Lawgiver and Judge of all" (Col. 1:24, F. 791, L. 6r–L. 10v; cf. 19:158). Or as Edwards handled this theme in relation to the history of redemption, "it may be looked upon as part of the success of Christ's purchase [of redemption] . . . that Christ did not rise as a private person but as the head of all the elect church; so that they did, as it were, all rise in him." As members of Christ's body the saints have a claim to eternal life. "As Christ rose from the dead, so he also ascended into heaven as the head of the body and forerunner of all the church; so they, as it were, ascend with him as well as rise with him" (9:358, 361; cf. "Misc." 691, 18:271).[8]

Moreover, the church has been bound to Christ in this way since the dawn of human history. For it has always been God's intention to secure a spouse for his only Son, thereby drawing the saints up into the Trinitarian life of God. As Edwards preached to his congregations in Northampton and in Stockbridge, "those that are saints now, they are of the same church with the apostles, and with David and Samuel and Moses, and Abraham, Is[aac] and Jacob. They are all but one church" (Eph. 5:25–27, F. 781, L. 3r). And as he spelled out in his sermon series *History of the Work of Redemption*, God has always adopted his saints by means of the same "covenant of grace," agreeing in mercy to count as righteous those who trust and cleave to his Son. "The religion that the church of God has professed, from the first founding of the church after the fall to this time, has always been the same" (9:442–44; cf. 9:290, 365–67, 443, 469–70, and passim). Even before the Incarnation, in the days of the Old Testament, God justified the saints by faith alone in the coming Messiah. Thus, in Edwards' view, the Old and New Testaments "don't differ as to the essence and substance of the covenant itself" but "only in manner and circumstances." Or as he noted in his "Miscellanies," no. [1353], the gospel itself is in the Old Testament, though "indirect" and "under a cover" (23:495; cf. "Misc." 439, 874, 13:487–89; 20:115–18).[9]

Likewise, the New Testament church "was first of all of the nation of Israel," not a new religious group with a different doctrine of salvation. "Therefore when the Gentiles were called they were but . . . added to Israel, to the seed of Abraham. They were added to the Christian church of Israel . . . and so were . . . only grafted on to the stock of Abraham and were not a distinct tree." Abraham served, in Edwards' view, as "the father of all the church, . . . a root whence the visible church thence forward through Christ, Abraham's root and offspring, rose as a tree distinct from all other plants." And though it is true, Edwards believed, that "after Christ came, the natural branches were broken off," and only those who placed their faith in Christ received God's pledge to Abraham, it is also true that Edwards believed in God's special concern for the Jewish people, interpreting the eleventh chapter of Romans as a promise of their conversion (9:376–77, 160, 469–70; cf. 11:113).

In short, the Old and New Testaments, the Hebrew Bible and Christian Scriptures, are for Edwards best interpreted in terms of continuity. To be sure, Edwards held firmly to the supremacy of Christ, the superiority of the New Testament, and the progressive maturation of the church since its beginning. In fact, in a fascinating entry in his unpublished "Notes on Scripture" (on Eph. 5:30–32), he went so far as to say the following: "Christ did as it were leave his Father in order to obtain and be joined to the church. . . . So he also left his mother, which was the church of the Jews, to cleave to the New Testament church as his wife. . . . The Old Testament church was as Christ's mother, but the New Testament church is his wife, whom he is joined to, and whom he treats with far greater endearment and intimacy" (15:181–82).[10] And in a lengthy, four-part sermon on Psalm 106:5 ("That I may see the good of thy chosen, that I may rejoice in the gladness of thy nation, that I may glory with thine inheritance"), Edwards told his congregation that while "God did great things of old to found the visible church of the Jews. . . . God hath done greater things to found his mystical, invisible church" (Ps. 106:5, F. 174, L. 12v).

But this did not mean for Edwards that the saints of the Old Testament did not belong to what he liked to call the "mystical, invisible church," only that this church had matured and, as it had, its distinction from the "visible church" had been clarified. As Edwards wrote in "Miscellanies," no. 710, "of old, under the Old Testament, the church of Christ was as a child (Gal. 4:1). So still under the gospel dispensation the church on earth is as a child, in comparison of what the church of glorified souls in heaven is when what is perfect is come" (18:338). The present-day church, in other words, remains immature as well, and will not be completely mature until it reaches heaven. Edwards explained this in detail in his best-known sermon on Christian love (entitled "Heaven Is a World of Love"):

> There is a twofold imperfect, and so a twofold perfect state of the Christian church. The Christian church in its beginning, in its first age before it was thoroughly established in the world, and settled in its New Testament state, and before the canon of Scripture was completed, was in an imperfect state, a kind of a state of childhood in comparison with what it will be in the elder and latter ages of the church, when it will be in a state of manhood, or a perfect state in comparison with what it was in the first ages. Again, the church of Christ, as long as it remains in its militant state, and to the end of time is in an imperfect state, a state of childhood . . . in comparison with what it will be in the heavenly state, when it comes to a state of manhood and perfection, and to the measure of the stature of the fullness of Christ. (8:366–67)

Edwards did enjoy describing the church as a "city on a hill," the "salt of the earth," and the "light of the world" (Matt. 5:13–16). Accordingly, he believed that the church "preserves" the world "from that utter ruin which its corruption and wickedness tends to." As he preached to his congregation regarding Christ's sermon on the mount, "the church is an occasion of a great restraint of the wickedness of the world." In fact, "the world would be destroyed if it were not for the church, inasmuch as all other things here below are for the church's sake." Edwards' comments here are striking: "the world was continued that the design of Christ's mediatorial kingdom might be carried on." Had God not elected to keep the world for the sake of his only Son, "the execution of the curse would be no longer delayed. God would uphold the world no longer, but would immediately let it perish and fall into utter ruin" (5:14, 19:539–59; Matt. 5:13, F. 427, L. 6r, L. 9r–v; and passim).

But, again, despite the church's importance to the health and welfare of the world, it too is beset by evil, sorely tried and tempted at present, and must do battle with the devil and his angels for survival. Like many theologians before him, Edwards distinguished between the church's so-called "militant state" on earth and its "triumphant state" in heaven (anticipated during the church's future millennium, or golden age). He wrote in his manuscript "Notes on the Apocalypse" (the biblical book of Revelation), "the church from Christ's time to the millennium, is in a state of warfare, or her militant state; but during that sabbatism, [she] shall be in a triumphant state. The proper time of the church's rest and triumph can't be said to be come, till all her enemies are subdued. As long as any considerable part of the world remains under the dominion of Satan, Michael and his angels will be at war with the devil and his angels" (5:178–79). Edwards frequently referred to the church in violent, martial terms, explaining in "Types of the Messiah" that "the church of the Messiah is often represented [in the Bible] as an army. They are represented as being called forth to war and engaged in battle" (11:303). And in a sermon to his parishioners, "Christians a Chosen Generation," Edwards repeated that "the church here upon earth is as an army that goes forth under Jesus Christ, the captain of their salvation, to resist the common adversary" (17:305; cf. 15:131, 255).

Indeed, not until heaven will the church receive its (final) glorification and live forever in perfect peace. As Edwards suggested in his sermon series *The History of the Work of Redemption*, "all that is before this, while the church is under means of grace, is only to make way for that, to prepare that success that is to be accomplished in the bestowment of glory. The means of grace are to fit for glory, and God's grace itself is bestowed on the elect to make them meet for glory." Further, "all those glorious things that were brought to pass for the church while under means of grace are but images and shadows of this" (9:493; cf. "Misc." 371, 13:443). In fact, as Edwards worked out in a little-known set of "Miscellanies" entries, even "the assembly" already in heaven, including saints as well as angels, "has all along been in a like progressive state with the church on earth, and is in a preparatory state." Or as he phrased this in an entry entitled "Confirmation of the Angels," the "affairs of the church on earth and of the blessed assembly of heaven are linked together. . . . when God gradually carries on the designs of grace in this world, by accomplishing glorious things in the church below, there is a new accession of joy and glory to the church in heaven." He put this most clearly perhaps in an entry he entitled "Saints in Heaven":

> The saints in heaven seem to be as nearly and immediately concerned in those glorious revolutions [i.e., spiritual revolutions on earth], as the saints on earth. And how meet and suitable is it . . . that, as Christ's mediatorial glory, and that reward he has for his own sufferings and righteousness, is progressive and is bestowed and advanced in various successive steps and degrees. . . . I say, how reasonable is it to suppose that the glory of the church in heaven, that part of the mystical body of Christ that is with him . . . and who are partaking of his reward, and whose glory and happiness is all a reward of the same righteousness, should be advanced by like steps and degrees, at the same time, and in the same dispensations of providence. ("Misc." 745, 18:390; "Misc." 515, 18:61–62; "Misc." 804, 18:506–7; cf. "Misc." 796, 18:497–98)

This gradual advancement of the church, both here on earth as well as in heaven, will culminate, in Edwards' view, after the final day of judgment, when God will gather all the elect to dwell with him forever in heaven. Even after the end of the world, the church will continue to grow toward God.[11] Its love affair with Christ will intensify through all eternity. But this affair will reach consummation when God has finished his work of redemption, or when the mystical bride of Christ has been made complete and is finally ready. As Edwards preached in Northampton, "when Christ shall bring his church into his Father's house in heaven after the judgment, he shall bring her there as his bride, having there presented her . . . without spot or wrinkle or any such thing [Eph. 5:25–27]. The bridegroom and the bride shall then enter into heaven, both having on their wedding robes, attended with all the glorious angels. And there they shall enter on the feast and joys of their marriage before the Father; they shall then begin an everlasting wedding day" (9:508).

Tellingly, Edwards' writings are full of this kind of erotic imagery. In fact, it would not be too much to say that Edwards was fascinated by the biblical doctrine of the church's "union" with Christ (more on this image below), for he spent hours upon hours working out its implications. He told his people that in heaven the saints "will have the perfect possession and enjoyment" of their beloved Jesus Christ. Likewise, "then shall Christ bring the church fully into his own possession. He will make it his own wholly and entirely." Indeed, he will "bring the church as near to himself as he desires" (Jer. 10:16, F. 355, L. 3r; Eph. 5:25–27, F. 781, L. 18v).[12] As Edwards describes it, in fact, the church's redemption and reunion with its most eager divine spouse proves so important to God himself that he has purchased it with his own blood—guaranteeing the safe arrival of his bride at the wedding feast. As Edwards preached in a vivid sermon in December 1745, "the church of God is purchased by the blood of God." God the Son has redeemed his bride from her former bondage to sin and Satan "at the price of his own life." Indeed, "he waded through a sea of blood to come at it" (Acts 20:28, F. 675, L. 1v; 14:431).

Consequently, God himself, in the person of Jesus Christ, the "stone which the builders rejected" (Matt. 21:42), has become the church's "chief corner stone" (Eph. 2:20), or the church's one "foundation" and guarantor of eternal life—even while Peter and the apostles remain "secondary" foundations. More specifically, for Edwards, God's decree to elect the church in Christ for the advancement of his glory is the church's guarantee that it will "persevere" to the end. As Edwards preached on Psalm 106, "the foundation on which it stands is God's eternal decree of election made known to them by the covenant of grace." He went on to ask rhetorically, "What can be more stable than what is eternal and has already stood from all eternity as God's love to his elect has, which is eternal in the same sense that God's being is eternal and, therefore, is as permanent and immutable as God's being?" Even during the church's militant state, "Christ has the dispensation of safety and deliverance in his own hands, so that we need not fear but that, if we are united to him, we may be safe." So Edwards assured his congregation that "the gates of hell never have been able to prevail against" the church. "God hath evermore had a holy seed that the devil never has been able to extirpate." Indeed, "many and great endeavors have been used in the world to extirpate the church, to root it out of the world, to leave neither root nor branch." There have been times when "God's church was almost swallowed up and carried away with the wickedness of the world." But "there is a secret life in it that will cause it to flourish again and take root downward, and bear fruit upward." In short, God loves the church too much to let it die (Is. 28:16, F. 285, L. 1v; Matt. 16:18, F. 488, passim; Ps. 106:5, F. 174, L. 31r; Is. 32:2, F. 289; Matt. 5:13, F. 427, L. 4v–5v; 9:174, 236; cf. "Misc." 79, 15:73; 10:311; 2:236; 5:155; 9, passim; Is. 37:31, F. 297, L. 2r).

As a Scripture-intoxicated man, Edwards knew well that this was why the Bible depicts the church variously as God's "portion," his "inheritance," his "treasure" and his "jewels," and depicts God, in turn, as the "portion" of his people. "God's people are God's portion," Edwards proclaimed to his congregation. "Such an honor have the saints that they are often called his portion, and his inheritance, and, sometimes, his precious treasure, his jewels and the like." While God "stands in no need of anything, and can't be made happier by the creature, yet God is pleased to set his heart upon the creature highly, to prize and value the saints as his portion and the lot of his inheritance" (Jer. 10:16, F. 355, L. 9r). Edwards went into more detail in his exegetical "Notes on Scripture":

> the church is not only represented as Christ's ornament, but God's people are often spoken of in the Old Testament as God's portion, inheritance, his treasure, his jewels, his garden of pleasant fruits, . . . the plant of his pleasures, his pleasant food as the first ripe figs . . ., a garden and orchard of spices, his bed or field of lilies among which he feeds, his fountain of gardens as refreshing streams from Lebanon, a garden where he gathers his myrrh and his spice, and where he eats his honeycomb with his honey, and drinks his wine with his milk. So the saints in the New Testament are spoken of as God's wheat and good grain, that he gathers into his garner. (15:578)

Edwards goes on, but by now his point is already quite well taken: God delights in the church and longs to enjoy her forever.

It should not need pointing out that Edwards borrowed straight from Scripture most of the imagery that he used to describe the bond between God and the church. A comprehensive catalogue of this imagery would consume too many pages, but a sampling may prove useful in filling out his view of the church. Like the Bible itself, Edwards depicted the church in many different ways, but returned regularly to a few particularly vivid illustrations. In a representative manuscript note on 1 Kings 6:7, for example, he referred to the church as "God's temple, a spiritual house, Jesus Christ being chief cornerstone, and all the saints as so many stones" (15:64). And in his book on *Religious Affections*, he employed the imagery of St. Paul in a way that has epitomized for many Edwards' mastery of biblical metaphor:

> All true Christians behold as in a glass, the glory of the Lord, and are changed into the same image, by his Spirit (II Cor. 3:18). . . . Christians that shine by reflecting the light of the Sun of Righteousness, do shine with the same sort of brightness, the same mild, sweet and pleasant beams. These lamps of the spiritual temple, that are enkindled by fire from heaven, burn with the same sort of flame. The branch is of the same nature with the stock and root, has the same sap, and bears the same sort of fruit. The members have the same kind of life with the head. . . . True Christians are as it were clothed with the meek, quiet, and loving temper of Christ; for as many as are in Christ, have put on Christ. And in this respect the church is clothed with the Sun, not only by being clothed with his imputed righteousness, but also by being adorned with his graces (Rom. 13:14). (2:347)

Edwards made frequent use of the "types" of the church he found throughout the Bible, especially the "images and shadows" of the church in the Old Testament. In his notebook on "Images of Divine Things," he wrote that the moon is a type of the church because it reflects the light of the sun/Son (Josh. 10:12-14). Movable tents are types of the church, "for here we are pilgrims and strangers, and have no abiding place" (Cant. 1:5). The burning of heifers in the Old Testament stands as a type of the church's participation in the sacrifice of Christ—as his body and by means of its own purgation (Num. 19). Many Old Testament patriarchs and matriarchs function as types of the Christian church, from Noah and his company to the likes of Rebekah and Deborah. As for Noah, the door of his ark "was open to receive all sorts of creatures—tigers, wolves, bears, lions, leopards, serpents, vipers, dragons—such as men would not by any means admit into the doors of their houses." Likewise, "Christ stands ready to receive all, even the vilest and worst." And "in the Christian church are gathered together persons of all nations, kindreds, tongues, and peoples, persons of all degrees, all kinds of tempers and manners." As for Rebekah, her "joining Isaac," who is himself a type of Christ, "represented a receiving of Christ" and typifies the New Testament lesson that the church "should leave all in this world to give up themselves to Christ, to be his spouse, and follow him into an unseen land" (11:134; 15:75, 279–81, 77, 297, 268–71; Gen. 24:58, F. 11, L. 2r–3r; 5:127).

As we have seen, however, in Edwards' view "the relation between Christ and his church is in Scripture represented by nothing so often as by that which is between an husband and wife." He once exclaimed in his "Miscellanies": "How greatly are we inclined to the other sex!" God has created human nature with powerful sexual inclinations. Christ himself has a human nature, and "that inclination which in us is turned to the other sex, in him is turned to the church. . . . Therefore when we feel love to anyone of the other sex, 'tis a good way to think of the love of Christ to an holy and beautiful soul." Edwards declaimed constantly in Northampton that "Christ is so united to the church that he is looked upon in some sense to be of the church." The saints are "members of his body, of his flesh and of his bone (Eph. 5:30)." The saints dwell "in" their Lord, much "as a man . . . is encompassed with the air that he breathes," or "as a man walks in the light of the sun," or "as a man bathes himself in cool waters in times of sultry heat for his refreshment and pleasure." Indeed, Christ is an "ocean of pleasure" in which his saints are submerged. The saints are "swallowed up" in him. In sum, "the day of a sinner's conversion may be called his wedding day." When God regenerates his elect, he truly ravishes their souls.[13] "By his Spirit [he] enters into their very souls and so makes them his temples" (Rev. 22:16–17, F. 932, L. 3v; 13:332; Col. 1:24, F. 791, L. 12r; Jer. 10:16, F. 355, L. 4v–5v; John 15:5, F. 645, L. 3r–v; Matt. 22:1–14, F. 1042, L. 1r.; cf. Hos. 3:1–3, F. 391, passim; 1 Cor. 1:9, F. 717, passim; Eph. 5:25–27, F. 781, passim; Eph. 5:30–32, F. 782, L. 1v; 15:92, 610–13; 19:779–80).[14]

In several manuscript notebooks as well as his work on the *End in Creation*, Edwards explored the implications of this amazing spiritual intimacy for the interpretation of Paul's assertion (in Eph. 1:23) that the church "is . . . the fulness of him that filleth all in all." Along the way, he echoed the strains of Janice Knight's "Spiritual Brethren," earlier Puritans centered in Cambridge who depicted the church in similar terms.[15]

What does it mean, Edwards wondered, to describe the church as the "fulness" of Christ, "as though he were not in his complete state without her" (*End in Creation*, 8:439–40)? Edwards was used to describing the Son of God as the "fulness" of his Father and the Holy Spirit as the "fulness" of the Godhead ("Misc." 104, 13:273, "Misc." 487, 13:528–32).[16] But how might the church itself function as the "fulness" of her Lord? In his "Notes on Scripture," Edwards suggested in a comment on this text that "Christ, who fills all things, . . . himself is filled by the church. He . . . receives the church as that in which he himself is happy. . . . as his glorious and beautiful ornament. . . . as that in which he has exceeding and satisfying delight and joy" (15:186–87). He commented further in his "Miscellanies": "We are incomplete without that which we have a natural inclination to. Thus, man is incomplete without the woman, she is himself; so Christ is not complete without his spouse" (13:272; cf. 14:155). And in another, extraordinary entry in his manuscript "Notes on Scripture" (dealing with Luke 1:35), Edwards added a comment so graphic that it is worth quoting here at length:

> As the blessed Virgin nourished her babe with milk from her paps, with nourishment from her breast, and as it were flowing from her heart, so Christ is as it were refreshed with the exercises of grace that flow from the hearts of the saints, and their good works, which are often represented in Scripture as the fruit and food that Christ expects, feeds on, and is delighted in. 'Tis that which is food to Christ in the heart, or the principle of grace there, which is as a newborn child, and causes it to grow. And the exercises and fruits of grace, that come from the hearts of the saints, do as it were nourish Christ's interest in the world, and cause Christ's mystical body, which is small as in infancy, to be strengthened and increased. (15:288–89)[17]

These exercises that fill, strengthen, and increase the body of Christ usually involve a great deal of redemptive suffering, according to Edwards. For as he ruminated in a couple of his other manuscript compendia, the church fills up her Lord's body by participating in and thus extending his own suffering for the salvation of the world. Edwards wrote in his "Miscellanies" that "the members of the body as well as the head, that have prayed and labored for the advancement of Christ's kingdom, and have suffered for it, and therein been made partakers with their head in his labors and sufferings, have filled up what is lacking in the sufferings of Christ." And in "Images of Divine Things," he explained, again by maternal analogy: "Women travail and suffer great pains in bringing children [forth], which is to represent the great persecutions and sufferings of the church in bringing forth Christ and in increasing the number of his children; and a type of those spiritual pains that are in the soul when bringing forth Christ." Edwards believed, in other words, that in its suffering with Christ, the church, which is his body, gives birth to the elect, contributing to God's work of perfecting the mystical bride of Christ (18:426–27; 11:55; cf. 15:53).

It should be clear at this point that Edwards always viewed the church as an intimate company of God's lovers, and thus abhorred the adulterous affairs of religious hypocrites. He embraced the diversity of this company. For as he said to his own congregation, "God sees [it] to be for the beauty of Christ's body . . . that it should be constituted of different members that have a different work and office." But he emphasized the unity of the body above all. As he wrote to a clergy friend in Scotland, "the church of God, in all parts of the work is but one," for "the distant members are closely united in one glorious head." Indeed, the concordance of the church proved the central theme of Edwards' transatlantic *Humble Attempt to Promote Explicit Agreement and Visible Union of God's People in Extraordinary Prayer* (1747). For as he explained within that volume, "as 'tis the glory of the church of Christ, that she, in all her members, however dispersed, is thus *one*, one holy society, one city, one family, one body; so it is very desirable, that this union should be manifested, and become visible; and so, that her distant members should act as one, in those things that concern the common interest of the whole body." Preaching in 1741, on a day of thanksgiving in Northampton, Edwards compared the church's unity "with the notes of a melodious tune": "the single notes separated one from another, and considered without any relation one to another, are without harmony. But they have their harmony from their being united fitly and aptly, united one to another, and the sweet relation they bear to each other" (14:270–72; 16:180; 5:365; Ex. 10:9, F. 22, L. 3r; cf. Col. 1:24, F. 791, passim, and Ps. 106:5, F. 174, L. 11v).

Further, the sweet and harmonious chords that make up the symphony of the saints were not to be intruded upon by the cacophony of those who refuse to play the Lord's song. For Edwards, "the church is heavenly and spiritual." Indeed, "she is not of this world." In fact, as he explained to his congregation in August of 1743, the saints "are a small number in comparison of the rest of the world." They "are a company . . . greatly distinguished." They "are strangers on earth (1 Pet. 2:11)." Though they "sojourn here," they clearly "don't belong here." In short, the saints "are in many respects separated from the rest of the world." Their symphony is set apart, a royal tune played only to God (5:186; Num. 23:9, F. 38, L. 3v–6v).

Consequently, Edwards emphasized throughout his doctrinal career the importance of realizing, or manifesting, the intimacy of the church in local congregational life. Long before his own dismissal, he was delineating forcefully between true and false religion, the invisible church and its visible counterpart, spiritual and carnal Christians, the heart's confession and that of the lips.[18] He did this most famously in the treatise *Religious Affections* (1746). But he did it earlier too, distinguishing consistently between *true* Christians and "all those that are called Christians, or are [Christ's] professed and visible people." In the winter of 1737, in a lengthy sermon series on Jesus' parable of the wise and foolish virgins (Matt. 25:1–12), Edwards explained in great detail that "the visible church of Christ is made up of true and false Christians," and that while "those two sorts of Christians do in many things agree," yet "in many other things" they "greatly differ."[19] He reminded his people frequently, both early and late in his ministry, that "they are not all Israel that are of Israel. . . . the part of the world that is called the Christian world is very large, comprising many whole nations. But Christ's flock is but small in comparison." Indeed, "they are but a handful. They are but thinly sewn here and there in the Christian world." Or as he put it to his parishioners in 1735, " 'tis not all them that profess Christianity, 'tis not all them that are Protestants, 'tis not all that are Presbyterians, 'tis not all that come to the sacrament that are really of the church. They are not all Israel that are of Israel (Rom. 9:6), but they only are of the church that are Israelites indeed in whom there is no guile" (Matt. 25:1–12, F. 505, L. 2r; Is. 45:25, F. 305, L. 1v–2r; Eph. 5:25–27, F. 781, L. 2r; cf. Ps. 106:5, F. 174, L. 10v–18r; Col. 1:24, F. 791, L. 2v–3r).

It is no wonder, then, that during and after New England's Great Awakening Edwards called for stricter standards of church membership in Northampton. He was never a Separatist (2:86; 4:474–83; 12:171; "Misc." 339, 13:414; 16:343), but even while perpetuating Solomon Stoddard's inclusive approach to church membership, he had always pushed for the purity of his parish. As Edwards wrote in the *Humble Inquiry*:

> I have formerly been of [Stoddard's] opinion, which I imbibed from his books, even from my childhood, and have in my proceedings conformed to his practice; though never without some difficulties in my view, which I could not solve: yet, however, a distrust of my own understanding, and deference to the authority of so venerable a man, the seeming strength of some of his arguments, together with the success he had in his ministry, and his great reputation and influence, prevailed for a long time to bear down my scruples. (12:169)

A paper trail of Edwards' "scruples" can be traced throughout his private notebooks beginning at least as early as 1728. For though he maintained his grandfather's policy on church membership for two decades, he had to live with a fair amount of cognitive dissonance as a result. In the summer of 1728, he wrote in a "Miscellanies" entry that membership in the local church was only for those who appear "true Christians." In the spring of 1730, he added that "none should be admitted to any church privileges, to have their children baptized, or to be looked upon as of the visible church of Christ, but those that come to the Lord's Supper," making clear his disagreement not only with Stoddard's membership policy but also with the more common use of New England's "Half-Way Covenant."[20] He continued, those who come to the Supper "ought all to be sufficiently instructed, that they must be Christians really, in order to come—for only the righteous have any right to the privileges of the church." They "must examine and prove themselves, whether or no they believe the gospel with all their hearts . . . and whether or no they are brought thoroughly to forsake all ways of sin . . . and whether they are fully and seriously determined so to do to the end, through all opposition; and whether they live in charity with all Christians." Edwards reiterated this notion at the acme of the Awakening: "they should profess their faith in Jesus Christ, including a credible profession of the Christian religion. . . . they ought to profess sincere, real faith or an hearty embracing [of] Christ, and reliance upon him as the Savior" ("Misc." 335, 13:411; "Misc." 338, 13:413; "Misc." 462, 13:503; and "Misc." 873, 20:112–15).

Such a profession of genuine faith was all that Edwards ever desired—despite the lingering misconception that he was ejected from his pulpit for reinstituting the requirement (upheld most famously by the Puritans) of a public conversion relation prior to one's admission into church membership.[21] As Edwards expressed his view to the Reverend Peter Clark before his dismissal, "the great thing which I have scrupled in the established method of this church's proceeding, and which I dare no longer go on in, is their publicly assenting to the form of words rehearsed on occasion of admission to the communion, without pretending thereby to mean any such thing as an hearty consent to the terms of the gospel covenant."[22] He explained:

> I can conceive of no such virtue in a certain set of words, that 'tis proper, merely on the making these sounds, to admit persons to Christian sacraments, without any regard to any pretended meaning of those sounds. . . . It doesn't belong to the controversy between me and my people, how particular or large the profession should be that is required. . . . I should content myself with a few words, briefly expressing the cardinal virtues or acts implied in a hearty compliance with the covenant, made . . . understandingly, if there were an external conversation agreeable thereto. Yea, I should think that such a person

solemnly making such a profession, had a right to be received as the object of a public charity, however he himself might scruple his own conversion, on account of his not remembering the time, not knowing the method of his conversion, or finding so much remaining sin, etc. . . . for I call that a profession of godliness, which is a profession of the great things wherein godliness consists; and not a professing his own opinion of his good estate. (16:344–45)

The details of one's conversion need not be rehearsed—let alone scrutinized—before the congregation. Indeed, they need not be understood by those who sought to join the church. Rather, such people needed simply to demonstrate *true* Christianity, the kind of faith that stemmed from a mystical, supernatural union with Christ. Or as Edwards summarized to his parish in the midst of this dispute, "'tis the mind and will of God that none should be admitted to full communion in the church of Christ but such as in profession and in the eye of a reasonable judgment are truly saints or godly persons" (Ezek. 44:9, L. 2v, Edwards Collection, Andover-Newton Theological School).

There is little evidence of any change in Edwards' doctrine of the church after the waning of the revivals. He had always opposed both separatism and hypocritical profession and had done so on the basis of the metaphysical principle of the church's unity as the mystical body of Christ. But it is no coincidence, either, that Edwards worked hardest to *align* Northampton's polity with his doctrine beginning in the early 1740s. For by the dawn of that fateful decade, he feared that his own church harbored an alarming number of Christian hypocrites, a number expanded in the heat of the revivals. Already in 1739, Edwards had overseen the first excommunication from Northampton's congregation in thirty years (i.e., since 1711), when Abigail Bridgman was removed for habitual drunkenness. In June 1740, he led in the founding of a local committee for "Considering causes and matters of difficulty that should arise in the Church," institutionalizing his concern to promote the purity of Christ's bride. The following month he publicly shamed another parishioner, Hannah Pomeroy, for transgressing the ninth commandment in "vilifying & Reproaching her neighbor Sarah [Clap]." In August 1741, he excommunicated Pomeroy for refusing to repent. In 1742, after a great deal of cajoling, he persuaded his congregation to renew its corporate covenant with their Lord, pledging again "to seek and serve God" by practicing Christian charity. In February 1743, he led in rebuking Bathsheba Kingsley, an itinerant minister from nearby Westfield who claimed immediate revelation and then neglected her wifely duties in the pursuit of a preaching ministry. In June 1743, he excommunicated yet another parishioner, Samuel Danks, for fornication and "contempt of the Authority of the Church." In 1744, he prosecuted Northampton's "Bad

Book" case, admonishing several young men in town for lascivious use of a midwives' manual. In 1747 and 1748, he took on two more cases of fornication, attempting (but failing) to require Lieutenant Elisha Hawley and Thomas Wait to marry the women they had impregnated, Martha Root and Jemima Miller. And in 1749, he excommunicated Hawley. In short, Edwards labored long and hard on the purity of his church, especially in the wake of the revivals. He preached quite often on matters of discipline. His ejection from Northampton in the summer of 1750 was but the tragic culmination of his struggle to embody in his local congregation what he took to be the nature of the true, or invisible, church.[23]

Likewise, Edwards' late decision to restrict the sacraments in Northampton to those who made a "true" profession proved novel only in its consistency with his doctrine of the church, and not as a deviation in his sacramental theology. For as Edwards had penned in his "Miscellanies" during the middle of the 1730s, "union with Christ, or a being in Christ, is the foundation of all communion with him." Or as he specified from the pulpit as early as 1735, "this is one end of Christ's appointing ordinances: that he might in them meet with his church, might bring her near to him, to behold him and to have communion with him. And this is especially one end of the Lord's Supper: that in that ordinance Christ might as it were bring his church to him, into his banqueting house, and present her to himself in sweet and holy communion." Indeed, for Edwards, the church's sacraments had always been interpreted best as "signs" and "seals" of real, spiritual fellowship with her Lord. They functioned as false, confusing signs when made available to the once-born. For as he reiterated when Northampton's communion controversy was brewing, "the Lord's Supper is a feast appointed to signify and seal Christians' union to Christ, and one to another," not any union that Christians might have with the unregenerate. The saints commune in the eucharist with "the universal church," and not with those who dwell completely outside the body of Christ. In fact, "the thing designed in the sacrament . . . is the communion of Christians in the body and blood of Christ," a participation in his passion, one that was intimate and intense, one that was not to be taken lightly or demeaned by unbelief ("Misc." 683, 18:247; Eph. 5:25–27, F. 781, L. 18r; 1 Cor. 10:16, F. 731, L. 2r–2v; 1 Cor. 10:17, F. 732, L. 1v; 1 Cor. 10:16, F. 730, L. 2v and 5v–6r; cf. 12:227–30).

When seen from this angle, then, it is clear that even Northampton's communion controversy had been impending for many years and cannot be understood without reference to Edwards' ecclesiology. As he summarized for his own church at the end of the Awakening, there are several realities that "appertain to the nature of the church" and that are rightly assessed only in relation to one another. Edwards listed these things as follows: "1. The members of the church of Christ. 2. Their relation and union to Christ. 3. Their distinction and separation from the world. 4. The causes and means of this distinction. 5. Their union and communion one with another. 6. The ends for which they are thus separated from the world and united to Christ and one another." As such exposition makes evident, Edwards maintained from first to last that the local church is most significant for its place in the body of Christ. Moreover, its worship and its sacraments involve a real participation in the glorification of God, *in* the person of the Son and by the power of the Spirit. To be sure, local history and popular religion played their part in Edwards' ejection from Northampton, but for him—and, no doubt, for many of his theologically inclined parishioners—Northampton's controversy had *most* to do with the doctrine of the church. Indeed, as was often the case in the life and work of Northampton's peculiar pastor, there was more to this dispute than meets the eye (Col. 1:24, F. 791, L. 3v–4r).

Notes

1. I am grateful to Kenneth P. Minkema for insightful comments on a draft of this chapter.

2. "Ecclesiology" is a technical, theological term that refers to the study of the church.

3. See also David D. Hall, "'Between the Times': Popular Religion in Eighteenth-Century British North America," in Michael V. Kennedy and William G. Shade, eds., *The World Turned Upside-Down: The State of Eighteenth-Century Studies at the Beginning of the Twenty-First Century* (Bethlehem, Pa.: Lehigh University Press, 2001), pp. 142–63.

4. Unless otherwise noted, the manuscript sermons quoted in this chapter are held in the Edwards collection of the Beinecke Rare Book and Manuscript Library at Yale University and are cited by biblical text, folder, and leaf. Further, inasmuch as Edwards' idiom is saturated with the phraseology of the King James Bible, and to avoid excessive editorial intrusion, I have tried as much as possible to limit my identification of his biblical phraseology *within quotations* to those instances where Edwards himself cited the Bible verses used.

5. Thomas A. Schafer, "Jonathan Edwards' Conception of the Church," *Church History* 24 (1955): 62.

6. For useful commentary on this notion, consult Sang Hyun Lee, *The Philosophical Theology of Jonathan Edwards* (Princeton: Princeton University Press, 1988). The term "Godhead" refers to the divine nature and divine life shared among the persons of the Holy Trinity (Father, Son, and Holy Spirit). The term "immanent Trinity" refers to the inner-Trinitarian life of God, or the activity of God within the Godhead. It is often distinguished from the term "economic Trinity," which refers to the life and activity of the Father, Son, and Holy Spirit within the "economy" of redemption (i.e., within the world).

7. On this point, see also Krister Sairsingh, "Jonathan Edwards and the Idea of Divine Glory: His Foundational Trinitarianism and Its Ecclesial Import" (Ph.D. diss., Harvard University, 1986). But note the correction to Sairsingh's account of this doxological dynamic in Stephen R. Holmes, *God of Grace and God of Glory: An Account of the Theology of Jonathan Edwards* (Grand Rapids: Eerdmans, 2001), p. 189.

8. See also Edwards' sermon "The Threefold Work of the Holy Ghost" (14:402–4), in which he adds that "this union of Christ to us . . . consists in two *things*, viz. union of nature, and love" (p. 403, emphasis mine).

9. On this theme, see also the two essays in Edwards' "Controversies" notebook entitled "Question: Wherein Do the Two Covenants Agree as to the Method of Justification, and the Appointed Qualification For It" and "The Things Wherein the Way of Justification by Mere Law and That by Grace Through Christ Differ as to the Qualification of the Subject that Primarily Entitles Him to Justification"(21:354–71).

10. But note that elsewhere Edwards refers to the church in general as Christ's mother. In his treatise *Religious Affections*, he wrote: "The ingenerating of a principle of grace in the soul, seems in Scripture to be compared to the conceiving of Christ in the womb (Gal. 4:19). And therefore the church is called Christ's mother (Cant. 3:11). And so is every particular believer (Matt. 12:49–50). And the conception of Christ in the womb of the blessed Virgin, by the power of the Holy Ghost, seems to be a designed resemblance of the conception of Christ in the soul of a believer, by the power of the same Holy Ghost" (2:161).

11. On this theme, see the important essay by Paul Ramsey, "Heaven Is a Progressive State" (8:706–38).

12. Edwards often extended his narrative description of this relationship into eternity, teaching that thenceforth Christ will "lead" his new bride in her "praises" of his Father. After their wedding day, moreover, the church shall reign with Christ forever, enjoying "dominion" with her king, "for they shall sit with him in his throne." Further, "as Christ is Lord of the angels, so the saints shall in some sort reign over angels in heaven." In fact, "this dominion will extend to all things that shall be theirs. Whatsoever they shall inherit as joint heirs with Christ, they shall in some respect reign over as kings with Christ" (Rev. 19:5–6, F. 920, L. 1v–2v; 18:300).

13. Correlatively, "Christ's heart is as it were ravished with the graces and holy exercises of his saints" (14:340).

14. On the Trinitarian foundations of this marital imagery in Edwards' writings, see especially Amy Plantinga Pauw, *The Supreme Harmony of All: The Trinitarian Theology of Jonathan Edwards* (Grand Rapids: Eerdmans, 2002). On the use of such erotic imagery among Edwards' Puritan forebears, see especially Richard Godbeer, " 'Love Raptures': Marital, Romantic, and Erotic Images of Jesus Christ in Puritan New England, 1670–1730," *New England Quarterly* 68 (1995): 355–84.

15. Janice Knight, in *Orthodoxies in Massachusetts: Rereading American Puritanism* (Cambridge, Mass.: Harvard University Press, 1994), describes the "Spiritual Brethren" in this way: "More emotional and even mystical [than their

New England counterparts, depicted by Knight as "Intellectual Fathers"], their theology stressed divine benevolence over power. Emphasizing the love of God, they converted biblical metaphors of kingship into ones of kinship. They substituted a free testament or voluntary bequeathing of grace for the conditional covenant described by the other orthodoxy" (p. 3).

16. Edwards affirmed that as the "fulness" of the Godhead, the Holy Spirit is also the bond of union both within the immanent Trinity and between God and his redeemed. On this doctrine and its ecclesiological import, see also Robert W. Caldwell III, "The Holy Spirit as the Bond of Union in the Theology of Jonathan Edwards" (Ph.D. diss., Trinity International University, 2003).

17. Lee, *The Philosophical Theology of Jonathan Edwards*, pp. 227–31, provides helpful commentary on the metaphysical basis of Edwards' interpretation of the church as "the completeness of Christ."

18. Much has been written on Edwards' view of the nature of true religion. For a brief introduction to this topic (discussed in relation to the writings of Edwards' Puritan predecessors and with a view to the importance of true religion for ecclesiology), see especially William K. B. Stoever, "The Godly Will's Discerning: Shepard, Edwards, and the Identification of True Godliness," in Stephen J. Stein, ed., *Jonathan Edwards' Writings: Text, Context, Interpretation* (Bloomington: Indiana University Press, 1996), pp. 85–99.

19. The best summary and analysis of this famous sermon series is found in Ava Chamberlain, "Brides of Christ and Signs of Grace: Edwards' Sermon Series on the Parable of the Wise and Foolish Virgins," in Stein, ed., *Jonathan Edwards' Writings*, pp. 3–18.

20. On the Half-Way Covenant and its history, see Robert G. Pope, *The Half-Way Covenant: Church Membership in Puritan New England* (Princeton: Princeton University Press, 1969). Samuel Hopkins, *The Life and Character of the Late Reverend Mr. Jonathan Edwards*... (Boston: S. Kneeland, 1765), p. 57, reported that Edwards went public with his change of mind on the Lord's Supper in the spring of 1744, and that this incited a great uproar in Northampton.

21. On the Puritans' practice of requiring a public relation of one's conversion experience before admission into the church, see especially Patricia Caldwell, *The Puritan Conversion Narrative: The Beginnings of American Expression* (New York: Cambridge University Press, 1983).

22. The "form of words" used for admission to church membership during Northampton's Stoddardean era may be found in the records of the First Church of Christ, Northampton, book 1, entry dated November 5, 1672, Forbes Library, Northampton: Massachusetts "A form of words to be used on the admission of members into full communion. You doe here publickly take hold of the covenant of the Lord, giving up your selfe unto him, to be one of his, subjecting your selfe to the teachings & government of Jesus Christ in this Church, & engage according to your place & power to promote the welfare thereof. & we do publickly acknowledge you a member of this Church in full communion promising to bear towards you in brotherly love, to watch over you for the good of your soule, to take care of your instruction & government in the Lord, & to make you partaker of all such priviledges as by the rules of [Christ] belong to you." For Edwards' opinion of "the

profession persons ought to make explicitly when they come into the visible church," see especially his discussion in "Miscellanies," no. 873 (20:112f.). For insightful commentary on Edwards' concern over Northampton's form of words, see Christopher Grasso, "Misrepresentations Corrected: Jonathan Edwards and the Regulation of Religious Discourse," in Stein, *Jonathan Edwards' Writings*, pp. 19–38.

23. On these cases of discipline and their significance, see the records of the First Church of Christ, Northampton, book 1, p. 25, Forbes Library, Northampton, Massachusetts; Deut. 29:18–21, F. 54 (a disciplinary sermon preached against Bridgman's drunkenness); "The Means and Ends of Excommunication" (22:68–79); "Miscellanies," nos. 485 (13:171–73, 527); "Copy of a Covenant, enter'd into and Subscribed, by the People of God at Northampton . . . on a Day of Fasting and Prayer for the gracious Presence of God in that Place. March 16, 1741, 2," Edwards Collection, Andover-Newton Theological School; Josh. 24:15–27, F. 66 (preached in March 1742 regarding Northampton's covenant renewal); "Fair Copy of Kingsley Case," Congregational Library, London, signed by a group of ministers, including Jonathan Edwards, in Westfield on February 17, 1742/43 (4:454–58); and "Some Reasons briefly hinted at, why Those Rules Exod. 22:16, & Deut. 22:28–29, relating to the Obligation of a man to marry a virgin that He had humbled, ought to be esteemed, as to the substance of them, as moral & of perpetual Obligation; with Hints of Answer to Objections," Edwards Collection, Andover-Newton Theological School (on the Hawley/Root fornication case of 1747/48). On Northampton's "Bad Book" case, see especially Ava Chamberlain, "Bad Books and Bad Boys: The Transformation of Gender in Eighteenth-Century Northampton," in David W. Kling and Douglas A. Sweeney, eds., *Jonathan Edwards at Home and Abroad: Historical Memories, Cultural Movements, Global Horizons* (Columbia: University of South Carolina Press, 2003).

Suggested Further Readings

Cooper, James F., Jr. *Tenacious of Their Liberties: The Congregationalists in Colonial Massachusetts*. Religion in America Series. New York: Oxford University Press, 1999.

Danaher, William J., Jr. "By Sensible Signs Represented: Jonathan Edwards' Sermons on the Lord's Supper." *Pro Ecclesia* 7 (1998): 261–87.

De Jong, Peter Y. "Jonathan Edwards: The Half-Way Covenant Attacked." In *The Covenant Idea in New England Theology, 1620–1847*, pp. 136–52. Grand Rapids: Eerdmans, 1945.

Hall, David D. "Editor's Introduction." *The Works of Jonathan Edwards*, 12, Ecclesiastical Writings. Ed. David D. Hall. New Haven: Yale University Press, 1994.

Haroutunian, Joseph. "Sinners and Saints in Full Communion." In *Piety Versus Moralism: The Passing of the New England Theology*, pp. 97–130. Hamden, Conn.: Archon Books, 1964.

Holmes, Stephen R. "The Community of God's Glory." In *God of Grace and*

God of Glory: An Account of the Theology of Jonathan Edwards, pp. 169–97. Grand Rapids: Eerdmans, 2001.

Jamieson, John F. "Jonathan Edwards and the Renewal of the Stoddardean Controversy." Ph.D. diss., University of Chicago, 1978.

———. "Jonathan Edwards' Change of Position on Stoddardeanism." *Harvard Theological Review* 74 (1981): 79–99.

McCoy, Michael Ryan. "In Defense of the Covenant: The Sacramental Debates of Eighteenth-Century New England (Puritanism)." Ph.D. diss., Emory University, 1986.

Sairsingh, Krister. "Jonathan Edwards and the Idea of Divine Glory: His Foundational Trinitarianism and Its Ecclesial Import." Ph.D. diss., Harvard University, 1986.

Schafer, Thomas A. "Jonathan Edwards' Conception of the Church." *Church History* 24 (1955): 51–66.

Stuart, Robert Lee. "'Mr. Stoddard's Way': Church and Sacraments in Northampton." *American Quarterly* 24 (1972): 243–53.

Tracy, Patricia J. *Jonathan Edwards, Pastor: Religion and Society in Eighteenth-Century Northampton*. New York: Hill & Wang, 1979.

Walker, George L. "Jonathan Edwards and the Half-Way Covenant." *The New Englander* 43 (1884): 601–14.

Thirteen

Typology

Janice Knight

THROUGHOUT HIS remarkable career, Jonathan Edwards celebrated the coherence and beauty of God's creation. In private notebooks, sermons, and treatises he contemplated "what was aimed at or designed in the creating of the astonishing fabric of the universe which we behold." He concluded that God ceaselessly reveals himself alike "by his *word* and *works*" and that the joy and duty of the Christian is to observe and praise this sacred design (8:419, 422). Eagerly discharging this task, Edwards searched the world as well as the Bible for signs of God's intent. He read the drama of Christ's death and resurrection in the cycles of the sun, the phases of the moon, and even in the emergence of the silkworm from its cocoon. In the hand-stitched journal he sometimes titled "The Images of Divine Things," sometimes "The Language and Lessons of Nature," Edwards made over two hundred entries showing how "the works of nature are intended and contrived of God to signify . . . spiritual things" (11:66). And in the thirty sermons that compose *A History of the Work of Redemption*, he traced God's providential design not only in traditional biblical chronicles but also in such events as the English Civil War. Though Scripture remained the surest guide to holy truths, in documents like these Edwards declared his faith that nature and human history are also legitimate sources of revelation, communicating God's purpose to his saints.

Typology was the interpretive key to these divine communications; Edwards argued that, properly understood, it could unlock God's intentions in the created world and in Scripture. In its narrowest definition, typology was a mode of biblical interpretation, an ancient science of reading that united the two Testaments. By means of this literary device, exegetes interpreted Jewish scripture in the light of Christian experience; they read specific events and persons of the Old Testament as symbolic prefigurations, or "types," of things fulfilled in the New. Thus David, as a type, anticipated the Messiah; the Exodus of the Jews from Egypt foreshadowed Christ's, sojourn in the wilderness. More than mere allegories or chance resemblances, such biblical types were divinely ordained prefigurations of specific future persons or events. Historically significant in themselves, they also prophesied the life of Christ.

While traditional exegetes allowed that God sometimes communicates spiritual truths through emblems in nature, they reminded their readers that revelation through natural types is unusual, limited to specific historical instances and scriptural stories. They explained, for example, that while the rock that Moses struck was indeed a divinely ordained type of Christ, ordinary rocks in nature hold no such honored place.[1] Countering this conservative tradition, Jonathan Edwards claimed that meaningful divine types overflow such narrow biblical boundaries. He described typology as a "certain sort of Language, as it were, in which God is wont to speak to us" (11:150). This divine speech is neither circumscribed by the Word nor completely fulfilled by the Incarnation. Edwards heard God's voice still sounding in nature, in human history, and in the flow of contemporary events.

Edwards contended, moreover, that God's extrascriptural communications are neither serendipitous nor occasional. Instead, they are part of a divinely instituted system of symbols that continuously prefigure and communicate the divine presence in nature and in history (8:564). God displays his will through a wide variety of types: "Thus God glorifies Himself and instructs the minds that He has made" ("Misc." 362, 13:435). In harmony with this emphasis on God's benevolent tutorship, Edwards identified sainthood with a new sense or knowledge of divine things. Grace endows the believer with a capacity to perceive God's presence in his own heart and in the wider world. With new eyes to see and new ears to hear, the true Christian can read sermons in stones and portents in the rituals of daily life.

Furthermore, God's communications accelerate as the work of redemption progresses; the unfolding of each successive period in sacred history brings greater knowledge of the divine, especially at the thresholds when one providential era gives way to the next. Describing the shift from the Old Testament world to that of the New, Edwards remarked, "[W]hat a great increase is here of the light of the gospel . . . [H]ow plentiful are the revelations and prophecies of Christ now to what they were in the first Old Testament period" (9:240). Prophecies become more exact; types become more frequent and more perfect in their prefiguring of the Messiah. This is, of course, a highly traditional interpretation of biblical types.

Less conventional was Edwards' claim that divine communications will continue to expand, in frequency and in kind, with the approach of the millennium. Just as the gospel light intensified with the first coming of Christ, so with the coming of his kingdom knowledge of heavenly things will increase, extending beyond the Bible to include revelation through nature and human history. In his most jubilant moods Edwards expressed faith that this process was already underway. He observed, for example, that "the late invention of telescopes, whereby heavenly objects are brought so much nearer and made so much plainer to sight . . . is a type and forerunner of the great increase in the knowledge of heavenly things that shall be in the approaching glorious times of the Christian church" (11:101).

Edwards trusted that this new age would be a "time wherein holiness should be as it were inscribed on everything, on all men's common business and employments, and the common utensils of life, all shall be dedicated to God" (5:338). In the latter days, the diverse discourses of nature, history, science, and business will be read as varieties of religious expression—varieties heralding the millennium by their very multiplication. Moreover, the company of saints will swell: "the whole earth shall be united as one holy city, one heavenly family, men of all nations shall as it were dwell together, and sweetly correspond one with another as brethren and children of the same father" (5:339). Simply stated, Edwards' theory of typology rested on a faith that the coming of the kingdom establishes God's glory on earth as it is in heaven.[2]

From this brief summary one would scarcely guess that for over forty years scholars have hotly debated the origins and orthodoxy of Edwards' typological theories. Perry Miller was the first to remark Edwards' extension of typology from Scripture to nature, and his 1948 introduction to *Images or Shadows of Divine Things* set the terms for the current critical disputes. To place the present article in context, it will help to comment on the pertinent scholarship before turning to Edwards' own exposition of his methods and purposes.

Miller argued that Edwards' embrace of nature as a type of the divine was a daring innovation that coupled Newton's claims of divine uniformity in nature with Locke's principles of sensational psychology. He observed that for Edwards "the pattern of the cosmos is infinite representation, and thereby intelligible"—intelligible, that is, to the regenerate sensibility. Natural imagery, theretofore regulated by conservative exegetes and "utilized only for similitude and metaphor," was transformed by Edwards into a coherent system of symbols. Nature "was a living system of concepts; it was a complete, intelligible whole." And, just as the new science generated attempts to standardize the system of human discourse, culminating in Dr. Johnson's *Dictionary*, so Edwards struggled to subject the language of nature "to the rule of the idea" and aspired to transcribe "a dictionary of divine discourse."[3] The typologizing of nature, then, was the fruit of Edwards' larger project of joining the lessons of the new science and psychology to the verities of the old piety.

To Miller, this "exaltation of nature to a level of authority coequal with revelation" separated Edwards from his Puritan ancestors. Though the deployment of scientific metaphors and the tendency to read traces of divinity in nature were common practices among New England divines,

Miller claimed that the system of analogies allowing Edwards to discern "the intention of God" in his creation violated the essential Puritan principles of divine sovereignty and mystery.[4] Only the metaphysics of the new science could account for Edwards' revolutionary claim that "the agreement between the animal creation and the divine idea would be exactly the same *kind* of agreement as between the types of the Old Testament and their antitype."[5]

Miller's interpretation has been subjected to extensive criticism and revision. Some scholars, disputing Miller's emphasis on Locke and Newton, insist that Edwards' immaterialism was inspired by such rationalist metaphysicians as Malebranche. They argue that Neoplatonism, not science, sanctioned his reading of the created world as a reflection of the spirit.[6] Though this position helps explain the source of Edwards' idealism, it does not account for his insistence on the historical dimension of types in nature. For Edwards, the material world never dissolves into pure spirit but instead becomes infused with greater sacred meaning as the millennium approaches. His Neoplatonism was always tempered by his keen interest in providential history.

Other critics object to Miller's stress on the new science as ceding too much importance to natural revelation and minimizing what they see as Edwards' conservative scripturalism and radical theism. They argue that orthodox theology must be based on a fundamental sense of God's power and transcendence. An unbridgeable gap separates the Creator from his creation; God's absolute sovereignty renders nature mute.[7] By their lights, Miller was simply wrong in suggesting that Edwards regarded nature as a reliable guide to spiritual truths. Yet, as I will show, Edwards maintained that God's sovereignty is never compromised by his delight in communicating himself through nature. Moreover, Edwards' position was completely orthodox; a century earlier, preachers like Richard Sibbes often observed that God's effulgent communications are witnessed throughout creation.[8]

Finally, scholars have reproved Miller for misreading Edwards' methods with respect to the typological practices of his contemporaries. In reconstructing the tradition of Protestant typology, these critics stress distinctions between natural and scriptural types they claim Miller blurred and emphasize even more strongly the innovativeness of Edwards' theories.[9] Separating natural symbols from biblical types, they identify the use of images from nature with liberal typology and specify that analogies between nature and spirit are ontological correspondences, not historical types. Conservative typology, on the other hand, is strictly historical, rooted in the biblical pattern of adumbration and fulfillment. These types "look forward in time, not upward through the scale of being," as do natural emblems. Briefly stated, conservative typology is one of historical existences while liberal typology is one of ontological essences.[10]

These same interpreters of Edwards claim that orthodox Protestants were skeptical about the allegorizing tendencies they associated with Catholic hermeneutics. Suspicious of the unrestrained use of ontological types, most reformers subjected imaginative and personal extension of typology to a strict standard of biblical and historical veracity. From this perspective, Edwards' embrace of natural types represented a loss of the historical dimension. While Miller argued that Edwards saw symmetry between ontology and history, these scholars claim that his natural typology "is in all respects a very different order of perception from the epistemology that is based on biblical exegesis and scriptural typology."[11]

The example of such orthodox spiritualizers as Edward Taylor and John Flavel notwithstanding, this construction implicitly suggests that Edwards' liberalized typology was somehow inconsistent with his highly conventional theology. Since the primary aim and achievement of such studies is to map Edwards' position with respect to orthodox tradition, they give less attention to the internal coherence of his theories. Consequently, Edwards is cast as a thinker divided against himself—a conservative theologian trying to liberalize the typological theories of his contemporaries.[12] Thus placed against the horizon of his period, Edwards becomes the great reconciler of warring traditions; read forward in time, he becomes the father of Emersonian idealism.

These valuable studies have corrected misapprehension and enriched our reading of Edwards. Yet taken together they are contradictory and raise as many questions as they answer about his typological practices. This difficulty arises at least in part from the focus of the studies; debate over Miller's claims too often sidetracks examination of Edwards' own writings. The alternative here proposed evaluates Edwards' typology within the context of his own first principles.

Contrary to revisionist claims, this approach reveals that Edwards' idealism was always balanced by a sense of the importance of nature as a vehicle of God's progressive communications. Furthermore, the desire to communicate does not compromise God's majesty but instead fulfills it. Finally, the most striking aspect of Edwards' reading of natural types is his complete inattention to the competing claims of Scripture and nature, history and ontology. Though the emphases differ from document to document, Edwards always wove ontological and historical types together in his writings. Despite the supposed strictures of Protestant typologists, he simply did not respect categorical distinctions, nor was this neglect motivated by desire to reform contemporary practice. Not the new science but his own certainty that a "lovely proportion and beautiful harmony" characterize God's world and his works enabled Edwards to posit a symmetry between the works of creation and redemption, nature and spirit.[13]

John Wilson has inaugurated the reappraisal of Edwards' typology, shrewdly emphasizing the intellectual coherence of his works.[14] More work must be done to locate typology within the larger architecture of Edwards' thought. This essay considers the relationship Edwards described between ontology and history and then explores the authority by which he blurred these traditional categories. When seen in the context of his thought, Edwards' typology seems less a forged union of opposites than an expression of a deeply felt, original harmony flowing from an integrated theology and expressed from the earliest to the final works.

There are several ways to test this assertion of the internal harmony of Edwards' thought. We can begin by examining documents that scholars have characterized as typologically liberal or conservative to see if those classifications will hold. More frequently rejecting than preserving these distinctions, Edwards merged ontology and history not only within the body of his texts but also within specific individual types. Key documents reveal that for Edwards these categories reflected human limitation; they did not measure divine things.

For example, Edwards undermined such artificial differences by presenting historical and ontological types side by side within a single text. Even in what critics consider his most conservative typological treatise, *A History of the Work of Redemption*, he freely mixed natural types with more traditional scriptural prefigurations. In the midst of a highly conventional discussion of the Old Testament church, he introduced the image of the moon's approaching conjunction with the sun to signify the decline of "the Jewish church from the time of its highest glory in Solomon's time" (9:229). Though in differing modes, these natural and scriptural types teach the same spiritual lesson: that a time of declining light or glory prepares the way, through contrast, for a greater period of illumination with the coming of the Son. No fanfare heralds the interjection of this ontological type to suggest that Edwards regarded it as a radical innovation. Rather, the image of the moon blends so organically with the historical types that it argues for an original wholeness in God's communications.

Similarly, Edwards drew an analogy between God's providence and "a large and long river, having innumerable branches beginning in different regions, and at a great distance one from another, and all conspiring to one common issue." Just as all dispensations of providence and all historical prefigurations flow from God as source or fountain, so they converge in Christ, who is the living water. The cycle is completed both in nature and in history with the passage to the "great ocean." God is "the head of the stream," as well as the "infinite ocean into which it empties itself" (9:520, 517).[15] The river is a perfect natural type for communicating the truth conveyed in scripture and realized in the history of redemption, that

God is the fountain "*of whom*, and *through whom*, and *to whom* is all being and all perfection" (8:551). These prepositions reveal that God is the essential conjunction, the active source and ultimate end of all things.

Such ontological types function as divinely instituted emblems, making immediately apprehensible the same spiritual truth that can be perceived with the unfolding of history (11:77). If the correspondence between these natural reflections and their spiritual realities was different *in kind* from historical adumbration and fulfillment, as some critics claim, Edwards did not seem to notice. Rather, these modes confirmed one another, offering the regenerate eye two ways of viewing a single truth. For the reader of Edwards' text or the auditor of his sermon, these natural types communicated in concentrated form (almost like a pictograph) the thesis unfolding in the treatise itself. The historical narrative and the natural image were merely alternative ways to understand the work of redemption and to retain it in the mind; the preacher, like God himself, used both to instruct and edify (11:191–95). Thus, while the "conservative" *Work of Redemption* predominantly examines historical, scriptural types, it by no means excludes the natural, ontological ones.

Similarly, in the documents critics identify with liberal typology, such as *Images or Shadows of Divine Things*, the historical dimension is not limited to a general or vague eschatological sense. Not only did Edwards include a number of traditional biblical types but several of his natural types exhibit the classic linear pattern of adumbration and fulfillment. One example, mentioned above, is "the late invention of telescopes," a "type and forerunner" of the millennial explosion of spiritual knowledge (11:101). Another is "the changing of the course of trade and the supplying of the world with its treasures from America." This material trade, too, anticipates the millennium, "when the world shall be supplied with spiritual treasures from America" (11:101). Such images prefigured the Second Advent in the same way that the Old Testament anticipated the New. In fact, as Edwards asserted in *Work of Redemption*, from the perspective of the Second Coming, "All that is before . . . are but images and shadows of this" (9:493).

This integration of ontological and historical types within the boundaries of a single text is only one of the ways that Edwards complicated the task of distinguishing liberal from conservative typology. Even more subtly, he blended these categories within specific, individual types. For Edwards, the most traditional biblical types retained an abiding ontological resonance, while the most radical natural emblems participated in the historical prefigurative pattern.

Edwards' reading of the "personal types" of Christ exemplifies this internal blending of categories in the biblical mode, a reading well within conservative practice. In *Work of Redemption* as well as in "Types of the

Messiah," Edwards presented Abraham and Moses, David and Solomon as divinely appointed, typical representations instituted "to exhibit and reveal" the coming Christ. Like everything in the Old Testament, these types are shadowy figures, "dark resemblances," "imperfect representation[s]" of Christ's light and glory (15:348). In the unfolding of time, with the approach of the Son, these shadows were infused with greater light, became more perfect images of the divine. David, as a "much greater type and ancestor of Christ" than Moses or Joshua, perfected the work that they began. "Of so much more glory was Christ accounted worthy" that there must be both a great number "of typical prophets, priests, and princes" and an increasing perfection among them in order to "complete one figure or shadow of that of which Christ was the antitype." In keeping with conservative theory, the Old Testament types were abrogated by Christ, "the substance of all the types and shadows" (9:218).

Yet there is an enduring value in these types of the Messiah that extends beyond their prefigurative function and must be termed ontological. Edwards observed that "like the lamps in the sanctuary," these figures will always radiate "a resemblance of spiritual light." They retain "a real value and excellency in themselves"; they endure as "mystical and symbolical representations of things of a higher and more divine nature," not just as that nature is revealed in time but also as it is manifested in the scale of being. Like the "gold and pearls, that were used in the sanctuary and priests' garments," Abraham and Isaac, David and Solomon forever retain a "resemblance of some real preciousness in the sight of God." Such continuing excellency and efficacy signified ontological value; as Edwards proclaimed, "the very nature of the thing makes it manifest" (11:306–7).

This enduring value is analogous to the continued efficacy of the moral law of the Old Testament, which endured beyond the fulfillment of ceremonial law. Just so, the exemplary value of christic types like David persisted beyond the Incarnation.[16] In this respect, Edwards' reading remained within the context of traditional typologizing. Yet, precisely at this juncture, even in conservative theory, the lines between ontology and history blurred. For Edwards, the tendency toward union of the two was even greater.

In the opening section of *Work of Redemption* Edwards shed light both on the distinction between exemplary and prophetic types and on the source of their continuing value. There he described a double process by which God effects his design. The first action is "[w]ith respect to the effect wrought on the souls" of men, by which "particular persons are actually redeemed." Identified with the covenant of grace, this personal "application of redemption" is "common to all ages from the fall of man to the end of the world." It is implemented "by repeating after continually working the same work over again, though in different persons from age to age" (9:120–21). The second action is "the Work of Redemption with respect to the grand design in general as it relates to the universal subject and end." Unlike the effect wrought on individual souls, this general work is carried on "not merely by the repeating and renewing the same effect on the different subjects of it, but by many successive works and dispensations of God, all tending to one great end ... altogether making up one great work" (9:121).

As Edwards explained, the *Work of Redemption* "chiefly ... insist[s] upon" the latter aspect—the unfolding of successive dispensations—"though not excluding" the repetitions common to all ages (9:122). This emphasis reflected a necessary textual economy rather than an essential preference. Indeed, Edwards fully explored the personal application of redemption in other works, such as *A Divine and Supernatural Light, Religious Affections,* and *Treatise on Grace.* Similarly, though these texts emphasized personal salvation, they did not exclude the grand historical design. As Edwards proclaimed, one aspect of redemption "necessarily supposes the other" (9:122). God effects redemption in the heart of each believer and through the successive ages of the church simultaneously.

This larger design established an intimate connection between ontology and history and confirmed the coincidental prefigurative and enduring value of the personal types. The evolution of types from shadows to ever more perfect images of the Messiah is part of the classic historical pattern of successive works by which the Old Testament scheme is brought to fulfillment in the New. In another sense, though still within this historical framework, the growing number and evolving perfection of the types reach beyond the Incarnation itself to foreshadow the glorious times of the church, marked by the "infinite progress and increase" of the body of saints, in whom "the image [of God] is more and more perfect" (8:443).

But Edwards refused to limit this progressive perfection of types to the historical dimension. He showed that a similar transformation is effected in every redeemed soul, but this change is, of course, ontological. It marks an ascent in the scale of being from an inferior to a superior state, from natural to spiritual creature. The effect wrought in this phase of redemption is "to restore the soul of man," to repair "the image of God [that] was ruined" by the Fall (9:124). This change in human essence is worked immediately by God, who restores "something of the same beautiful proportion in the image, which is in the original" (2:365). "The image is a true image," in which the redeemed soul mirrors spiritual excellency. While perfecting this reflection is reserved for the saints, the Old Testament figures nonetheless glow with the same spiritual light and become "themselves burning shining things" (2:343). They are ontological types of the internal and spiritual transformation that repeats within every saint from age to age. In this respect, the types of the Messiah manifest their enduring exemplary value and efficacy. Thus, in the personal types of the Messiah, as in the *Work of Redemption* itself, ontology is inextricably linked with history, and Edwards always presented the two in vital union. As historical prefigurations, these types are abrogated by Christ. But as images of individual redemption, they endure. For Edwards, the two senses of typology were not divisible even within the most conventional biblical examples.

By the same token, this interpenetration of categories is to be found in the natural types. Perhaps the most dramatic example is entry number fifty in *Images or Shadows* "The rising and setting of the sun is a type of the death and resurrection of Christ" (11:64). Scholars have used this image to illustrate the inviolable distinction between historical types and ontological analogies.[17] Yet Edwards' explication of this type in the conservative "Notes on the Bible" makes clear that he did not recognize a dichotomy of categories; rather than abandoning the pattern of adumbration and fulfillment, he argued instead for the historical veracity of the natural type. Like scriptural prefigurations, God instituted the setting sun "to be a type of Christ" (11:64). Since the work of creation preceded the work of redemption in the divine economy and in historical time, there is justice in asserting that God established a linear pattern in which nature anticipates Christ in the same way the Old Testament prefigures the New (9:509–10). The correspondence is more than analogical; Edwards explained events in the Savior's life in the language of antitypical fulfillment: "that the sun is a type of Christ was probably one reason why Christ's resurrection was about the time of the rising sun, i.e., because the rising of the sun is a type of the resurrection of Christ, as the sun setting is a type of the death of Christ"(11:64).

Contrary to the rules of conservative typologizing, but in keeping with his own sense of the coherence of God's revelations, Edwards insisted that the repetition of the type in nature does not violate its original prefigurative function: "it is no sign that it is not a type of the resurrection of Christ that is but once, for it is fit that the type should be repeated often but that the antitype should be but once" ("Note on Luke 23:44" in the "Blank Bible," vol. 24 of the Yale edition). He argued instead that a similar repetition of types is just as easily found in Scripture: "there must be a number of typical prophets ... to complete one figure or shadow of that of which Christ was the antitype" (9:218). In both nature and the Bible, the reason for this repetition is the same: "to signify the great importance of the antitype" (11:95). Moreover, the sense of equity discussed above with respect to the personal types of Christ also applies to natural ones. Just as the figure of David remains exemplary, so the seasons of the sun continually re-present a "lively" image of the divine (11:114).

As do biblical types, these natural figurings of Christ display degrees of perfection: "there is a like difference and variety in the light held forth by types as there is in the light of the stars in the night" (11:114). Edwards explicitly established a similarity between the calibration of perfection in nature and in Scripture. It is important to note that while scriptural prefigurations grow more perfect through time, the natural types ascend the scale of being, moving from the lower to the upper end of creation "in an infinite variety of degree" (11:114). Here again, Edwards' typology sanctified the blending of ontology and history. And this indissoluble bond finds its greatest earthly expression in the saint, who, as crown of creation and chief actor in history, is both an ontological and a historical anticipation of the perfection of Christ.

Even this brief examination of the typological texts suggests that Edwards married ontology to history in a depiction of the divine plan continually and simultaneously moving up the chain of being and through the unfolding of time. His typology unified seemingly diverse categories; it proved that the worlds of existence and of essence are one. Scripture joins with nature, just as the Old Testament joined with the New, in a linear prefiguration of God's grace and his glory.

Another way to consider the problem of Edwards' typology is to ask a slightly different, perhaps more philosophical question: for Edwards, what guaranteed this unity of seemingly disparate discourses? The answer is, of course, God himself. This answer, though obvious, is worth exploring. One must ask not only what in the specific constitution of God's nature upholds creation and makes the pattern of the universe intelligible but also what makes this diversity of discourses delightful.

While it may be true that Edwards' Lockean epistemology informed his new typology, it is more fundamentally correct to say that his conception of God inspired his innovations. Edwards ended "Types of the Messiah" with an assertion that "[t]he principles of human nature render TYPES a fit method of instruction," but he began that treatise with a prerequisite observation that "it has ever been God's manner from the beginning of the world, to exhibit and reveal future things by symbolical representations." Types are rendered a fit medium of communication not first by human nature but by God's manner of being. The creature's natural delight in, and disposition to receive, impression and instruction originate in God's inclination to glorify and communicate himself ("Misc." 370, 13:441–42).

Traditional piety, Neoplatonic idealism, and Lockean experimentalism are fused in Edwards' simply stated belief that "God is a communicating

Being" ("Misc." 332, 13:410). This attribute is primary in the divine nature and inspires human nature. Edwards' deity is not essentially an omnipotent sovereign or a benevolent judge, nor can excellency or beauty alone be considered his primary attributes. Scholars focusing on these qualities or on the Neoplatonic origins of Edwards' typology underestimate the dynamic nature of his deity and the prophetic, historical dimension of the types.[18] Edwards' fundamental conviction of God's effulgence underwrote his theory of divine communications that overflow the human categories of history and ontology. The first and essential attribute—the impetus in God's self-generation and his generation of the world—is being and its communication.

Only recently have scholars such as Sang Hyun Lee begun to appreciate the centrality of this dynamic conception of the deity to Edwards' thought.[19] It was implicit, for example, in Edwards' description of God's various attributes. Will and reason, though part of God's infinite being, are nonetheless mere aspects of his nature displayed "according to our way of conceiving of God" (2:255). Neither God's natural perfections (consisting of "his power, his knowledge whereby he knows all things, and his being eternal, from everlasting to everlasting, his omnipresence, and his awful and terrible majesty") nor his moral perfections (consisting in his "holiness . . . his purity and beauty as a moral agent . . . his righteousness, faithfulness and goodness") should be perceived as commanding an essential primacy (2:255). Instead, these are aspects of God's being exhibited to each believer in proportion to his or her disposition either to love God's holiness or to fear his power: "Like the two opposite scales of a balance," "God has wisely ordained, that these two opposite principles of love and fear, should rise and fall," and with them God's nature is manifested as either "amiable" holiness or "terrible majesty" (2:255, 179, 256). With respect to these attributes, the issue is not one of ontological primacy in God's nature but of limited perception in man's. As a part of his loving care and desire to be received, God reveals himself as each believer requires.

The apparent multiplicity of God's essence is a divine concession to human frailty and emerges as an aspect of God's creation of the world. God delights in displaying to his creature the attributes of power and prudence, wisdom and love. As Edwards explained, "If the world had not been created, these attributes never would have had any exercise." But Edwards also took great pains to prove that establishing an arena in which to exercise these faculties is not God's *ultimate* end in creating the world; they therefore cannot be regarded as primary in his nature. While it was true that "after the world is created, after intelligent creatures are made . . . then that disposition which is called his faithfulness may move [God] in his providential disposals towards them," Edwards insisted that

"that perfection of God which we call his faithfulness, or his inclination to fulfill his promises to his creatures, could not properly be what moved him to create the world" (8:429, 412). Nor can such a claim be made for the perfection of God that is designated as his power.

Rather, underlying these subordinate and consequential ends is the original and chief end for which God created the world and in which his primary nature consists: God's "disposition to communicate himself, or diffuse his own *fullness*" so that "there might be a glorious and abundant emanation of his infinite fullness of good *ad extra*, or without himself" (8:433). It is this natural disposition "to cause the beams of His glory to shine forth, and His goodness to flow forth" that is fundamental to the Godhead. Edwards contended that "we must conceive of God's determination to glorify and communicate Himself as prior to the method that His wisdom pitches upon as tending best to effect this"—either through the creation of the world or the work of redemption ("Misc." 1062, 20:432). This essential understanding of God as being and being's inherent need to communicate itself was fundamental to Edwards' thought. The divine impulse precedes the creation of the world and informs the history of redemption.

Just as Edwards converted the language of Locke into divine discourse, so here he read Newton's tropes of mass and force as types of God's glory. Contrary to many scholars' claims, Edwards' embrace of Locke and Newton is not evidence of his liberalism or modernism—quite the opposite. For Edwards, God's disposition to communicate himself inspired and sanctified all human idioms, so that even the vocabulary of science became theologically resonant. Thus, he described God as "that being who has the most of being, or the greatest share of universal existence"—the entity of greatest possible mass (8:550). Inherent in the mass of entities was an attractive force, an emanation of energy. In God's nature, too, this property of emanation or communication is implicit. Edwards identified being and its communication as God's glory; it not only signified what is "internal . . . inherent in the subject"—God—but also stood for the "emanation, exhibition or communication of this internal glory" (8:513). Edwards derived this meaning of glory from his translation of the Hebrew word *kavod*, which he rendered as "heaviness, greatness, and abundance." Converting ancient faith into modern metaphors, Edwards took the next step of translating *kavod* as gravity to signify both the degree of being and of emanation inherent in the glory of God (8:512–13).

This formulation of glory was central to Edwards' theology and is especially useful for understanding his typological innovations. It maintained the important distinction between being and emanation, deity and nature; yet it allowed for God's delight in his creation. Moreover, it sanctioned the union of Neoplatonism with prophetic historicism that is the hallmark of Edwards' typological practice. His conviction of God's essential effulgence produced a theory in which divine communications simply overwhelm the descriptive categories of history and ontology.

This basic configuration of being as glory and its emanation informed many aspects of Edwards' thought, including his account of the Trinity. Though in its deepest sense the Trinity remained a sacred mystery to Edwards, one "so infinitely above our reach" and one that language was inadequate to explain, he nonetheless did try to describe the process by which God the Father, as "the deity subsisting in the prime, unoriginated and most absolute manner, or the deity in its direct existence," becomes three-in-one (21:131, 139).[20]

Edwards began *An Essay on the Trinity* by declaring that the happiness of the Father consists in his perception and enjoyment of himself, in "beholding and infinitely loving, and rejoicing in, His own essence" (21:113). The verb tenses underscore the active nature of his perception, "that God perpetually and eternally has a most perfect idea of Himself." God must become his own "eternal and necessary object." As Edwards declared, perception requires an other: "[t]here must be a duplicity." In the act of thinking and therein projecting an image of himself the Father begets his Son. One God becomes two: "[t]here is God and the idea of God" (21:114).

But this first emanation does not satisfy God's desire for effulgence; from the two a third entity overflows, born of the attractive force between them: "so the Holy Spirit does in some ineffable and inconceivable manner proceed, and is breathed forth both from the Father and the Son, by the Divine essence being wholly poured and flowing out in that infinitely intense, holy and pure love and delight that continually and unchangeably breathes forth from the Father and the Son" (21:185–86). The structure of this sentence, with its rolling cadences and dynamic expansion by verbal addition, reflects the effulgent nature of being.

Edwards' Godhead is most properly described, then, as a holy society, formed from "the great design of glorifying the deity and communicating its fullness" ("Misc." 1062, 20:431). The ineffable source of the Trinity is the inherent disposition of being in its "prime, unoriginated and most absolute manner" to be effulgent, to flow out even within itself. This is properly called the glory of God manifested *ad intra*, within the deity (21:131).

It is testimony to the integrity of Edwards' thought that effulgence *ad intra* is "agreeable" to "that which proceeds from God *ad extra*" ("Misc." 1218, 23:153). Such external communication consists not just in God's immediate relation with his creature but also in the larger works of creation and redemption. Emanating from the Trinity according to the order of subsistence and the economy of action, each of these works is identified primarily with a single person of the Godhead. First, Edwards described the work of creation as the emanation of God the Father, who intended "that his works should exhibit an image of himself their author, that it might brightly appear by his works what manner of being he is" (8:422). Like Christ himself, the created world corresponds to God's idea or projection of his own original being. Following creation in the economy of the Trinity is the work of redemption, first as it was virtually purchased by Christ and through time, and then as it is made actual by the Holy Ghost in the heart of each believer. Edwards identified these two aspects of salvation with the historical work of redemption and the ontological transformation wrought by grace. Like the persons of the Trinity, the two aspects are distinct but not separate. While they are "by no means to be confounded one with another," they do necessarily suppose each other (8:422). As Edwards made clear, the work of redemption in its unfolding through successive ages is essentially a part of the office of Christ. The covenant of grace, signifying the ontological change in the soul, is primarily the office of the Holy Spirit.

Implicated in the agreement between God's communications *ad intra* and *ad extra* is the question of how ontology is related to history. The source of the ineffable, indissoluble union of these two modes is contained, though not explained, in the sacred mystery of the Trinity, which not only makes one God three but also insists that priority of existence and equality of essence are eternally joined. History can no more be severed from ontology than the idea of God can be divorced from his love. The coupling of natural and historical types, which does indeed seem anomalous with respect to human reasoning, is resolved *ad intra*, that is, within God's nature.

Glory can be read as the subtext for much of Edwards' writing. As he declared, the ultimate end of God's work is of so sublime a nature that it simply exceeds our conceptual boundaries. Such a great design is "better understood, by using many words and a variety of expressions," Edwards remarked. "Though it be signified by various names, yet they appear not to be names of different things but various names involving each other in their meaning, either different names of the same thing, or names of several parts of one whole, or of the same whole viewed in various lights" (8:526–77).

It is also in this context that Edwards' anthropology may be better understood. As he translates *kavod*, glory embraces human nature as well as the divine: it is "the knowledge or sense, or effect of [emanation or communication of internal glory] in those who behold it; to whom the exhibition or communication is made" (8:513). Anthropology is implicated in theology, as the creature perceives God's fullness and participates in his glory.

Moreover, the saint's capacity to be a psalmist, to return God's fullness, is also a part of glory: "In the creature's knowing, esteeming, loving, rejoicing in, and praising God, the glory of God is both exhibited and acknowledged; his fullness is received and returned." The proportion between God's nature and man's is not one of power and dependence, nor one of justice and responsibility; rather, "here is both an *emanation* and *remanation*" (8:531). God as a communicating being not only "loves to see Himself, His own excellencies and glories" but also "loves His creatures so, that He really loves the being honored by them" ("Misc." 208, 13:342). Reciprocity is inherent in the notion of communication. Not only has God "exhibited himself, in his being, his infinite greatness and excellency" but he "has given us faculties, whereby we are capable of plainly discovering [his] immense superiority to all other beings" (8:551).

This configuration of the creature's relation to God threads throughout Edwards' writings. The saint's role as perceiver of the divine is nowhere more evident than in Edwards' explication of the Fall and its effects. In *The Doctrine of Original Sin* he described prelapsarian nature, in which "two kinds of principles" existed: the "*inferior* kind . . . being the principles of mere human nature" and the "*superior* principles . . . wherein consisted the spiritual image of God" (3:381–82). Superior principles are described in the terminology of glory: they "immediately depend on man's union and communion with God, or divine communications and influences of God's Spirit" (3:382). Human disobedience forfeited the spiritual principles and severed communion with the divine; God withdrew the creature's capacity to perceive or to act in terms of moral excellence. But the infusion of grace, which is the "Holy Ghost dwelling in the soul and acting there as a vital principle," restores the ability to perceive "the true beauty and loveliness" and the "moral excellency" of divine things (2:256–57; *Grace*," 21:196). The regenerate saint receives nothing less than "a principle of a new kind of perception or spiritual sensation," one in which he is given "eyes to see and ears to hear" and a taste to relish the "glory and beauty of God's nature" (2:205, 206, 248).

Rather than the *forma ab extra* of Lockean epistemology, then, God's essential effulgence provides a surer foundation for Edwards' notion of grace as a new sense. Moreover, Edwards' understanding of the sacramental ordinances, of prayer, and even of the singing of hymns was rooted in the twin process of divine exhibition and human apprehension (2:114–16).

Lastly, Edwards' innovations in typology can be understood in terms of these principles. The extension of typology to nature is of a piece with God's role as a communicator and the saint's joy in spiritual knowledge. Natural types allow that "wherever we are, and whatever we are about, we may see divine things excellently represented and held forth" (11:74). To be sure, this expanded perception rests upon a gracious transformation within each heart. God's voice is always resonant in nature, and his visage was from the first stamped on the face of creation; yet sin blinds humankind to these divine traces. Grace restores the senses of perception; it "unstop[s] the ears of the deaf, and open[s] the eyes of them that were born blind," so that one can once again discern and delight in the full range of God's communications (2:206).

But more: as the work of redemption unfolds in time, there will be an acceleration of communication, an explosion of knowledge of divine things.[21] "It is evident from the Scripture, that there is *yet remaining* a great advancement of the interest of religion and the kingdom of Christ in this world, by an abundant outpouring of the Spirit of God, far greater and more extensive than ever yet has been" (5:329). "It is represented as a time of vast increase of knowledge and understanding, especially in divine things" (5:338). This increasing celerity of emanations is implicit in the definition of glory as "gravity" and is directly related to the growing numbers composing the community of saints. Just as God must be understood as a holy society, so human beings cannot be considered as unitary; each saint is part of the dynamic community of believers, a society to be enlarged over time and most particularly by seasons of awakening.[22] Just as "the *degree* of the *amiableness* or *valuableness* . . . is not in the *simple* proportion of the degree of benevolent affection seen, but in a proportion *compounded* . . . of the degree of *being* and the degree of *benevolence*," so the beauty of the single regenerate soul is not as pleasing to God, who "esteems, values and has respect to things according to their nature and proportions," as a community of saints "consisting of many millions" (8:548, 422–23).

At one point in the *Nature of True Virtue* Edwards used the metaphor of gold to show that the degree of preciousness is directly related to quantity or mass, but the more proper description of this increasing value is the one with which he concluded *The End for Which God Created the World* (8:549). There the calculus of the millennium is revealed: the emanation of God and the remanation of the community of saints are properly understood in terms of glory-as-gravity. Edwards proposed that "there never will be any particular time" when union with God will be perfectly consummated. Indeed, how can there be, when the very principle of communication requires both subject and object? Rather, "the eternally increasing union of the saints with God" must be represented "by something that is ascending constantly towards that infinite height, moving upwards with a given velocity; and that is to continue thus to move to all eternity" (8:534).

In place of consummation, Edwards posited an eternal dynamic, in which the bond of attraction between the two entities—God and creature, or more properly the society of the Godhead and the community of saints—grows ever stronger as the mass increases and the distance diminishes. When those glorious days of the earthly church arrive, "wherein the whole earth shall be united as one holy city," God will perforce be drawn down from his heaven, even as the saints ascend. Those days, described at the outset of this essay, not only will be accompanied by an increase of knowledge but will be caused by that increase (5:339).

The expansion of typology to include nature, history, current events, and even commerce is part of this temporal process "wherein holiness should be as it were inscribed on everything" (5:338). Now God's discourse comes to embrace more and more of the idioms of everyday life. When seen within the context of Edwards' own master trope rather than in the terms of current critical debates, aspects of Edwards' typology that seemed in conflict "appear not to be names of different things," but like the multiple definitions of glory itself are "various names involving each other in their meaning . . . [are] names of several parts of one whole" (8:526).

A "certain sort of Language, as it were, in which God is wont to speak to us": typology is best understood as a form of divine speech, as part of "a communicative disposition in general" in God's nature and in his universe (8:435). Typology allowed Edwards' saint to perceive and delight in God's love, revealed in the lessons of nature as in the words of the prophets. In the end, Edwards confessed to having little faith in the meager powers of human expression. He concluded that the greatness of God must always elude mortal description, "words being less fitted to express things of so sublime a nature." But for Edwards, the immortal glory of God himself resides in the ceaseless desire to communicate, in the "disposition in the fullness of the divinity to flow out and diffuse itself" through all time and all creation (8:527, 435).

Notes

1. William G. Madsen, "From Shadowy Types to Truth," in *The Lyric and Dramatic Milton: Selected Papers from the English Institute*, ed. Joseph H. Summers (New York: Columbia University Press, 1965). For other books on typology, see the suggested further reading below.

2. See Alan Heimert, *Religion and the American Mind from the Great Awakening to the Revolution* (Cambridge, Mass: Harvard University Press, 1966), passim.

3. Perry Miller, introduction to Jonathan Edwards, *Images or Shadows of Divine Things* (New Haven: Yale University Press, 1948), p. 27.

4. Ibid., pp. 27–28. Though he acknowledged that the Puritans believed that God reveals his will through special providences as well as through the Bible, Miller emphasized that these communications are intermittent and do not lend themselves to a systematic reading of nature.

5. Ibid., pp. 27, 35, 23.

6. See Norman Fiering, "The Rationalist Foundations of Jonathan Edwards' Metaphysics," Wilson H. Kimnach, "Jonathan Edwards' Pursuit of Reality," and Stephen J. Stein, "The Spirit and the Word: Jonathan Edwards and Scriptural

Exegesis," all in *Jonathan Edwards and the American Experience*, ed. Nathan O. Hatch and Harry S. Stout (New York: Oxford University Press, 1998).

7. Reclaiming Edwards for a traditionalist Christian context, Stein faults Miller for an "antipathy to the scriptural dimension of Edwards's work" in "The Spirit and the Word," p. 125. Taking a more radical view, R. C. De Prospo objects to Miller's modernist reading of Edwards as a precursor to the transcendentalists. De Prospo insists that Edwards operated within atheist discourse that continues indefinitely to generate hierarchical duplicities. *Theism in the Discourse of Jonathan Edwards* (Newark: University of Delaware Press, 1985), pp. 12–13, 59, 68, 75, 83. As reviewers have noted, this provocative view does not account for Edwards' immaterialism or his pleasure in the beauty of the typical world.

8. Such scholars as James F. Maclear, in "'The Heart of New England Rent':The Mystical Element in Early Puritan History," *Mississippi Valley Historical Review* 42 (1956): 621–52, and Geoffrey Nuttal, in *The Holy Spirit in Puritan Faith and Experience* (Oxford: Blackwell, 1946), have repeatedly called attention to a long and equally orthodox tradition within theist discourse that stressed God's effulgent love.

9. Most notably, Lewalski's *Protestant Poetics* and Lowance's *Language of Canaan* have revised our understanding of the tradition of typology. Lowance's reading of Edwards' historical types is especially insightful; for the purpose of this essay, his analysis of the ontological types is less helpful. Like Miller, Lowance reads Edwards in terms of the conflict between science and orthodox theology and therefore emphasizes the disjunction between Edwards' liberal typology and his conservative doctrines.

10. Madsen, "Shadowy Types," p. 99.

11. Lewalski, *Protestant Poetics*, p. 140; Lowance, *Language of Canaan*, p. 260.

12. Ibid., pp. 249–76.

13. See also Edwards' extended discussion of secondary beauty in *True Virtue*, (8:561–74).

14. See Wilson's superb introduction to Edwards' *Work of Redemption* for an insightful reading of some of the issues considered in this essay (9:1–100).

15. Wilson has identified several "master models" that appear in liberal and conservative treatises alike. As he argues, the branching of a tree, like the motion of a river, is a recurrent type of providential dispensation (9:50–52). These images appear in both *Work of Redemption* and *Images or Shadows of Divine Things*, indicating that at the most basic level the exclusive claims of history and nature were not as significant for Edwards as modern critics persistently assume.

16. Jesper Rosenmeier, in "Veritas: The Sealing of the Promise," *Harvard Library Bulletin*, 16 (1968): 31, discusses the persistence of moral value in prefigurative types.

17. "A type is a historical person or event, not a mythical person or a recurrent event like the rising and setting of the sun." Madsen, "Shadowy Types," p. 99. With respect to Image no. 50, Lowance concurs with this distinction, arguing that "although his ensuing argument attempts to prove that there is more than a simple analogy between the sun rising and the coming of Christ (for example, an

instituted resemblance), Edwards here has clearly abandoned the historical scheme of adumbration and fulfillment." *Language of Canaan*, p. 268.

18. For example, Roland Delattre's *Beauty and Sensibility in the Thought of Jonathan Edwards: An Essay in Aesthetics and Theological Ethics* (New Haven: Yale University Press, 1968) provides a brilliant discussion of the role of beauty in God's nature but does not fully consider the dynamism implicit in divine self-exhibition.

19. See Lee, *The Philosophical Theology of Jonathan Edwards*, exp. ed. (Princeton: Princeton University Press, 2000), for a complementary reading of Edwards' conception of God's dynamic communicative nature. I am pleased to find that a number of the ideas suggested here are confirmed and elaborated there, but I dissent from his formulation in one fundamental respect. While Lee argues that Edwards' dynamism exemplifies a more radical modernism than even Miller suspected (p. 3), I argue that it is rooted in an older tradition of pietism that reaches back to the writings of Sibbes. In the conclusion of my doctoral dissertation, "A Garden Enclosed: The Tradition of Heart-Piety in Puritan New England" (Harvard University, 1988), I show how Edwards' emphasis on God's dynamic effulgence and on grace as a new perception, as well as his linkage of communication and communalism to the postmillennial reign, echoes earlier pietist positions. Edwards was far more traditional in these formulations than most scholars acknowledge.

20. For a slightly different reading of glory, see David Pierce, "Jonathan Edwards and the 'New Sense' of Glory," *New England Quarterly* 41 (1968): 84–95.

21. See also p. 338: "It is represented as a time of vast increase of knowledge and understanding, especially in divine things."

22. For the fuller consideration of this aspect of Edwards' thought, see Heimert's *Religion and the American Mind: From the Great Awakening to the American Revolution* (Cambridge, Mass.: Harvard University Press, 1966).

Suggested Further Readings

Bercovitch, Sacvan. *The Puritan Origins of the American Self*. New Haven: Yale University Press, 1975.

———, ed. *Typology and Early American Literature*. Amherst: University of Massachusetts Press, 1972.

Brumm, Ursula. *American Thought and Religious Typology*. Trans. John Hoaglund. New Brunswick, N.J.: Rutgers University Press, 1970.

Lewalski, Barbara Kiefer. *Protestant Poetics and the Seventeenth-Century Religious Lyric*. Princeton: Princeton University Press, 1979.

Lowance, Mason I., Jr. *The Language of Canaan: Metaphor and Symbol in New England from the Puritans to the Transcendentalists*. Cambridge, Mass.: Harvard University Press, 1980.

Miller, Perry. Introduction to Jonathan Edwards, *Images or Shadows of Divine Things*. New Haven: Yale University Press, 1948.

Fourteen

History

John F. Wilson

IN ORDER TO comprehend "history" in the thought of Jonathan Edwards, one must necessarily begin where he ended. This means attending to Jonathan Edwards' "Letter to the Trustees of the College of New Jersey," written in the last months of his life. In it he reflected upon the projects from which he would have to turn aside should he accept their invitation to preside over the fledgling college at Princeton. He believed that such a move would decisively affect his intellectual aspirations, in particular the broad plans he had to publish several major studies. One among the projects put at risk by relocation to New Jersey would be a so-called "History of the Work of Redemption" that he had long intended to write. In this letter Jonathan Edwards sketches out in some detail a multilevel inquiry in which he would trace the progress of the world's redemption, both on earth and through associated events in heaven and hell, culminating with the completion of all things and presumably the end of time itself. This encompassing vision has captured the imagination of generations of scholars and general readers alike, providing the point of departure for unending conjectures and countless assertions about Jonathan Edwards' and his view of history.

Jonathan Edwards' name for this particular project, "A History of the Work of Redemption," is identical with one version of his working title for a series of sermons he had preached in 1739. The presumption has been irresistible that this sermon series itself should be understood as the initial draft of his never-completed project. The sermon series, as transcribed by Jonathan Edwards, Jr., and edited in Edinburgh by the Scottish cleric John Erskine, was published some fifteen years after Edwards' death. This "History" is among the first sustained book-length projects Edwards drafted, even though it was not issued in his lifetime.

The burden of this essay is to untangle, for the benefit of twenty-first-century readers, several interrelated questions about Jonathan Edwards and his interpretation of history. It may help if these issues are parsed at the outset, indeed listed analytically, so as to assist those who wish to appreciate the place of history within the range and reach of Jonathan Edwards' thought. The following topics will be discussed in turn.

First, the genesis and content of the sermon series titled "The Work of Redemption," preached for the first and only time in Northampton in 1739 and edited for publication in Edinburgh in 1774. To avoid confusion, the sermon series will be identified as the "Redemption Discourse" and the posthumously published version as *A History of the Work of Redemption*.

Second, what we can know about the project Jonathan Edwards termed a "History of the Work of Redemption" from the letter he wrote to the Trustees at Princeton, and the relationship of this project to the unpublished "Redemption Discourse."

Third, Jonathan Edwards' broader reflections about God's purpose in creating the world, conceived by him as divine energy flowing out from, and eventually returning to, the godhead, a process comprising human history, indeed, the history of the cosmos itself.

Fourth, Jonathan Edwards' relatively infrequent references to "history" in the corpus of his writings.

Finally, the many interpretations modern writers have placed upon Jonathan Edwards' purported interest in "history," some claiming it to be the unifying center of his thought.

A critical understanding of Jonathan Edwards necessarily includes exploring these separate but interrelated dimensions of "history." Indeed, it is imperative not to conflate these separate topics into a single and coherent view of "history."

As Jonathan Edwards matured in the Northampton pulpit after the death of Solomon Stoddard (his grandfather), his preaching branched out in several directions. One of these was to develop carefully constructed series of sermons, that is, pulpit discourses extending across numerous preaching units. One early example is a noteworthy series titled "Charity and Its Fruits," preached in 1738, that stretched across fifteen separate occasions (8:125–397).[1] It was an expository exegesis of 1 Corinthians 13, the so-called "Hymn to Love" attributed to the apostle Paul. In the middle of the nineteenth century Tyron Edwards published the series, introducing them as "lectures."[2] This and other such efforts were very much in the mold of Puritan exegetical preaching from the sixteenth century forward. In the following year (1739), Jonathan Edwards launched an even more ambitious project, a series of thirty sermons he preached on a single scriptural verse, Isaiah 51:8.[3] From this text he drew forth a "doctrine," namely, that "The Work of Redemption is a work that God carries on from the fall of man to the end of the world." Jonathan Edwards characteristically referred to this project as his "Redemption Discourse." More generally, it was organized around a strong story line comprising a "history" that carried "from the fall of man to the end of the world." In effect, he took the sermon structure that had been perfected by Puritans over several centuries (including major elements like text, doctrine, observations, improvements, applications) and utilized it as the scaffolding for an entire "edifice" of thirty sermon units. When published in Edinburgh (in 1774), well after Jonathan Edwards' death, the editor had stripped away many characteristics of the sermon form. This redaction accentuated the strong story line identified in *A History of the Work of Redemption*. In retrospect, the several sermon series from the late 1730s mark a stage in Jonathan Edwards' writing practices that would eventually lead to the longer treatises and tracts that he published in the next decades.

For those with an interest in history, Jonathan Edwards' story line about the work of redemption appears as a comprehensive or universal account of the life of humankind "from the fall of man to the end of the world." His sources for this "history" are what came to his hand and might be anticipated. The early sections rest almost exclusively on biblical accounts (in the Hebrew scriptures that Christians know as the Old Testament). Jonathan Edwards' command of these materials was daunting; he quoted long passages from memory, and his working notebooks make it clear that his scrutiny of texts was searching and imaginative. While the center of the story line concerns the life and death of Jesus the Christ, he draws upon extrabiblical sources in the Graeco-Roman period to enrich his presentation and to make his references more universal. For the postbiblical period, he utilizes an assortment of sources ranging from scriptural prophecies, through histories of the papacy and the church, to discussions of those European peoples that he knew about. In such a perspective his burden was to assemble an account of humankind as God wrought the redemption of the world through Christ. Thoughtful and critical readers will want to ask, however, whether this way of expressing the case distorts Edwards' logic, putting the cart before the horse, so to speak. Edwards was less concerned with the fate of humankind, that is, with charting its trials and tribulations, than he was with the "work" that Christ does on God's behalf in renewing the creation. To be sure, humankind's redemption would be achieved as a *by-product* of Christ's work—but his perspective gives an altogether different emphasis to the subject, decidedly more in accord with the doctrinal world of Reformed theology.

For the period preceding Christianity's explicit founding up through the life and work of Jesus, Edwards' chief interpretive strategy is to use typology. He finds Christ and his coming foreshadowed through the events and persons of the Old Testament. Edwards' appropriation of the rich vein of typology is relatively elastic, permitting him to render links more tightly as well as more loosely. Familiar with its limitations, and aware of the seventeenth- and eighteenth-centuries debates about it, he nonetheless uses typology with remarkably few constraints. The burden of these sections of his discourse is to argue that all "historical" events and persons point to the coming of a Christ. The middle section, defined as the great time of Christ's coming, finds its controlling center in the "work" that in principle will be accomplished through it—namely, the redemption of the world. He mines extrabiblical sources, aligning them with biblical ones, to chart this great work that goes on in the life and death of Jesus of Nazareth as the Christ. Finally, the period that follows the decisive work of Christ, namely, the period after his death and resurrection, is punctuated and structured through infusions of the Spirit. These are gracious gifts to the postbiblical church, directly anticipating the final return of Christ and the eventual end of history. It is evident that Edwards' chief means for interpreting postbiblical events as a coherent history was through the application of biblical prophecies to them.

Such a story line can indeed be construed as universal, that is to say, as the core of world history. In principle it can incorporate materials from outside the canonical sources, necessarily subjecting them to interpretation in light of a determining theological framework. In this abstract sense, it is possible to assimilate *A History of the Work of Redemption* to the genre of universal histories that the Enlightenment era had spawned.[4] This step is especially easy to take when the text utilized is the published version (1774) of the original sermon series (1739), for, as has been indicated, Erskine stripped away many elements of the original sermons that Edwards had composed—and presumably delivered.

If we seek to understand Edwards' mind, however, our datum should be the "Redemption Discourse," the 1739 manuscripts from which he preached the series of thirty sermons, there being no evidence that he ever undertook to repreach, let alone to recast or redraft, them. (Indeed, the only intrusions in the actual sermon booklets—aside from Edwards' own revisions and deletions made when he drafted them, and in the same ink—appear to be a very few marks made by Jonathan Edwards, Jr., presumably while transcribing them.) Interpretation of these sermon booklets more properly situates the project as a "discourse" (Edwards' term) about the redemption of the world. Its intellectual burden is his theological doctrine about the divine "work" through which God redeems the creation. In this sense, the "Work of Redemption" traces out through time, and in several stages, Christ's achievement in redeeming the world. Thus, Edwards' strong interest in "history," as expressed in the Redemption Discourse, is essentially framed theologically, driven by his doctrinal convictions. It points to comparable interests broadly shared with Calvinists on both sides of the Atlantic.

Those who read the pertinent section of Jonathan Edwards' "Letter to the Trustees of the College of New Jersey" will find a much fuller account of what he planned to do with his "History of the Work of Redemption" than appears in the Redemption Discourse itself.[5] It is important to interpret the substantial paragraph he devoted to the topic by offering commentary on its most critical sentences. Jonathan Edwards recounted that for many years he had thought about a major project ("a great work") on this topic, having first begun it "not with any view to publication." This seems to be a clear reference to the 1739 sermon series, his "Redemption Discourse." Immediately he declares that the project to which he wishes to turn will be "a body of divinity in an entire new method, being thrown into the form of an history" (16:727). This assertion has fostered some disagreement about its meaning. Edwards' prose style (he assembles long series of parallel phrases and clauses without significant punctuation) allows a reader to project his or her own emphasis upon the text through subordinating one to another. Which term should readers take as controlling for Edwards—*body of divinity* or *history*? In this case the first alternative seems compelling. Clearly it was to be a body of divinity, "history" specifying the "new method" in terms of which he would construct it. This view is confirmed by what follows, for his subject is the "affair of Christian theology," more particularly "as the whole of it, in each part, stands in reference to the great work of redemption by Jesus Christ." This, Edwards goes on, he supposes to be "the grand design of all God's designs, and the *summum* and *ultimum* of all the divine operations and degrees [sic]" (16:727–28). Especially note that Edwards is proposing that the "work of redemption" encompasses all of God's operations. So this project from which Jonathan Edwards must turn away if he accepts the position at the college is a grand theological disquisition about the most fundamental of all doctrines, namely, that about God's redemption of the world. It is to be done through a new method, by charting the relevant stages of redemption as they appear through time.

The paragraph of his letter continues, expanding upon the subject so defined. Edwards emphasizes that he had thought to arrange "all parts of the grand scheme in their historical order." He intends to trace back divine dispensations to their beginning in eternity, identifying their manifestations in "the wonderful series of successive acts and events" primarily in the "church of God," but not excluding the "revolutions in the world of mankind, affecting the state of the church and the affair of redemption." This will require attention to accounts in "history or prophecy" and will conclude with a consummation in "that perfect state of things." Edwards insists that the "history" he so describes will encompass "all three worlds, heaven, earth, and hell," and that it will consider the "connected, successive events and alterations, in each so far as the Scriptures give any light." Above all, this approach will introduce "all parts of divinity in that order which is most scriptural and most natural." Thus, "every divine doctrine will appear to the greatest advantage in the brightest light, in the most striking manner, showing the admirable contexture and harmony of the whole" (16:728).

With the project delineated in this manner, its relationship to the 1739 Redemption Discourse is readily apparent. This grand design appears to have expanded the original scope of the preaching series, the proposal having become both more encompassing in its intent and inclusive in its contents. Further indications of Edwards' ideas for and about this project are embedded in three notebooks, undoubtedly dating to the late Stockbridge period, that he constructed from scrap paper.[6] Writing in the margins of book sheets, or on the verso of already used paper, he jotted a series of notes to himself about what might be included in the "History of the Work of Redemption." None of the entries is sustained, and together they add little to our overall understanding of the objective he sketched in the letter to the trustees. At most the notes indicate particular points he would address or striking insights he might expand. It is appropriate to conclude that while Edwards had clearly resolved to turn to this task imminently, in fact he had accomplished very little on "History of the Work of Redemption" before moving to Princeton.

Read searchingly, Edwards' plans for a "History of the Work of Redemption," like the Redemption Discourse itself, suggest that he would have produced a comprehensive body of divinity emphasizing the work of redemption as the most fundamental doctrine of the Christian religion. He proposed that the work was to be viewed "historically," that is, as a dynamic process that would be explored as it was manifested through time. So he advanced the view that history was the theatre of divine salvation, where those with opened eyes might see God's actions. As such his chronicle would continue in the tradition of ecclesiastical histories from across the Christian era, albeit in a decidedly Protestant mode. In his letter to the trustees, there was no suggestion that history per se held special meaning. The special meaning was given in the Reformed understanding that the world's redemption was a divine work, one that was, if possible, even more fundamental than its creation. Edwards' purpose was to explicate this basic theological position, not to propose an innovation in historiography that would itself be part of the cultural project generated out of the Enlightenment.

If Edwards had made little or no headway on his "History of the Work of Redemption" while residing in Stockbridge, he did complete two essays, written "for the learned and inquisitive," that are statements of his mature thought. Neither was published in his lifetime, but through the collaboration of two protégées and close associates, Samuel Hopkins and Joseph Bellamy, they were published in Boston in 1765 as *Two Dissertations*.[7] The second of them, titled *The Nature of True Virtue*, addressed a preoccupation that can be traced back to Edwards' college years. The first essay, *Concerning the End for which God Created the World*, exhibits another dimension of interest in "history." At root, Reformed theology proposed that God's purpose in creating the world was simple: he did it for his own glorification. In the logic of theology, this position established that divine activity was self-motivated and self-actualized rather than responsive to, or in any particular dependent upon, the actions of humans. Edwards took up this staple doctrine in the first essay, exploring rational and scriptural aspects of the subject in a suitably sustained fashion. The core of this account is his claim that in creation "divine fullness" initially emanates from the Godhead and that it is received by and then returned to God through the creature: "Here is both an *emanation* and a *remanation*. The refulgence shines upon and into the creature, and is reflected back to the luminary" (8:531).[8] So for Edwards "history" is the medium of time (and space) in which divine energy flows out to create the world, eventually completing the process in returning to the Godhead itself; God's outflowing energizes creation, and human response points toward return of the created order to God. Thus it is a process within the divine economy, indeed, more properly speaking, it is the economy of the world that is divinely generated. This entire process has direction in time as history (the return of the creation to and its unification with God), but its eventual destiny, its end, lies beyond time. While implicated in it, humans do not of themselves contribute to its achievement.

In such a fashion, Reformed theology informs—indeed, provides an even more inclusive frame for—Edwards' understanding of the history in which he cast his reflections about the "Work of Redemption." "History" is the modality in which the ultimate and most basic purpose of the creation is experienced and known because it is identical with, and takes place within, so to speak, God's self-glorification. In this sense, the claim can be advanced that Edwards shifts attention to the "meaning" of history. For human experience and consciousness take place "within" a cosmic process so understood. This does represent a kind of opening to modern thinkers' preoccupation with history as the condition under which humankind lives in time. It also connects with the strong emphasis that mid-twentieth-century religious thinkers like the Niebuhr brothers, Reinhold and Richard, gave to time and history. In such a framework, history functions as the "metaphysical medium" in which meaning is displayed. If someone wishes to link Edwards' thought about "history" with more recent religious reflection, the "First Dissertation" will prove to be the most promising connection. But it is appropriate, even necessary, to recognize that Edwards anchors his reflections about history in

Reformed doctrine about the "End for which God Created the World." Thus, the interest he has in time and history as a condition of human consciousness is situated within a theologically defined cosmos. In projecting his "history" of the work of redemption, Edwards was certainly prepared to make use of extrabiblical sources, but only because they might flesh out (in the sense of providing particulars for) his account of the church's role in the larger redemptive process. He did not construe such sources as materials for modern critical historiography.

In light of this discussion it is imperative to explore whether Edwards chose to deal with history as a subject anywhere else in the vast corpus of his writings. Yale's critical edition of his works is nearing completion (at least as projected). It will include all of the writings published during his lifetime and most that were issued posthumously, as well as his significant notebooks and compilations of scriptural materials. This will position those who are interested to achieve an overview of his developing thought.[9] For the first time it may now be possible for the serious general reader (as opposed to the specialized and dedicated scholar) to achieve a relatively comprehensive grasp of Edwards' intellectual world. Accordingly, one means of gauging the place of history in his mental landscape is to review the indexes of the published volumes. What stands out, in high relief, is the virtually complete absence of references to "history" as a subject. It is certainly evident that, as part of his voracious reading, Edwards availed himself of such historical accounts as were available to him about matters such as the popes of the Middle Ages or the churches of European nations. But aside from references to his own "History of the Work of Redemption," very few topics are explicitly cited as "historical," and few passages can be identified where issues of "history" are discussed. When the notebook that chronicled his reading is published in the Yale series, it will become possible to chart his habits of mind even more fully. Of course, events like those associated with the awakening of 1734, or the later removal from Northampton to Stockbridge, or occasional events in world history, are amply cited in requisite locations, as are individuals with whom Edwards interacted in one or another fashion. In sum, though others have often selected the term "history" to characterize Edwards' thought, it was not a term that he used very much in his own writings, personal or professional. Serious students of Edwards would be ill advised, however, to stop there in their quest. They should look beyond "history" as a term to more technical designations that are relevant to Edwards' strategies of interpretation throughout his writings. Among such designations are those associated with prophecy and apocalypse, methods of interpreting them, such as figuralism and typology, and categories like eschatology, including freighted concepts like the millennium.

Note well, however, that these designations are constitutive elements in Edwards' theological program; he does not utilize them as historiographical devices in a modern sense.

Terms like scriptural account, figural representation and typological thinking, revelation, apocalypse (or unveiling), millenarianism most certainly concern history in the broadest sense; they make it possible to identify the significance of events that humans experience in time. But especially as used by Jonathan Edwards they place constructions on events, interpreting them within framework of a broadly Christian, and more specifically a Reformed, view of the world. So the experience of ancient Israel becomes prototypical for the life of God's people in the new dispensation inaugurated by Jesus, who is understood to be the Christ. Prophetic visions of the future serve to isolate and explain intervening events. Apocalyptic denunciations of ancient enemies of Israel carry fresh meaning as applied to the antagonists of the latter-day church. And the vision of a millennial fulfillment assures the faithful that a fuller age is to be anticipated, preparatory to the final consummation of all things. These historical references are meaning-bearers for the faithful, conferring eternal or lasting significance on the mundane. In this sense they are intensely "historical," because they condense in symbolic form specific projections about the whole, providing the faithful with a coherent world.

In her introduction to those "miscellanies" Edwards composed largely during the 1730s, Ava Chamberlain formulates a helpful insight (18:29–34). On the basis of these notebooks, which are filled with his reflections, she suggests that Edwards' thought developed markedly, especially in the later years of that decade. Initially centered on rational argumentation as a line of defense against his antagonists (particularly the deists), it shifted to demonstrations of the power of the Christian religion as these were chronicled in salvation history. Of course, his own experience with the revivals in Northampton (as prelude to the broader awakening occasioned by Whitefield's itinerancy) represents an immediate social context for this shift. Thus, Chamberlain proposes that Edwards moves from basing his defense of Christianity upon rational arguments to propounding that fulfillments in Scripture and of prophecies, both displayed in historical events, offer convincing proof of its truth. In this she neatly indicates *the particular kind of history* that Edwards makes the bearer of theological truth: historical events that embody the story line of a Godhead creating, sustaining, and redeeming the world as the outflowing self-expression of internal glory.

This essay is written for use by readers who wish to appreciate Jonathan Edwards, and especially to understand the place of history as a category in his thought. Thus, it first directed attention to his own expressions of an interest in history. Accordingly, we noted the relevant paragraph in Edwards' "Letter to the Trustees of the College of New Jersey" about his projected "history," and we explored its relationship to the major series of sermons preached in 1739 as the Redemption Discourse. Recognizing the significance Edwards attached to scripture history and prophecy, we then turned to a brief analysis of his essay the *End for which God Created the World* that established its cosmic context—framed as it was in terms of Reformed doctrine. In turn, this led back to a brief discussion of Edwards' general "atonality" with respect to history, at least as moderns use the term critically, for he believed that events explicated scriptural accounts or followed divine promises. In one sense this series of topics completes a survey of the place of "history" in Jonathan Edwards' thought.

But there is another sense in which this account is only the introduction to a larger story. For, especially in recent times, a number of interpreters have emphasized the centrality of history to Edwards' worldview. They have believed it to be both a means to understand his intellectual endeavors and a promising approach to connecting this eighteenth-century theologian with more recent intellectual preoccupations. The concluding section of this essay will selectively review claims that have been advanced about history in Edwards' thought, seeking both to clarify it further and to interpret the diversity of opinions others have formed about it, particularly in the second half of the twentieth century. Accordingly, the concluding discussion will identify and introduce the claims that some interpreters have made about Edwards' interest in history.

H. Richard Niebuhr published *The Kingdom of God in America* in 1935, having composed it as a sequel to *The Social Sources of Denominationalism* (1929).[10] In the earlier work he explored the "nature of the relation of religion to culture" by reviewing the factors that produced the "complexity of American Christianity." In the latter study he undertook to interpret "the meaning and spirit of American Christianity as a movement which finds its center in the faith in the kingdom of God."[11] While Jonathan Edwards was certainly not the first person to express the idea that America would play a special role in realizing God's kingdom on earth, Niebuhr argued that, possibly more than any other figure, his influence had been critical in orienting the emerging nation to that possibility. Edwards was instrumental specifically because of his connection with the Great Awakening, in which he made the "millenarian tendency" the "common and vital possession of American Christians."[12] Niebuhr cast Edwards' *History of the Work of Redemption* as central to his case, quoting a substantial section of one paragraph. By the middle decades of the twentieth century, then, an influential theologian had identified

Jonathan Edwards as making a signal contribution to American culture by emphasizing that God's kingdom would be realized through (and possibly in) American history. In subsequent years other scholars have developed this insight.[13]

Perry Miller, whose biographical study, *Jonathan Edwards*, was published shortly after World War II, made the most far-reaching claims about the place and significance of Edwards' views concerning history.[14] Framing his analysis in terms of dichotomies and tensions between events in Edwards' "external biography" and the intellectual achievements of his interior life, Miller vigorously argued that Edwards had achieved a range of insights that were ahead of his time. Miller traced the relationship of Edwards' ideas to those of such figures as Locke, Berkeley, and Newton, crediting the eighteenth-century theologian with approaching a twentieth-century comprehension of human acting and thinking as well as of nature. The final chapter makes the boldest claims about Edwards' intellectual achievements (pp. 307–30). Miller proposed, in effect, that Edwards' most noteworthy but underappreciated insight lies in his radical philosophy of history, his understanding of it as a unitary process, comprehending an end as well as a beginning, and transcending time. Of course, Miller acknowledged that Edwards expressed this insight in the idiom of his own day, and that he advanced it through symbols rather than by means of abstract and rational arguments. Specifically, he identified the millenarian views that Edwards advocated, portraying them as embers smoldering in the colonial undergrowth, eventually to burst forth and blaze brightly in the phenomenon of the Great Awakening. Perry Miller's Jonathan Edwards stood forth as an outsize figure at the foundation of American civilization. Edwards' intellect was worthy to be compared with the great minds of Europe; the fact that such an intellect could be nurtured in the New World proved that American cultural life had not been entirely barren, altogether lacking in magisterial figures.

Within the decade, there was a direct response of sorts to this extraordinary assessment of the importance of Jonathan Edwards' understanding of history. In the Jefferson Memorial Lectures at Berkeley in 1966, Peter Gay offered his interpretation of "Puritan Historians in Colonial America" under the title *A Loss of Mastery*.[15] Gay argued that the craft of writing history declined among colonial historians between, on the one hand, the homely but effective chronicle of William Bradford or the popularizing history of Edward Johnson and, on the other, the substantial and more pretentious works of Cotton Mather or—more especially—Jonathan Edwards. Gay suggested the term "pathetic" as appropriate for Mather, the term "tragic" for Edwards: "What made Edwards a tragic hero was [a] ruthlessly intelligent search for the meaning of Puritanism, pursued without regard to the cost." In Gay's view, any evaluation of

Edwards as historian must rest on *A History of the Work of Redemption*. And he opined that: "However magnificent in conception, however bold in execution, . . . [it] is a thoroughly traditional book, and the tradition is the tradition of Augustine."[16] Peter Gay's association of Edwards' approach to history with the tradition of Augustine, an association earlier made by H. Richard Niebuhr, speaks directly to the crux of Miller's argument. For it had been the burden of Augustine's *City of God*, informed by Scripture, to present history as unitary, requiring interpretation from some point outside itself. In this Jonathan Edwards stood in the company of the bishop of Hippo. Where he departed from Augustine was in looking toward the future for the external reference point (specifically, to the creation's return to the Godhead through the millennium) rather than to the past. But Gay's more fundamental point about the tradition in which Edwards stood cannot be challenged.

More recently a number of scholars have evaluated these claims and counterclaims and offered their own interpretations of Edwards' approach to history. One example is Gerald R. McDermott, who elucidates what he calls "The Public Theology of Jonathan Edwards" in *One Holy and Happy Society*.[17] In this endeavor, he touches on Edwards' undoubted commitment to the broader Puritan tradition, expressed in its colonial variant, that presumed a "national covenant," which is to say, claimed religious warrant for the nation as vessel of divine purposes.[18] But even more significant for those who seek to understand Edwards' view of history, McDermott explores with some care the millennial dimension of his thought.[19] He usefully summarizes much recent scholarship on various aspects of this topic, including questions surrounding the various chronological schemes (to which Jonathan Edwards was heir) for dating the arrival of the millennium, the location of texts pertaining to the issue in Edwards' corpus of writings, and Edwards' presumed view about its eventual realization. Accordingly, McDermott's interests center in how Edwards viewed the stages of historical development and more especially their relevance to his claims about Edwards' public theology. In a second book, titled *Jonathan Edwards Confronts the Gods*,[20] the same author systematically explores Edwards' thought as a response to deism, which represented the continuing and central challenge to his Reformed worldview. Thus, he was preoccupied with squaring particularistic Christian claims with deism's implicit universalism, and this meant construing God's redemption of the world in terms that took account of the range of non-Christian faiths about which he knew, including pagans, followers of Muhammad, and Chinese sages no less than Jews. McDermott's is a rounded inquiry into Edwards' commitment to sustain the authority of revealed religion in an era becoming skeptical about any claim that truth might be particular.

In a contrasting study, Michael McClymond approaches aspects of Edwards' theology in a monograph titled *Encounters with God*.[21] Two chapters of this book bear directly on the topic of history. The first reviews Edwards' essay *End of Creation* and its dependence on such theorists as Shaftesbury and Hutcheson. McClymond concludes that "*End of Creation* presupposes principles of Calvinist particularism that are neither expounded nor justified in the course of the argument."[22] McClymond appears to be much more positively impressed by the *History of the Work of Redemption*, for he directs attention to the several schemes that Edwards utilized to bring unitariness to history. But the theological premises of the effort are still acknowledged; indeed, McClymond makes a point of contrasting Edwards' perspective with more properly Enlightenment historiography, exemplified by figures such as Voltaire and Gibbon.[23] Thus, McDermott and McClymond directly analyze Jonathan Edwards' interest in history, but in a manner characteristic of recent scholarship, both draw back from making claims as far-reaching as Perry Miller's. The long shadow of Peter Gay's critique falls across their work.

The most comprehensive discussion of Jonathan Edwards' view of history is to be found in recent writings by Avihu Zakai, an Israeli specialist in American culture who teaches at the Hebrew University. Zakai brings several noteworthy strengths to this task. He has studied in great detail the English background to colonial American Puritanism and has explored with care the ideological orientation of the early settlement of Puritan New England, the legacy appropriated by Jonathan Edwards. He also stands at a sufficient cultural distance to appreciate Edwards' relationship to broader European intellectual currents.[24] The thrust of his interpretation is that Edwards stood securely in the Christian tradition of understanding history that was distinctively reshaped as a consequence of the Protestant Reformation. The Reformed view built upon older ecclesiastical history in which the church was understood to bear witness to the divine salvation of the world as well as to provide the means of eventually bringing humanity to eternal life. The English Puritans gave particular expression to this tradition, many among them believing that England was to be God's "elect nation," with a special destiny in the later stages of world history. Such heightened religious nationalism, cast in a historical mode, found expression in the English civil struggles of the seventeenth century and contributed to the impulse that transported some members of the "elect" across the Atlantic Ocean, particularly the settlers of New England. Indeed, apocalyptic and millennial convictions energized the impulse to "independency" and "visible sainthood" that marked the struggles to realize "the New England Way."

Viewed in this perspective, Jonathan Edwards was less an outright innovator in his thought and activity than he was one seeking to repristinate the core of New England Puritanism, which was being challenged on several fronts in the eighteenth century. In particular, he reexpressed older ideals and objectives with a force and clarity that lent them great authority. In no regard was he more effective in doing this than in his situating the convictions held by orthodox Puritans within the larger framework of historical expectation that gave tangible point and meaning to their theological quest. Zakai's *Jonathan Edwards' Philosophy of History: The Reenchantment of the World in the Age of Enlightenment* presents a remarkably full delineation of his distinctive proposals about the meaning of history. It is by far the best-balanced and most comprehensive analysis of this contested topic and stands as its definitive interpretation.

The argument offered by Avihu Zakai makes the important point that, while Jonathan Edwards was surely a figure of his own time, he was also indelibly imprinted with the specific understanding of salvation history that came to him from seventeenth-century England and New England. Through his forceful exposition of a new redemptive framework that would give universal significance to the religious effervescence of his time, Jonathan Edwards placed his own era in proximity to the presumed completion of history. In this way, he commended specific expectations that would take on a life of their own, especially as the popular culture of the nineteenth century was transformed by the presumptions and coloration of the Enlightenment. In this new cultural situation, religious convictions about the end of history served effectively to frame antiprogressive—as well as progressive—views of the American future. At the same time, these beliefs became detached from interpretive strategies like typology and figural exegesis of Scripture. In this way, and separated from its deeper sources, Edwards' thought seems to have heralded the nineteenth century, even as, in a critical historical perspective, his concerns thoroughly exemplified the seventeenth. Looked at in this light, Jonathan Edwards turns out to have been a creature of history even more than the creator of a new historiography.

Notes

1. A critical edition of *Charity and Its Fruits* is published in *The Works of Jonathan Edwards*, 8, ed. Paul Ramsey (New Haven: Yale University Press, 1989). The introduction explores technical aspects of the manuscript as well as presenting the editor's interpretation of Edwards' ethical writings.

2. Ramsey reproduces Tyron Edwards' original introduction (8:125ff.).

3. The critical edition of *A History of the Work of Redemption* is published in *The Works of Jonathan Edwards*, vol. 9, ed. John F. Wilson (New Haven: Yale University Press, 1989). The text reproduces (insofar as possible in typeface) a

transcription of the original sermon booklets from which Edwards preached the series of sermons that comprises the Redemption Discourse. The following discussion draws upon the critical introduction (9:3–109), which should be consulted for details and specific citations.

4. Figures like Hume, Voltaire, and Gibbon are frequently cited as exemplifying this new interest in history that underlies, and eventually produces, modern critical historiography.

5. The text of this letter in the Yale edition (16:725–30, item no. 230) reproduces a version published by Samuel Hopkins; no manuscript copy appears to have survived. The section that concerns "History of the Work of Redemption" is on pp. 727–28, and the quoted phrases that follow are taken from that text.

6. For a more extensive discussion of the "Notebooks" Edwards kept in planning his *History of the Work of Redemption*, see appendix B to volume 9 of the Yale edition (pp. 543–56), where they are described and discussed.

7. *Two Dissertations* may be consulted in *The Works of Jonathan Edwards*, 8, *Ethical Writings*. Paul Ramsey provides a critical discussion of the text(s) as well as offering commentary upon them. The discussion that follows about the first of them, *End for which God Created the World*, draws on these materials.

8. The quotation comes in the summary (section 7) of the initial dissertation.

9. *The Works of Jonathan Edwards* will comprise twenty-seven volumes of his published and unpublished writings. It will exclude incomplete and less formal materials, although the editorial board plans to eventually have those transcribed, at least roughly, and made electronically accessible.

10. *The Social Sources of Denominationalism* (New York: Henry Holt and Co., 1929); *The Kingdom of God in America* (New York: Harper and Brothers, 1935).

11. *Kingdom of God*, p. vii.

12. Ibid., p. 143.

13. See, as a prominent example, Ernest Lee Tuveson, *Redeemer Nation, the Idea of America's Millennial Role* (Chicago: University of Chicago Press, 1968).

14. New York: William Sloane Associates, 1949.

15. Berkeley: University of California Press, 1966.

16. Ibid., pp. 104, 94.

17. University Park: PA. Pennsylvania State University Press, 1992.

18. Ibid., chapter 1, "God's Manner with a Covenant People: The National Covenant," pp. 11–36.

19. Ibid., chapter 2, "That Glorious Work of God and the Beautiful Society: The Premillennial Age and the Millennium," pp. 37–92.

20. New York: Oxford University Press, 2000.

21. New York: Oxford University Press, 1998.

22. Ibid., chapter 4, "Valuation: Ethics and Divinity in *End of Creation*," p. 63.

23. Ibid., chapter 5, "Narration: Drama and Discernment in *History of Redemption*," p. 79.

24. Zakai analyzes the background to New England Puritan thought in his *Exile and Kingdom: History and Apocalypse in the Puritan Migration to America* (Cambridge: Cambridge University Press, 1992). His extensive discussion of

history and eschatology in Edwards' thought is published as *Jonathan Edwards' Philosophy of History: The Reenchantment of the World in the Age of Enlightenment* (Princeton: Princeton University Press, 2003).

Suggested Further Readings

Conforti, Joseph A. *Jonathan Edwards, Religious Tradition, and American Culture.* Chapel Hill: University of North Carolina Press, 1995.
Lee, Sang Hyun. *The Philosophical Theology of Jonathan Edwards*, pp. 211–41. Princeton: Princeton University Press, 2000.
Miller, Perry. *Jonathan Edwards*, pp. 307–30. New York: William Sloan Associates, 1949.
Wilson, John F. "Editor's Introduction." In *The Works of Jonathan Edwards, 9, A History of the Work of Redemption.* Ed. John F. Wilson. New Haven: Yale University Press, 1989.
———. "History, Redemption, and the Millennium." In *Jonathan Edwards and the American Experience*, ed. Nathan O. Hatch and Harry S. Stout, pp. 131–41. New York: Oxford University Press, 1988.
———. "Jonathan Edwards as Historian." *Church History* 46 (March 1977): 5–18.
Zakai, Avihu. *Jonathan Edwards' Philosophy of History: The Reenchantment of the World in the Age of Enlightenment.* Princeton: Princeton University Press, 2003.

Fifteen

Eschatology

Stephen J. Stein

THERE IS A BIT of an anachronism in the title of this essay. Jonathan Edwards never used the term "eschatology" in his private reflections or in his public writings concerning the "last things." The word was not coined in English before the fifth decade of the nineteenth century.[1] But the religious and theological issues embraced by the term today preoccupied Edwards from his earliest recorded years until the close of his life. The issues in question cover the full range of concerns dealing with the ultimate destiny of individuals and of the entire created order.

For Edwards the obvious "last things" included a series of interconnected concepts: death, judgment following death, and final, eternal destiny, either heaven or hell. His notion of time was a corollary concern, because questions regarding the passage of time arise naturally in the discussion of eschatological issues. But his ruminations on the end of things also inevitably invited reflection on penultimate issues. "Last things" often seem to mirror next-to-last things, sometimes even first things.

"Last things" demand attention to proximate matters, and sometimes even to first things. And in the world of eschatology—whether the word existed or not—such proximate matters and first things may often consume as much or more attention than ultimate concerns. In the case of Edwards, the proximate or "almost last things" included a series of religious and theological issues that engaged his thought and reflection throughout his ministry. How, for example, does God effect the ultimate outcome in the divine economy? What historical forces move the divine plan forward? What are the critical stages in the progress toward the end? What roles do the respective parties on earth and in heaven play in this drama? Where does the world stand at the present moment in the divine plan? What are the responsibilities of the faithful in all this? Similarly, first things were the object of Edwards' theological attention. For what purpose did God create the world? How does that objective relate to the processes of history? These and other questions occupied Edwards through the years.

The particular eschatological categories Edwards employed were a product of the religious and theological culture of the first half of the eighteenth century. Few of the concepts were unique or distinctive to his thought; he was a participant in the larger eighteenth-century discussion concerning "last things."[2] His eschatological ideas, which ranged widely over his own lifetime, were in general random and occasional. Late in his career he intended to write something more systematic, but smallpox snuffed out his life before he was able to fulfill plans for a coherent, organized statement on "last things." Scattered draft materials in his working notebooks and a posthumous publication provide some limited assistance. The historian must therefore reconstruct Edwards' eschatological views largely from scattered and occasional observations. At best one can only project tentatively the fuller and more complete statement he might have made had he survived as president of the College of New Jersey. Even with this limitation, however, Edwards' eschatology has a describable form and content.

In what follows, a chronological framework will be used to sketch the continuities and discontinuities in Edwards' reflections on eschatological matters. Three time periods provide the organizing scheme: Edwards' early years of theological reflection, from the time of his schooling to 1733; the years dominated by his involvement with local revivals and with the Great Awakening in New England, from 1734 to 1748; and the last decade of his life, the period often identified as his most productive." Edwards' eschatological views during these three phases will be characterized as random, occasional, and somewhat systematic, respectively. A brief summary statement closes the essay.

The authors who deal with Edwards' eschatology are divisible into two camps: those who celebrate and identify with his views and those who adopt a more detached and/or critical perspective. Edwards' students and disciples were among the first to pay focused attention to his writings on the "last things." Samuel Hopkins and Joseph Bellamy, both of whom studied with Edwards, shared his preoccupation with eschatology, and both published works dealing with such matters.[3] In the nineteenth century, Sereno Dwight, Edwards' grandson and his editor, adopted a similarly positive view of Edwards' concern with the "last things."[4] In the twentieth century, those who celebrated Edwards' eschatological judgments often hailed from the evangelical religious camp (for example, Iain H. Murray and John H. Gerstner) or from the ranks of systematic theologians (for example, Robert W. Jenson and Sang Hyun Lee).[5] During Edwards' lifetime his published views on such matters sometimes attracted negative commentary from theological opponents. Critical scholarly attention, however, dominated the literature on his eschatological views during the closing decades of the twentieth century. The agenda for debate was established by the works of Perry Miller, C. C. Goen, and Alan Heimert;[6] and a host of reactive studies have been and continue to be published.[7] Theological and cultural developments at the turn of the millennium provided additional incentive for reflection on eschatological issues, including Edwards' judgments about such matters.

Edwards began writing his earliest comments on eschatological issues in late 1722, when he was serving as a supply minister in New York City. In the years that followed, before he assumed the position of assistant minister to his grandfather Solomon Stoddard in Northampton, Massachusetts, he established a lifelong pattern of study, constructing a series of private notebooks in which he recorded theological observations and judgments. He maintained these study habits and expanded the number of notebooks in later years, even when he faced an increasingly demanding set of public responsibilities after he succeeded his grandfather as the sole minister in Northampton and as his reputation expanded.

Edwards' earliest observations on eschatology in these notebooks appear almost completely random. Among the first entries in the "Miscellanies," for example, is an "Exposition" of Revelation 5:10 in which he described the saints' reigning with Christ during the thousand years as a "spiritual resurrection," by contrast with a "natural resurrection." He regarded this interpretation as an encouragement for martyrs and saints who suffered under pagan and antichristian violence (13:167–68). From early on, Edwards left nothing to the imagination regarding the identification of the Antichrist: in a related entry he identified the Antichrist with the Church of Rome and argued that the Roman church's profession of the Christian faith made it all the more anti-Christian; it was a "loathsome, poisonous, crawling monster" (13:185–86). In another early note on anti-Christian "hatred and malice," he observed that the Papists often even refused to bury the dead whom they killed in their religious conflicts—proof of their being compared to those who mocked the faithful witnesses in Revelation 11:8–10 (13:191).

In these earliest eschatological observations, Edwards seized upon images from Revelation. He identified the "woman in the wilderness" in Revelation 12:6 with the evangelical church "in the valleys of the Piedmont" (13:196). He equated the target of the third vial poured out in Revelation 16 with the "fountains of Popery," which were the Catholic universities, the Jesuit order, and France, all of which provided support for the Church of Rome (13:195–96). In a less vitriolic and more positive strain, Edwards interpreted the "four living creatures" of Revelation 4:6ff. as four divine attributes responsible for the management of the world: "wisdom, power, goodness, and justice." These control the wheels of providence. This image reinforced Edwards' confidence concerning the final outcome of history, even though at the moment the church's prospects appeared dim (13:191–95).

In view of his early focus on Revelation, it is not surprising that by spring or early summer of 1723 Edwards began a separate notebook devoted exclusively to the Apocalypse. The opening portion of that manuscript he filled with notes, proceeding chapter by chapter through the entire text of Revelation. His entries, which defy easy generalization, have the collective practical effect of reassuring Christians in every age that despite the horrific evils perpetrated against the church by her enemies—paganism, Judaism, antichristianism, "Mahometanism," and others—the faithful will triumph. Writing about the church triumphant in chapter 21, Edwards asserts, "Hereby is signified that all the changes, dangers, doubts, difficulties, storms and tempests, sorrows and afflictions of this world shall forever vanish and be abolished" (5:124). About this same time in the "Miscellanies," Edwards described the vision of an earthly millennium "all over the world" during which divine and human knowledge will spread so widely that even in the most distant, remote, and uncultivated regions the reign of truth will prevail, and "the glories of the Creator" will resound everywhere ("Misc." 26, 13:212–13). This confidence about the ultimate outcome of history marks Edwards' eschatology from beginning to end.

Among Edwards' earliest reflections on the "last things" are a variety of comments on the nature of the happiness that will be enjoyed by the saints in heaven. Some will enjoy greater happiness than others, but that will not be "a damp to the happiness of those that are inferior," for everyone will be "completely satisfied and full of happiness" ("Misc." 5, 13:201–2). In a later note he contrasted the bodily perfection of the saints in heaven with the excruciating, "intolerable pain" that will befall "the bodies of the wicked" after the resurrection ("Misc." 95, 13:263). Edwards repeatedly focused on the contrast between the two eternal abodes. In heaven, sensual pleasures will be "vastly more ravishing and exquisite" ("Misc." 182, 13:328); in hell, the torments will be "vehement beyond conception." To the latter comment Edwards added the interesting speculation "that this earth, after the conflagration," probably will be "the place of the damned" ("Misc." 275, 13:376).

Edwards' earliest commentary on the Bible displayed his predisposition to view the text through a typological lens. For him, biblical types found their fulfillment in antitypes—biblical, historical, natural, or other. The hermeneutical advantage typology offered was immense. Virtually any detail in the Bible, no matter how significant or seemingly insignificant, might be set into a typological framework and linked to something of greater import. Edwards' consuming interest in typology was one of his motives for starting yet another notebook, devoted to the general interpretation of Scripture, and with special attention to matters of typology.

Near the beginning of 1724 he constructed the first section of what became "Notes on Scripture," which includes numerous entries in the broad category of eschatology. For example, Edwards linked "the lord therefore of the vineyard cometh," a passage from the parable in Matthew 21:40–41, with the "end of the world" and the beginning of "the new heavens and new earth" (15:49). He associated the "monstrous births" recorded in Genesis 6:4 with the Church of Rome, "that monstrous beast," which joins the profession of Christ with "most odious devilism" (15:50). He employed typology to suggest that the Pharisees and the "Jewish church," denounced as "hypocritical, superstitious, corrupt, haughty, [and] persecuting," correspond to the apostatized Church of Rome (15:56). He made use of the Jews in a different manner when describing the victory of Mordecai and Esther over the coalition of Haman: the first two were "figures of the glory, peace, and prosperity of the church after the final overthrow of Antichrist," identified with Haman (15:63). These entries confirm the adversarial nature of his view of other religious traditions. They were enemies and opponents in the cosmic drama leading up to the eschaton.

Edwards expanded his commitment to the study of the Bible in 1731 when he acquired an interleaved Bible from his brother-in-law Benjamin Pierpont. This manuscript, formally entitled "Miscellaneous Observations on the Holy Scriptures," informally cited by Edwards as the "Blank Bible," became the location in which he wrote more than five thousand entries and references relating to all sections of the Bible.[8] Included among these were manifold observations directly or indirectly related to his eschatological interests. For example, he regarded Deuteronomy 32 as typical of the final apocalyptic events. He found biblical evidence in 1 Kings 18:44–46 that the latter-day events would begin in the West, specifically in America. He interpreted Psalm 137:9 as a statement of God's pleasure with those who seek to overthrow the Church of Rome. Luke 21:24 became the basis for his conviction that the defeat of the Antichrist and the conversion of the Jews would happen at about the same time in the progress toward the end of time. He used 1 John 4:3 to confirm his belief that the pope was the Antichrist. His commentary on Revelation in the "Blank Bible" was filled with eschatological observations, including the use of Revelation 13:18 to equate "the number of the beast" with numerical equivalents derived from the word "Lateinos."[9]

In these early years this pattern of random observations on diverse eschatological topics prevailed. Edwards' most concentrated cluster of such materials is in "Notes on the Apocalypse." In over sixty entries at the beginning of a series of numbered notes, Edwards continued his bitter polemic against Roman Catholicism with multiple excoriating comments. In one such summary judgment he declared that "the Church of Rome is the mother of the apostasy of the Christian church" (5:136). He frequently resorted to ridicule in these entries. He spoke of Catholic worship as "ridiculous ceremonies" and as "sorceries" worked by the priests (5:140). Edwards attempted to correlate episodes in Revelation with historical events, both past and present. His abiding instinct to historicize the biblical accounts began in this early period. For example, he thought the third trumpet sounded in Revelation 8:7 signified the scourge of the Goths and Vandals on the Western empire (5:128). He identified the "two witnesses" of Revelation 11 with "the Waldenses and Albigenses" (5:137). In this notebook Edwards also reflected on the sequence of end-time events. He wrote entries on the millennium, the first and the second resurrections, and the New Jerusalem. Each of these apocalyptic themes would continue to attract his attention in later years. These early random entries and interests anticipate his lifelong preoccupation with such eschatological issues.

In the years between 1734 and 1748, Edwards stepped into the broader public arena in New England, the English colonies in North America, and the wider English-speaking world. A series of his publications moved him into the religious spotlight, even though he was relatively isolated on the New England frontier in western Massachusetts. His publications were of two kinds: sermons and lectures given in Northampton, Boston, New Haven, and elsewhere that were published and circulated widely, and more general apologetic works that described and defended the local revival in Northampton in 1734–35 and later the colonywide evangelical upsurge commonly associated with the First Great Awakening. The revivals and the awakening occupied a great deal of his intellectual energies in these years and also reinforced his continuing interest in eschatological concerns. He judged the evangelical successes to be signs and instruments of history moving toward its conclusion. At the same time that he was increasingly occupied with public responsibilities, he continued his private program of study, writing an astonishing amount in his notebooks and beginning yet others.

Religious events in Northampton vaulted Edwards into the public arena. Beginning in late 1733, a dramatic spiritual change swept through the town. Before long, Edwards later reported, "a great and earnest concern about the great things of religion and the eternal world became universal in all parts of the town, and among persons of all degrees and all ages; the noise among the dry bones waxed louder and louder" (4:149). Edwards' descriptions of the local revival in Northampton and of similar occurrences in other towns along the Connecticut River brought attention to him as a leader of these movements and as their defender. Though he did not elaborate extensively on eschatological themes in his description of the Northampton revival, he did take note that the residents of the town were greatly concerned with getting into "the kingdom of heaven" and equally fearful of "dropping into hell" (4:150). Edwards was cautious in his public assessment of the local revival, dismissing the report of some that this "remarkable concern" was evidence "that the world was near to an end" (4:190). But in his private notes Edwards acknowledged that revivals are employed by God to move the course of history toward its proper end.[10]

The local revivals of 1734–35 came and went, leaving their supporters, including Edwards, with a sense of disappointment that the "late" religious surge had not sustained itself. Edwards found himself attempting to explain to his congregation how God works out his larger plan of salvation. In 1739 he preached a series of thirty sermons based on Isaiah 51:8, with the doctrinal statement "The Work of Redemption is a work that God carries on from the fall of man to the end of the world" (9:116), for the purpose of demonstrating the theological significance of the divine control of history. In the sermons he set out to identify and describe the "various dispensations of God" that belong to that work down through the centuries, and the closing words of the thirtieth sermon cite the final words of the Book of Revelation that express the desire that Christ would come quickly. In between the Fall and the eschaton comes a series of events that are orchestrated as part of God's larger plan for history and for the work of redemption. Included in the sequence are events that typologically anticipate later events fundamental to the progress of the church—"almost last things." Central in this drama of redemption are the rise, opposition, and eventual fall of the Antichrist, after which the millennial age begins.[11] Edwards' description of the thousand years of the church's prosperity on earth reads a bit like the account of the Northampton revival writ large. It will be a time of "vital religion" prevailing everywhere, with holiness, peace, harmony, and love uniting all nations and all parts of the church throughout the world (9:481–86). These 1739 sermons manifested in public the investment Edwards had been making in his private study of the Bible, his predisposition to interpret Scripture typologically, and his integration of prophecy and history. Throughout it all he expressed an unshaken confidence in the ultimate outcome of the work of redemption. Edwards' confidence in the triumph of the church over the forces of the Antichrist was confirmed, among other ways, by his study of Moses Lowman's *Paraphrase and Notes on the Revelation*, a work he cited at length in his notebooks and alluded to in his sermons (5:219–52, 9:422–23).

With such confidence and a longing in his soul for a return of the revivals, it is no surprise that Edwards was thrilled when the itinerant Anglican preacher from England, George Whitefield, about whom American colonists had read so much, arrived in America and began a highly publicized preaching tour. Stimulated by these and other evangelical successes throughout New England, Edwards used the occasion of an invitation to the commencement of Yale College in 1741 to address the question of how to distinguish authentic from unauthentic religious experiences. He sought to provide guidance for those caught up in religious excitement and to situate the current evangelical successes in a larger perspective. One premise of his method for discerning the true works of the Spirit was his belief that the "last and greatest outpouring of the Spirit of God . . . in the latter ages . . . will be very extraordinary" (4:230). Although much of his discourse focused on problematic expressions of enthusiasm in the revivals, he called on his audience to support the "remarkable and wonderful work" (4:270), and he cast that exhortation in the framework of Christ's second coming, "a spiritual coming, to set up his kingdom in the world" (4:271). Although he hedged on whether the revivals were "the beginning of that great coming," he affirmed that they are similar to it in that they are a work of the Spirit (4:272).

Edwards emerged in the early 1740s as a leading supporter and spokesperson for the awakening in New England. The fact that the religious community divided over these revivals became the occasion for him to write an even more extensive description and defense of them. Responding to critics who lashed out at the unrestrained enthusiasm in the revivals and what they regarded as inappropriate behavior that did not conform to the established religious culture of the day, Edwards published in 1742 *Some Thoughts Concerning the Present Revival of Religion in New England*, affirming it as "a glorious Work of God" and exhorting New Englanders to acknowledge and promote it (4:290). His extended analysis tied the evangelical awakening to scriptural types and precedents. Even more important from the standpoint of his interest in "last things," he cast the revivals in an eschatological framework. In perhaps his most speculative comment of its kind, Edwards wrote, " 'Tis not unlikely that this work of God's Spirit, that is so extraordinary and wonderful, is the dawning, or at least a prelude, of that glorious work of God, so often foretold in Scripture, which in the progress and issue of it, shall renew the world of mankind" (4:353). In other words, the awakening in New England might be an anticipation, or even the start, of the long-promised millennial age. "And there are many things," he added, "that make it probable that this work will begin in America" (4:353). He followed that suggestion with several comparisons of the "two great habitable continents" (4:354) that worked out to the advantage of the "new world." But that was not the end of his speculation; he then added that perhaps New England will be the location "whence this work shall principally take its rise" (4:358).

Little surprise that critics of the awakening seized on Edwards' rather audacious judgments. They ridiculed the notion that the revivals, which they equated with wild enthusiasm, were to be the beginning of the millennial age. Charles Chauncy, minister of Boston's First Church, derided Edwards' suggestion.[12] Other opponents railed at the idea that the outbursts of newly convicted sinners were the first stages of the blissful millennium. Edwards was usually restrained in his public statements concerning eschatological issues, reserving his more speculative ideas on these matters for his private notebooks. His exchanges with critics of the revivals, however, ultimately led him to write his monumental defense of evangelical religion, the *Treatise Concerning Religious Affections*, which attempts to establish the signs of an authentic work of God's Spirit. That treatise, however, is not essentially eschatological; rather, its focus is on Christian life in the here and now.

Despite his hopes for the awakening, Edwards was again forced to watch the revivals ebb within a short period of time. In late 1745, Edwards wrote to a correspondent in Scotland that in New England God "has now in a great measure withdrawn," with the result that religion was experiencing "innumerable and inextricable difficulties" (16:181). Warfare among the powers of Europe—conflicts that spilled over into the New World—added to the uncertainties of the day. And yet Edwards did not despair. In these times of religious decline and imperial strife, he joined with other evangelicals in Great Britain who were proposing that prayer might well be the means for promoting the kingdom of God. A number of ministers in Edinburgh were organizing a "concert of prayer" in which Christians from all corners of the world would unite on a given day to pray for an outpouring of the Spirit. This united effort began early in the 1740s, but it was the decline of the revivals that led Edwards to join the undertaking.

In 1747–48 Edwards wrote a treatise in support of the concert of prayer, the title of which summarizes its substance and eschatological framework: *An Humble Attempt to Promote Explicit Agreement and Visible Union of God's People in Extraordinary Prayer for the Revival of Religion and the Advancement of Christ's Kingdom on Earth, pursuant to Scripture-Promises and Prophecies concerning the Last Time*. From Zechariah 8:20–22 he argued that the prophecy concerning the prosperous times of the church on earth had yet to be fulfilled and that Christians have a responsibility to seek God's Spirit by fervent prayer. Edwards assembled a variety of reasons for participating in the effort, including the notion that God promised to pour out the Spirit in great abundance in the latter days. In the treatise Edwards defended the concert of prayer against criticism that it was pharisaic, requiring public prayer at particular times. He also tied his reasoning to an interpretation of the Book of Revelation and in doing so, parted company with Moses Lowman, who argued that the fall of Antichrist would not take place before the year

2000. The practical effect of Lowman's chronology was to put off the return of Christ; Edwards was disturbed of the thought of Christ's return being so far off. In the *Humble Attempt* he took issue with Lowman's dating of the events depicted in the Apocalypse. In "Notes on the Apocalypse" he began a new section entitled "Events Probably Fulfilling the Sixth Vial on the River Euphrates, the News of which was Received since October 16, 1747." His entries, drawn from newspapers published in the colonies, recorded military successes of the English and others against the Catholic powers of Europe. For example, he noted that the Boston *Evening-Post* on December 7, 1747, reported that an English privateer captured "a Spanish ship with a valuable cargo, supposed to be worth 50,000 pound sterling" (5:256). Here in the naval and economic news he saw a triumph which for him heralded the approach of the "last things."

In this second period Edwards found himself operating increasingly in the public eye. He emerged as a champion of the revivals and a defender of the awakening in New England. For him these public events intersected in instructive ways with the years of effort he had invested in private study, confirming the larger historical and eschatological framework of his thought.

The third period of Edwards' life opened on a note of conflict, moved through a highly creative period, and culminated in unexpected professional prominence, followed by personal tragedy. The conflict was with the congregation in Northampton over the issue of qualifications for communion. When Edwards departed from the practice of his predecessor and grandfather Solomon Stoddard by requiring stricter standards of qualification, he created a furor in the congregation that ultimately led to his dismissal. After a period of some professional uncertainty, in 1751 he accepted the position of minister at the mission to the Housatonic Indians in Stockbridge, Massachusetts. This move, on first blush, appeared negative because Stockbridge was a frontier outpost, but with the passage of time it proved otherwise. Although Edwards was consumed with new responsibilities and found himself locked in controversy about the policies governing the mission, his years in Stockbridge proved a boon to his program of study and to his writing projects. At Stockbridge he crafted a second defense of his position in the communion controversy (12:349–503), published a massive exposition of the bondage of the will (1:129–439), and wrote a treatise on original sin (published posthumously; 3:102–437). He also drafted two shorter dissertations that appeared in print several years after his death, one of which—*Concerning the End for Which God Created the World*—addresses the ways in which first things shape the understanding of "last things" (8:399–627).

In addition, these were years that saw Edwards continue his private studies and his entries in his notebooks, including many on eschatological themes. He also planned several major projects that were intended to present in more systematic fashion ideas he had been developing in the preceding two periods. The primary clue to these plans as they bear on "last things" lies in his 1757 letter to the trustees of the College of New Jersey, who invited him to be the president of the college. In that letter he described two major projects he contemplated, one of which was to be "a body of divinity in an entire new method, being thrown into the form of an history." This work, called *A History of the Work of Redemption*, would deal with

> the course of divine dispensations, or the wonderful series of successive acts and events; beginning from eternity and descending from thence to the great work and successive dispensations of the infinitely wise God in time, considering the chief events coming to pass in the church of God, and revolutions in the world of mankind, affecting the state of the church and the affair of redemption, which we have an account of in history or prophecy; till at last we come to the general resurrection, last judgment, and consummation of all things. . . . This history will be carried on with regard to all three worlds, heaven, earth, and hell. (16:727–28)

Herein lies Edwards' plan for a more systematic statement on prophecy and history in the work of redemption. In this project he intended to move beyond the random and the occasional to a new and different form for Christian theology cast in a historical mode. This was not systematic theology in the usual sense, but for Edwards it was systematic in that it spanned all of history and proceeded in chronological order, from creation to the end of time. Eschatology, or the "last things," figured centrally in its design.

Historians have speculated what Edwards' "great work" would have been had he survived his smallpox inoculation and continued for a number of years in the presidency at Princeton. Some have suggested that his 1739 sermons were the "great work" in an early version, a legitimate enough view. On the other hand, Edwards invested an immense amount of time in study between 1739 and 1758, when he died. Therefore, it seems probable that a fuller expression of his views was forthcoming, tying together his mature historical and eschatological reflections. The remainder of this essay will sketch some of the particulars that, no doubt, figured in his plans for the sections of the history that dealt with "last things."

One topic of continuing eschatological concern for Edwards was the millennium, "the glorious times of the church on earth after the fall of Antichrist." Specifically, he focused repeatedly on the possible length of time implied by the biblical "thousand years." Edwards recognized that the primary text involved, namely, Revelation 20:5, was subject to both a literal and a figurative interpretation, because that is "the manner of Scripture prophecy." But he also compiled a list of reasons why the reference was not to "any space of time vastly longer than a thousand years," even if the words were intended figuratively. Among his reasons was the fact that the earth's population would explode over time, and as a result the earth would be unable to "hold the inhabitants" ("Misc." 836, 20:50–51). Written perhaps in 1752 or early 1753, the last entry in the "Miscellanies" indexed by Edwards under "Millennium" pursues the same issue. He suggested that an overly lengthy millennium would tempt the saints "not to behave themselves as pilgrims and strangers on earth" ("Misc." 1224, 23:156). In other words, they would relish this world and forget the promise of heavenly treasures. For these and other reasons, he asserted that the millennium probably would be approximately a thousand years.

Through the years, Edwards' reflections on the day of judgment moved back and forth between the astounding drama and power of Christ's physical reappearance as the mighty judge and the differing responses of the saints and the wicked at the divine tribunal. The sound of the trumpet, the flaming fire, the shaking of the universe, the opening of graves, the glory and majesty of Christ's being—all of these "terrify the ungodly" at the same time that they "increase the confidence of the saints" ("Misc." 949, 20:204–8, "Misc." 1138, 20:512–13). Both groups face the Judge, who will open the books and bring to light "the secrets of all hearts" and "the hidden things of darkness." Then the righteous will be blessed and the wicked cursed. At that point, adding to the drama, "The righteous, before they go into heaven, shall stay to see the execution of the sentence on the wicked." The wicked exit to "everlasting punishment," and then the righteous gain "life eternal." This, Edwards declares, is "the finishing work of redemption" ("Misc." 949, 20:204–8).

Edwards spent an inordinate amount of time and thought throughout his career on the subject of heaven. His written notes describe heaven as the "eternal residence" of God ("Misc." 743, 18:376–80), located in "the uppermost part of the universe" and in "the highest or outermost part of it" ("Misc." 743, 18:380–81). Heaven is also "the habitation of the angels" ("Misc." 745, 18:390), and it will be the eternal abode of the saints. Edwards was also preoccupied through the years with the nature of the happiness of the saints in heaven. He asserted that their happiness will be progressive, and that it will consist "very much in BEHOLDING the manifestations that God makes of himself in the WORK OF REDEMPTION" ("Misc." 777, 18:427). They will also rejoice when they observe the "victory of the church on earth over her enemies" ("Misc." 777, 18:434)—evidence that Edwards rejected any notion of soul sleep, for the departed saints are present and aware in heaven even before the Day of Judgment. The final "consummate glory" of the church "will be at the end of the world" ("Misc." 777, 18:432).

One feature of both heaven and hell is similar, in Edwards' judgment: both are progressive states. He asserted that the "MISERY OF DEVILS AND SEPARATE SOULS IS PROGRESSIVE," like the happiness of the saints in heaven. One pivotal moment in that progressive misery of the wicked is "at the fall of Antichrist [when] the [misery of the] separate souls of persecuting popes, and other popish persecutors, shall especially be increased" ("Misc." 805, 18:508). Edwards never tired of contemplating the defeat of Antichrist. He also never seemed to tire of describing the "EXTREMITY OF HELL TORMENTS." In a strange sort of construction, he reasoned that "the greater the misery" of the damned in hell, "the more glorious the salvation" of the saints in heaven—an inverse ratio specifically so ordered by God ("Misc." 572, 18:111). Not just the EXTREMITY but also the "ETERNITY OF HELL TORMENTS" was a major theme occupying Edwards' attention. He used Luke 20:36 and other biblical passages to argue that a proper eternity excludes "any end." Revelation 21:4 also states that "there shall be no more death" in eternity, thus no escape from the torments by that means ("Misc." 1004, 20:328). It appears that Edwards' depiction of the unending tormented state of the damned brought a kind of eschatological pleasure and/or closure to him.

Edwards' eschatological views are a product of his years of study and of his response to life circumstances. Disciplined study and meditation on the texts of the Bible, with special focused interest on Revelation, resulted in certain thematic and topical continuities over time. His view of prophecy informed all of his reflections, for he saw himself in the midst of a historical process that had been anticipated typologically in the pages of Scripture. Edwards' eschatological views, while not systematically expressed, invite generalization by the historian. Five related observations are in order.

> 1. The controlling principle in Edwards' eschatology, is the connection between first and last things. In the dissertation *Concerning the End for which God Created the World*, published posthumously, he affirmed the constancy of divine intention and the controlling sense of purpose for the entire created order (8:403–536). God created the world "for his own glory," as Edwards stated in a very early "Miscellanies" entry ("Misc." 106, 13:276). God's glory, first exhibited in the intra-Trinitarian relationship with the Son and the Spirit, is replicated in time and space through the creation of the physical universe. The creation therefore magnifies the glory of God, displaying the excellencies of the divine. That glory is never more evident than in the progression from first things to "last things." God's final purpose for the elect is redemption, or the unending pleasure of the divine presence and glory in heaven. The goal of "an infinitely perfect union" of the saints with God is "what God aimed at in the creation of the world" and what will continue as an "eternal

and increasing union" throughout eternity (8:535–36). Therefore, creation and redemption are linked for Edwards from the beginning.

2. Divine providence controls the course of events between first things and "last things." The entire path of history is in that sense eschatological as it moves toward its ultimate end or objective. Providence, as a concept, involves the notion of God's continuing creation, what Edwards described as "a present, remaining, continual act" ("Misc." 346, 13:418). Everything in the universe is subject to "the immediate influence of God" ("Misc." 177, 13:326). Therefore, the course of history is not determined simply by the laws of cause and effect but by the divine purpose and order that governs the whole creation. This is why Edwards was concerned with penultimate issues as well as ultimate ones. Of all such issues, perhaps his view of the millennium is most striking in its consistency with the goal of creation and the work of redemption. He described the millennium as a future age when the truth of the gospel will cover the entire world, when "divine and human learning" will be diffused widely, and when "the glories of the Creator" will sound throughout all nations ("Misc." 26, 13:212–13). This millennial age anticipates the heavenly state ("Misc." 262, 13:369). Longing for such a moment encourages the efforts of the church to advance "Christ's kingdom" on earth ("Misc." 351, 13:427).

3. The Holy Spirit, in Edwards' view, is the primary agent whereby Christ's kingdom on earth advances. The church, the bride of Christ, is the object of God's love and delight. Ministers have the task of nurturing the saints by proclaiming to them the word of God, by administering the sacraments, and by exhorting them to lead godly lives. By these means the Holy Spirit effects conviction and conversion, according to Edwards. It was the general and widespread success of God's Spirit in the 1740s that lifted Edwards' spirit and raised his hopes, leading to his controversial speculation that the world might be on the threshold of the millennial age and that perhaps New England would be in the vanguard of that renewed outpouring of the Spirit (4:353–58). That speculation aside, Edwards firmly believed that revivals were the means for advancing the kingdom. He regarded the fruits of God's Spirit evident in the colonial awakenings and in the transatlantic revivalistic successes as evidence of progress in the work of redemption and therefore appropriately subject to eschatological interpretation.

4. Forces of evil opposed to the work of redemption, according to Edwards, impeded the progress of the gospel and the advance of Christ's kingdom. That opposition took many forms in history: Satan, the author of sin in the Garden; Pharaoh, who enslaved the children of Israel; the kingdoms of the ancient Near East that carried captive the Israelites; the Jews who crucified Christ; the Romans who persecuted the early Christians; the spiritual Babylon presided over by the papal Antichrist; the forces of "Mahometanism"; hypocrites within the church itself. Religious conflicts in Edwards' own day were bitter and

intense, and his hostility to groups he identified as enemies of the elect or of the true church was aggressive and unambiguous. His use of military imagery was consistent with biblical language, in which warfare was a prevailing metaphor. Conflict, drama, fear, excitement, suspense, and uncertainty appear in his eschatological reflections, but they are more than matched by a sense of confidence, joy, happiness, assurance, certainty, and victory. Despite the prolonged and seemingly unending conflict, Edwards confidently affirmed the ultimate triumph for Christ and the church. His eschatological vision left no doubt about the outcome of the work of redemption.

5. For Edwards the final stage of the eschatological process—a stage involving the return of Christ to judge the world, the consummation of the union between Christ and the church in heaven, and the consignment of the wicked to hell—will not, in fact, be final. In that sense, therefore, the use of the word "eschatology" when speaking of Edwards is not only anachronistic but also inaccurate. Both heaven and hell are progressive states and will continue forever. In the former, "the glorified saints shall grow in holiness and happiness" ("Misc." 105, 13:275). In the latter, the damned will experience unending "Hell Torments." There is literally no final point in eternity. The saints will sing the praises of God in unending choruses; at the same time, the wicked will suffer everlasting punishment. Both of these situations, in Edwards' judgment, are apt reflections of the glory of God and consistent with the controlling purpose of creation.

Notes

1. *Oxford English Dictionary*, 2d ed.
2. See, for example, Reiner Smolinski, "Apocalypticism in Colonial North America," in Stephen J. Stein, ed., *The Encyclopedia of Apocalypticism*, vol. 3, *Apocalypticism in the Modern Period and the Contemporary Age* (New York: 1998), pp. 36–71.
3. Samuel Hopkins, *A Treatise on the Millennium. Showing from Scripture prophecy, that it is yet to come; when it will come; in what it will consist; and the events which are first to take place, introductory to it* (Boston, 1793); and Joseph Bellamy, *Sermons upon the following subjects, viz. The divinity of Jesus Christ. The millenium* [sic]. *The wisdom of God, in the permission of sin* (Boston, 1758).
4. In *The Works of President Edwards; with a memoir of his life*, 10 vols. (New York, 1830), Sereno Dwight published Edwards' letter of March 5, 1744, to his Scottish correspondent, William McCullough, in which Edwards used Scripture to defend his views on the millennium against his critics and underscored the importance of prophecy and its relationship to history (1:211–19).
5. Iain H. Murray, *Jonathan Edwards: A New Biography* (Edinburgh, 1987); John H. Gerstner, *The Rational Biblical Theology of Jonathan Edwards*, 3 vols.

(Powhatan, Va., 1991–93); Robert W. Jenson, *America's Theologian: A Recommendation of Jonathan Edwards* (New York, 1988); and Sang Hyun Lee, *The Philosophical Theology of Jonathan Edwards* (Princeton, 1988).

6. Perry Miller, *Jonathan Edwards* (New York, 1949); C. C. Goen, "Jonathan Edwards: A New Departure in Eschatology," *Church History* 28 (1959):25–40; and Alan Heimert, *Religion and the American Mind from the Great Awakening to the Revolution* (Cambridge, Mass., 1966).

7. See, for example, the publications listed in "Suggested Further Readings" and in note 5.

8. *The Works of Jonathan Edwards*, 24, *"The Blank Bible,"* ed. Stephen S. Stein (New Haven, 2005).

9. For Edwards' annotations to the biblical passages cited here, see the "Blank Bible," pp. 167, 281, 454, 732, 753, 881, 892, and 755, respectively.

10. See, for example, his entry on Is. 37:30–31, where he identifies "revivals of the church" as "shadows and resemblances of the last resurrection" ("Blank Bible," p. 507).

11. Edwards' written reflections concerning the millennium extend across his entire adult life, his earliest comment coming in "Miscellanies," no. 26. Perhaps undue attention has been paid to this one aspect of his eschatological thought because of the early pivotal essay by C. C. Goen which declared Edwards' postmillennialism to be a new departure in American thought. Subsequent revisions of that view have reduced the stark contrast drawn between pre- and postmillennialism. To the extent that Edwards anticipated the spread of the gospel and the eventual dominance of the church before the end of time, he can be labeled a postmillennialist. The casual characterization of the two forms of millennialism as pessimistic and optimistic, respectively, has less validity than earlier scholars have suggested. See Stein, "American Millennial Visions."

12. See *Seasonable Thoughts on the State of Religion in New-England, a treatise in five parts* (Boston, 1743), p. 372.

Suggested Further Readings

Bloch, Ruth H. *Visionary Republic: Millennial Themes in America Thought, 1756–1800*. Cambridge: Cambridge University Press, 1985.

Davidson, James West. *The Logic of Millennial Thought: Eighteenth-Century New England*. New Haven: Yale University Press, 1977.

Goen, C. C. "Jonathan Edwards: A New Departure in Eschatology." *Church History* 28 (March 1959): 25–40.

Hatch, Nathan O. *The Sacred Cause of Liberty: Republican Thought and the Millennium in Revolutionary New England*. New Haven: Yale University Press, 1977.

Jenson, Robert W. *America's Theologian: A Recommendation of Jonathan Edwards*. New York: Oxford University Press, 1988.

Lee, Sang Hyun. *The Philosophical Theology of Jonathan Edwards*, pp. 236–41. Princeton: Princeton University Press, 1988.

Lee, Sang Hyun, and Allen C. Guelzo, eds., *Jonathan Edwards in Our Time: The Shaping of American Religion*. Grand Rapids: Eerdmans, 1999.

McDermott, Gerald R. *One Holy and Happy Society: The Public Theology of Jonathan Edwards*. University Park: Pennsylvania State University Press, 1992.

Pauw, Amy Plantinga. *The Supreme Harmony of All: The Trinitarian Theology of Jonathan Edwards*. Grand Rapids: Eerdmans, 2002.

Scheick, William J., ed. *Critical Essays on Jonathan Edwards*. Boston: G. K. Hall, 1980.

Smolinski, Reiner. *The Kingdom, The Power, & The Glory: The Millennial Impulse in Early American Literature*. Dubuques, Ia.: Kendall & Hunt, 1998.

Stein, Stephen J. "American Millennial Visions: Towards Construction of a New Architectonic of American Apocalypticism." In *Imagining the End: Visions of Apocalypse from the Ancient Middle East to Modern America*, ed. Abbas Amanat and Magnus Bernhardsson, 187–211. London: I. B. Tauris, 2002.

———. "Transatlantic Extensions: Apocalyptic in Early New England." In *The Apocalypse in English Renaissance Thought and Literature: Patterns, Antecedents and Repercussions*, ed. C. A. Patrides and Joseph Wittreich, pp. 266–98. Manchester: Manchester University Press, 1984.

———, ed. *Jonathan Edwards: Text, Context, Interpretation*. Bloomington: Indiana University Press, 1996.

Wilson, John F. "History, Redemption, and the Millennium." In *Jonathan Edwards and the American Experience*, ed. Nathan O. Hatch and Harry S. Stout, pp. 133–41. New York: Oxford University Press, 1988.

Zakai, Avihu. *Jonathan Edwards: The Reenchantment of the World in the Age of the Enlightenment*. Princeton: Princeton University Press, 2003.

Sixteen

The Sermons: Concept and Execution

Wilson H. Kimnach

IN CONSIDERING Jonathan Edwards' sermons, it is important to begin where Edwards himself began: with the Puritan sermon as it was handled in New England, and particularly in the Connecticut Valley, during the first decades of the eighteenth century. For Edwards inherited this distinctive literary form at the end of nearly a century of assiduous domestic cultivation and within a half-century of its demise, and during the relatively brief span of his preaching career he fully exploited its potential without seriously altering its form, thus contributing more than any other individual to its definition in the history of our national literature.

Basically, the form comprises three divisions or movements: a Scripture text, usually "opened" or subjected to detailed explication; a Doctrine, or theological axiom predicated by the text, which is in turn interpreted and confirmed by arguments from Scripture and human experience; and finally an Application, a systematic inculcation of the more practical implications of the Doctrine. It is the sermon form of William Perkins and William Ames, though Richard Bernard's *The Faithfull Shepherd* offers the most penetrating discussion of it, while the diagrams in John Wilkins' *Ecclesiastes* provide the most useful representation of its all-important bone structure.[1] Employed in the seventeenth century by virtually all of New England's great preachers, the form was then commonly expanded at the level of the statement of doctrine so that a single sermon contained two, three, or sometimes several doctrinal "branches" or propositions: moreover, each of the Doctrines usually demanded its own Improvement. Generally, in such cases, a final Application of the Whole trimmed the underbrush in conclusion, though this device hardly restored the sermon to a clean-limbed symmetry.

During Edwards' youth, several changes in handling the sermon form were observable among New England's leading preachers. In the Connecticut Valley, the trend was toward the relative simplicity espoused by Wilkins, while preserving the formal statement of doctrine. Since the statement of doctrine, and not the subject text, had always been to the sermon what the thesis statement is to the essay, this move tended to strengthen the thematic focus and rhetorical unity of the sermon, though it inevitably reduced its philosophical range and literary complexity. Still, the sermon could be a very complicated structure in the hands of Timothy Edwards or Solomon Stoddard. The elder Edwards had a penchant for subheads, for instance, and wrote sermons containing as many as seventy numbered heads; Stoddard, on the other hand, loved rhetorical dialogue (*dialogismus* and *prosopopoeia*) and frequently slows the rhetorical momentum of his sermons in order to conduct question-and-answer sessions. Of all those who are likely to have had a direct influence over Edwards at an early age, perhaps it is his respected kinsman, William Williams of Hatfield, whose sermons most strictly adhere to the form adopted by Edwards.[2]

Over a period of years, Edwards developed a sure sense of movement from Text to Doctrine to Application which is a grand march down from the mountain: from Holy Writ to abstract principles to personal values and actions; from the realm of God to the realm of human understanding to the sensibility of the human heart; from the eternal to the temporal to the existential moment. Eventually, he would not only recognize the nature of the form but exploit its dynamic potential more artfully than any other American preacher.

Although the complete working papers of a colonial preacher are rarely found today, the methodicalness of Jonathan Edwards and the filial piety of his family have made it possible to amass what is undoubtedly the bulk of his sermon manuscripts and related papers.[3] The twelve hundred or so sermons and the attendant sermon notebooks, scripture notebooks, and miscellaneous manuscript writings now collected at the Yale Beinecke Library vividly illustrate the day-to-day working life of a great, but not unrepresentative, New England preacher.

The extant collection of Edwards' sermon manuscripts was originally codified by Edwards himself. His notebook references indicate that the sermon manuscripts were stored in a file by text, and this minimal system of classification was supplemented by a series of sermon notebooks which, in addition to storing ideas for future sermons, apparently served as topical indexes for those already written. "Sacrament," "Lecture," "Virgins," "Peace," "Singing," "Fast," "Contention," "Children," "Moral Honesty," "Covenant," "Rulers," "Affliction," "Education," "Ordination," "Natural Persons," and "Relative Duties" are typical of the varied headings for entries in the three extant sermon notebooks. Many references to particular sermons, identifying them in relation to theological concepts, are also found in the substantive notebooks, such as the voluminous "Miscellanies." Thus Edwards maintained a library of his own sermons, which he studied and utilized variously in his efforts to fulfill the preacher's unremitting duties.

A sermon selected from the file often has, in addition to the identifying text (located near the upper lefthand corner of the first page), a brief record of its pulpit history, sometimes in longhand, sometimes in shorthand, and occasionally in a combination of both. About four hundred sermons, or one-third of the canon, are thus annotated, usually on the first page if space permitted. These notes indicate that many of the sermons were repreached once, twice, or three times, and a number are marked as having been repreached five, six, and even seven times. Occasionally, the repreachings involved delivery in several towns, but many sermons were repreached once or twice at Northampton, usually with alterations and after intervals of several years. After Edwards' remove to Stockbridge, the notes indicate, almost all of the sermons delivered to the white congregation were repreachings of early Northampton sermons. Edwards generally wrote new sermons in abbreviated or outline form for the Indians at the Stockbridge mission; however, even these outlines are frequently abstracts of earlier Northampton sermons.

When Edwards decided that a sermon could be preached once again, he usually made alterations in the manuscript. In addition to merely aesthetic improvements, many revisions were made to adapt the sermon to a new occasion and, frequently, a different auditory. Some vivid instances of Edwards' concern for occasional nuances are to be found by comparing the outlines prepared for delivery to his Indian congregation with earlier Northampton source sermons: passing references to local farming and business affairs become, in the Indian sermons, allusions to nature, hunting, and tribal customs. Indeed, both sermons and sermon notebooks testify that Edwards considered every sermon to be occasional, regardless of its burden of abstract theology, and the immediate occasion of each sermon is indelibly stamped upon it by shadings of diction, choice of metaphors, and allusions, even when prepared by the author for the press.

Edwards many times revised his sermon with great deftness and artistic economy, altering or adding only a few small passages here and there, yet effecting substantial changes in the sermon's rhetorical impact. A fine example of such alterations occurs in a sermon on John 8:34, *Wicked Men's Slavery to Sin* (10:339–50). Edwards wished to impress upon his congregation how sinners are abused by the very master they serve, although he did not discover his most apt illustration until after the sermon was written:

> [Satan and his cohorts] do by you as I have heard they do in Guinea, when at their great feasts they eat men's flesh. They set the poor, ignorant child, who knows nothing of the matter, to make a fire, and while it stoops down to blow the fire one comes behind and strikes off his head, and then he is rosted by that same fire that he kindled, and made a feast of and the scull is made use of as a cup, out of which they make merry with their liquor. Just so Satan, who has a mind to make merry with you.

In this brief interpolation, consisting of a scene and a sententious reflection upon it, Edwards provided his sermon with its most vivid illustration, a verbal emblem which subtly adjusts the tone of the entire sermon by stressing the black comedy of the paradoxically "innocent" sinner's predicament. The image of the cannibal feast (perhaps inspired by a current travel book) becomes, in the sermon's context, a satanic parody of the sacrament; the victim is analogous to an inverted saint, and his symbolic situation is a suggestively reflective water image of the Christian life. By such brilliantly economical strokes, Edwards could significantly redirect the thought and enhance the impact of his sermons.

Among the sermons in which major revision for repreaching required the addition of new sheets to the manuscript is the well-known *God Glorified in Man's Dependence* (17:200–14). Having been invited to preach the Thursday lecture in Boston, Edwards selected a sermon from the file of sermons preached at Northampton and revised it—an almost invariable practice when he was to appear as a guest speaker. The additions made for Boston are on three and one-half leaves and consist of three passages. The first passage differentiates the "objective" good which the redeemed have in God from their "inherent" good in Him. The second is an entirely new and quite lengthy Proposition II in support of the doctrine; it focuses the auditory's attention on the work of redemption as a glorification of God, the redeemed being no more than adjuncts to the process of divine self-fulfillment. The third addition is the insertion of a new Inference 2 in the Application, involving deletion of two paragraphs from Inference 1 and the necessary renumbering; its first sentence reads, "Hence those doctrines and schemes of divinity that are in any respect opposite to such an absolute and universal dependence on God, do derogate from God's glory, and thwart the design of the contrivance for our redemption."[4] So much for Arminians and liberals!

The Northampton sermon and that preached in Boston in July 1731 are the same sermon, but the revised version is obviously more erudite and radical in its argument. In effect, it is more suited to the public lecture before other ministers and Boston intellectuals whom Edwards wished to impress with his doctrinal stance. As in many other cases, what Edwards did through revision was to fit his sermon to the audience and occasion.

Less frequent, though significant, is revision to the point at which a sermon's identity is altered, and the sermon is virtually recast, the old elements being made into a new sermon. One of the most interesting examples of this recasting process involves a sermon on Canticles (Song of Solomon) 1:3. It exists in two forms in two separate booklets, the first dated 1728, the second 1733. First preached at Northampton, Edwards later recast it for delivery in Boston.

The first difference one notes between the versions is in the Opening of the Text, "Thy name is as ointment poured forth." In the Northampton version Edwards provides a densely detailed exegesis of biblical references to the ancient Hebrew use of oil, considering its composition and especially its typological signification, the anointment of Christ with the Holy Ghost. The Opening of the Text in the version intended for Boston, on the other hand, is more fluent and discursive. It begins with two paragraphs on the Canticles as the Song of Songs, the most excellent of the 1,005 songs attributed to Solomon, "as the subject of it is transcendently of a more sublime and excellent nature than the rest, treating of the divine love, union, and communion of the most glorious lovers, Christ and his spiritual spouse, of which a marriage union and conjugal love (which, perhaps, many of the rest of his songs treated of) is but a shadow." The broader frame of reference, encompassing the entire song rather than merely the concept of anointment; the more discursive speculation on the relationship between Christ and the redeemed, and the more sustained exposition, after the manner of an essayist rather than an expositor, contribute to make the Boston version a much more effective literary performance. If one collates the two sermons, he finds that the differences increase as the sermons develop, and in their conclusions the Applications are quite dissimilar. That of the Northampton version is a long and heated exhortation to seek Christ; the Use in the Boston version is more like an aid to reflection: "The Use that I would make of what has been said is to move and persuade to an acceptance of the Gracious offer that Christ makes of himself to us." Edwards was an evangelical pastor in Northampton; in Boston he was an eloquent interpreter, presenting his understanding of a portion of the Word for the consideration of fellow inquirers.

After comparing the sermons, one may return to the statements of doctrine only to find that he has missed a subtle distinction in the interpretation of the text, "Thy name is as ointment poured forth." Edwards informed his Northampton hearers that the words meant "That Christ Jesus is a person transcendently excellent and *desireable*." But for Bostonians the text meant. "That Christ Jesus is a person transcendently excellent and *lovely*." (italics supplied). This degree of rhetorical discrimination is characteristic of Edwards and is merely the homiletical equivalent of the forensic precision of proofs in his treatises.

An easier, yet sometimes more radical, technique is "cannibalism," Edwards' not infrequent practice of fleshing out sermons with the physical components of other sermons.

The simplest variety of cannibalism is that in which parts of different sermons were temporarily joined, perhaps without any tampering with the sermon booklets. That this practice was common appears from Edwards' shorthand notes in the sermon manuscripts. A sermon on Numbers 14:22–23 contains the statement, "Doctrinal part the second time"; another, on Mark 9:44, notes, "Preached the Application a second time." It seems that many times Edwards carried two sermons into the pulpit so that he might preach the Doctrine from one and the Application from the other, thus making a "new" sermon. These ephemeral sermons are largely unidentifiable, for the shorthand notes seldom refer to the accompanying sermon. Some sermons contain telltale stitching holes, showing that Edwards occasionally went to the trouble of detaching portions to be preached, stitched them into a single booklet for the preaching, and then reversed the process when the performance was over. At least once he neglected to set things right. A sermon on Romans 5:7–8 has a full Text and Doctrine, but no Application. Its Application is now stitched to the end of a sermon on 2 Corinthians 9:15.

A slightly more complex procedure can be seen in the booklet of Nehemiah 2:30. It originally contained two sermons, one on the first part of the verse, the other on the remainder. Each sermon has its own Doctrine and Application. Hidden in the booklet, however, is a third sermon, discoverable by following the directions of a shorthand note and reading only those passages marked by vertical lines in the lefthand margins. The passages comprise about six pages from the Doctrine of the first sermon and about seven pages from the Application of the second. Making this "hidden" sermon required more effort in the study than the procedure described above, but it gave Edwards a single, fairly small sermon booklet containing a choice of three sermons for a single pulpit appearance, or a pair for delivery in the usual morning-afternoon Sabbath service.

In the most literal variety of cannibalism, the identity of the original sermon is virtually destroyed as it is incorporated in a new sermon. A vivid example is a sermon on Matthew 21:5, written in 1727 when Edwards was decreasing the size of his sermon booklets from octavo to duodecimo. He seems to have begun writing in one of the duodecimo booklets, in which he got through the Text and Doctrine sections. When it came to the Application, however, he turned to his sermon file and took the Application from a sermon written five years earlier in an octavo booklet. Having cut off the pages needed, he then wrote a new concluding section for the Application on a duodecimo leaf. Placing the leaves in order he stitched the whole together, making a sandwich of the new and the old.

How frequently Edwards performed this operation is hard to tell, particularly if the sermons involved were written at about the same time and thus manifest no significant disparities in hand, ink, or paper. There are, however, gaps in the chronology of the extant manuscript sermon canon not easily attributed to lapses in Edwards' sermon production, and there are sermons specifically referred to in the sermon notebooks which no longer exist, though it would perhaps be too harsh to attribute all such evident losses to the custodial irresponsibility of Edwards' heirs. No doubt, a number of his sermons were cannibalized in this manner; moreover, they may have been good ones, since he thought they contained material worth repreaching. At any rate, a few forlorn Applications, Doctrines, and assorted subheads are stored with the sermons in the file, probably remnants of such cannibalistic enterprise.

One particular variant of cannibalism appears in only a few instances, but deserves mention because of the light it sheds upon Edwards' capacities as an ingenious manipulator of sermonic materials. This technique involves a combination of cannibalism and recasting, the end product of which is a rather strange bifurcated sermon.

Revelation 21:18 is a two-booklet sermon of the early octavo quires, having the normal development of a single sermon through the two booklets. But it also contains inserted leaves from another sermon, two in the first booklet (containing the Text and the first part of the Doctrine) and one in the Application in the second booklet (containing the remainder of the Doctrine and the Application). It is evident that Edwards took two sermons, cut up one, and inserted the desired parts in the body of the other. The result is a single sermon that could be preached from either one of two beginnings. Edwards might have started with the "main" sermon and preached on Revelation 21:18 and the doctrine that "There is nothing upon earth that will suffice to represent to us the glories of heaven." Or, he might have started with the grafted-on segment of the second sermon and preached upon I John 3:2, his doctrine being "That the Godly are design'd for unknown and inconceivable happiness." In either case, he would have preached most of the Doctrine and Application of Revelation 21:18, but when preaching from that text he probably omitted most or all of the exposition of the inserted excerpts from I John.

What would have been the value of such a strategy? It would have enabled Edwards to carry two sermons in the booklets normally allotted to one. Moreover, the fact that the sermons share many passages would have made it easy to preach them alternately, with a minimum of preparation. And when would such considerations have been in Edwards' mind? When he was on the road, preaching in several towns in comparatively quick succession, with fatiguing days on horseback between his pulpit appearances. A note on the back of the first booklet, written in a typical mixture of shorthand and longhand, seems to confirm this speculation: "Preached at Scantick, at New Haven, at Fairfield, [at] New York, at Bolton, and Glastonbury." All the notes appear to have been made at the same time, or at least within a few weeks.

Like his less famous colleagues, Edwards labored with diligence and sometimes surprising ingenuity to meet the demands of the pulpit. His sermon file was also a generator of sermons, since the reexamination of old sermons inevitably facilitated and shaped the production of new ones. Indeed, it was almost certainly through the study and reworking of old sermons that Edwards developed his homiletical style. His peculiarly fine mind, verbal sensitivity, and poetic sensibility are evident in his literary practices, as presented above. But what of his distinctive approach to the business of preaching, and the foundations of his strategy within the tradition of the inherited sermon form? For answers we must look to Edwards' personal background and distinctive training.

As the son of the Reverend Timothy Edwards, Jonathan witnessed the delivery of innumerable sermons during his formative years, and later as a colleague and "journeyman preacher" under his renowned grandfather, the Reverend Solomon Stoddard of Northampton, he rapidly developed and perfected his own sermon style. This background certainly contributed more to the character of Edwards' sermons than texts on rhetoric or homiletics that he may have studied at Yale College. Indeed, there are many indications that Timothy Edwards and Solomon Stoddard were the determinative factors in Jonathan Edwards' ultimate conception of the sermon.

> Let us labour in a very particular, convincing and awakening manner to dispense the Word of God; so to speak as tends most to reach and pierce the Hearts and Consciences, and humble the Souls of them that hear us . . .

The words are Timothy Edwards', though they might easily have been Stoddard's. They occur in the one sermon he published, *All the Living Must Surely Die*,[5] and they remind us that, although Timothy never attained widespread fame, he was a powerful evangelical preacher. Indeed, Benjamin Trumbull, in his *History of Connecticut*, attests that "no minister in the colony had been favoured with greater success than he [in promoting awakenings during the years before the Great Awakening]."[6] Whether or not he was so outstanding, he certainly did use the basic sermon form later adopted by his son.

The handful of extant sermons by Timothy Edwards reveal him to have been a rather pedestrian, if intelligent and learned, preacher.[7] The form of his sermons might be described as classical Puritan, corresponding in principle and structure to the Ramistic diagrams in John Wilkins' *Ecclesiastes* (a middle-of-the road Puritan text, if such there be). His sermons have the three basic divisions of Text, Doctrine, and Application, each structured internally through a succession of brief, numbered heads. In comparison with Jonathan's sermon structure, however, Timothy's is multiply bifurcated.

Jonathan Edwards' first sermon, on Isaiah 3:10 (10:296-307), written after he left home but before he came under the influence of Stoddard, shows that he immediately reduced the number of heads and subheads to permit greater development within heads; likewise, he reduced the frequency of Scripture citation. Perhaps these moves reflect the influence of his training in rhetoric at Yale, but the form is obviously that which was branded deep in his mind by his father's example, whatever refinements may have been acquired at college.

When Edwards joined his grandfather as colleague in 1727, he had written over thirty sermons, though his style was not yet fully developed. In these early sermons, the preoccupation with formal structure and the transitions it required is manifested in a certain woodenness in the diction. There are some effective passages and even some fine sermons, but professional consistency and polish are not yet evident. During the next two years, however, Edwards was to develop with great rapidity under Stoddard, so that he was possessed of much of his ultimate mastery by the time of the old master's death in 1729.

Solomon Stoddard was probably the most impressive man Edwards met in his youth—perhaps in his life. Stoddard was one of the great preachers of the latter days of the theocracy, and it was largely because of him that the atmosphere of theocracy lingered a little longer in the Connecticut Valley than in the East. "Pope Stoddard," as he was only half-irreverently called, evidently preached in a manner in some respects reminiscent of Thomas Hooker. The form of his sermons is the same as that used by Timothy Edwards, the only notable difference being a reduced number of heads and subheads: Stoddard also apparently needed more space for development than Timothy Edwards. Still, in comparison with the sermons of Jonathan Edwards, those of Stoddard are heavily structured and formally conservative.

Within the formal structure, however, Stoddard found ample range for the exercise of his oratorical and literary powers. He infused the "plain style" with a strong tincture of his own personality and, being gifted with a capacity for pungent, epigrammatic expression, he created, without relying extensively on the graces of imagery and metaphor, a colloquial idiom that is still vital. In *The Benefit of the Gospel to those that are Wounded in Spirit*, as in many other sermons, Stoddard asks all the "right" questions and supplies all the answers.[8] The very momentum of successive answers carries the minds of the congregants from stage to stage of the argument. It is not logic, but a rhetorical structure which has some of the inevitability of logic. Very often, moreover, the conclusion of an inquiry is vigorously propounded in an epigrammatic climax, corresponding in effect to the conclusion of a syllogistic demonstration:

> If they were thoroughly scared, they would be more earnest in their Endeavours; Senselessness begets Slightliness.[9]

Or in another passage:

> The Pretence that they make for their Dullness, is, that they are afraid there is no Hope for them . . . but the true Reason is not that they want Hope, but they want Fears.[10]

Such expressions are not soon forgotten; like his grandson and successor in the Northampton pulpit, Stoddard reveals his notion of religion to have been sensational.

Stoddard could also use imagery and metaphor with real artistry when the occasion arose:

> their hearts be as hard as a stone, as hard as a piece of the nether milstone, and they will be ready to laugh at the shaking of the Spear.[11]

Finally, he could employ repetition effectively, often achieving striking results through incremental repetition of an important word, though not necessarily a "poetic" one:

> They may have a large understanding of the Gospel, yet not be set at Liberty by it. Men may be affected with it, yet not be set at Liberty by it. Men may be stirred up to reform their Lives, yet not be set at Liberty. There be but a few comparatively that are set at Liberty by it....[12]

In technique—and indeed in theme—Stoddard's sermons are strikingly close to those later preached by Edwards. His grandson never used the Question–Solidus Answer device as much as he, preferring the continuous line of argument, but certainly all of the above passages are more than a little reminiscent of Jonathan Edwards.

In addition to being an excellent example of the Puritan preacher himself, Stoddard was something of a critic and even a theorist in the art of prophesying. For instance, in 1724 he published a sermon, *The Defects of Preachers Reproved*, which elucidates the paradoxical doctrine that "There may be a great deal of good Preaching in a Country, and yet a great want of good Preaching." In this sermon Stoddard equates good preaching with revival preaching, insists upon the minister's preaching from personal experience rather than from a mere theoretical understanding, and fervently advocates the "hellfire" strategy. Thus, he argues:

> When men don't Preach much about the danger of Damnation, there is want of good Preaching.[13]

More than that:

> Men need to be terrified and have the arrows of the Almighty in them that they may be Converted.[14]

He urges preachers to deal "roundly" with their congregations and "rebuke sharply" those who need reproof. Finally, he defends his conception of the sermon from the accusations of a new faction arising in the East:

> It may be argued, that it is harder to remember Rhetorical Sermons, than meer Rational Discourses; but it may be Answered, that it is far more Profitable to

Preach in the Demonstration of the Spirit, than with the enticing Words of man's wisdom.[15]

"Rational Christianity" and the essay-sermon may have been riding the tides into Boston harbor at the beginning of the eighteenth century, but they would not inundate the Connecticut Valley if Solomon Stoddard could help it. In his hands, the traditional Puritan sermon retained the outward form of Ramean logic, but it had become a meticulously prepared instrument of psychological manipulation; consequently, he was not about to trade it for what he saw as a psychologically superficial and intellectually simplistic, though stylish, mode of discourse. For Solomon Stoddard, rhetoric was power.

There can be little doubt that Stoddard made a great impression on his grandson through his advice and example, shaping Edwards' conception of the sermon at a crucial point in his literary development. Without really deviating from the classic Puritan sermon form that Timothy Edwards employed, Stoddard discovered hidden rhetorical resources in the "plain style" by insisting upon the evaluation of rhetoric in psychological terms that were more comprehensive and subtle than either the old logic or the new Reason. Although widely divergent in talent and personality, Timothy Edwards and Solomon Stoddard fortuitously complemented one another in their sequential impact upon Edwards. Most important of all, perhaps, is their insistence upon the sermon as a heart-piercing implement (represented by the image of the arrow or spear), a simple, efficient, yet terrible device.

The man who won the epithet "Fiery Puritan" achieved that dubious distinction largely through the resonance of one small publication, despite the counterinfluences of other and greater works, and a lifetime devoted to sweetness and light. The reputation of the piece seems to be all out of proportion, and learned students of Edwards sometimes wish that the whole embarrassing phenomenon would go away. The public, on the other hand, continues to pay *Sinners in the Hands of an Angry God* (22:400–35) as much attention (not all of it positive) as anything Edwards wrote. No doubt, the sermon is significant, but just what is significant about it, in contrast to many other sermons by Edwards and his contemporaries, has remained something of a mystery.

Sinners is usually identified as one of Edwards' "hellfire" sermons, perhaps the best; however, comparison with other examples of the breed among Edwards' sermons reveals that *Sinners* is not even a proper "hellfire" sermon, let alone the best. Sermons such as *The Eternity of Hell Torments* and *The Future Punishment of the Wicked Unavoidable and Intolerable*, as well as several manuscript examples, serve to mark the distinction between a true hellfire sermon and the proto-eschatological concern of *Sinners*, consumed as it is with the here and now. Perhaps

Edwards himself supplied the proper category when, subsequent to the Enfield preaching, he gave it a titular identity as a "hands" sermon. It is, after all, neither the "slipping foot" image of the text nor the keen implication of the statement of doctrine's "mere pleasure" that so fixes the mind. Moreover, in establishing the sermon's identity through this particular image, Edwards probably touched his contemporaries more deeply than if he had made the fires of God's wrath his keynote, for "hands" sermons appear to have had a significant tradition, both more poignant and less hackneyed than "hellfire" sermons.

The hand image had been fully sanctioned by the Bible and was clearly associated with the power of God to act *in this life*—particularly in terrible, retributive acts. Seemingly brutal, the language is suited to extreme situations, such as addresses to condemned convicts. Having undoubtedly been exposed to the convention throughout his youth, Edwards was prepared, in the spring of 1741 when his own congregation no longer responded adequately to his exhortations, to unleash the power of this traditional, but somewhat uncommon, variant of the awakening sermon. In order to appreciate the nature of this tradition, we should consider a few of the elements of *Sinners in the Hands of an Angry God* that have been most remarked: Edwards' use of imagery involving physical suspension and pressure; the insistence upon temporal pressure from passing time, both through mere assertion and through metaphor; and finally, the figural intensity resulting from repetition of various sorts. The notion of the unawakened sinner's being upheld by God's hand implies both the sinking weight of the sinner and the lowering, virtually depressive presence of a disapproving Deity tenuously counterbalanced by mere mercy. In sermons Edwards was familiar with, these conditions were conventionally treated as interrelated.

Just as Edwards obviously utilized the traditional language and imagery of the Bible for his most successful effects in *Sinners*—the importance of the spider image has been greatly exaggerated—so he exploited the subgenre of the execution sermon for this special address to the unconverted—than whom, in Edwards' eyes, no type of human could be more completely or surely condemned. The tradition in which he preached is subtly yet openly acknowledged by Edwards in several ways. There is, of course, the imminent confrontation with eternity, then the many variations upon the theme of suspense-suspension-hanging, and inevitably the there-but-for-the-grace-of-God-go-I motif common to the type.

But the most significant conventional element, one that Edwards not only acknowledges but intensifies and exalts in his reification of the form, is the insistence upon the union of power and authority in the governing entity. From the statement of doctrine, with its phrase "mere pleasure" suggesting the formulaic identification of sovereign right but elevating "majesty's" to the supreme "mere," to the prominent thread of references throughout the sermon comparing the relative impotence of earthly princes to the omnipotence of God in dealing with rebels and otherwise condemned persons, Edwards displays considerable artistry in ringing new changes upon this central element of the execution sermon. Not only does God have a personified Justice threatening death, but the earth, the elements, indeed all the creation, including devils, hell, death, and invisible fields of Newtonian force: all are contrived within the closed system of God's sovereignty to the end of ultimately destroying the condemned. The unregenerate sinner has no further court of appeal, no alternative system of values with an objective foundation; the sole escape is through the door where Christ beckons (not the trap in the floor).

If Edwards displays recognition of the traditional "hands" sermon in his use of the conventional biblical imagery, and if he paid the customary tribute of genius by discovering new potentialities within the old form, then it is within the telescoped traditions of the Puritan sermon form and the execution sermon that he discovers the most significant dimension of his innovation in *Sinners*. The occasional form required by the sub-genre of the execution sermon, with its careful distinctions between the community and the condemned, the public law and the private will, and the necessity of condemning the crime while offering hope to the condemned where possible, made this variant of the Puritan sermon a difficult business indeed, and there are few sermons of outstanding literary merit among the extant examples of the type.[16]

However, in *Sinners in the Hands of an Angry God*, Edwards finally achieved an absolutely sustained tone, a sharply delimited range of imagery, and a syntactical structure tightly meshed through both small and large patterns of repetition. As a matter of fact, had Edgar Allan Poe been so inclined he might have used this sermon more plausibly than Hawthorne's tales to illustrate his theory of the "single effect."[17] The sheer centripetal force of meditation upon the governing idea of the sermon—a quality apparent in many of Edwards' writings—is unequalled in intensity elsewhere. In a series of subtle adjustments of focus spanning the entire sermon, Edwards gradually removes the psychological supports of virtually all involved witnesses, and suddenly the entire community finds itself suspended over the pit of mortality, wholly vulnerable within and without, while the eternal moment of God's real time dispels the last illusions of progression in life or discourse. As the final paragraphs warn, even while indicating the concomitant of hope found in all depictions of divine wrath, there is only the moment to awake and turn to Christ before being turned off by the hangman.

The work of pastor Edwards only started with the sinner's awakening, of course, and it must be stressed that no sermon, however great, is to be taken in isolation. Sermons were preached in course, in cycles of awakening, instruction, consolation, celebration, and on a host of special occasions, both civil and ecclesiastical. But in these courses of sermons Edwards made his theological speculations public for the first time, and this publication in the pulpit in turn further shaped his private speculations. Finally, though some would tend to separate the great treatises on philosophical theology from mere pastoral homiletics, it is worth considering that virtually all of Edwards' major treatises were prefigured in his ordinary sermons, in whole or in several parts. For Edwards, the sermon was the essential literary form.

Notes

1. *The Faithfull Shepherd* (London: Thomas Pavier, 1621); *Ecclesiastes, Or, A Discourse Concerning the Gift of Preaching as it falls under the Rules of Art*, 2nd ed. (London: M. F., for Samuel Gellibrand, 1647), pp. 5–7.

2. In addition to purely formal resemblances, the sermons of Williams frequently resemble those of Edwards (or vice versa) in the wording of formulaic transitions between heads. A good example of a Williams sermon is his ordination sermon, *A Painful Ministry* (Boston: B. Green, 1717).

3. The history of Edwards' manuscripts and the extent of the collection now at the Yale Beinecke Library are discussed by Thomas A. Schafer in "Manuscript Problems in the Yale Edition of Jonathan Edwards," *Early American Literature* 3 (Winter 1968–69): 159–71.

4. The three additions are found on pp. 207–10 (excepting most of the scripture proofs on p. 209), 210–12, and 212–13, respectively. A second layer of inserts, all of a comparatively minor nature, was added for the printed version. Unless otherwise indicated, the sermons discussed in this essay remain in manuscript at the Beinecke Rare Book and Manuscript Library, Yale University.

5. *All the Living Must Surely Die: Election Sermon* (New London: T. Green, 1732), p. 25.

6. *History of Connecticut* (New Haven: Maltby, Goldsmith, and Wadsworth, 1818), 2:140.

7. Four sermons were printed from manuscripts by John A. Stoughton in *"Windsor Farmes": A Glimpse of an Old Parish* (Hartford: Clark & Smith, 1883), pp. 121–45.

8. *The Benefit of the Gospel to those that are Wounded in Spirit* (Boston: Thomas Fleet, 1713), pp. 116–17.

9. Stoddard, *Benefit*, p. 180.

10. Stoddard, *Benefit*, p. 181.

11. *The Defects of Preachers Reproved* (New London: T. Green, 1724), p. 13.

12. Stoddard, *Benefit*, pp. 175–76.

13. Stoddard, *Defects*, p. 13.

14. Stoddard, *Defects*, p. 14.

15. Stoddard, *Defects*, pp. 24–25.

16. There are a number of printed eighteenth century sermons that were preached before convicts condemned to execution, and most have a rhetorical family resemblance as "hands" sermons, though comparison shows how rare is a sustained intensity. Noteworthy are Cotton Mather's sermon in *Pillars of Salt* (Boston: Green and Allen, 1699); Increase Mather's *The Folly of Sinning* (Boston, 1699), especially the second sermon, and his sermon on a fatal accident (rather than an execution), *The Times of Men are in the Hand of God* (Boston, 1675).

17. In a review of Nathaniel Hawthorne's *Twice-Told Tales* published in *Graham's Magazine* (May 1842), Poe theorizes that, in short fiction, a truly skillful artist conceives of an effect to be achieved and then works toward it with great discipline: "If his very initial sentence tend not to the outbringing of this effect, then he has failed in his first step." Significantly, Poe is generally credited with establishing a new level of artistic discipline in this argument, anticipating the technical excellence of the modernists.

Suggested Further Readings

Kimnach, Wilson H. "General Introduction to the Sermons: Jonathan Edwards' Art of Prophesying" and "Preface to the New York Period." *The Works of Jonathan Edwards*, 10, *Sermons and Discourses, 1720–1723*, pp. 3–293. New Haven: Yale University Press, 1992.

———. "Jonathan Edwards' Early Sermons: New York, 1722–1723." *Journal of Presbyterian History*, 55: 255–56.

———. "Jonathan Edwards' Pursuit of Reality." In *Jonathan Edwards and the American Experience*, ed. Nathan O. Hatch and Harry S. Stout, pp. 102–17. New York: Oxford University Press, 1988.

Westra, Helen. *The Minister's Task and Calling in the Sermons of Jonathan Edwards*. Studies in American Religion, no. 17. Lewiston, N.Y.: Edwin Mellen Press, 1986.

See also the editors' prefaces to the Yale Works: volume 14 (*Sermons and Discourses, 1723–1729*, ed. by Kenneth P. Minkema); volume 17 (*Sermons and Discourses, 1730–1733*, ed. by Mark Valeri); volume 19 (*Sermons and Discourses, 1734–1738*, ed. by M. X. Lesser); volume 22 (*Sermons and Discourses, 1739–1742*, ed. by Harry S. Stout and Nathan O. Hatch, with Kyle P. Farley); and volume 25 (*Sermons and Discourses, 1743–1758*), ed. by Wilson H. Kimnach (forthcoming).

Seventeen

Missions and Native Americans

Gerald R. McDermott

IN HIS APPENDIX TO *The Life of David Brainerd*, Jonathan Edwards observed that the revival among Brainerd's Indians at Crossweeksung (New Jersey) from August 1745 to October 1746 was more impressive than much of what had passed for revival during the Great Awakening, because the Indian awakening was deeper and more enduring (7:500–41).[1] He speculated that the "wonderful things" which God had done among the Indians "are but a forerunner of something yet much more glorious and extensive of that kind" (7:533). By this he meant a "general revival of religion" that would be "very glorious . . . special and extraordinary" and would produce the "flourishing of Christ's kingdom on earth" (7:532).

This revealing claim indicates that missions to Native Americans were for Edwards simply a chapter in the larger story of the history of revival, which was the main story line in the history of humanity itself, all of which Edwards included in what he called the history of redemption. In this essay I will relate first how missions generally functioned in Edwards' history of redemption and then look more closely at Edwards' own mission to Native Americans. Along the way we will see both how Edwards regarded indigenous religion and how he came to grow in affection for the Indians whom he pastored. At the end I will comment briefly on the importance of Edwards' mission to Protestant missions in later centuries.

For Edwards, mission is the principal moving force of the history of redemption. Although this history never really had a beginning (since "God's electing love and the covenant of redemption never had a beginning") and will have no end, its chief purpose is to repair the damage by the Fall and restore God's image in humanity (which means its nature and soul) and the world (9: 119, 123–24). The history of redemption has four other purposes: to gather together all things into union in one body joined to Christ, to effect the triumph of good over evil, to perfect the beauty of the elect, and to glorify the Trinity (9:124–25). Missions, therefore, are the principal means used by God to secure these purposes in history.

The history of missions is energized by periodic revivals powered by the Holy Spirit, who first inspires men and women to pray for them. The revivals usually come after times of irreligion and moral laxity, are directed by a prophet or some other eminent person, and proceed mainly through preaching (9:142–43, 195, 279). All of this takes place gradually, over the course of millennia, which is the best and only way to demonstrate to finite beings the infinite range of God's perfections (9:355). Edwards argued that if God's glory and beauty were displayed all at once, it "would dazzle our eyes and be too much for our sight" (9:356).

Several elements of this schema are noteworthy. First, all of history since the Incarnation is seen as the actualization of "Christ's purchase" (9:502). History since Christ, in other words, is the story of the application of the work of the Cross. Everything that occurred before the time of Christ was simply preparation for this work, and everything in so-called secular history since the Cross applies it (9:513).

Hence, the purpose of history is redemption, which begins with conversion, which is procured by missions. The conversion of one soul, Edwards declared, is more glorious "than the creation of the whole material universe" and brings more happiness than "all that a people could gain by the conquest of the world" (4:345). Therefore the work of missions, which stimulates revival, is the hidden dynamic driving history and the fruit of missions produces more human happiness than the ablest statecraft.

Second, Edwards' missiology was innovative in two respects. While there were others such as Richard Baxter who had called for modern missions (and theologians such as Samuel Willard and Cotton Mather who had urged missions to Native Americans), Edwards provided new, high-profile sophistication to the claim that the church should be on mission. The standard theological textbooks of Ames, Wollebius, and Calvin were silent on missions, and no other major work of Protestant dogmatics in the English-speaking world gave missions a prominent place. Many Reformed thinkers, including Edwards' ally Thomas Prince in Boston, believed missions were largely limited to the apostolic age.[2]

By giving such prominent place to the laity's intercession for revival, Edwards was also one of the first Protestant thinkers to apply the Great Commission (Matt 28:18–20) to all church members and to invest that call with such universal vision. In his *Humble Attempt to Promote Explicit Agreement and Visible Union of God's People in Extraordinary Prayer for the Revival of Religion and the Advancement of Christ's Kingdom on Earth* (1747), Edwards gave first place to the church's intercession and only marginal place to preaching as the stimulus which prompts outpourings of the Holy Spirit upon the earth. Edwards' enormous prestige in the century after his death, combined with the numerous reprints of *Humble Attempt*, contributed significantly both to nineteenth-century Anglo-American

Protestantism's lay enthusiasm for foreign missions and to the resulting expansion of Christendom to what we now call the third world.

Perhaps Edwards' most productive stimulus to missions generally—and Indian missions in particular—was his extraordinary historical optimism and fervent expectation of imminent revival. Beginning in the late 1730s and continuing through the Great Awakening and much beyond, Edwards prophesied that the world was on the verge of massive religious revival. The era was like that of the first century, he wrote: there had just been a great leap in learning, and it was a dark time again for religion. No biblical prophecy had to be fulfilled before this great outpouring of the Spirit; only prayer and preaching were needed. The revival would bring the "church's prosperity" and at the same time violent opposition, because the "great revival" will "mightily rouse the old serpent" (5:425). The long-term result would be awakening in every nation—among Jews, Muslims, and heathen, and throughout Africa, Asia, and Australia. Repeatedly he projected the conversion of American Indians, as well as the inhabitants of Africa and western Asia: "Many of the Negroes and Indians will be divines, and . . . excellent books will be published in Africa, in Ethiopia, in Turkey" (9:480).

In his 1742 defense of the Great Awakening, *Some Thoughts Concerning the Present Revival of Religion in New England*, Edwards famously opined that in the New England revivals of the early 1740s, "the New Jerusalem in this respect . . . extraordinary degrees of light, love and spiritual joy . . . has begun to come down from heaven" (4:346). Largely because of this remark, most interpreters have held that Edwards believed that the millennium had already arrived, or was about to come to or through America. But Edwards' eschatology has been grossly misunderstood, and was misunderstood even in his own day, as he himself complained in a letter to a Scottish correspondent in 1744 (16:134f.). Just a few pages after this notorious remark in *Some Thoughts*, Edwards referred to "this work of God's Spirit" as "the dawning, or at least a prelude, of that glorious work of God, so often foretold in Scripture, which in the progress and issue of it, shall renew the world of mankind" (4:353). In other words, this work was to be dynamic and progressive, not static and completed as in the millennium.

Later in *Some Thoughts* Edwards refers to the New England revival as perhaps "the dawning of a general revival of the Christian church" (4:466)—again, not the finished and quiescent period typically understood as the millennium. In 1744 Edwards distinguished between the work of God's Spirit that will precede the millennium and the millennium itself and denies that he ever said the millennium had begun (4:558–60). By 1747 Edwards was writing that the great work of God's Spirit, preceding the millennium, might take 250 years, and might not even begin for several hundred years to come—but that in the meantime there would be many happy revivals well worth praying for (5:410–12, 427). At this point Edwards was describing the millennium in strictly international terms. When New England and America were mentioned, they were the most egregious examples of peoples who were spiritually bankrupt and most in need of awakening to save them from perdition (5:357–58).[3]

Long before he arrived at his mission post in Stockbridge, Edwards began to think that what God was doing among Native Americans might be a "forerunner" of the great work of God's Spirit at the end of the age. His interest was piqued in part by Solomon Stoddard and David Brainerd. Stoddard, Edwards' grandfather and the senior pastor under whom he served as assistant for three years, had long envisioned a multiracial American church, with Indians in full communion with whites. In 1723 Stoddard published a blistering attack on New England for its failure to heed God's command to evangelize the Indians.[4]

David Brainerd was so convinced of the extraordinary graces God had shown to the Indians among whom Brainerd worked that his diary persuaded Edwards that "something very remarkable" was occurring among these subjects of Satan (9:434). Brainerd had related stories of Susquehanna Indians who manifested a "disposition" to hear the gospel and Indians on Juniata Island who were remarkably free of prejudice against Christianity (7:294). He had written of an Indian "powwow" (medicine man), clad in bearskin and mask, beating a rattle and dancing "with all his might," who felt his fellow Indians had become corrupted and sought to restore their ancient religious ways. This powwow opposed their consumption of alcohol and affirmed many, though not all, of Brainerd's Christian doctrines. Brainerd believed that he was "sincere, honest and conscientious," and concluded "there was something in his temper and disposition that looked more like true religion than anything I ever observed amongst other heathens" (7:329–30).

Brainerd's Indian converts seem to have impressed Edwards as well. One Indian woman was a textbook example of Edwardsean spirituality. "She has seemed constantly to breathe the spirit and temper of the new creature . . . [and manifested] a true spiritual discovery of the glory, ravishing beauty, and excellency of Christ" (7:371). One medicine man had been a "murderer" and "notorious drunkard" and had purposely steered other Indians away from Brainerd's preaching. Brainerd compared him to Simon Magus and confessed that he had secretly wished for his death. But then the medicine man had gained a "lively, soul-refreshing view of the excellency of Christ," challenged another powwow to embrace

Christ, and like St. Paul spent his days preaching the faith he once attacked (7:398, 391–95).

Brainerd's greatest boast was in his own Indian congregation, made up of those who had welcomed his preaching. Here, Brainerd claimed, was Christian love of greater strength than in the early church (7:387) and a sense of the presence of God stronger than in any white congregation: "I know of no assembly of Christians where there seems to be so much of the presence of God, where brotherly love so much prevails, and where I should take so much delight in the public worship of God, in the general, as in my own congregation" (7:367–68).

As we have already seen, Edwards believed these events were "but a forerunner of something yet much more glorious and extensive of that kind" (7:533). In other words, Brainerd was underestimating the importance of his work when he concluded that "the living God, as I strongly hoped, was engaged for [the Indians' salvation]" (7:255). Not only was God acting in demonstrative ways to redeem the devil's people,[5] but this redemption had world-historical significance. It would presage the last, mighty work of the Spirit across the world at the end of time.

In the meantime "something remarkable" was appearing among the Indians of New England (9:434). Their approach to things of the Spirit was not following the usual Reformed pattern. Even their moral character was different, for they displayed far less ingenuity in evil than Europeans: "The poor savage Americans are mere babes and fools (if I may so speak) as to proficiency in wickedness, in comparison of multitudes that the Christian world throngs with" (3:183). But of far more significance was their religious sensibility. Beginning in his sermon series on the history of redemption in 1739, continuing into the 1740s, and then multiplying during the Stockbridge years, Edwards was repeatedly struck by what seemed to be a regenerate disposition among otherwise unconverted Indians. In the forties he was commenting on what he had heard from Brainerd, but in the fifties he reported his own observations from his frontier mission outpost among the Indians.

Edwards first made public comment about "remarkable" things among the Indians in a 1739 sermon on the work of redemption. There he noted that among "many Indians" there was a "remarkable . . . *inclination* to be instructed in the Christian religion" (9:434; emphasis added). His use of the word "inclination" is suggestive, because later, in *Religious Affections* (1746), he uses the same word for the central orientation of the self, that which signals the basic direction of the soul, either toward or away from God (2:12–13, 100, 107, 310, 312, and passim).

Whether or not Edwards meant in 1739 that this promising inclination was evidence of a regenerate disposition, his choice of a text for his first sermon to the Indians at Stockbridge[6] suggests that in 1751 he was considering that possibility. The new missionary pastor chose to preach on Acts 11:12–13, the story of the Roman centurion Cornelius, who is described by Luke as a God-fearing, "devout man" whose prayers and alms were approved by God (Acts 10:2–4, KJV)—and whom Edwards, at least as early as 1740, had regarded as already regenerate just before Peter told him about Jesus ("Misc.," 840a; 20:56). Edwards told his Indian auditors that Cornelius "had heard something of the true G. before Peter came to Him but he knew but little[.] he did not know anything about J[esus] X[Christ]." But Cornelius "was willing to be instructed" and "had a mind to know more." Therefore, he "prayed to G. that he might be brought into the Light."

After explaining how Cornelius and his family were converted through Peter's preaching, Edwards proclaimed, "Now I am come to preach the true Relig. to you & to your Childr. as Peter did to Cornelius & his family that you & all your chil. may be saved" (Sermon on Acts 11:12–13, Jan. 1751.) We don't know if any of the Indians who heard him that day "were willing to be instructed" and "had a mind to know more," but we do know that Edwards was convinced shortly thereafter that Indians at Onohquaga[7] had such a mind. In the following year he wrote the Reverend Isaac Hollis that "many" members of that tribe "that used to be notorious drunkards and blood-thirsty warriors, have of late strangely had their *dispositions* and manners changed through some wonderful influence on their minds." They were now uninterested in war and had forsaken drunkenness. What's more, they had "a *disposition* to religion and a thirst after instruction" (16:499). Once again, Edwards' vocabulary is suggestive. "Disposition" was a word Edwards used synonymously for "inclination," both in sermons and in his most developed analysis of religious experience, the *Religious Affections*. To say that the Onohquagas had a disposition to religion and a thirst after instruction recalls the nearly identical description of Cornelius, and therefore suggests that the Spirit was working in these Indians to prepare them for conversion.

A similar suggestion is made in his 1753 letter to Andrew Oliver, the secretary of the Board of Commissioners for Indian Affairs. A Mohawk sachem had informed him that the Onohquagas were more religious and virtuous than the Mohawks, Edwards wrote, and he himself had found this testimony to be true. "They have appeared to be far the best *disposed* Indians we have had to do with, and would be *inclined* to their utmost to assist, encourage and to strengthen the hands of missionaries and instructors, should [any] be sent among [them], and do all they can to forward their success among themselves and other Indians round about" (16:583). Two days later Edwards wrote a Scottish minister that another group of Indians had a Cornelian desire to hear and assimilate the gospel: they "have a great desire that the gospel should be introduced and settled in their country" (16:595).

Edwards apparently pondered these things in his heart and deduced that the Indians would have a glorious future in the work of redemption. His optimism was not shared by many. In fact, Samuel Kirkland, "the most effective Protestant missionary to the Iroquois," concluded that the Indians were under the curse of Ham and as a people would never be called to God at the millennium.[8] Edwards, in contrast, added no qualifications when he predicted that the Indians of America, along with "the nations of Negroes and others," shall "serve the true God and praises shall be sung to the Lord Jesus Christ" (9:472).

Therefore he was confident that God would work through preaching to redeem the devil's people. During his seven years at Stockbridge he preached more than one hundred and eighty-seven new sermons and on another twenty occasions preached from earlier manuscripts.[9] It is clear from the extant manuscripts that Edwards worked hard to adapt his rhetoric to the abilities of his hearers. As Rachel Wheeler has noted, the Stockbridge sermons tell more stories than the Northampton sermons;[10] they are also simpler in presentation and employ more imagery derived from nature. For example, a 1751 sermon on 2 Peter 1:19 ("We have a more sure word of prophecy") illustrates all three of these devices:

> When G. first made man He had a principle of Holiness in his Heart. That holiness that was in Him was like a Light that shone in his Heart so that his mind was full of Light[.] But when man sinned against G. He lost his Holiness & then the light that was in His mind was put out. . . . Truly good men . . . not only have the light Shining round about em but the Light Shines into their Hearts. . . . wicked men . . . altho the Light shines round about em yet it dont Shine into 'em but [they] are perfectly dark within.

The imagery is of light and darkness, there is (allusion to) the story of the Fall, and the difference between the regenerate and unregenerate is put in starkly simple terms.

Imagery drawn from nature can be seen in another sermon from the same month. Preaching on Genesis 1:27, Edwards declared that "The Holiness of God is like the brightness of the Sun & Holiness in men is as when you hold a Glass in the light of the Sun whereby the Glass shares with some Image of the suns Brightness" (Sermon on Genesis 1:27, Aug. 1751). Perhaps referring to the Indian susceptibility to drink, Edwards compared humans to swine: "Men when they are drunk do vile [things] & behave thems[elves] in a Beastly manner like a pig that wallows in the mire" (ibid.). Describing regeneration, he used the graphic images of snakes, toads, and excrement: "That which is filthy like a toad or serpent is made to shine bright with some of [Christ's] beauty & brightness. That which is like a Heap of dung is made a[s] one of G[o]ds precious Jewels" (ibid.).

If Edwards preached more simply to his Indian congregation, accommodating the form of his message to an audience unfamiliar with the religious and cultural traditions of white Europe, he did not sacrifice content. The aesthetic dimension of his theological vision, for example, was not an elitist mystery reserved for learned adepts but stood at the heart of his understanding of true religion, to which even the most rusticated soul was given access. He told the Stockbridge Indians in his first sermon, for instance, that they must have "their Eyes opened to see how lovely [Christ] is" (Sermon on Acts 11:12–13). In an October 1751 exposition of Psalm 119:18 ("Open thou mine eyes, that I may behold wondrous things out of thy law"), the preacher explained that the "chief things" that our eyes must be opened to see are Christ's "Glory and Excellency." In a sermon on the two ways of life—one that leads to life and happiness, and the other that leads to death and misery—he explained that even those who go to church may be headed for death. This is true for all those who attend meetings but into whose hearts the Light has not shone, so that they "are blind & dont see the Glory & Loveliness of G[od] and [Christ]" (Sermon on Matt. 7:13–14, Jan. 1751) And in a communion lecture to the Stockbridge Indians, he asserted that a good man "Loves G[od] above all else for his own Beauty" (Lecture before the sacrament, on Ps. 27:4 [2], 1). Hence, if Edwards preached a gospel at once aesthetic and mystical, he considered his Indians capable of understanding such rarefied themes. His outlines were less complex and his imagery earthier than in his sermons to white audiences, but the vision he tried to evoke was no less sublime.

Some scholars have alleged that Edwards became a missionary "largely by default."[11] Yet Edwards had at least three other job offers before deciding on Stockbridge, two for comfortable pulpits in New England and one for a post in Scotland. We have already seen that missions were integral to Edwards' vision of history, and we know that he showed keen interest in the Stockbridge mission from its very inception. He was present at the creation of the original plan, in 1734, to evangelize the Stockbridge Indians. Edwards and his uncle, Colonel John Stoddard, who knew the Indian tribes better than any other white man in the region, met with others in Stoddard's home to strategize. They decided to send John Sergeant, who had studied in the Edwards parsonage, as their first missionary. Other early missionaries to the Indians either studied at the manse or attended church with Edwards, who was recognized by the Boston Commissioners[12] as a missionary trainer. Edwards was in close contact with the Stockbridge mission for seventeen years before he took it over in 1751, sent progress reports about it to his correspondents in Scotland, and passed along gleanings of missionary successes elsewhere around the world. He took the lead in starting another mission, finally unsuccessful, to the Iroquois. And he deferred work on his premier theological project of the period, *Freedom of the Will*, in order to edit Brainerd's diary, for the sake of missionary work among the Indians. As he was about to begin his work at the Stockbridge mission, he referred to it as "the important service I have undertaken in this place" (16:387).

Hence Stockbridge was not a forced exile, as has been sometimes reported. But neither was it, as still others have claimed, a quiet retreat. In some ways it was, as Charles Chaney put it, a "living hell." Although Edwards believed in the mission, and grew in genuine affection for his Indian parishioners, life was difficult there. Stockbridge was crowded with refugees (from the colonial wars with the French and their Indian allies) and soldiers, some of whom took shelter in the Edwards home. One Sunday morning in 1754 Indians ("doubtless instigated by the French," Edwards charged) attacked and killed three white worshipers between services. In addition, the mission was wracked by recurrent party strife between Edwards and the same Williams clan that had helped drive him out of Northampton.

When Edwards arrived at Stockbridge in June 1751, he inherited a troubled mission. John Sergeant had died in 1749, leaving behind 218 Mahicans, descended from the once-mighty Algonquin tribe. In the next two years, ninety Mohawks of the Iroquois "Six Nations" arrived from the Mohawk River, some forty miles west of Albany—many lured by the promise of education for their children at a boarding school run by the incompetent "Captain" Martin Kellogg, who was supported over Edwards' protests by Sergeant's widow, a member of the Williams clan. When Kellogg refused to defer to his replacement, Gideon Hawley, half the Mohawks left the mission. Then the boarding school burned mysteriously; arson was suspected. By the end of 1753, all of the Mohawks were gone, but not without expressing their support for the embattled Edwards.

Troubles within and without did not prevent Edwards from applying himself assiduously to his missionary tasks. For the seven years until he departed for Princeton in January 1758, Edwards held four services most Sundays: two for his Indian charges and two for the white congregation. During the week, while pursuing his theological projects, he expended considerable time and effort defending Indians against greedy whites who were manipulating the Stockbridge mission for their own aggrandizement. Despite recurrent health problems and public vilification of his efforts, Edwards wrote numerous letters to Boston and London pleading his Indian parishioners' rights to education and justice. He obtained land and had it plowed for Indian families, for example, so that they could send their children to school, and made sure that five Indian boys found lodging in white homes so they could receive an education. Edwards took at least one of the boys into his own home (16:634, 638).

In 1751 Edwards wrote to the speaker of the Massachusetts Assembly to urge that body to honor its treaty obligations to the Housatonnuks (the name given by white settlers to the Stockbridge Indians, most of whom were Mahicans). When a friend of one of the whites seeking to exploit the mission struck an Indian child on the head with a cane, it was Edwards who managed to convince the offender to pay damages. After an Indian was killed by two whites, he labored to obtain indemnity money to pay the griefstricken family (16:644). Edwards spent hours listening to the broken English and sign language of Indian children and asking questions in his own broken Indian dialect, so that he could accurately report to the Boston commissioners that his Indian scholars did not have enough blankets or food, that some boys had no breeches and many were going ragged to meetings, and that all the boys were being forced to work six days per week. Once a week he sat the Indian children down for instruction in religion, experimenting with new methods that emphasized narrative and Socratic questioning instead of rote learning, which until then had been the method of choice. Edwards was concerned that the lessons would "cease to be a dull, wearisome task, without any suitable pleasure or benefit" (16:407–8). Sadly, Edwards and others (John Sergeant and Timothy Woodbridge) who fought for Indian rights "were all but powerless against the aggressive [Ephraim] Williams [ironically, a relative of Edwards] and his supporters . . . [who] cheated the Indians out of their land and drove them from their town."[13]

In one respect, however, his Indian congregation might have sensed in Edwards something less than respect for their culture. He adamantly refused to learn their language, claiming that his time would be spent more profitably teaching them English and that they themselves agreed with his decision. One wonders if those who disagreed felt free to voice their disapproval to one who was director of the mission compound on which they lived. Perhaps some Indians also wondered why Edwards encouraged his own son to learn Mahican, and how such an industrious scholar could not make more effort to learn the language of those he hoped to win (16:562, 666–67).

Edwards shared the overwhelming white consensus that Indian culture was inferior and despicable. Even John Eliot, the apostle to the Indians, referred to Indians as "doleful creatures," the very ruins of mankind.[14] Edwards was raised in a society that recounted tales of Indian ritual torture and cannibalism. They told of the Hurons, for example, who urged all the members of their villages to participate in the torture of captives.[15] Both Hurons and Iroquois believed that if their victims did not exhibit terror, their gods would be displeased and send misfortune to the captors. Sometimes the captives' bodies were cut up, cooked, and eaten, in an effort to replace a tribal member lost to war or disease and "devour" what they symbolized as the source of their rage.[16] (One suspects that fewer stories were told of white atrocities inflicted on Indians.)[17] Edwards no doubt also recalled the Indian murder of one of his aunts and two cousins and the captivity of an uncle and four more cousins.[18]

Indians were also guilty of "idolatry"; they showed reverence for the numinous in nature, which Edwards and other Reformed Christians interpreted as sinful worship of the creature rather than the Creator.[19] As a result, Edwards and most Protestant missionaries failed to see anything in Indian religion that could serve as common ground or a point of contact in evangelism. They studiously discounted similarities between Indian and Christian religion, such as moral government, retribution, heaven and hell, and the necessity of a virtuous life.[20]

Nevertheless, Edwards won the affection of his Indian parishioners, and he returned the sentiment. Early in his tenure at Stockbridge, shortly after being ejected from the Northampton pulpit by parishioners who complained of his "unsociable" ways, Edwards seemed encouraged that "the Indians seem much pleased with my family, especially my wife" (16:420). Later he referred to them as "my people," and noted happily that they "steadfastly adhere to me," despite the concerted efforts of the Williams family—his own relatives—to alienate them from him (16:610). Edwards also numbered the white Stockbridge congregation among his supporters, but he preached a kinder and gentler message to the Indian congregation. In her careful study of the Stockbridge sermons, Rachel Wheeler notes that while Edwards told the Indians repeatedly of Christ's desire to save them, he spent far more time in his sermons to the "English" congregation at the mission warning them of God's wrath. The missionary preacher emphasized to his Indian auditors not God's judgment but the divine invitation; he was careful to apprise them that God's election did not depend on skin color or nationality. There is "forgiveness offered to all nations," he assured them.[21]

In the last decade of his life, then, Edwards signaled a change in emphasis. No longer were Indians stellar members of Satan's kingdom. The majority of them may still have been denizens, but they were no more prominent in that infernal realm than legions of white hypocrites. Among the worst of these were the greedy English and Dutch traders, who purposely kept Indians from instruction "for the sake of making a gain of you. For as long as they keep you in Ignoran[ce] 'tis more easy to cheat you in trading with you." Of course, the French weren't any better. According to Edwards, they made sure the Indians didn't learn to read so that they would not see that French ways "are not agreeable to the Scriptures.... When the Bible is hid from em they cant cheat em & make em believe what they have a mind to" (Sermon on 2 Peter 1:19; Aug. 16, 1751). Edwards concluded that Indian hostility to whites in North America was God's judgment on Euro-Americans for their treatment of Native Americans: defrauding and killing them, poisoning them with alcohol, and depriving them of the gospel (16:434–47).

To confer moral equivalence on English and French sins was, for many New Englanders, a kind of communal treachery. Edwards would, of course, in the same breath join his compatriots in denouncing the French as benighted pawns of the papal Antichrist. Yet his willingness to condemn both English and French exploitation of the Indians acknowledged the humanity of Native Americans in a way that most of his compatriots did not. He never came close to the fraternal humility of John Woolman, who respected the religious *knowledge* of Indians and considered their spiritual condition as (in some ways) superior to his own.[22] But he shared some of the sensitivity of Roger Williams, who said that Indians had not sinned against gospel light and were closer to grace than the "unchristian Christians" of the Massachusetts Bay Colony.[23]

Jonathan Edwards came to believe that what God was doing among Native Americans, who were the first real heathen that Western Christians had lived with in the second millennium, was tangible evidence that the great work of God's Spirit may have begun. These "remarkable" scenes in the drama of redemption were being performed on the New England colonial stage, and for Edwards were dramatic previews of the final act in which all those held prisoner by Satan would be triumphantly liberated.

These remarkable scenes—if not so much in Edwards' direct experience as in his depiction of the Brainerd experience—came to have an equally remarkable impact on later Protestant missions. Edwards' *Life of David Brainerd*, which was probably the first full missionary biography ever published, became the best-known of all his literary works. Never out of print in the two and a half centuries since its publication, it provided "the Protestant icon of the missionary, its ideal type."[24] William Carey (1761–1834), English Baptist missionary to India and principal founder of Anglo-American missions, drew up a covenant for his missionary band that included the words, "Let us often look to Brainerd." According to one of his biographers, Carey so devoured Edwards' life of Brainerd that it became almost a second Bible to him. He repeatedly cited

Brainerd's experience among the Indians as an example of the power of the gospel to convert the heathen before they were civilized.²⁵ The Bible and the *Life of Brainerd* were the only two books that Gideon Hawley, one of Edwards' protégés, carried within his saddlebag while working among Native Americans. John Wesley published an abridged version of the *Life* in 1768 (and then seven more separate editions), excising Calvinist passages but writing that preachers with Brainerd's spirit would be invincible. The list of missionaries who testified to Brainerd's influence is a Who's Who of Anglo-American missions in the last two centuries: Francis Asbury, Thomas Coke, Henry Martyn, Robert Morrison, Samuel Mills, Robert M'Cheyne, David Livingstone, Adoniram Judson, Theodore Dwight Weld, Andrew Murray, and Jim Elliott. Joseph Conforti argues that the *Life of Brainerd*'s enormous impact on American missionaries is "summed up by the fact that when the American Board of Commissioners for Foreign Missions established its first Indian post, among the Cherokees in 1817, the missionaries named it Brainerd."²⁶

Some of Edwards' other works were also influential in modern missions. Carey used the *Humble Attempt* to discount the contention that certain prophecies had to be fulfilled before the heathen could be converted. *The Humble Attempt* inspired the founders of the London Missionary Society, the (English) Baptist Missionary Society, and the Scottish Missionary Society, as well as the most celebrated of all Scottish evangelicals, Thomas Chalmers. Edwards' *History of the Work of Redemption*, though not well received until the nineteenth century, became one of the most popular manuals of Calvinist theology during the Second Great Awakening and excited renewed interest in missionary work both at home and abroad. Its encouragement of human contribution to redemption through individual conversion and revivalism helped "universalize" the revivals of the Second Great Awakening.²⁷ Hence a full range of Edwards' treatises was important to the growth of the nineteenth-century missionary movement in England and America. If candidates to the Church Missionary Society "managed to get through their missionary training and had still not read Edwards, future missionaries were given a book allowance out of which they were expected to buy certain books, including 'Edwards' Works.' "²⁸

For some of these reasons Edwards has been called the "grandfather" of modern Protestant missions. Because he lived between two great missionary cycles, the great age of Roman Catholic missions and the Anglo-American Protestant missionary movement, Edwards cannot be called its father—at least in any direct sense. Yet the latter movement was "a child whose appearance and personality point to the paternity of Edwards"²⁹— if not directly at least indirectly, through his theology of missions, which underscored the world-historical importance of his and Brainerd's missions to Native Americans.

Notes

1. Since Native Americans now use "Indian" and "Native American" interchangeably, I do the same in this essay.
2. The dates of the Crossweeksung revival and other details in this essay are from Davies.
3. For a full exposition of Edwardsean eschatology and America's role in it, see McDermott 1992, pp. 37–92.
4. Stoddard, *Question: Whether God Is Not Angry with the Country for Doing So Little towards the Conversion of the Indians?* (Boston, 1723), esp. pp. 6–12. Earlier, however, Stoddard had evinced less than generous attitudes toward Indians. In 1703 he wrote to Governor Dudley suggesting the English might hunt Indians "with dogs . . . as they doe Bears," because Indians don't fight fairly, "after the manner of other nations." They are thieves and murderers, he wrote, who "don't appear openly in the field to bid us battle, . . . [and] use those cruelly that fall into their hands." Stoddard concluded that since they act like wolves, they should be treated like wolves. Massachusetts Historical Society *Collections*, 4th ser., II, pp. 235–37.
5. Edwards believed that the devil had isolated the Indians in North America to keep them away from the gospel, and that they had become Satan's peculiar people (9:472).
6. This was a congregation of one to two hundred Mahican and Mohawk Indians.
7. This was the name for several villages along a ten-mile stretch of the Susquehanna River. By the mid-1750s, Tuscagoras, Mahicans, Shawnees, and Oneidas lived in these villages. Colin G. Calloway, *The American Revolution in Indian Country: Crisis and Diversity in Native American Communities* (Cambridge: Cambridge University Press, 1995), pp. 108–11. Unless otherwise indicated, sermons referred to in this essay are in the Beinecke Rare Book and Manuscript Library, Yale University.
8. Axtell 1985, p. 72.
9. Rachel Wheeler, "'Friends to Your Souls': The Egalitarian Calvinism of Jonathan Edwards" *Church History* 72.4 (2003): 749.
10. Ibid., pp. 750–51.
11. Andrew F. Walls, "Missions and Historical Memory: Jonathan Edwards and David Brainerd," in David W. Kling and Douglas A. Sweeney, eds., *Jonathan Edwards at Home and Abroad: Historical Memories, Cultural Movements, Global Horizons* (Columbia: University of South Carolina Press, 2003), p. 250. Pettit charged that Edwards was interested not in Brainerd's mission but merely in his commitment to a holy cause (Pettit, p. 13).
12. These men were commissioners of the Society in London, for Propagating the Gospel in New England, and the Parts Adjacent.
13. Lion G. Miles, "The Red Man Dispossessed: The Williams Family and the Alienation of Indian Land in Stockbridge, Massachusetts, 1736–1818," *New England Quarterly* 67.1 (1994): 74–75. This was the same Williams family that engineered Edwards' expulsion from Northampton. Ephraim Sr., head of the

Stockbridge branch of the family, was an uncle to Solomon Williams, who wrote a challenge to Edwards' *Humble Inquiry* on communion qualifications—the material issue that led to Edwards' removal.

14. Cotton Mather, *Magnalia Christi Americana*, 2 vols. (Hartford, 1820), 1: 504, cited in *Life of Brainerd* (7:26).

15. Bowden, p. 71.

16. Matthew Dennis, *Cultivating a Landscape of Peace: Iroquois-European Encounters in Seventeenth-Century America* (Ithaca: Cornell University Press, 1993), pp. 89f. For "routine" tortures inflicted on captives, see John Demos, *The Unredeemed Captive: A Family Story from Early America* (New York: Alfred Knopf, 1994), pp. 80–81, and Daniel K. Richter, *The Ordeal of the Longhouse: The People of the Iroquois League in the Era of European Colonization* (Chapel Hill: University of North Carolina Press, 1992).

17. On white atrocities, see Francis Jennings, *The Invasion of America: Indians, Colonialism, and the Cant of Conquest* (Chapel Hill, N.C.: Institute of Early American History and Culture and University of North Carolina Press, 1975), pp. 160–70, esp. p. 160: There were no Indians in Ireland when Cromwell's armies made it a wilderness, nor were there Indians with Wallenstein and Tilly during the Thirty Years' War in central Europe. If savagery was ferocity, Europeans were at least as savage as Indians. . . . Many of the aspects of so-called savage war were taught to Indians by European example.

For white use of torture and savagery in warfare in King Philip's War, see Jill Lepore, *The Name of War: King Phillip's War and the Origins of American Identity* (New York: Random House, 1998). For British torture of their own soldiers, see Francis Jennings, *Empire of Fortune: Crowns, Colonies, and Tribes in the Seven Years War in America* (New York: W. W. Norton, 1988), pp. 208–9. Indians apparently invented scalping, but whites encouraged the practice by paying for scalps; see James Axtell, *The European and the Indian: Essays in the Ethnohistory of Colonial North America* (New York: Oxford University Press, 1981), pp. 16–35, 207–41.

18. On February 29, 1704, Kahnawake Indians from near Montreal killed 48 people at Deerfield, Massachusetts, and took another 112 as captives to Canada. Among the killed were the Reverend John Williams's wife and two children. He and his four other children were taken captive; all were eventually returned to Massachusetts except Eunice (age four at capture), who chose to remain for the rest of her life among the Kahnawake. See Demos, pp. 80–81.

19. See, for example, sermon on Deut. 32:29, July 1752.

20. Ola E. Winslow, *Jonathan Edwards 1703–1758: A Biography* (New York: Macmillan, 1940), p. 29; Hutchison, p. 32. Most Europeans did not expect to learn anything from "heathen" religions. Jennings, pp. 53; Bowden, p. 122.

21. Rachel Wheeler, "Disappointment: The Stockbridge Indians and Jonathan Edwards," chap. 3 in "Living upon Hope: Mahicans and Missionaries, 1730–1760," (Ph.D. diss., Yale University, 1998); Sermon on Luke 24:47, October 1751.

22. Woolman, *The Journal of John Woolman and A Plea for the Poor* (1774; Secaucus, N.J.: Citadel Press, 1972); cited in Hutchison, p. 33.

23. Hutchison, pp. 36–37.

24. Walls, p. 253.
25. Stuart Piggin, " 'The Expanding Knowledge of God': Jonathan Edwards' Influence on Missionary Thinking and Promotion," in Kling and Sweeney, pp. 266–96.
26. Joseph A. Conforti, *Jonathan Edwards, Religious Tradition, and American Culture* (Chapel Hill: University of North Carolina Press, 1995), p. 75.
27. Ibid., pp. 48–49.
28. Piggin, p. 279.
29. Ibid., 266.

Suggested Further Readings

Axtell, James. *The Invasion Within: The Contest of Cultures in Colonial North America*. New York: Oxford University Press, 1985.
Beaver, R. Pierce. "American Missionary Motivation before the Revolution." *Church History* 31 (1962): 216–26.
———. *Pioneers in Mission: The Early Missionary Ordination Sermons, Charges and Instructions*. Grand Rapids: Eerdmans, 1966.
Bowden, Henry Warner. *American Indians and Christian Missions: Studies in Cultural Conflict*. Chicago: University of Chicago Press, 1981.
Chaney, Charles L. *The Birth of Missions in America*. South Pasadena, Calif.: William Carey Library, 1976.
Davies, Ronald E. "Prepare Ye the Way of the Lord: The Missiological Thought and Practice of Jonathan Edwards (1703–1758)." Ph.D. diss., Fuller Theological Seminary, 1989.
Hutchison, William R. *Errand to the World: American Protestant Thought and Foreign Missions*. Chicago: University of Chicago Press, 1987.
McDermott, Gerald R. *Jonathan Edwards Confronts the Gods: Christian Theology, Enlightenment Religion, and Non-Christian Faiths*. New York: Oxford University Press, 2000.
———. *One Holy and Happy Society: The Public Theology of Jonathan Edwards*. University Park: Pennsylvania State University Press, 1992.
Pettit, Norman, ed. Editor's Introduction. *The Works of Jonathan Edwards, The Life of David Brainerd*. Ed. Norman Pettit. New Haven: Yale University Press, 1985.

Eighteen

The Puritans and Edwards

Harry S. Stout

THE TITLE OF MY essay is one of those beguilingly simple phrases that in a disturbingly brief period of time can recall virtually the entire corpus of colonial New England religious studies. Edmund Morgan tells us, only half in jest, that there will soon be one published book for every forty colonial New England families. Similarly, in his reference guides to Edwards scholarship, M. X. Lesser records over three thousand books, articles, and dissertations, a majority of which were completed in the past forty years.[1] In short, if any subject has enjoyed more sustained and concentrated study than the Puritans in New England, it would be Jonathan Edwards.

As so much scholarly attention has been devoted both to the Puritans and to Edwards, it is not surprising that the interrelationship between the two has frequently been examined. Equally predictable is the fact that the conclusions have differed widely. Writing in the 1920s and 1930s, "progressive" historians, led by Vernon Parrington, had no problem seeing Edwards as an "anachronism" retarding America's progress to enlightened liberalism. At the other extreme was Perry Miller's 1949 intellectual biography of Edwards, which concluded that he was so far ahead of his time that our own is barely catching up. So successful was Miller's rehabilitation that a generation of scholars set themselves to explore the question of Edwards' "modernity."[2]

Over the past decade, more balanced assessments have appeared that seek to place Edwards in his eighteenth-century American and British context. While conceding Edwards' genius and confirming his standing as America's first great philosopher, they also point to the many ways in which his thought moved along the plane of seventeenth- and eighteenth-century Puritan theology. In one important respect, however, Miller's revisionists agree with him in separating the Puritans and Edwards. Both find that Edwards repudiated the "national" covenant of his Puritan predecessors. The term "national covenant" was first used by Perry Miller to distinguish the Puritans' sense of two covenants. One, the "covenant of grace," referred to individuals and personal salvation in the life to come. The other, the national covenant, applied to nations and governed their temporal success in this world. In early Puritanism these two contradictory covenants—one of faith, the other of works; one unconditional, the other conditional—existed in creative tension, but by 1740, if not sooner, they became hopelessly divided into two opposing parties. One group (the "liberals" or "rationalists") emphasized corporate morality and God's outward covenant with New England. The other group (called "pietists" or "evangelicals") rejected the "federal theology" and focused their preaching solely on personal salvation and the life to come.

As America's foremost evangelical theologian, Edwards fell into the camp of those who rejected the national covenant. Indeed, according to Miller, Edwards initiated the evangelicals' rejection of federal theology: "Every New Englander before Edwards was a 'Federalist,' and because [Edwards] put aside all this sort of thinking, he became a new point of departure in the history of the American mind." Surprisingly, this view has gone virtually unchallenged. In the most complete analysis of Edwards' thoughts on the covenant to appear since Miller, Conrad Cherry concludes that the federal theology "did not assume for [Edwards] the same importance for an understanding of the saints' social and political life as it had for his forefathers."[3]

In the remarks to follow I will suggest that Edwards was more of a Puritan than Miller or his revisionists concede. In fact, he was every bit the federal theologian that his Puritan predecessors were. Throughout his career as pastor and teacher, he adhered exactly to the logic and tenets of the national covenant and reiterated them in exactly the same terms as did his predecessors in the New England pulpit. Nor was he alone among evangelicals in doing so. A corollary to my thesis is that evangelicals generally accepted the federal logic and applied it to their own New England in times of great national trial and stress. Indeed, the federal theology enabled evangelicals and rationalists to come together on a common footing when faced with external enemies.

That historians have missed the connections between Edwards and the federal theology is owing largely to the types of evidence they consulted. For the most part, scholars have approached Edwards' preaching from the vantage point of his published sermons. With the exception of a handful of ordination sermons, these printed works were exclusively "regular" or Sunday sermons that had as their central theme the great drama of salvation. Comments on the national covenant and corporate morality were generally considered inappropriate for Sunday preaching, and therefore did not appear in the text. The appropriate time for social commentary and discussion of covenant conditions was election day or a fast day, when communities would meet on a weekday to hear about the current state of God's covenant with New England.[4] Unlike many rationalist ministers, who often had their fast (or election) sermons published,

Edwards never published a fast sermon, nor was he ever invited to deliver an election sermon. If we were to judge only from the printed record, then, Edwards never preached on the federal covenant.

For the most part, Edwards and his fellow evangelicals preferred to publish selections from their regular Sunday sermons. But this does not mean that they did not deliver fast sermons in times of great calamity or national uncertainty, any more than it means that rationalists did not preach salvation on Sundays. To the contrary, evangelicals delivered fast sermons on weekdays with the same faith and seriousness with which rationalist ministers delivered conversion sermons on Sundays. Edwards was no exception.[5] When his fast and thanksgiving sermons are examined in their entirety, it becomes apparent that Edwards, together with his rationalist counterparts, approached New England as a "peculiar" nation who, like Israel of old, enjoyed a special covenant relationship with God.

Edwards absorbed the logic and terminology of federal covenants from an early age, when he sat under the ministry of his father, Timothy Edwards. Like his son, Timothy Edwards was widely recognized as an evangelical preacher who concentrated on the New Birth. But in times of national or local crisis, he wielded the logic of the fast, with its distinctive jeremiad, as efficiently as any other minister of his age. In an unpublished fast sermon delivered in 1709, following "Our fatal disappointment in our expedition against our French and Indian Enemies," Timothy explained that defeat came as a result of New England's sin: When God's people fail to acknowledge their corporate dependence on Him,

> [God] trys afflictions and the Rods of anger. He makes use of many angry frowning dispensations. [He] chastens, corrects em and sends calamitys and Judgments of various Kinds and Sorts . . . to bring e'm [sic] back from their Sinfull Wanderings unto the Straight path of their duty . . . especially those of 'em that he has taken nearest himself, and thus he dealt with that sinfull and Rebellious people of his, the children of Israel.[6]

Threats like this were frightening. But from the parallel with Israel, New England could also take hope. Disappointments and defeats were different from utter destruction; they were not signs of divine desertion so much as urgent calls to reformation: "Sincere Repentance and hearty and Real returning unto God is the proper voice and Loude call of the Judgments of God . . . the Judgments of God do with a Loud voice call upon a Sinfull and disobedient people to Repent and Return unto the Lord." If God's people sincerely reformed, then according to the logic of the federal covenant, they could depend on victory in the end.

Contained in Timothy's fast sermon were all the elements of federal rhetoric that Jonathan would later employ in his own pulpit. First was the parallel with Israel. National covenants did not cease with Israel but would continue to the end of time. The people of New England were such a covenant people, but their corporate standing before God was precarious. God was angry at them because of their sins; if they refused to repent, their trials and calamities would become progressively more severe and culminate in divine desertion. But if they repented and reformed their lives, God would be merciful and deliver them. What at first glance seems to be a rhetoric of condemnation and guilt turns out on further analysis to be the necessary first step to deliverance and triumph.[7]

The earliest of Jonathan's extant fast sermons was given soon after his ordination at Northampton in 1726. In November 1727, New England experienced the "Great Earthquake." The quake began, according to several accounts, with a "flash of light," which was then followed by a "horrid rumbling" and "weighty shaking" that continued to reverberate throughout the evening. Weymouth's Thomas Paine recalled how: "The motion of the Earth was very great, like the waves of the sea ... The strongest Houses shook prodigiously and tops of some Chimneys were thrown down ... It affected the People of N-E, especially those near the Center of it, with more Fear and Amazement than ever is thought to have befallen the Land since it had that Name." Awakened sleepers poured into the streets in huddled groups, certain that the Day of Judgment had come. The aftershocks continued for nine days, which, Paine observed, "mightily kept up the Terror of it in the People, and drove them to all possible means of Reformation."[8]

On the day following the earthquake, fasts were called spontaneously throughout the land and repeated several times in the ensuing weeks. In Northampton Edwards mounted the pulpit and preached from Jonah 3:10: "And God saw their works, that they turned from their evil way; and God repented of the Evil that he had said he would do unto them, and he did it not" (14:222).[9] While in regular sermons Edwards' primary concern was the individual soul, his concern on this occasion was the temporal estate of New England, which he believed was governed by its corporate covenant with God. Even as his text was devoted to the nation of Nineveh and God's mercy to it because it repented, so also was his concern that day with the nation of New England and the warning contained in its earthquake.

Like the other ministers in 1727, Edwards perceived both natural and supernatural meanings in the great earthquake. On the one hand, he drew from the most recent scientific literature to explain that earthquakes were not in themselves miracles but natural convulsions that occurred when bodies of water met with "subterraneous Fires" in underground caverns to produce rumblings at ground level.[10] On the other hand,

Edwards explained, God also used earthquakes to warn a covenant people: "earthquakes and lights in the heaven may often have natural causes yet they may nevertheless be ordered to be as a forerunner of great changes and judgments." Such was clearly the case with New England's recent convulsion, leading Edwards to the doctrine that "when God gives a sinful people warnings of impending judgments, the only way to have them averted is reformation."

A little later in the sermon, Edwards made plain that he was speaking in temporal and collective terms to the people of Northampton, not in eternal terms, and in so doing illustrated the different ends and logics of the two covenants:

> If a nation or people are very corrupt and remain obstinate in the evil way, God generally if not universally exercises these threatenings. God is more strict in punishing of a wicked people in this world than a wicked person. God often suffers particular persons that are wicked to prosper in the world and discharges them to judgment in the world to come. But a people as a people are punished only in this world. Therefore God will not suffer a people that grow very corrupt and refuse to be reclaimed to go unpunished in this world. (14:217)

Here it was appropriate to think of New England "as a people" in temporal terms of rewards and punishments. Corporate morality could not win or merit eternal salvation, but it could ensure success on earth.

With his temporal argument firmly in mind, Edwards returned again to the earthquake and rehearsed the corruptions that gave rise to the divine warning. The earlier revivals of his grandfather had clearly passed, leaving Edwards to conclude that "our Land is very much defiled." In particular Edwards cited an "abundance of cheating and injustice" that had increased since his arrival in Northampton a year earlier. Equally offensive was an increase in swearing and insensitivity to the great concerns of religion. This insensitivity was "especially among the young people," who most needed to consider the state of their souls. Too many of the inhabitants had grown "secure in riches." Therefore, "God shows us that we are in his hand every moment by this shaking the foundation of the earth . . . [He could] plunge us down to the pit when he pleases" (14:225).

In his regular Sunday preaching, Edwards used the language of destruction and "the pit" to drive sinners to conversion. Here, however, he employed similar terminology to encourage a whole community to turn away from sin and thus avoid further punishments "in this world." As with personal repentance, hypocrisy was the sin most to be avoided in outward shows of repentance and humiliation. Mere external observance of the fast was not enough if New England was to escape temporal punishments: "'Tis only their reformation that will prevent them [from destruction] . . . A people's praying that judgments may be averted is insufficient . . . and all the while to go on sinning and provoking God." The severity of the earthquake confirmed how God's patience was being pushed to the breaking point: "God has a long time been warning us and has been waiting to be gracious to us . . . And yet there has been no general reformation. We have kept many days of fasting and humiliation . . . and have pretended to humble ourselves for our backsliding. But yet [we] have not grown any better." If New England did not repent as a people, then God would annul his covenant and there would be no defense. Individuals in New England might still be saved for eternity (that was another story and another covenant), but they could not escape destruction in this earthly life: "And how can you expect . . . that you can escape the wrath of the God that can shake a whole land and make the earth to tremble . . . Do you flatter yourself that God may bring judgments upon this land, yet you shall escape the public calamities?" Clearly the answer was no. All must repent and reform before it was too late. The wicked must turn to God or face "the cold arms of death and the hot flames of hell" (14:225–26).

Throughout the 1730s and 1740s, most of the misfortunes New England endured were of internal origin. Apart from occasional attacks from the Indians, New England's borders were safe, and the chief concerns in these years were natural calamities like drought, fire, disease, and pestilence, and internal discord over questions of revival and the New Birth. Already in 1736 Edwards employed a fast sermon to plead for harmony and the elimination of a "party spirit among us." While differences of opinion were inevitable, "yet there is no necessity of making parties and raising tumults because of this . . . How much more comfortable and pleasant living is in a society that lives in love and peace than when there are brawls and perpetual contention."[11]

Despite New England's precarious peace in the 1730s and 1740s, all recognized the possibility of war and presented it as the divine affliction most to be avoided. With the possibility of war ever present, congregations needed to be constantly reminded of their national standing before God. Edwards' congregation was no exception.

At a fast sermon delivered in March 1737, Edwards outlined federal theology and its temporal corollaries. Ancient Israel was the model and prototype for all subsequent covenant people, so Edwards turned to 2 Chronicles 23:16 for his text: "And Jehoiada made a covenant between him and between all the people, and between the king, that they should be the Lord's people." That text, Edwards explained in his opening remarks, occurred at a point in Israel's history when they had turned away from worshiping false idols and returned to God. Earlier, Judah had worshiped Baal, and God had allowed the enemy nations to attack his people for their idolatry. Now they had returned to God, renewed the covenant, implored his mercy, and received outward blessings in return. In brief compass, Edwards explained to his listeners what was meant by a covenant people:

> [S]ome are distinguished of God as a covenant people. So were the people that were spoken of in the text. God entered into covenant with Abraham and Isaac and Jacob, and brought them out of Egypt, and in a solemn manner entered into covenant with them in the [desert] and separated them from the [other] nations on the earth to be a covenant people, a peculiar people to the Lord.[12]

As God's people, Israel could depend on divine protection and "temporal blessings," as long as they honored the terms of the covenant. Indeed, Edwards went on, it was the enjoyment of "covenant blessings" that distinguished covenant peoples from profane societies.

From ancient Israel, Edwards turned to New England, observing that the federal theology did not cease with the Old Testament but continued throughout history. Citing God's promise in Exodus 19:6, Edwards assured his listeners that "if you keep my covenant ye shall be unto me . . . an holy nation." Clearly New England was such a "nation," its inhabitants called of God to be a "peculiar people":

> We have been greatly distinguished by God as a covenant people. God has distinguished us by making known his covenant to us. We have been in a very [clear] manner a land of light . . . The land of our forefathers has been a land of such light . . . You are a people that have been distinguished of God as a covenant people for a long time and have been distinguished in the means that God has used with you.

For a people thus blessed, the lessons to be learned in the fast were obvious: "Hence learn such causes we have to lament the degeneracies and corruptions of this land." Through fasting Edwards hoped to inculcate true humbling, which, as earlier, he distinguished from "hypocritical fasting." If God's people were to continue receiving the blessings of the land, they must heed the words of their pastors and repent: "You are a people that have been distinguished of God as a covenant people for a long time. You have for a long time enjoyed the preaching of God's word and the visibility of the gospel in a steady course." Only by honoring that word and reforming the evil in their communities could God's people expect to continue receiving temporal rewards and prosperity. If they failed to acknowledge the words of God's prophets on days of fasting and humiliation, they would surely suffer the same fate as Israel at the hands of neighboring enemies. Even now, Edwards warned, there were "great numbers of papists" to the north, creating in North America an ominous "mixture of dark with light."

As long as peace prevailed on New England's borders, fast sermons were usually centered on calls for internal harmony and repetitions of the terms for temporal and material blessings. All of this changed in the spring of 1745, when New England forces mounted an assault on the French fortress at Louisbourg. From that point on, Edwards' generation of ministers faced an ongoing succession of wars and rumors of wars. Fast days would be called with renewed urgency in New Light and Old Light congregations alike, and the chief concern was no longer internal contention, drought, or blasted crops but national survival. The stakes were high in the mounting struggle between France and England for control of the New World, and nowhere were they higher than in New England, where the harshest fighting was sure to take place. The new circumstances charged the old rhetoric of the fast with a new urgency.[13] If New England was to survive its long ordeal for liberty and self-determination, it must remain a covenant people.

In articulating the terms of victory, Edwards and other New Light ministers proved to be as quick to claim federal promises as were their Old Light counterparts. For Edwards, no less than for the rationalists, New England was a "visible people of God," a "city set on a hill," and was under great obligations to its covenant God. On the eve of the Louisbourg expedition, Edwards delivered a series of sermons on Leviticus 26:3–13 with the overriding theme that "temporal blessings" accrue to a people of God. Included in those blessings was military defense: God's people could depend upon "safety . . . with reference to enemies" and eventually would inherit "the blessings of peace."[14] Edwards' 4 April "fast for success in [the] expedition against Cape Breton" followed the traditional formula in defining a righteous war and then promising ultimate victory. From 1 Kings 8:44 he demonstrated how "a people of God may be called to go forth to war," and that such action was "lawful and a duty." With flawless logic he pressed the point that "if it be lawful for a particular person to defend himself with force, Then it is lawful for a nation of people made up of particular persons." In situations where God's people were threatened, they should look to God for deliverance, because "God and he only determines the event of war and gives the victory." If they went to war in dependence on God and honored the terms of his covenant, then they could claim the victory: "God is ready in such a case to hear the prayer of his people and give them success."[15] Like his earlier fast sermons, those that marked the start of the Louisbourg expedition were unoriginal; they offered nothing new in terminology or logic. When facing outward enemies and the horrors of war, Edwards, like his peers, instinctively fell back on federal promises in their simplest, most elemental form.

Throughout the spring of 1745 all ears eagerly awaited news from Louisbourg. On 21 May, following another series of fast sermons, New Englanders rejoiced to learn the "news from Cape Breton that ye royal Battery is taken [and] ye English army encamped before ye Town."[16] Through a fortunate set of circumstances, including good sailing weather and French miscalculations, the New England troops were able to set in a siege and wait out the outnumbered and undersupplied French. Finally, on 17 June, the unthinkable happened: pressed by dwindling goods and constant bombardment, the "Gibraltar of the New World" fell and passed to the command of the colonial commander William Pepperell. The impossible had been achieved: with no assistance from England, New England troops had succeeded in humbling one of the most powerful French fortresses in the New World and, in the process, had fixed their self-image as a divinely assisted people of war.[17]

News of the surrender did not reach Boston until 3 July, just as many ministers were convening there for the annual college commencement. The ensuing celebration was unrestrained. Westboro's Ebenezer Parkman witnessed "all manner of Joy thereat . . . The Bells were rung, Guns fired etc. Commencement was rendered the most gladsome Day." Thomas Prince later recalled that "when the Tydings came . . . we were like them that dream: our mouth was fill'd with Laughter, and our Tongue with Singing." Throughout the evening the sky over Boston was illuminated by bonfires and fireworks. Religious controversies which as late as 6 April were, in Parkman's words, "hotter than ever" melted away as all New England joined to celebrate the victory. Over the next two weeks, towns and churches throughout new England gathered for thanksgiving sermons and services of celebration.[18]

Like the earlier fast sermons, thanksgiving sermons were quick to portray the victory in apocalyptic terms and ascribed it to God's historic covenant with New England. No other explanation seemed adequate to explain the "train of providences" accompanying the New England troops on their feared expedition. Again, differences between rationalists and evangelicals disappeared in the occasional pulpit. Following news of the surrender, Edwards turned to history for comparable achievements. So magnificent a victory, he concluded, came "the nearest to a parallel with God's wonderful work of old, in Moses', Joshua's, and Hezekiah's time, of any that have been in these latter ages of the world" (5:362).

Edwards's chief antagonist, Charles Chauncy, used similar terms to describe the recent events. The colonists' victory "in this part of the dominion of Antichrist" was so stupendous that the only historical precedent for Chauncy—as for Edwards—were the victories of ancient Israel: "I scarce know of a conquest, since the days of *Joshua* and the *Judges*, wherein the finger of God is more visible. . . . let the inspired language of *Moses*, and the *whole Body of the Jewish Nation*, be ours upon this memorable occasion."[19]

In a sermon preached in Northampton in August 1745, following the safe return to the congregation of twenty soldiers, Edwards again traced the train of remarkable events attending the colonial victory—"enough to convince any infidel" that God fought "for his people that go forth to war and returns them to the people and house of God in prosperity." Later that month Edwards employed his quarterly lecture on Psalm 111:5 ("he will ever be mindful of his covenant") to explain how "God is engaged to do great things for his people," and that he "never fails in any instance of faithfulness of the covenant engagements he has entered into." The exhortation portion of his sermon notes were left blank for extemporaneous enlargement, save for the simple phrase, "to exhort all to be mindful of their covenant with God."[20]

So monumental was the Louisbourg victory in building New England's self-confidence and sense of mastery that in annual Thanksgiving sermons in the following fall ministers reiterated the glorious victory, and again, Edwards was no exception to the general pattern. For his Thanksgiving Day discourse on 5 December 1745, Edwards selected Jeremiah 51:5: "For Israel hath not been forsaken, nor Judah of his God, of the Lord of hosts; though their land was filled with sin against the Holy One of Israel." That prophecy, Edwards explained, came at a time in Israel's history when Babylon was about to be destroyed and the children of Israel "set at liberty from their captivity."[21] The destruction of Babylon, moreover, "was an evidence that God had not forsaken his people." From there Edwards reiterated the familiar conclusion that all nations were not alike in the sight of God; some were set aside to be in a "special relation" to him as a professing people: "A professing people are a covenant people of God and stand in special relation to him as his people in distinction from others that are not in covenant with him as it was of Israel of old." But Israel was not the last professing people; such covenant communities continued into the New Testament period and throughout history. New England was such a people and could claim God's promise "to guard them from their Enemies and . . . keep them from being swallowed up by them." In his mercy God sustained covenant relations with a nation until they absolutely rejected him, thus leading Edwards to the doctrine that "the mercy of God towards a professing people is very wonderful when he don't forsake them tho their land be filled with sin against him." Quite simply, God will not forsake a covenant people unless they first forsake him.

From the model of Israel contained in his text, Edwards turned the application portion of his sermon to a consideration of New England. "How wonderful God's mercy is to our nation and land, for this that is spoken of in the text and doctrine seems to be the case with us." Despite grievous sins and lapses in piety, New England remained a covenant people. To locate them in the vast history of redemption, Edwards proceeded to trace the history of professing peoples in England and New England. In the grand manner of the election sermon preacher, he unveiled the long train of covenants that culminated with the birth of New England. Beginning with the apostasy of Rome and the papal "Antichrist," he turned to movements for reform in England, from John Wycliff to Henry VIII. Despite the contrary ambitions of Queen Mary, Edwards continued, England continued on a Reformed course under Elizabeth and thwarted "a grand design formed by the Papish party in Europe to bring the Protestant nations under the yoke of the church of Rome." Again there was peace and prosperity until the reign of King James, when "England began in many respects to be false against the holy one of Israel." Increasingly through the reign of King Charles, "the nation began very much to depart from the purity of doctrine," leading to calls for reform sounded by the "Puritans as they were called." The Puritans suffered "great cruelty" and persecution by the Church of England. Many escaped to New England, and just "when the nation seemed to be on the brink of ruin, God was pleased wonderfully to appear and bring about a great reformation." The revolution brought reform to England, through "the Assembly of Divines" that met at Westminster and the confession of faith they produced.

From the English Revolution and the Westminster Confession, Edwards turned to England in the eighteenth century. Queen Anne's War between 1702 and 1713 was, he observed, a dangerous time that brought the nation "back to brink of Ruin," but again they were spared and peace returned. Now, under the reign of King George I, there was freedom of religion and "Liberty of Conscience," allowing God's people to thrive both in England and, more importantly, in New England. Edwards reminded his congregation of the great revival in Northampton in 1735 and the "more general Revival of Religion" that came later. Despite regrettable lapses in piety and immorality, the revivals ensured God's continued presence in New England and promised victory over "the French nation."

Throughout 1746, Edwards continued to use fast days to justify war as both a natural right and sacred duty. In June 1746 he employed a text from Nehemiah 4:14 ("remember the Lord, which is great and terrible, and fight for your brethren, your sons, and your daughters, your wives, and your houses") to establish the doctrine that: "When a people of God are molested and endangered by injurious and bloody enemies; for them cheerfully to exert and expose themselves in a war tending to their defence of safety is a good work and a duty they owe to God, their country and themselves." Besides temporal success, Edwards saw in the war with France an apocalyptic significance whereby " 'Tis to be hoped that the time of his own throne is approaching."[22]

While victory over France was certain so long as New England remained a covenant people, the timing was not certain. No one saw the 1748 treaty with France as anything more than an armistice, postponing for a time the dreaded struggle that was sure to follow. Formal peace did nothing to solve the territorial disputes between France and England, nor did it ease the hatreds—both national and religious—that had been accumulating for over a century. Rationalists and evangelicals would continue to divide strenuously over questions of pulpit style and theology, but they agreed about their common enemies in this world, and this concurrence released energies for joint action. All believed that, as God's covenant people, New Englanders had a glorious mission to fulfill in the world, and that mission required the preservation of their liberties against external enemies. Civil and religious liberties were interconnected in New Englanders' minds, and both were essential to their corporate identity as the New Israel. It did not matter which was threatened: remove one and the other was sure to follow. When that happened, God's Word would cease to reign as the law of the land, and New England would relinquish its special covenant.

During the interwar years between 1749 and 1754, Edwards struggled furiously against the tide of "Arminianism" as it found expression in the Half-Way Covenant (or Stoddardeanism) and denial of original sin. His well-known opposition to the policy of open communion initiated by his grandfather was so uncompromising that it earned him a dismissal from his Northampton congregation and resettlement among the Stockbridge Indians in 1751. Yet throughout his opposition to the Half-Way Covenant, he never wavered in his acceptance of the federal theology and his conviction that New Englanders were a special people who enjoyed peculiar blessings and responsibilities in this world. Fast sermons that were delivered in the 1740s to his Northampton congregation were repeated verbatim to Stockbridge congregation in the 1750s.[23] Throughout, he approached New Englanders as a people bound in covenant, whose blessings and calamities would be commensurate with their performance of covenant conditions.

By March 1755 it was clear to Edwards and other colonial leaders that New England's armistice with France was about to end. To the members of his Stockbridge congregation, set on the outer rim of English civilization, the dangers of renewed war were especially frightening. At a special fast day called in March 1755, Edwards repeated a sermon he delivered in 1744 "on occasion of war with France." It is, Edwards began, "owing to the protection of heaven that our nation and land have not been destroyed before now by the same kind of Enemies with those that . . . now oppose [us]."[24] With war again approaching, frightened New Englanders had to remember only one lesson, that "sin above all other things weakens a people in war." When "vice prevails among a people," defeats are sure to follow, because among professing peoples, success or failure "corresponds to" their covenant keeping. If they break the covenant, they can expect the worst, "destruction by the sword of the enemy is a most just . . . recompense for the rebellion of a people against God." Conversely if the people of Northampton or of Stockbridge turn back to God, he will be proved to deliver them and, "in a special manner to show his hand in the government of the world in disposing [of] the enemies of war."

Within three months of Edwards's fast sermon, New England entered another time of trial. In July 1755, at the very time that Edwards was completing the *True Virtue* dissertation and beginning his massive treatise *Original Sin*, General Edward Braddock and his British regulars were decisively defeated on the banks of the Monongahela River by a combined force of French and Indian troops. Thus began the fourth and final war for North American hegemony. In New England, one out of every three men able to bear arms was enlisted for service—a figure far exceeding the conscription rates for other regions and other colonies. Before the Seven Years' War (or French and Indian War) was over, virtually every New England family had one member engaged in what would become the largest war fought to that time on North American soil.[25]

The spectacular shouting matches between rationalists and evangelicals disappeared in the face of renewed war with France. As before, New Englanders were brought together by war, and the chief instrument of cohesion was the local sermon delivered on days of fasting and troop musterings. From the commencement of hostilities, the clergy were united in stirring martial resolve and specifying the terms and nature of divine assistance. In this war, as in others, they did not discourage armed conflict but encouraged it, for nationalistic and prophetic reasons. Their rhetorical task on weekday fasts and in addresses to artillery and militia companies was twofold. First, they had to establish the justice and necessity of war with France in terms drawn both from secular writings on civil liberties and property rights and from Scripture prophecies foretelling terrible wars between God's New Israel and the forces of Antichrist. Second, they had to prepare their people for the possibility of short-term defeats and great sufferings before victory would be ultimately won. Temporary defeats signaled the need for repentance and dependence on God; victories confirmed New England's chosen status as the unconquerable people of God. In either case the national covenant was confirmed.

Of the righteousness of New England's cause there could be no doubt. Despite its many wars, ministers insisted that New England was not a militaristic culture pursuing armed conquest for the sake of vainglory. Its wars were just, fought in defense of life, property, and civil and religious liberty. At a fast service in July 1755, Edwards repeated a sermon he had delivered earlier (on the eve of the Louisbourg expedition) underscoring the doctrine that "it is lawful and duty in some cases for one nation to wage a war with another . . . Reason and the light of nature shows it . . . it follows from the law of self-preservation."[26] Clearly war with France was such a case. In 1755 as in 1745, "it is of vast importance to us that the expedition should be [a] success on many accounts." God's people must be fervent in their prayers, but they must also be willing to lend their arms in the sacred cause. In closing, Edwards sought "to excite all to seek to God for success in this . . . enterprise."

However just the "enterprise," success was not immediately forthcoming. Following Braddock's defeat, Anglo-American forces suffered one disappointment after another. So devastating were the defeats that in a fast sermon from 1756, Edwards turned to Psalm 60:9–12 ("Give us help from trouble, for vain is the help of men") to establish the consoling doctrine that "it becomes a people after defeat in war to relinquish all other dependence and to look to him for help."[27] The times, Edwards conceded, were dark. "It is now a time distinguished from all others that ever have been in the Respect that this [is] a time wherein the civil and Religious Liberties of the British Plantation in America and all that is dear to us [is] being threatened." But the times were not hopeless. Despite temporary setbacks and smaller armies, Edwards assured his listeners that "the race is not to the swift," and that even as God delivered his people Israel in time of distress, even so would he continue to provide "a peculiar Encouragement for God's people." New Englanders could be sure that immediate losses in battle were not a final sentence of doom, because Scripture clearly foretold the downfall of Antichrist.[28]

Edwards's death on 22 March 1758 prevented him from witnessing the final victory over France, though he would certainly not have been surprised. Like other thanksgiving preachers in 1759 and 1760, he would have ascribed the triumph to New England's covenant with God and their ongoing status as a "peculiar people." That same image of a chosen people would sustain New Englanders through their next crisis: the controversy with England. Had Edwards lived to witness the unfolding conflict with England, he would have certainly supported the "sacred cause" of liberty and turned his pen to calls for moral reformation and promises of national success. Such calls for national reformation and triumph would never have displaced Edwards' primary concern with the great and all-consuming question of personal salvation in the world to come, but they would have assumed a crucial significance in questions bearing on New England's temporal estate in this world. The covenant made that inevitable.

If anything is clear from the foregoing analysis of Edwards' fast and thanksgiving sermons, it is that he was a child of New England's federal theology. The federal covenant—unlike questions of epistemology, psychology, and moral philosophy—was not a philosophical problem for Edwards, but part of the taken-for-granted reality in which New England society grew and took shape. In fact, *no* eighteenth-century established minister dared to deny the federal covenant and New England's attendant identity as a special people with a messianic destiny. The external threats were too direct and the fears of national extinction too real for any to challenge this master organizing principle of New England culture. If the formulaic terms of covenant promise and chosen peoplehood sound hopelessly repetitious and formal—or simply wrongheaded—it must be remembered that in New England they gained force with retelling and military success. Quite simply, New Englanders, like "Americans" later, never lost the big battles. As long as they continued to win, the covenant was validated and the myth lived on. The vision of a redeemer nation and a covenant people was dazzling, and none, including Edwards, could escape its glare. As one voice among thousands, Edwards helped perpetuate that quintessentially Puritan notion of a righteous city set high upon a hill for all the world to see. That notion apparently has yet to run its course. In this sense, we continue to inhabit a world formed largely by the Puritans and defenders of the Puritan legacy like Edwards.

Notes

1. See Edmund S. Morgan, "The Historians of Early New England," in Ray Allen Billington, ed., *The Reinterpretation of Early American History: Essays in Honor of Jonathan Edwin Pomfret* (New York: W. W. Norton, 1968), pp. 41–42; and M. X. Lesser, ed., *Jonathan Edwards: A Reference Guide* (Boston: G. K. Hall & Co., 1981).

2. See V. L. Parrington, *Main Currents in American Thought,* vol. 1, *The Colonial Mind* (New York: Harcourt, Brace & Co., 1927; rpt. 1954), pp. 153–62; and

Perry Miller, *Jonathan Edwards* (New York: William Sloane Associates, 1949). For a fine summary of the debate over Edwards' "modernity," see Donald Weber's introduction to the new edition of Miller's *Jonathan' Edwards* (Amherst: University of Massachusetts Press, 1981).

3. Perry Miller, *Jonathan Edwards*, p. 76, and "The Marrow of Puritan Divinity," reprinted in *Errand into the Wilderness* (New York: Harper, 1965), pp. 50, 98. See also Conrad Cherry, "The Puritan Notion of the Covenant in Jonathan Edwards' Doctrine of Faith," *Church History* 34 (1965): 329, and *The Theology of Jonathan Edwards: A Reappraisal* (Garden City, N.Y.: Anchor Books, 1966), p. 109.

4. The major distinctions in form, content, and function between regular (Sunday) sermons and occasional (weekday) sermons have not been sufficiently emphasized in studies of Puritan preaching. For a discussion of the very different purposes and logics of these two categories of sermon, see Harry S. Stout, *The New England Soul: Preaching and Religious Culture in Colonial New England* (New York: Oxford University Press, 1986), pp. 13–31.

5. I am grateful to James F. Cooper, Jr., for assistance in compiling the listing of fast and thanksgiving sermons in the Edwards Papers at Yale University's Beinecke Library. In all, sixty-eight sermon manuscripts survive, of which twenty-six were thanksgiving sermons and forty-two fast sermons. These sermons span Edwards' careers in Northampton and Stockbridge (1727 through 1757).

6. Timothy Edwards' sermon notes are printed in John A. Stoughton, *"Windsor Farmes": A Glimpse of an Old Parish* (Hartford: Clark & Smith, 1883), pp. 143, 122, 126.

7. Sacvan Bercovitch discusses the ways in which Puritan rhetoric was simultaneously condemnatory and optimistic in *The American Jeremiad* (Madison: University of Wisconsin Press, 1980).

8. Thomas Paine, preface to *The Doctrine of Earthquakes* (Boston, 1728). The earthquake fasts are described in W. D. Love, *The Fast and Thanksgiving Days of New England* (Boston: Henchman, 1895), pp. 185–95.

9. Sermon on Jonah 3:10, 21 December 1727, Edwards Papers, Beinecke Rare Book and Manuscript Library, Yale University. All subsequent references to Edwards' unpublished sermons are taken from the Beinecke collection unless otherwise noted.

10. John Barnard, *Two Discourses Addressed to Young Persons* (Boston: S. Gerrish, 1727), p. 78. The conventional logic of earthquake sermons is summarized in Maxine Van De Wetering, "Moralizing in Puritan Natural Science: Mysteriousness in Earthquake Sermons," *Journal of the History of Ideas* 43 (1982): 417–38.

11. Sermon on Acts 19:19, 1 April 1736; published as "A Through Reformation of Those Things That Before Were Amiss," in Michael McMullen, ed., *The Blessing of God: Previously Unpublished Sermons by Jonathan Edwards* (Nashville, Tenn.: Broadman & Holman, 2002); the quote appears on p. 263.

12. Sermon on 2 Chronicles 23:16, March 1737.

13. The significance of the Louisbourg campaign is discussed in S.E.D. Shortt, "Conflict and Identity in Massachusetts: The Louisbourg Expedition of 1745," *Histoire Sociale* 5 (1972): 165–85.

14. Sermon on Leviticus 26:3–13, 28 February 1745.
15. Sermon on 1 Kings 8:44–45, 4 April 1745, published as *The Duties of Christians in a Time of War, the Works of Jonathan Edwards*, 25, *Sermons and Discourses, 1743–1758,* ed. Wilson H. Kimnach (New Haven: Yale University Press, forthcoming).
16. Recorded in G. L. Walker, ed., *Diary of Rev. Daniel Wadsworth, 1734–1747* (Hartford, 1894), p. 123.
17. See Shortt, "Conflict and Identity in Massachusetts."
18. Frances G. Walett, ed., *The Diary of Ebenezer Parkman, 1703–1782* (Worcester, Mass.: American Antiquarian Society, 1974), 3 July 1745, p. 120, and 6 April 1745, p. 114; and Thomas Prince, *Extraordinary Events . . . ,* 2d ed. (Boston, 1747), p. 34.
19. Charles Chauncy, *Marvelous Things* (Boston: T. Fleet, 1745), pp. 11, 20.
20. Sermon on 2 Chronicles 20:27–29, August 1745; and Sermon on Psalm 111:5, August 1745.
21. Sermon on Jeremiah 51:5, 5 December 1745.
22. Sermon on Nehemiah 4:14, June 1746. See also Edwards' thanksgiving sermon Sermon on Exodus 33:19, August 1746.
23. See, e.g., "Sermon on Joshua 7:12," 28 June 1744, repeated March 1755; "Sermon on Jeremiah 51:5," repeated November 1757; "Sermon on Exodus 33–9," August 1746, repeated November 1754; "Sermon on 1 Kings 8:44," 4 April 1745, repeated July 1755; "Sermon on Isaiah 33:19–24," 16 October 1746, repeated July 1756.
24. Sermon on Joshua 7:12, 28 June 1744.
25. On the costs of war in New England, see Fred Anderson, "A People's Army: Provincial Military Service in Massachusetts during the Seven Years' War," *William and Mary Quarterly* 40 (1983): 499–527.
26. Sermon on 1 Kings 8:44ff, 4 April 1745, *The Works of Jonathan Edwards*, 25 (forthcoming).
27. Sermon on Psalm 60:9–11, 28 August 1755, published as *God's People Tried by a Battle Lost*, in *the Works of Jonathan Edwards*, 25 (forthcoming).
28. For equations of France with Antichrist, see Nathan O. Hatch, *The Sacred Cause of Liberty: Republican Thought and the Millennium in Revolutionary New England* (New Haven: Yale University Press, 1977), pp. 41–42; and Thomas M. Brown, "The Image of the Beast: Anti-Papal Rhetoric in Colonial America," in Richard O. Curry and Thomas M. Brown, eds., *Conspiracy: The Fear of Subversion in American History* (New York: Holt, Rinehart and Winston, 1972), pp. 1–20.

Suggested Further Readings

Foster, Stephen. *The Long Argument: English Puritanism and the Shaping of New England Culture.* Chapel Hill: University of North Carolina Press, 1991.
Holifield, E. Brooks. *Theology in America: Christian Thought from the Age of Puritans to the Civil War.* New Haven: Yale University Press, 2003.

Knight, Janice. *Orthodoxies in Massachusetts: Rereading American Puritanism.* Cambridge, Mass.: Harvard University Press, 1994.
Miller, Perry. *Errand into the Wilderness.* Cambridge: Harvard University Press, 1956.
———. *The New England Mind: From Colony to Province.* Cambridge, Mass.: Harvard University Press, 1953.
Noll, Mark. *America's God: From Jonathan Edwards to Abraham Lincoln.* New York: Oxford University Press, 2002.
Stout, Harry S. *The New England Soul: Preaching and Religious Culture in Colonial New England.* New York: Oxford University Press, 1986.
Stout, Harry S., and D. G. Hart, eds. *New Directions in American Religious History.* New York: Oxford University Press, 1997.

Nineteen

Edwards' Theology after Edwards

Mark Noll

THE FORMIDABLE CREATIVITY of Jonathan Edwards' theological writings, along with his centrality in the first evangelical awakening, guaranteed that his work would remain of great interest to later Protestant theologians, to many lay evangelicals, and even to some intellectuals who were not Christian.[1] To be sure, when Edwards died at Princeton, New Jersey, on March 22, 1758, there died as well his singular combination of intellectual convictions: theocentric theology, idealist philosophy, Calvinist soteriology, affectional psychology, deontological ethics, and regenerate ecclesiology. Yet much that he had affirmed continued to attract the interest of later thinkers. Into the mid-nineteenth century his arguments concerning the nature of the human will dominated the agenda of America's formal religious thought. During the second half of the twentieth century, his written oeuvre, unpublished as well as published, became the object of a remarkable intellectual revival. For a wide circle of believing Christians, his particularly Calvinist works as well as his writings on revival have been read, debated, contested, and admired to the present day. In addition to his very large place in America's theological and religious history, Edwards remains one of the few American theologians to have been read abroad, first in Scotland, England, Wales, and the Netherlands, but then in more recent decades also in many other far-flung parts of the globe.[2] Any account of "Edwards' Theology after Edwards" must be partial, but even a rapid survey of the generations immediately following Edwards can suggest the many levels on which his influence advanced. By then treating at somewhat greater length the controversial uses of Edwards during the nineteenth century, it is possible to understand more clearly why his significance endured and then, in the latter half of the twentieth century (again treated rapidly here), proliferated.

The Multinational Basis for a Multivalent Influence

Edwards' influence exerted greatest force on two of his own students and closest professional friends, Joseph Bellamy (1719–1790) and Samuel

Hopkins (1721–1803), who themselves came to be regarded as the founders of a "New Divinity." Their most substantial publications, Bellamy's *True Religion Delineated* (1750) and Hopkins' *System of Doctrine* (1793), were written as self-conscious extensions of Edwards' main teachings on, respectively, the nature of genuine godliness and the interaction of divine and human motives in redemption. Yet as they pursued their Edwardsean projects, Bellamy and Hopkins were also reacting to changes in American circumstances. The result was that they modified the Edwards they were hoping to vivify. Instead of Edwards' definitive picture of God as perfect beauty, Bellamy conceived God more as the world's ultimate giver of law. For his part, Hopkins translated Edwards' main ethical principle ("love to Being in general") from its contemplative focus on God to its practical usefulness on earth (Hopkins' phrase was "disinterested benevolence"). Hopkins also suggested that human sinfulness should not be viewed in terms of flawed human character but as a function of sinful actions. In both cases, the later theologians were feeling the weight of Enlightenment standards of justice that came to dominate public life during the political and social upheavals of the Revolutionary period.

In their turn, the students of Edwards' students made more adjustments. Jonathan Edwards, Jr. (1745–1801), who studied with both Bellamy and Hopkins, defended a governmental view of the atonement in which the work of Christ was pictured as restoring the balance in God's justice rather than as placating the divine wrath. Nathanael Emmons (1745–1840) was known as an "exercise" theologian, because (following Edwards) he exalted God as the absolute determiner of all events, but (against Edwards) reduced human morality simply to what humans do (instead, as with Edwards, who they are). In a contrasting effort to keep divine sovereignty and human responsibility together, Asa Burton (1752–1836) propounded a "taste" scheme, arguing that actions proceeded from an underlying "nature" or "heart" oriented for or against God.

Overlapping this generation of metaphysical Edwardsians were some of the leading theological educators of the early American republic. Founders of Andover Seminary (1808) like Jedidiah Morse (1761–1826) wanted to revive Edwards' orthodox Calvinism. Later professors at Andover, especially Edwards Amasa Park (1808–1900), constructed elaborate intellectual genealogies to track and defend what they considered the best interpretations of Edwards' theology. By contrast, the founders of Connecticut's East Windsor Seminary, Asahel Nettleton (1783–1844) and Bennet Tyler (1783–1858), were committed to traditional modes of Christian proclamation that they thought Edwards had modeled in his self-consciously evangelistic Calvinism. Although their stress on the all-sufficiency of divine action in salvation and on the sinfully bound human will soon faded in the nineteenth century, precisely those emphases have been revived in the last half-century by evangelical students of Edwards in both Britain and America.

The most accomplished nineteenth-century thinkers who regarded themselves as followers of Edwards were known as the New Haven theologians: Timothy Dwight (1752–1817), president of Yale College, and his two most famous students, Nathaniel William Taylor (1786–1858), the first theological professor at the Yale Divinity School and a strong proponent of revival, and Lyman Beecher (1775–1863), the energetic revivalist and social reformer. These New Haven stalwarts did, in fact, modify Edwards considerably, especially by defending a modern concept of freedom (the power to choose among potential actions) as opposed to the view that Edwards upheld (the power to do what you have chosen to do in consistency with your character). But Taylor especially combined better than anyone in the nineteenth century what Edwards had also combined to such great effect: an ability to reason metaphysically about human nature in subtle philosophical terms alongside a deep commitment to evangelism and church renewal. The major difference was that Taylor and Beecher lived and wrote in an America where "common sense" about the "faculties" of the self led to beliefs about the limits of divine prerogative and the capacities of human willing that Edwards, a century earlier, had resisted.

Subtle as was Edwards' philosophical theology and extensive as was his legacy among elite theologians, his greatest impact on the broader public was always exerted through his activities as leader and chronicler of the colonies' First Great Awakening. The Edwards who preached eagerly for conversion, who experimented with new methods for revival, and who depended manifestly upon the power of God to change people's lives remained a steady inspiration to later generations who also led, or who hoped for, revivals. Congregationalists like the Connecticut pastor Benjamin Trumbull and Joseph Tracy, historian of the colonial Awakenings, no less than the Presbyterian theologian of revival William Sprague looked back to Edwards for such inspiration.

Edwards' influence was also mediated to a very large circle of serious Christian readers by his work as editor and publisher of the diary of David Brainerd. What Edwards, as a grieving friend and future father-in-law, found in the diary after Brainerd's death seemed a perfect instance of what he had taught about the ideal Christian life. With a little editing to cut out Brainerd's occasional lapses into despair, Edwards produced a work that has never been out of print. It was read with heartfelt appreciation by many leaders of domestic evangelism (like the Methodist Francis Asbury), domestic reform (the Baptist Francis Wayland), and missionary service abroad (Samuel J. Mills, Adoniram Judson, Mary Lyon, A. J. Gordon).

The work's great appeal remains its intense testimony concerning "love to Being in general," which Edwards thought was exemplified in Brainerd's missionary labors among the Mahican and Delaware Indians.

In light of the fact that Edwards' first significant writing on revival—the *Faithful Narrative of Surprising Conversions* (1737)—was published in England, it is not surprising that he exerted considerable interest among Calvinist and evangelical believers there. Since Edwards and his first British promoters were paedobaptists, however, it is somewhat surprising that this influence would work most strongly among Baptists. When the Northamptonshire Baptist Andrew Fuller read Edwards on the will in the 1770s, he found a way to affirm both inherited Calvinism and a new evangelistic urgency. The key was Edwards' distinction between natural human ability (unimpaired by the fall) and moral human ability (damaged so as to require the quickening work of the Spirit). Edwards' influence on Fuller and several other Baptist contemporaries was also one of the key factors that inspired William Carey to publish a rousing appeal for foreign missionary service in 1792 and then the next year to become the pioneer English missionary to India.

Edwards' English appeal extended, however, well beyond the Baptists. To John Wesley he posed difficulties, since Wesley very much wanted to promote Edwards' accounts of revival but wanted nothing to do with his Calvinism. The way out was editing with the penknife: after massive cutting, Wesley included four of Edwards' works in the "Christian Library" he prepared for the Methodist Connexion, and he also eagerly promoted his abridgment of the *Life of David Brainerd*. Later, a very different sort of interest in Edwards would appear in England. In the wake of the French Revolution, William Godwin published his radical *Enquiry Concerning Political Justice*, in which he borrowed a great deal from Edwards on freedom and virtue. To the consternation of the theologically orthodox, Godwin used Edwards to deny that supposed criminals could be held accountable for their crimes and to argue that social inferiors did not owe any sort of gratitude to their social superiors.

Scotland's interest in Edwards began early and continued strong for a long time. As early as the late 1730s, Edwards was corresponding with a circle of ministers that included William McCulloch of Cambuslang and James Robe of Kilsyth, towns that witnessed revivals in the early 1740s very similar to those of Edwards' Northampton in the mid-1730s. Younger ministers like John Erskine soon joined in promoting Edwards' ideas. In fact, the Scots' interest was so great that they would later publish several of Edwards' manuscripts that his New England associates simply ignored. Edwards was also praised as a subtle metaphysician by leading members of the Scottish Enlightenment, including Henry Home (Lord Kames) and Dugald Stewart, the major force behind the *Encyclopedia Britannica*.

When defenders of Lord Kames used the arguments of Edwards' *Freedom of the Will* to support the opinions Kames had published on "Liberty and Necessity" in his *Essays on the Principles of Morality and Natural Religion* (1751), Edwards himself was stirred to action. A long letter to John Erskine, arguing that his understanding of moral necessity was very different from Lord Kames', has been regularly added as an appendix to later printings of Edwards' work.

In summary, through the first generations after Edwards' death, readers as diverse as Lord Kames, William Carey, Samuel Hopkins, and Francis Asbury were finding much to ponder in what he had written. During the first two-thirds of the nineteenth century, that interest would continue unabated and, when inflated by controversy, would even grow.

Battles Royal in the Nineteenth Century

Controversy arose in the context of the nineteenth century's great struggles to control the heritage of Reformed Calvinism. New Divinity, New Haven, and—in general—New England theologians enjoyed a natural advantage in the use of Edwards since they were his lineal intellectual descendents. The other great party of American Calvinists in this era were the mid-Atlantic states Presbyterians. These eager and often winsome dogmatists always thought New Englanders were too much enamored with metaphysics, but despite that opinion, many of America's leading Presbyterians held Edwards in highest regard. To the founder of Princeton Seminary, Archibald Alexander (1772–1851), Edwards was an honored predecessor as theological evangelist. To later Princeton theologians, like Charles Hodge (1797–1878) and Lyman Atwater (1813–1883), Edwards represented the triumph of historic Calvinism over idle philosophy. To Henry Boynton Smith (1815–1877) of Union Theological Seminary in New York, who came to advocate a more romantic, Christ-centered theology, Edwards represented the best kind of theologian, because he had reasoned with sophistication while maintaining humble trust in God's sovereign wisdom and in the saving power of the Holy Spirit.

The controversial use of Edwards began with questions about revival, but soon spread rapidly to broader theological issues. Almost as soon as Charles G. Finney (1792–1875) began to itinerate in 1824, he began to praise the example of Jonathan Edwards. By the time he published his *Lectures on Revivals of Religion* in 1835, Finney had already been harshly criticized by leaders of the older Calvinist churches, who regarded his novel methods as a serious problem. But against such critics, Finney enlisted a long parade of former worthies, including the late "President Edwards," who was a "great man . . . famous in his day for new measures." Finney signaled out especially Edwards' refusal to baptize children of unregenerate parents and his willingness to encourage lay preachers as innovations that paved the way for Finney's own "new measures," such as protracted meetings and the anxious bench. Just as retrograde conservatives had opposed Edwards in his day for his innovations, now Finney thought other petty-minded naysayers were obstructing the means of "seeking out ways to do good and save souls."[3]

The victims of Finney's jibes did not wait long to retrieve Edwards for themselves. In the late 1820s and 1830s, conservative Congregationalists like Asahel Nettleton joined activist colleagues like Lyman Beecher and Princeton Presbyterians like Samuel Miller and Albert Dod in efforts to strip Finney of his Edwardsean pretensions.[4] Dod's criticism was the most sweeping: for Finney to "use of the name of this great man" to defend his new measures was "to slander the dead." Finney might claim that Edwards sanctioned the widespread use of "lay exhortation," but this claim merely illustrated his "ignorance of Edwards' opinions and writings." To prove his point, Dod quoted the very works on revivals that Finney himself had cited, where "Edwards makes known, with all plainness his opposition to lay exhortation." Finney's "bold misrepresentation" of Edwards was merely one further "illustration of that unscrupulousness in the use of means for the attainment of his ends, which he too often manifests."[5]

Finney and other Jacksonian evangelicals valued Edwards for his place in the history of revival, even though they felt it was necessary to set aside the specific convictions of his theology. New England Congregationalists, by contrast, valued Edwards as a revivalist and perceived precisely in his exposition of revival his most important theological contributions. For their part, the more conservative, or Old School, Presbyterians valued Edwards' specifically theological pronouncements but worried that these had been compromised by his revivalistic excesses. Nineteenth-century Scots, along with the more romantic, or New School, Presbyterians, had yet another perspective. To them it was important that Edwards had combined the strictness of Old Calvinist theology with the experimental piety of revival.

Soon the opponents of Finney were arguing among themselves at a deeper level. By mid-century the conservative Presbyterians and the mainstream New England Congregationalists had clearly diverged. The institutions of New England Calvinism, like the Andover and Yale seminaries, reflected an eclectic intellectual heritage compounded of the mingled Puritan-Enlightenment legacy of eighteenth-century Yale and Harvard, the more recent assumptions of philosophical Common Sense philosophy, a smattering of the new century's new thought (often as filtered through Samuel Taylor Coleridge), and the conflicting ideals of republican freedom, establishmentarian tradition, and ecclesiastical Independency. The institutions of the Old School Presbyterians, like Princeton Seminary and the College of New Jersey, looked consciously to Scripture, the Reformed confessions, and Common Sense moral intuitions, as well as (less consciously) to republican ideals of freedom.

Although New England's bond to Edwards was closer than that of Princeton, it was the Presbyterians who made the first contentious claims for Edwards' theological mantle. Presbyterian attention to Edwards arose within the context of church politics, especially Presbyterian division into Old and New School denominations in 1837 and their reunion in the North in 1868. At issue was the extent to which the Presbyterians had been infected by New England's theological orientation and the specific ideas of Yale's N. W. Taylor. To Princeton, Taylor's theology was dangerous in the extreme; Presbyterian guardians were alert to any hint of its appearance in their midst. It was especially galling that the New Haven theologians and the proponents of other faulty New England systems would view themselves as the descendents of Edwards, who, the Old Schoolers felt, had taught pretty much what they themselves did.

From the time of the Presbyterian division in 1837, Princeton authors wrote steadily about Edwards.[6] As they saw it, Edwards had too easily tolerated enthusiasm in the colonial Awakening; he had promoted eccentric views of a common humanity in his *Original Sin*; he had fostered unsound habits of metaphysical speculation; and his *Dissertation on the Nature of True Virtue* had exerted an especially bad influence on later New England theologians. Yet to the Presbyterians these were all relatively minor matters compared to Edwards' sterling fidelity as an orthodox theologian, one who had distinguished himself in the "full and zealous maintenance of the old Calvinistic doctrines." By contrast, later New England theologians had abandoned Edwards' dearest convictions and, drawing unwarranted conclusions from his foibles, promoted serious error. As one Princeton author asked pointedly in 1840, "Shall we not heed his counsels as well as revere his name?"[7]

These jabs had the inevitable consequence. New England reasserted its claim to Edwards, and for more than twenty years the battle was joined. In the course of the exchange, Princeton usually got the better of debate on the question of the will. Try as they might, New Englanders could not convincingly link their belief in what Taylor called the will's "power to the contrary" with the arguments for moral necessity in Edwards' *Freedom of the Will*.[8] New England, on the other hand, maintained that Princeton did not understand Edwards' ethical principles. Its theologians mounted a convincing case to demonstrate the continuity from Edwards' *True Virtue* to their more up-to-date theories of benevolence.[9]

Of the many contributors to this debate, the two most important were Park of Andover and Atwater of Princeton. Park was goaded into especially vigorous action in 1851 after Charles Hodge had claimed that Park and his Congregationalist contemporaries taught an "anti-Augustinian" system that contradicted the major positions of Edwards.[10] Park responded with a prodigy of exegesis, tracing the continuities of theology in New England from Edwards to Park's own generation. In a very abridged summary, he contended that New Englanders from Edwards onward believed (1) that there is, strictly speaking, no sinful nature lying behind individual acts of sin—all sinfulness arises from the acts of evil themselves; (2) that as a consequence, no guilt, or absolutely foreordained certainty to sin, passes down from Adam throughout the whole human race—guilt before God is not imputed from Adam but is each person's own responsibility; and (3) that by nature people have the power to do what God's law demands—there is no bondage of the will to the sinful inclinations of a sinful nature.[11]

Even in his own day, Park's effort to make Edwards conform to later New England views on free will, the voluntary character of sinfulness, and imputation was not persuasive. A fellow Congregationalist, Parsons Cooke, concluded, for example, that in Park's construction of New England's theological history, "We have rarely met with an instance in which so distinguished an author as Edwards has met with so much injustice at the hand of a commentator."[12] Edwards, in fact, did believe in the moral bondage of the will and that a sinful nature underlay sinful deeds; and he did hold to something like traditional views on the imputation of Adam's sin.

Park himself provided a clue as to why Princeton could regard his views as diverging so far from those of Edwards. Park's "scheme," as he put it, benefited from "the philosophy of Reid, Oswald, Campbell, Beattie, Stewart . . . *the philosophy of common sense.*" The great strength of this Scottish contribution was "to develop 'the fundamental laws of human belief.' " Moreover, it "has aided our writers in shaping their faith according to those ethical axioms, which so many fathers in the church have undervalued." The result was that "the metaphysics of New England theology . . . is the metaphysics of common sense."[13] So great was Edwards that Park could not give him up, even if Edwards had denied Park's understanding of the natural and universal moral sense. Yet so powerful had modern moral philosophy become that Park's only course was to read Edwards through the lenses it provided.

In addition, however, Park's account of New England theology did properly spotlight a major Princeton misreading of Edwards. It had become standard for Old School Presbyterians to treat Edwards' *Dissertation on the Nature of True Virtue* as a badly flawed effort. On several occasions Princetonians described this essay as a late and ill-conceived product of Edwards' pen that encouraged antinomianism, egotistic utilitarianism, revivalistic excess, and theological absurdities (e.g., Samuel Hopkins' "willingness to be damned for the glory of God"). Park showed, by contrast, that *True Virtue* was a mature product of Edwards' thought and that it lay at the heart of his general theological concerns.[14] Park's effort to translate this victory into a defense of his substantive theological affirmations were not convincing, but he did expose a persistent Princeton inability to grasp an important element of Edwards' thought.

Park was fooling himself if he felt that his counterattack would silence the Old School. In 1858, Lyman Atwater offered the definitive Old School account of Edwards. Atwater was originally a Connecticut Congregationalist and had been both a parishioner and student of N. W. Taylor, but this early training had not taken, and he stood foursquare with the Old School Presbyterians. From 1840 to 1868 Atwater was the major voice in the *Princeton Review* defending Edwards and attacking the later New England theologians. His review of theological history spared no tender feelings in New England:

> Edwards held and devoted his labours to prove the doctrines commonly known as Old Calvinism, with the single exception theologically, that he taught Stapfer's scheme of the mediate imputation of Adam's sin; and with the further qualification, that he held an eccentric philosophical theory of the nature of virtue, as consisting wholly in love to being in general. . . . Neither of these peculiarities, however, was allowed to act upon or modify other parts of his theology. . . . We think it easy to show . . . that the distinctive features of this New Divinity, in all its successive forms, are utterly abhorrent to his entire system.[15]

Atwater surmised that New Englanders perceived such a connection only because Jonathan Edwards, Jr., bore his father's name as he led succeeding generations away from the elder Edwards' views.[16] In the course of his account, Atwater paused to make explicit what had been implicit in Princeton's earlier attacks on New England. If the Congregationalists succeeded in disposing of original sin and the imputation of Adam's guilt, the heart of Christianity was imperiled: "the whole doctrine of atonement and justification is implicated with that of imputation."[17] The battle for Edwards, in Atwater's view, was part of a much larger struggle for the faith itself.

The clash between Princeton and New England over Edwards continued for several more years, with the last full exchange a tedious skirmish in 1868 about the true bearing of N. W. Taylor's theology.[18] But the basic positions remained constant. Princeton held up Edwards as a great exponent of orthodox Calvinism, despite his lack of caution concerning revivals and religious experience. By contrast, New Englanders held that from first to last Edwards belonged to them.

While Princeton debated with Andover and Yale as to who had the best claim on Edwards, a more diverse group of theologians was attending to Edwards in order to reject him. During the nineteenth century at least forty-one substantial refutations of Edwards' major books appeared, ranging from Charles Chauncy's offended rejection of Edwards' *Original Sin* in 1795 to Lewis French Stearn's attacks on the moral determinism of *Free Will* in 1890.[19] While most of Edwards' principal treatises came under attack, the *Freedom of the Will* bore the brunt.

The central objection was that Edwards' "iron network of philosophical necessity," though reflecting an intelligence of "gigantic power," led to conclusions that violated the commonly perceived morality of the universe.[20] To this central objection commentators added manifold protests concerning Edwards' use of logic, a number of complaints about the imprecision of his language, and a few counterarguments from the Bible. But the main criticism usually circled back to how Edwards' conclusions violated the moral conscience. This was the specific charge that appeared repeatedly in response to *Freedom of the Will*. Nevertheless, of Edwards' works only the life of Brainerd was printed more frequently in the nineteenth century, and it was largely through this treatise that theocentric theology survived in America, in spite of Kantian philosophy, utopian republicanism, and the blooming of romanticism. Henry Philip Tappan, sometime president of the University of Michigan, and author of the century's most extensive attack on Edwards' view of the will, testified to the stature of this book in the introduction to his refutation:

> There is no work of higher authority among those who deny the self-determining power of the will; and none which on this subject has called forth more general admiration or acuteness of thought and logical subtlety. I believe there is a prevailing impression that Edwards must be fairly met in order to make any advance in an opposite argument.[21]

To make such an advance was then what Tappan, along with twenty-eight other authors, tried to do.

Despite the chorus of dissent from his views, Edwards did not lack for defenders, proponents, and admirers throughout the nineteenth century. In the United States, the New School Presbyterian Henry Boynton Smith, from his post at Union Theological Seminary in New York, came closest to filling the role of a true successor. A mediator by temperament and conviction, Smith did not fear to draw resources from the Edwardsian tradition, from Old School Calvinism, and from contemporary Europe. Yet his theology was consistently conservative. Smith had almost as much difficulty with N. W. Taylor's New Haven views as did Princeton. Theologically, he differed from his American contemporaries by placing unusual stress on the person and work of Christ as the heart of theology. Princeton, by contrast, regularly moved from authority (whether creedal or scriptural) to Christ, while the path for New England began with consciousness.

As an instance of his attitude, Smith in a programmatic exposition of method, "The Relations of Faith and Philosophy," singled out Edwards as one who saw "the necessity of bringing the subtlest researches of human reason into harmony with the truths which lie at the basis of all piety. . . . Intellect and faith acted together in him, distinct, yet as consentaneous as are the principles of life and the organic structure of our animal economy."[22] In his theology, Smith followed where Edwards had led. Neither philosophy without faith (which was Smith's harsh assessment of New Haven) nor faith without philosophy (his milder criticism of Princeton) provided for the nineteenth century what Edwards had offered to his.[23]

In only one other venue did a significant number of nineteenth-century theologians appropriate Edwards as Smith did. This was in Scotland, where Edwards had been famous before his death and where he continued to be widely read into the twentieth century. Scottish interest in Edwards was no mystery. Scotland shared with New England a Calvinistic heritage rooted in the English Reformation. Both New England and Scotland were cultural provinces of London, yet both long resisted English alternatives to the older Calvinism. Scotland was also home to the variety of Enlightenment thought that Americans domesticated for themselves, and regular exchange occurred between the two locales throughout the eighteenth and nineteenth centuries.

The two most conspicuous Scots to make use of Edwards were Thomas Chalmers (1780–1847), Scotland's most influential divine during the first half of the century, and John McLeod Campbell (1800–1872), its most creative theologian of the era. They were thinkers who shared a common respect for Edwards and made a common criticism of his works, and yet they developed his insights in very different ways.

Edwards' impact on Chalmers was especially profound. Chalmers had been a young ministerial student with a predilection for liberalizing theology when in 1796 he encountered Edwards' *Freedom of the Will*. The result was electric. As an old man Chalmers recalled that there was "no book of human composition which I more strenuously recommend than his Treatise on the Will,—read by me forty-seven years ago, with a conviction that has never since faltered, and which has helped me more than any other uninspired book, to find my way through all that might otherwise have proved baffling and transcendental and mysterious in the peculiarities of Calvinism."[24] Edwards' lasting bequest to Chalmers was twofold: he gave Chalmers a sense of how God's omnipotence was manifest in every aspect of creation, and he greatly impressed Chalmers by embodying both intellectual acuity and spiritual fervor. Chalmers eagerly took up the phraseology of an American correspondent when in 1821 he wrote that Edwards was "perhaps, the most wondrous example, in modern times, of one who stood richly gifted both in natural and spiritual discernment."[25]

For all their respect, the Scottish theologians shared a common reservation about Edwards. Chalmers expressed it indirectly when writing about his adolescent encounter with *Freedom of the Will*:

> I remember when a student of Divinity, and long ere I could relish evangelical sentiment, I spent nearly a twelve-month in a sort of mental Elysium, and the one idea which ministered to my soul all of its rapture was the magnificence of the Godhead, and the universal subordination of all things to the one great purpose for which He evolved and was supporting creation. I should like to be so inspired over again, but with such a view of the Deity as coalesced and was in harmony with the doctrine of the New Testament.[26]

Chalmers' indirect criticism became more pointed in John McLeod Campbell. McLeod Campbell remains an important figure in the history of the Kirk because of a spectacular theological trial in 1831, which led to his being dismissed from the ministry, and because of the creativity of *The Nature of the Atonement* (1856), the book that summed up his heterodox views. A good part of Campbell's *Atonement* carries on a dialogue with Edwards, particularly in an effort to render Edwards' conception of Christ's redeeming work more human.[27] Built into Campbell's constructive theology was, in other words, an answer to the criticisms raised by Chalmers about Edwards' neglect of New Testament themes.

For Campbell, following Edwards' course meant exchanging the older views of a legal, penal atonement for an ethical, subjective one. McLeod Campbell's theology rose from a practical need. Several of his most faithful parishioners felt trapped by the fear that they were not of the elect, and others seemed to pursue good works only in order to win safety for themselves. In response, Campbell began to reassess the nature of Jesus' death for sinners. Was it true, as the Kirk held, that Christ died only for the elect? Did his death not rather suggest the possible reconciliation between God and all humanity? Was it not possible to think of Christ's sacrifice as a kind of supererogation of suffering which opened the way to God? In working out his positive answer to these questions, McLeod Campbell made specific use of a suggestion Edwards had raised in a treatise on *The Necessity and Reasonableness of the Christian Doctrine of Satisfaction for Sin* (published with the collected works in the nineteenth century). There Edwards suggested that for the greatness of evil "either an equivalent punishment or an equivalent sorrow and repentance" must exist.[28] Although Edwards had not considered the second possibility,

McLeod Campbell took it seriously and argued that the atonement was best explained by the infinite nature of Jesus' sorrow for sin. This solution pushed Edwards' Calvinism out of its own orbit, away from an objective to a subjective view of the atonement. And it certainly took the enormity of sin less seriously than had Edwards. Yet McLeod Campbell still made a remarkably fruitful effort to put Edwards to use in a situation where the problem was not, as for Edwards, waking the unconcerned to their spiritual need but assuring the faithful of God's love.

Whether Chalmers and Campbell were as successful as Edwards in their theological efforts is not at issue here. What is clear is that these Scottish theologians had read Edwards with profit. They, along with H. B. Smith, did not try to duplicate his work nor to dignify their innovations by associating them with his name. Rather, they drew together piety, learning, and doctrine to make the effort Edwards had made, which was to give each of these elements due attention in an integrated theological exposition. They were, in that sense, Edwards' most faithful disciples in the nineteenth century.

The Twentieth Century

After the great theological struggles of the nineteenth century, opinions of Edwards among elite American academics sank very low, until a brilliant Harvard professor of English, Perry Miller, set out in the 1930s to rehabilitate the Puritans, including Jonathan Edwards. The two volumes of Miller's *The New England Mind* (1939, 1953) were accompanied by an influential intellectual biography of Edwards (1949). Miller was an agnostic and could not share Edwards' faith in God, but he argued passionately that Edwards had addressed the world in the most realistic terms imaginable. In the wake of this attention from Miller, and then from the Yale philosopher John E. Smith along with many other first-rate academics, a great revival of interest has occurred. The number of doctoral dissertations on Edwards has been doubling every decade for the last half-century. Ever better-grounded and ever more compelling monographs tumble from the presses. In 1957 Yale University Press began to publish a new edition of his works. Under the editorship of Perry Miller and his successors, John E. Smith and Harry S. Stout, this series has issued more than twenty volumes and has become—by considerable measure—the most significant publishing project ever in American theological history.

Alongside the twentieth-century academic recovery of Edwards has come also fresh attention and respect from the mainline Protestant churches. Here the pioneer was Joseph Haroutunian, a Turkish-born theologian at McCormick Seminary in Chicago, who in 1932 published *Piety versus Moralism*. It argued that supposed improvements made by Edwards' New England successors had in fact obscured Edwards' own enthralling vision of the greatness and goodness of God. Haroutunian, who was also a promoter of John Calvin and Karl Barth, was soon joined by theologian-historian H. Richard Niebuhr, whose *Kingdom of God in America* (1935) likewise held Edwards up for special commendation, and ethicist Paul Ramsay of Princeton University, who in several key studies, including two important contributions to the new Yale edition, championed selective aspects of Edwards' ethical views. To these and now many others, Edwards became not a brooding presence to flee but a landmark to recover and—reservations, emendations, omissions, and modifications duly noted—to recommend.

It may seem strange in view of Edwards' intense commitment to revival, but twentieth-century evangelical Protestants came late to the recovery of Edwards. Several pioneers were especially important for this phase of the Edwards retrieval. Martyn Lloyd-Jones, the Welsh physician who preached at London's Westminster Chapel from 1939 to 1968, promoted Edwards as one of the exemplary Puritans whom he hoped to rehabilitate for the benefit of British church life. Richard Lovelace of Gordon-Conwell Seminary described Edwards in his *Dynamics of Spiritual Life* (1979) as someone who practiced the kind of thoughtful activism that modern evangelicals needed to imitate. John Gerstner of Pittsburgh Theological Seminary, through years of lecturing and publishing, introduced thousands of students to Edwards' theology as an impeccable version of classical Calvinism. The Banner of Truth Trust, led by its editor, Iain Murray, who has authored one of the most important modern biographies of Edwards (1987), has also been a formidable force in bringing Edwards back to life for contemporary evangelicals. The influential speaking and writing of John Piper, a Baptist theologian-pastor from Minneapolis, has emphasized Edwards as an altogether salutary guide to seeking God's own glory as the highest purpose of human life (see, for example, *Desiring God*, 1986). At the start of the twenty-first century, evangelical Protestants, who in many ways are the modern constituency closest to Edwards' own religious concerns, have at last begun to learn from him themselves.

The end result of the twentieth-century revival of Edwards is the profound and wide-ranging reconsideration to which the other essays in this book testify so elegantly. When in 1957, Perry Miller introduced Paul Ramsey's edition of *Freedom of the Will* as the first volume in Yale University Press's new edition of Edwards' works, he went out of his way to assure readers that his own enthusiasm for Edwards did "not . . . imply that today the precise doctrines that Edwards maintained, in the language in which he cast them, have been or should be extensively revived." It was rather that Miller intended to demonstrate that "Edwards—the greatest philosopher-theologian yet to grace the American scene—deserves to be heard."[29] Through the efforts of Miller and now many successors, that goal has been accomplished, and with supernal effect. Indeed, some of those who have worked so hard that Edwards might be heard will also take the step that Miller foreswore and affirm that he deserves to be followed as well. In the breadth of his learning, piety, and intellectual rigor, Edwards is more comprehensively alive today than ever in his own lifetime or since.

Notes

1. General information in this essay is taken from the two volumes cited in note 2; Thomas H. Johnson, *The Printed Writings of Jonathan Edwards, 1703–1758: A Bibliography* (Princeton, 1940); and the works listed below under "Suggested Further Readings." Portions of this essay revise sections of what I have published before, including "Jonathan Edwards and Nineteenth-Century Theology," in *Jonathan Edwards and the American Experience*, ed. Nathan O. Hatch and Harry S. Stout (New York, 1988), pp. 260–87; "The Contested Legacy of Jonathan Edwards in Antebellum Calvinism: Theological Conflict and the Evolution of Thought in America," *Canadian Review of American Studies* 19 (Summer 1988): 149–64; and "The Claimers and Reclaimers of Edwards," *Christian History* no. 77 (special Edwards issue 2003): 260–28.

2. For superb documentation, see M. X. Lesser, *Jonathan Edwards: A Reference Guide* (Boston, 1981); and Lesser, *Jonathan Edwards: An Annotated Bibliography, 1979–1993* (Westport, Conn., 1994).

3. Charles G. Finney, *Lectures on Revivals of Religion* (2nd ed., New York, 1835), pp. 241–42.

4. *Letters of the Rev. Dr. Beecher and Rev. Mr. Nettleton, on the "New Measures" in Conducting Revivals of Religion* (New York, 1828), pp. 14, 20, 29. Samuel Miller to W. B. Sprague, 8 Mar. 1832, in Sprague, *Lectures on Revivals of Religion* (London, 1959), pp. 24–25, 28–30, 41–42 of separately numbered appendix. Miller, *Life of Jonathan Edwards* (New York, 1849; orig. 1837), p. 193.

5. Albert Dod, "Finney's Lectures," *Biblical Repertory and Princeton Review* 7 (Oct. 1835): 657–58. *Biblical Repertory and Princeton Review* is hereafter cited as *BRPR*.

6. Miller, *Life of Jonathan Edwards*, James Waddel Alexander and Albert Dod, "Transcendentalism," *BRPR* 11 (Jan. 1839): 38–43; Charles Hodge, *The Constitutional History of the Presbyterian Church in the United States of America* (Philadelphia, 1851; orig. 1840), 2:39–101; Anon., "The Law of Human Progress," *BRPR* 18 (Jan. 1846): 26; Anon., Short Notices, *BRPR* 27 (Oct. 1855): 701–2.

7. Miller, *Life of Jonathan Edwards*, 245; Lyman Atwater, "The Power of Contrary Choice," *BRPR* 12 (Oct. 1840): 549.

8. For the debate over free will, see Atwater, "The Power of Contrary Choice," pp. 532–49; Atwater, "Dr. Edwards' Works," *BRPR* 15 (Jan. 1843): 57, 64; Atwater, "Modern Explanations of the Doctrine of Inability," *BRPR* 26 (Apr. 1854): 36–46; and Atwater, "Whedon and Hazard on the Will," *BRPR* 36 (Oct. 1864): 679–703. Congregationalist responses are found in Edward Beecher, "The Works of Samuel Hopkins," *Bibliotheca Sacra* 10 (Jan. 1853): 76–80; and Edwards Amasa Park, "New England Theology," *Bibliotheca Sacra* 9 (1852): 170–220. *Bibliotheca Sacra* is hereafter cited as *BS*.

9. Princeton misreadings of *The Nature of True Virtue* are found in Miller, *Life of Jonathan Edwards*, pp. 241–44; Archibald Alexander, *Outlines of Moral Science* (New York, 1852); Atwater, "Outlines of Moral Science by Archibald Alexander," *BRPR* 25 (Jan. 1853): 19–23; and Hodge, *Systematic Theology* (Grand Rapids, 1979; orig. 1872–73), 1:432–34. Convincing replies came from Beecher, "Works of Hopkins," pp. 77–78; Anon., "Dr. Alexander's Moral Science," *BS* 10 (Apr. 1853): 390–414; and Anon., "President Edwards' Dissertation on the Nature of True Virtue," *BS* 10 (Oct. 1853): 705–38.

10. Hodge, "Professor Park and the Princeton Review," *BRPR* 23 (Oct. 1851), as reprinted in Hodge, *Essays and Reviews* (New York, 1857), pp. 631–32.

11. Park, "New England Theology," pp. 174–75.

12. Cooke, "Edwards on the Atonement," *American Theological Review* 11 (Feb. 1860): 118.

13. Park, "New England Theology," pp. 191–92.

14. A representative statement of Park's argument is found in ibid., pp. 196–97.

15. Atwater, "Jonathan Edwards and the Successive Forms of New Divinity," *BRPR* 30 (Oct. 1858): 589.

16. Ibid., pp. 602, 613.

17. Ibid., p. 617.

18. Charles Hodge, "Presbyterian Reunion," *BRPR* 40 (Jan. 1868): 52–83; George Park Fisher, "The Princeton Review on the Theology of Dr. N. W. Taylor," *New Englander* 27 (Apr. 1868): 284–348; Fisher, "The Augustinian and the Federal Theories of Sin Compared," *New Englander* 27 (June 1868): 468–516 (with reference to Edwards, p. 507); Timothy Dwight, "Princeton Exegesis: A Review of Dr. Hodge's Commentary on Romans V. 12–19," *New Englander* 27 (July 1868): 551–603; Lyman Atwater, "Professor Fisher on the Princeton Review and Dr. Taylor's Theology," *BRPR* 40 (July 1868): 368–97; and Fisher, "Dr. N. W. Taylor's Theology: A Rejoinder to the Princeton Review," *New Englander* 27 (Oct. 1868): 740–63.

19. Charles Chauncy, *Five Dissertations on the Scripture Account of the Fall; and its Consequences* (London, 1785), pp. 191–99, 260–64 (see Lesser, *Edwards: Reference Guide*, 1785.1); Lewis French Stearns, *The Evidence of Christian Experience* (New York, 1890), pp. 84–87 (see Lesser, *Edwards: Reference Guide*, 1890.10).

20. Fisher, "The Philosophy of Jonathan Edwards," *North American Review* 128 (1879): 300; Albert Taylor Bledsoe, *An Examination of President Edwards' Inquiry into the Freedom of the Will* (Philadelphia, 1845) (see Lesser, *Edwards: Reference Guide*, 1845.2).

21. Henry Philip Tappan, *A Review of Edwards' "Inquiry into the Freedom of the Will"* (New York, 1839), p. xi.

22. Smith, *Faith and Philosophy: Discourses and Essays* (Edinburgh, 1878), pp. 59–61, 90.

23. This formulation of Smith's concerns is from George M. Marsden, *The Evangelical Mind and the New School Presbyterian Experience* (New Haven, 1970), p. 163.

24. Chalmers to William B. Sprague, *Annals of the American Pulpit* (New York, 1854), 1:334.

25. Chalmers, *The Christian and Civic Economy of Large Towns* (Glasgow, 1821), 1:318.

26. Quoted in William Hanna, *Memoirs of the Life and Writings of Thomas Chalmers* (Edinburgh, 1851), 1:17.

27. John McLeod Campbell, *The Nature of the Atonement and Its Relation to Remission of Sins and Eternal Life* (London, 1959; orig. 1856), pp. 51–75.

28. Ibid., p. 137.

29. From Perry Miller's "General Editor's Note" to the Yale edition of *The Works of Jonathan Edwards* (1:viii).

Suggested Further Readings

Conforti, Joseph A. *Jonathan Edwards, Religious Tradition, and American Culture.* Chapel Hill: University of North Carolina Press, 1995.

Foster, Frank Hugh. *A Genetic History of the New England Theology.* Chicago: University of Chicago Press, 1907.

Guelzo, Allen C. *Edwards on the Will: A Century of American Theological Debate.* Middletown, Conn.: Wesleyan University Press, 1989.

Kuklick, Bruce. *Churchmen and Philosophers from Jonathan Edwards to John Dewey.* New Haven: Yale University Press, 1985.

Noll, Mark A. *America's God, from Jonathan Edwards to Abraham Lincoln.* New York: Oxford University Press, 2002.

Sweeney, Douglas. *Nathaniel Taylor, New Haven Theology, and the Legacy of Jonathan Edwards.* New York: Oxford University Press, 2002.

Sweeney, Douglas, and David Kling, eds. *Jonathan Edwards at Home and Abroad: Historical Memories, Cultural Movements, Global Horizons.* Columbia: University of South Carolina Press, 2003, esp. D. W. Bebbington, "Remembered around the World: The International Scope of Edwards' Legacy."

The Works of Jonathan Edwards (Yale Edition)

Harry S. Stout, *General Editor*
Kenneth P. Minkema, *Executive Editor*

Volume number; publication date	*Volume Title*	*Volume Editor(s)*
1 (1957)	Freedom of the Will	Paul Ramsey
2 (1959)	Religious Affections	John E. Smith
3 (1970)	Original Sin	Clyde A. Holbrook
4 (1972)	The Great Awakening	C. C. Goen
5 (1977)	Apocalyptic Writings	Stephen J. Stein
6 (1980)	Scientific and Philosophical Writings	Wallace E. Anderson
7 (1985)	The Life of David Brainerd	Norma Pettit
8 (1989)	Ethical Writings	Paul Ramsey
9 (1989)	A History of the Work of Redemption	John F. Wilson
10 (1992)	Sermons and Discourses, 1720–1723	Wilson H. Kimnach
11 (1993)	Typological Writings	Wallace E. Anderson and Mason I. Lowance, Jr., with David H. Watters
12 (1994)	Ecclesiastical Writings	David D. Hall
13 (1994)	The "Miscellanies," a–500	Thomas A. Schafer
14 (1997)	Sermons and Discourses: 1723–1729	Kenneth P. Minkema
15 (1998)	Notes on Scripture	Stephen J. Stein
16 (1998)	Letters and Personal Writings	George S. Claghorn
17 (1999)	Sermons and Discourses, 1730–1733	Mark Valeri
18 (2000)	The "Miscellanies," 501–832	Ava Chamberlain
19 (2001)	Sermons and Discourses, 1734–1738	M. X. Lesser
20 (2002)	The "Miscellanies," 833–1152	Amy Plantinga Pauw
21 (2003)	Writings on the Trinity, Grace, and Faith	Sang Hyun Lee

22 (2003)	Sermons and Discourses, 1739–1742	Harry S. Stout and Nathan O. Hatch, with Kyle P. Farley
23 (2004)	The "Miscellanies," 1153–1360	Douglas A. Sweeney
24 (2005)	"The Blank Bible"	Stephen J. Stein
25 (2005)	Sermons and Discourses, 1743–1758	Wilson H. Kimnach

List of Contributors

Kenneth P. Minkema is Executive Editor of *The Works of Jonathan Edwards*.
Peter J. Thuesen is Associate Professor of Religious Studies, Indiana University-Purdue University, Indianapolis, Indiana.
Amy Plantinga Pauw is Henry P. Mobley Professor of Doctrinal Theology, Louisville Presbyterian Theological Seminary.
Richard R. Niebuhr is Hollis Professor of Divinity Emeritus, Harvard University Divinity School.
Sang Hyun Lee is Kyung-Chik Han Professor of Systematic Theology, Princeton Theological Seminary.
Robert J. Jenson is Senior Scholar for Research, Center of Theological Inquiry, Princeton.
Robert E. Brown is Visiting Assistant Professor of Religion, Bucknell University.
John E. Smith is Professor of Philosophy Emeritus, Yale University, and former General Editor of *The Works of Jonathan Edwards*.
Allen C. Guelzo is Henry R. Luce Professor of the Civil War Era, Gettysburg College.
Douglas A. Sweeney is Associate Professor of Church History and History of Christian Thought and Chair of the Department, Trinity Evangelical Divinity School.
Janice Knight is Associate Professor of English Language and Literature and Chair of Undergraduate Studies, University of Chicago.
John F. Wilson is Collord Professor of Religion Emeritus, Princeton University.
Stephen J. Stein is Chancellor's Professor of Religious Studies, Indiana University.
Wilson H. Kimnach is Presidential Professor in the Humanities, University of Bridgeport.
Gerald R. McDermott is Professor of Religion and Philosophy, Roanoke College.
Harry S. Stout is Jonathan Edwards Professor of American Christianity, Yale University, and General Editor of *The Works of Jonathan Edwards*.
Mark Noll is Carolyn and Fred McManis Professor of Christian Thought, Wheaton College.

Index

ability, natural vs. moral, 123
Abraham, 172, 197
accountability, 116, 124, 125
action, 104, 115, 117, 126
Acts, Book of, 263, 265
Adam, 14, 299, 300. *See also* imputation
Addison, Joseph, 19; *Guardian*, 25
ad intra/ad extra. *See* God
aesthetics, 38, 53, 93, 112, 265
affections, 111; emphasis on, 8; and God, 162; gracious, 105; gracious vs. natural, 151; instinctive, 162; and JE's upbringing, 1; kind, 157, 161; and Locke, 109; and love, 104; marks of, 151, 154; between men and women, 161; and morality, 157; and passions, 103, 104; true vs. false, 105; as unity of idea and feeling, 105; and virtue, 162; and will, 104
Alexander, Archibald, 296
Alexandrians, 73, 79, 84n.6
Alsted, Johann Heinrich, *Scientiarum Omnium Encyclopaediae*, 19
America, 219–20
Ames, William, 243, 259; *Medulla Sacrae Theologiae*, 19
ancients, 11, 29, 50–51, 212
Anderson, Wallace E., 22, 37
Andover Seminary, 293, 297, 301
angels, 57, 77, 173–74
Anglicanism, 20, 26
Anselm, 74, 76, 106
anthropology, 14, 204
Antichrist, 232, 234–35, 238, 287
antinomians, 12
Antiochenes, 73, 79, 84n.6
apocalypse, 217, 218, 229, 230, 234–35, 282. *See also* eschatology; millennium
apprehension, 110, 112. *See also* perception
Arianism, 25
Aristotle, 18, 60, 65, 67, 68, 84n.10, 116–17, 131
Arminianism, 11, 14, 285; in "Account Book," 25; atonement in, 140; context of, 118–19; destruction of, 121; and Drummer's collection, 20, 21; and fatalism, 126; and freedom of moral agents, 120; and justification, 145; and Lord's Supper, 119; polemic against, 7; and Trinity, 49; and will, 118, 124, 125
Arminius, Jacobus, 117
Arnauld, Antoine, *La Logique, ou L'art de penser*, 18
Asbury, Francis, 294, 296
astronomy, 19, 96, 191–92, 196. *See also* science
atheism, 126
atonement: Anselmian understanding of, 74; in Arminianism, 140; in Campbell, 303–4; dual nature of, 137; and the Father, 55; in JE's followers, 293, 300; by Jesus Christ, 55; need for, 140; as overcoming estrangement, 76; and punishment vs. sorrow, 303–4
attractive force, 202, 206
Atwater, Lyman, 296, 299, 300
Augustine, 106; *City of God*, 117, 221; *Confessions*, 117
Augustinian tradition, 46, 47, 48, 52
autonomy, 108, 116

backsliding, 7, 279
Bacon, Francis, 118
Bad Book affair, 12, 183–84
Banner of Truth Trust, 305
baptism, 12, 297
Baptists, 294, 295
Barth, Karl, 305
Bartlett, Phoebe, 10
Baxter, Richard, 259
Bayle, Pierre, *Historical and Critical Dictionary*, 20, 94
beauty, 40; appreciation of, 153; and being, 157; complex, 38; of creation, 190; of elect, 258; of God, 4, 46, 51–53, 57, 61, 69, 70, 93, 105, 201, 259, 293; and good, 77; knowledge of, 112; and love, 155, 157; and morality, 41, 112, 157; of nature, 37; as object, 41; as object of knowledge, 112;

beauty (cont.)
particular vs. general, 155; primary, 160; primary vs. secondary, 157; as relational, 53; sense of, 107; simple, 38; spiritual, 112; of Trinity, 53, 54; and true virtue, 40, 41, 154, 155; of union with Christ, 139; and virtue, 156; of world, 208n.7

Bedford, Arthur, *Scripture Chronology Demonstrated by Astronomical Calculations*, 28, 94

Beecher, Lyman, 294, 297

being, 3; and beauty, 157; benevolence as consent to, 156; and consciousness, 35, 36; consent to being by, 36, 150; consent to being in general by, 155; disagreement to, 39; and emanation, 202, 203; excellence of, 34; extension of, 156; as glory, 203; God as prime and original, 44; intelligent, 63; and knowledge, 35, 36; natural phenomena as shadows of, 36; particular and general, 39; and plurality vs. pluralism, 36; proper, real, and substantial, 36; as proportion, 34, 39, 40

being in general: benevolence to, 41, 156; consent to, 41, 155, 159; and heart, 41, 156, 160, 161, 163; love to, 155, 156, 293, 295; propensity to, 41; union with, 159; and virtue, 40–41, 155

believer, 73–76, 140, 201. *See also* faith

Bellamy, Joseph, 13, 25, 28, 119, 215, 227, 292–93; *True Religion Delineated*, 293

benevolence, 164n.8, 165n.9, 298; to being in general, 41, 156; as consent to being, 156; disinterested, 151; and heart, 159; and kind affections, 161; and love, 41, 151–52, 156; in morality, 154; natural, 150; pure, 156; union with other in, 159; virtuous, 156

Bengel, Johann, 97

Berkeley, George, 3, 220

Bernard, Richard, *The Faithfull Shepherd*, 243

Bible, 87–99; in "Account Book," 24; accuracy of, 11; aesthetic quality of, 93; affective apprehension of, 94; authenticity of, 92, 95, 96; authorship of, 28, 94–95; canonicity of, 95; chronology of, 28; and church, 171, 172, 176–77, 195; and conservatism, 193; critical scholarship on, 27, 28, 92, 94–97, 98; and deism, 91–92; as divine revelation, 88, 91–94, 95; as divine speech, 93; and eschatology, 94, 228–31, 238; exegesis of, 14, 96, 97–98, 98; and geography, 28, 96; and God's indwelling presence, 6; as good, 93; historical context of, 94–97, 98; and history, 28, 92, 96, 213; and human culture, 91; importance of, 24; influence of, 17; as inspired, 91, 95; JE's engagement with, 16; Jesus Christ in, 72, 81; in Locke, 27; love in, 154; Messianic prophecies in, 28; moral law of, 197; and nature, 194; new apprehension of, 69; perfection in, 200; as polite reading, 27; prefiguration in, 200; primacy of, 47; prophecy in, 95; providence in, 190; and Puritans, 17; and redemption, 213; in "Redemption Discourse," 212, 213; and Reformation, 91; revelations in, 191; and rhetoric, 90; saints in, 171, 172; and science, 96; as self-authenticating, 91; in sermons, 243, 244, 246–47, 248, 250, 254; as source, 106; spiritual transformation in, 198–99; as sufficient, 91; and theology, 90; and Trinity, 47, 50, 51; truth of, 28; and typology, 97, 190, 193, 195, 196, 197, 198, 212, 213, 229–31, 232, 233. *See also specific books*

Blount, Charles, 27
Bonaventura, 106
Braddock, Edward, 286, 287
Bradford, William, 220
Brainerd, David, 10, 258, 261–62, 266, 269–70, 294–95, 301
Breck, Robert, 7, 119
Bridgman, Abigail, 183
Brown, Robert E., 28; *Jonathan Edwards and the Bible*, 98
Burgersdijck, Franco, 18
Burr, Aaron, Sr., 14
Burr, Esther Edwards, 26
business, 192, 196, 207

Calmet, Augustin, 98
Calvin, John: and Haroutunian, 305; justification in, 140, 141, 142; and missions, 259; nature in, 37; will in, 117
Calvinism, 4, 26; accountability in, 125; in "Account Book," 24; in Church of England, 20; curriculum of, 19; and fatalism, 126; grace in, 130; and JE, 18;

JE's boyhood questioning of, 2;
JE's citations of, 29; justice of, 121;
More's rejection of, 18; particularism
of, 222; and Presbyterians, 298; and
Scotland, 302; and Wesley, 295; will
in, 116, 124
Cambridge Platonists, 23
Campbell, John McLeod, 302, 303–4; *The
Nature of the Atonement*, 303
Canticles (biblical book), 177, 186 n.10, 246
Carey, William, 269–70, 295, 296
Cartesian logic, 18
cause, 22, 23, 59, 116, 118, 123–24, 239
Chalmers, Thomas, 270, 302–3, 304
Chamberlain, Ava, 218
chance, 117, 124
Chaney, Charles, 266
Channing, William Ellery, 150
chaos, 123, 124
charity, 131, 142, 147, 154. *See also* love
Chauncy, Charles, 105, 113, 118, 234, 282–83, 301
Cherry, Conrad, 127, 135, 275
choice, 104, 121, 123, 124, 294.
See also will
Christianity, 14, 51, 190, 218, 221
Christians, true vs. false, 181, 182
christology, 72–84, 97. *See also* Jesus Christ
2 Chronicles (biblical book), 279–81
Chubb, Thomas, *A Collection of Tracts*, 28
church: admission to, 2, 11–12; and Bible, 176–77; as bride, 69–70, 170, 171, 175, 178, 180, 186n.12; as children, 171, 173; as city on a hill, 173; dangers to, 11; definitions of, 168–69; and end of world, 237; enemies of, 229; erotic imagery concerning, 175; and evil, 173–74, 176; and Father, 171; and final judgment, 174–75; foundation of, 175–76; as fullness of Jesus Christ, 178–79; glorification of, 174; and God, 168–69, 173; as God's lovers, 180; and grace, 168, 174; and Great Awakening, 181–83; and history, 171; and Holy Spirit, 169; and Jesus Christ, 69–70, 168–71, 172, 174, 175, 177, 178–80, 183, 184, 185, 240; membership in, 2, 167, 168, 169, 181–85, 187n.22; as militant, 173–74, 176; and missions, 259; as mother of Jesus, 172, 186n.10; and New Testament, 171, 172; and Old Testament,
171, 172, 177, 195; present-day, 173; preservation of world by, 173; purity of, 183, 184; and redemption, 171, 217; in Revelation, 228; and revivals, 168; as saints, 168; and society, 1; suffering of, 179; as triumphant, 173–74, 229; true vs. visible, 169; types of, 177–78; unity of, 180; visible vs. invisible, 11, 172
Church of England, 5, 20, 49, 118
Clap, Sarah, 183
Clark, Peter, 182
Clarke, Samuel, 18, 19, 20, 26, 27; *Discourse Concerning the Unchangeable Obligations of Natural Religion*, 25; *The Scripture-Doctrine of the Trinity*, 49
clergy, 1, 17, 239, 286
Coates, Thomas, 140
cogitation, 110
Coleridge, Samuel Taylor, 107, 297
College of New Jersey, Princeton, 14, 15, 298
Collins, Anthony, 27
Colossians, Epistle to, 178, 181
Common Sense philosophy, 297, 298, 299
communication. *See* God
communion, 53, 92, 93, 205. *See also* Lord's Supper; union
compatibilism, 126, 130, 134
complacence, 41, 164n.8, 165n.9
Concert of Prayer, 10
Congregationalism, 2, 12, 17, 297, 299, 300
Connecticut Collegiate School, 3, 17
conscience, 157, 159–60, 162, 163, 165n.17
consciousness, 35, 36, 84n.10, 115, 302
consent: to being in general, 41, 155, 159; of being to being, 36, 150; and creaturely excellency, 53; and excellency, 52; of God to creation, 54; of Trinity, 56
conversion: caution concerning, 9; and church membership, 182–83; and communion, 2; and Holy Spirit, 239; of Indians, 261, 263; of JE, 118; JE as inspiration in, 294; melancholy in, 7; in missions, 259; nature of, 2; practice as sign of, 69; psychology of, 7; as reconstitution of soul, 93; and revivals, 1; in sermons, 254; and Trinity, 53; true marks of, 8
conviction, 107, 108
Cooke, Parsons, 299

1 Corinthians, Epistle to, 8, 112, 178, 184, 211
2 Corinthians, Epistle to, 112, 248
cosmology, 3, 14, 169. *See also* universe
cosmos. *See* universe
Council of Chalcedon, 72–73, 78
Council of Trent, 132
covenant, 8, 12; admission to, 11; federal, 276, 281, 282, 288; of God with New England, 275, 276, 277–78, 279, 280, 282, 283, 284, 285, 286, 287, 288; of grace, 171, 197, 274, 275; with Israel, 279–81; meaning of, 280; national, 274–75; nature of, 2; and redemption, 55–56, 135, 258
creation: beauty of, 190; as constituted by laws, 60; continuous action of, 14, 22, 60; as emanation, 204; and eschatology, 69–70; as frame for God's self-enlargement, 59; and God, 53–54, 59, 60, 67; and God's communication of self, 203; God's consent to, 54; God's end in, 63–65, 67–68, 69, 130, 144, 145, 147, 153, 170, 201–2, 216, 226, 238–39; God's pleasure in, 66; harmony of, 194; and history, 216; and Jesus Christ, 78; and millennium, 239; in Neoplatonism, 64; and space, 216; and time, 216; and Trinity, 61–62, 69, 203–4. *See also* creature(s); human being(s); nature; universe
creature(s): excellency of, 53; happiness of, 63; natural, 198; relation with God of, 44, 48, 205; spiritual, 198; union with each other, 44. *See also* creation; human being(s)
cross, work of, 259
Cudworth, Ralph, 19; *The True Intellectual System of the Universe*, 29
Cutler, Timothy, 4–5, 20, 21

Dana, James, 127
Danks, Samuel, 183
David, 197
Defoe, Daniel, 20; *Family-Instructor*, 26; *Religious Courtship*, 26
deism, 44; and Bible, 91–92; and God, 92, 108; JE's opposition to, 10; JE's reading of, 27–28; morality in, 92; and nature, 108; and reason, 51, 91; and revelation, 91, 92, 94; and Trinity, 50; universalism of, 221

Delattre, Roland, 38, 128
dependence: of existence on divine perception, 22; on God, 6, 49–50, 54; in redemption, 56
De Prospo, R. C., 208n.7
Descartes, René, 18, 42n.4
desire, 115, 117
determinism, 124, 128, 301. *See also* necessity
Deuteronomy, Book of, 230
devil, 107, 173–74, 230, 239, 261, 268, 271n.5
disposition: of believer, 201; divine as sovereign and self-sufficient, 63; finite and created, 63; God as, 61–62, 63, 65, 68, 131; grace as new, 131; heart as, 155; of holiness, 137; Holy Spirit as, 130, 131, 132–35, 136, 137, 145; of Indians, 263; and law, 59, 60, 63, 135; reality as network of, 59–60; in sinner, 142; and virtue, 40. *See also* habit; inclination
Dod, Albert, 297
Drummer, Jeremiah, 20–21, 22, 23
Dudley, Paul, 5
Dugard, William, *Rhetorices Elementa*, 18
duty/obligation, xvi, 92, 139–140, 151, 152, 190, 276, 281, 284, 285, 287
Dwight, Sereno, 87, 88, 227
Dwight, Timothy, 294

earth. *See* world
East Windsor Seminary, 293
Edwards, Jonathan (JE): and Boston preaching, 246, 247; and colonial leadership, 10; at Connecticut Collegiate School, 3, 17; conversion of, 118; cultural context of, 1, 2, 3, 226–27; dismissal of, 12, 119, 235, 285; education of, 3–4, 17–19; family environment of, 17; and First Congregational Church of Northampton, 5–8, 9, 10, 11–12, 24, 118, 228, 235, 245, 246, 247, 251, 264, 285; and Hawley, 7; at Indian mission in Stockbridge, 12–13, 119, 120, 235–36, 245, 261–69, 285; intellectual background of, 16–30; and Johnson, 3; later reception of, 292–306; marriage to Sarah Pierpont, 5; ordination of, 5; as pastor at Bolton, 5; physical frailty of, 5; prayer booth of, 2; as preacher, 4, 244, 246–48,

249, 250, 256; provincialism of, 24; reputation of, 7, 127–28, 231, 233; sermons of, 5–6; and Stoddard, 5, 6, 11, 17, 181, 228, 235, 251, 253; as supply minister in New York, 228; at Yale College, 5, 17–18, 116; writing style of, 21; at Wethersfield, 18
Jonathan Edwards, works: "Account Book," 24, 25, 26, 27; "Beauty of the World, The," 37; "Blank Bible," 28, 89, 94, 95, 98, 199, 230; "Catalogue of Reading," 23–24, 25, 27, 29, 94; *Charity and Its Fruits*, 8, 52, 133, 147, 154, 211; commentary on Revelation, 5; *Concerning the End for Which God Created the World*, 13, 67, 89, 98, 147, 154, 169, 178–79, 206, 216, 222, 235, 238; "Confirmation of the Angels," 174; "Controversies," 139, 141; "Discourse on the Trinity," 45, 46, 47, 48; *Discourses on Various Important Subjects*, 26, 27; *Distinguishing Marks of a Work of the Spirit of God*, 10; *Divine and Supernatural Light*, 6, 45, 106, 198; *Doctrine of Original Sin*, 205; *Ecclesiastical Writings*, 167, 168; *Essay on the Trinity*, 203; *Eternity of Hell Torments*, 253; *Excellency of Christ*, 56; "Exposition on the Apocalypse," 79; *Faithful Narrative of a Surprising Work of God*, 7, 168; *Faithful Narrative of Surprising Conversions*, 295; *Farewell Sermon*, 12, 14, 119; *Freedom of the Will*, 13, 14, 22, 28, 89, 108, 116, 120–21, 123, 124, 125, 127, 128, 155, 266, 296, 298, 301, 302–3, 305; *Future Punishment of the Wicked Unavoidable and Intolerable*, 253; *God Glorified in Man's Dependence*, 49–50, 246; *God Glorified in the Work of Redemption*, 6, 14; *Harmony of the Old and New Testaments*, 11, 14, 28, 90, 91, 95; "Heaven Is a World of Love," 173; *History of the Work of Redemption*, 8, 11, 14, 16, 90, 91, 95, 99, 171, 174, 190, 195, 196–98, 199, 210, 211, 212, 213, 219, 221, 222, 236, 270; "History of the Work of Redemption," 210, 215; *Humble Attempt to Promote Explicit Agreement and Visible Union of God's People in Extraordinary Prayer for the Revival of Religion and the Advancement of Christ's Kingdom on Earth, pursuant to Scripture-Promises and Prophecies concerning the Last Time*, 10, 234, 259, 270; *Humble Inquiry*, 12, 167, 181; *Images of Divine Things*, 37, 89, 177, 179, 190; *Images or Shadows of Divine Things*, 192, 196, 199; "Interleaved Bible," 11; *Justification by Faith Alone*, 7, 27, 137, 139, 141; "Language and Lessons of Nature," 190; Lecture before the sacrament, on Psalm 27:4 [2], 1, 265; "Letter to the Trustees of the College of New Jersey," 210, 213–14, 219, 236; *Life of David Brainerd*, 10, 12, 258, 269–70, 294–95, 301; "Living to Christ," 168; "Love the Sum of All Virtue," 147; "Mind," 34–35, 39, 40, 42n.1; "Miscellaneous Observations on the Holy Scriptures," 230; "Miscellanies," 4, 6, 9–10, 11, 27, 45, 88–89, 92, 94, 95, 98, 178, 228; "Miscellanies" No. z, 79; "Miscellanies" No. 5, 229; "Miscellanies" No. 13, 179; "Miscellanies" No. 26, 229, 239; "Miscellanies" No. 27b, 132; "Miscellanies" No. 48, 63; "Miscellanies" No. 79, 176; "Miscellanies" No. 94, 44–45, 49; "Miscellanies" No. 104, 61, 62, 179; "Miscellanies" No. 105, 240; "Miscellanies" No. 106, 238–39; "Miscellanies" No. 107, 61; "Miscellanies" No. 126, 93; "Miscellanies" No. 177, 239; "Miscellanies" No. 182, 229; "Miscellanies" No. 202, 94; "Miscellanies" No. 204, 92, 93; "Miscellanies" No. 208, 205; "Miscellanies" No. 241, 59, 60; "Miscellanies" No. 262, 239; "Miscellanies" No. 275, 229; "Miscellanies" No. 276, 94; "Miscellanies" No. 332, 54, 201; "Miscellanies" No. 333, 93; "Miscellanies" No. 335, 182; "Miscellanies" No. 338, 182; "Miscellanies" No. 346, 239; "Miscellanies" No. 351, 239; "Miscellanies" No. 370, 200; "Miscellanies" No. 371, 174; "Miscellanies" No. 445, 63; "Miscellanies" No. 448, 55; "Miscellanies" No. 462, 182; "Miscellanies" No. 487, 79–82, 81, 179; "Miscellanies" No. 530, 149; "Miscellanies" No. 539, 52–53; "Miscellanies" No. 547, 76; "Miscellanies" No. 553, 63;

Jonathan Edwards, works (*cont.*)
"Miscellanies" No. 572, 238; "Miscellanies" No. 629, 134, 135; "Miscellanies" No. 683, 184; "Miscellanies" No. 710, 168, 172; "Miscellanies" No. 743, 237–38; "Miscellanies" No. 776, 170; "Miscellanies" No. 777, 237; "Miscellanies" No. 782, 106, 110, 111; "Miscellanies" No. 805, 238; "Miscellanies" No. 832, 50; "Miscellanies" No. 836, 237; "Miscellanies" No. 873, 182; "Miscellanies" No. 949, 237; "Miscellanies" No. 958, 78; "Miscellanies" No. 1004, 238; "Miscellanies" No. 1015, 94; "Miscellanies" No. 1020, 94; "Miscellanies" No. 1062, 55, 202, 203; "Miscellanies" No. 1067, 11, 28; "Miscellanies" No. 1068, 11, 28; "Miscellanies" No. 1081, 54; "Miscellanies" No. 1138, 237; "Miscellanies" No. 1218, 61, 203; "Miscellanies" No. 1224, 237; "Miscellanies" No. 1245, 170; "Miscellanies" No. 1263, 60; "Miscellanies" No. 1337, 92; "Miscellanies" No. 1338, 51; "Miscellanies" No. 1350, 28; "Miscellanies" No. 1353, 172; "Miscellanies" No. 1359, 29; "Miscellanies" no. 1060, 28, 95; *Misrepresentations Corrected, and Truth Vindicated*, 12, 119–20; *Morning-Exercise Against Popery*, 26; "Natural Philosophy," 37, 60, 96; *Nature of True Virtue*, 13, 41, 89, 111, 147, 153, 154, 206, 215–16, 286, 298, 299–300; *Necessity and Reasonableness of the Christian Doctrine of Satisfaction for Sin*, 303; "Notes on Scripture," 11, 28, 89, 94–95, 98, 172, 176, 179, 230; "Notes on the Apocalypse," 173, 230–31, 235; *Observations Concerning the Scripture of Œconomy of the Trinity and Covenant of Redemption*, 55–56; "Of Atoms," 35; "Of Being," 35; "OfInsects," 37; "Of Light," 37; "Of the Rainbow," 37; *Original Sin*, 13–14, 89, 98, 286, 298, 301; *Personal Narrative*, 2, 17, 39, 45, 106; *Present State of the Republick of Letters*, 25; *Pressing into the Kingdom*, 7; "Rational Account of the Principles and Main Doctrines of the Christian Religion," 50; "Redemption Discourse," 211–12, 213, 214; "Saints in Heaven," 174; Sermon on Acts 11:12–13, 263, 265; Sermon on Matthew 7:13–14, 265; Sermon on 2 Peter 1:19, 264, 269; *Sinner Is Not Justified in the Sight of God Except Through the Righteousness of Christ Obtained by Faith* (Master's *Quaestio*), 4, 6–7, 14, 136–37; *Sinners in the Hands of an Angry God*, 9, 253–55; *Sinners in Zion*, 9; *Some Thoughts Concerning the Present Revival of Religion in New England*, 10, 111, 233, 260; "Spider Letter," 37, 96; "Subjects to Be Handled in the Treatise on the Mind," 60; "Traditions of the Heathen," 11; *Treatise Concerning Religious Affections*, 10, 21, 22, 45, 89, 103, 110, 111, 133, 136, 137, 154, 177, 181, 198, 234, 262, 263; *Treatise on Grace*, 132–33, 136, 198; *Two Dissertations*, 147, 215; "Types of the Messiah," 174, 196–97, 200; *Wicked Men's Slavery to Sin*, 245–46

Edwards, Sarah Pierpont, 5, 10, 26
Edwards, Timothy (father), 1, 2, 5, 17–18; *All the Living Must Surely Die*, 250; sermons of, 244, 250, 253, 276–77
Edwards, Timothy (son), 15
Edwards, Tyrone, 211
elect, 170, 180; beauty of, 258; in Campbell, 303; dearness of, 152; and final judgment, 175; Jesus Christ as head of, 171; as one with God, 67–68; and redemption, 69, 238. *See also* regenerate person(s); saints
Eliot, John, 267
Elohim, 50
emanation, 54, 55, 56, 82, 202, 203, 204, 205, 206, 216
emanationism, 64, 65
Emerson, Ralph Waldo, 194
Emlyn, Thomas, *Humble Inquiry into the Scripture-account of Jesus Christ*, 50
empiricism, 16, 22, 31n.16. *See also* science
England, 49, 281, 285
Enlightenment: history in, 222; influence of, 21, 22, 23, 26, 27, 29–30; justice in, 293; legacy of, 297; Miller on, 16; polite learning of, 19–20, 25; reason in, 50; and Scotland, 302; universal history in, 213, 215; and will, 116

enthusiasm, 12, 107, 233, 298
Ephesians, Epistle to, 168, 175, 178, 181, 184
Epicurean philosophy, 19
epistemology, 69, 108–9
Erskine, John, 14, 29, 33n.34, 119, 120, 295, 296
eschatology, 69–70, 217, 226–40; and Bible, 94, 228–31, 238; as dynamic and progressive, 260–61; and history, 226, 228, 229, 231, 232, 235, 238, 239; and Jesus Christ, 78; and love, 153; and revivals, 231–32, 233, 235; as term, 226, 240; and time, 226; and Trinity, 56; and typology, 229–31, 232, 233, 238. *See also* millennium
essence, 35, 200, 204
ethics, 69, 298
evangelical movement, 9, 10, 26, 227, 232–33, 234, 275, 276, 282, 285, 286, 295, 297, 305. *See also* revivals
evil: in Calvin, 117; and church, 173–74, 176; and determinism, 124; as disagreement to being, 39; in fast sermons, 280; and God, 126; and hell, 238; and last judgment, 237; as opposed to redemption, 239–40; as violation of obligation, 140; and will, 125. *See also* sin
excellence/excellency, 45; and consent, 52; and consent of being to being, 36; creaturely, 53; of divine objects, 108; of God, 4, 51–53, 93, 105, 140, 201, 238; love as, 40; as object of knowledge, 112; and plurality, 34, 40, 52; as term, 38; of Trinity, 54; and true virtue, 154
excommunication, 183
exegesis, 28. *See also* Bible; typology
existence: dependent on God's perception, 22; and essence, 35, 200, 204; God as cause of, 60; God as direct, 61; in God's mind, 35, 37; of God through himself, 35; mystical conception of, 23; priority of, 204
Exodus, Book of, 280
experience, 107; authentic, 233; and conscience, 160; and doctrine, 105; and ideas, 109; in Locke, 109; and sense, 110; and understanding, 105, 106; and will, 124

faculty, 104, 205
faith: act of as good, 138, 139, 141–42; and church membership, 183; conviction of, 108; as disposition, 142; as disposition of holiness, 137; free act of, 136; God's infusion of, 142; and grace, 130, 136; grace grounded in, 138; and Holy Spirit, 140–41; and Jesus Christ, 138; and justification, 5, 74–75, 136–45, 146n.8, 172; notional understanding of, 103; profession of, 11; as reception, 75; redemption through, 4; as union with Christ, 138–39; as virtue, 137. *See also* believer
fall, 148, 168, 205, 232, 258
fallen creature, 130, 131. *See also* sin; wicked, the
family, divine, 56
fast, 275, 276, 277, 278–79, 280, 284–86
fatalism, 126
Father: and atonement, 55; and church, 171; Clarke on, 49; and community of spirits, 82; creation as emanation from, 204; defined, 61–62; as first true actuality of God, 61–62; glorification of, 56; honor of, 48; hypostasis of, 72; imitation of, 151; and Jesus Christ, 80; and love, 52; marriage of Jesus and church before, 70; in Mather, 46; and redemption, 54; self image of, 203, 204; self knowledge of, 62, 67; self love of, 67; and Son, 82, 203; Son as fullness of, 179; Son as idea of, 46, 48; Son as one substance with, 49; Son as repetition of, 48, 62; Son loved by, 62, 76; and timelessness, 67; in Trinity, 203; as unoriginated, 62. *See also* Trinity
Fiering, Norman, 18, 22, 23
figuralism, 217, 218, 223. *See also* typology
final judgment. *See* judgment
Finney, Charles G., *Lectures on Revivals of Religion*, 296–97
First Congregational Church of Northampton, 5–8, 9, 10, 11–12, 24, 228, 235, 245, 246, 247, 264, 285
fitness, moral vs. natural, 138, 139, 145
Flavel, John, 194
forgiveness, 170, 268
form, concept of, 142
fornication, 183, 184

Foxcroft, Thomas, 120
France, 13, 228, 266, 269, 276, 281, 282, 284, 285, 286, 287
freedom, 11, 115–28, 135, 136, 143, 294, 295
Fuller, Andrew, 295

Galatians, Epistle to, 173
Gale, Theophilus, 29
Galileo Galilei, 118
Gassendi, Pierre, 19
Gay, Peter, *A Loss of Mastery*, 220–21, 222
Genesis, Book of, 28, 178, 230, 264
geometry, 19, 38
Gerstner, John H., 227, 305
Gibbon, Edward, 222
Gillies, John, *Historical Collections*, 29
glory: appreciation of, 153; and church, 174; and communication, 204; of God, 6, 54, 63–64, 70, 107, 144, 145, 169–70, 185, 191, 192, 200, 202, 203, 204–5, 216, 238, 246, 259; as gravity, 202, 206; and Trinity, 53, 238, 258
God: actuality of, 61, 62, 63, 65, 66; ad extra activity of, 56, 63, 64, 68, 169, 170, 202, 203, 204; ad intra activity of, 63, 203, 204; and affections, 162; analogies for, 47; awful sweetness of, 4; beauty of, 4, 46, 51–53, 57, 61, 69, 70, 93, 105, 201, 259, 293; being of, 105; as being of beings, 35; as benevolent, 201; and causation, 22, 23, 59, 60; and church, 168–69, 173; as communicating being, 205; communication from, 191; communication in nature by, 193, 194; communication of purpose of, 190; communication of self, 48, 61, 62, 63, 66, 131, 144, 169, 170, 193, 200, 202, 204; communion with, 92, 93, 205; as community of persons, 47; consent to, 155; consent to creation by, 54; continual maintenance by, 4; continual recreation of world by, 22; control of events by, 116, 117, 125, 232, 293; covenant with New England, 275, 276, 277–78, 279, 280, 282, 283, 284, 285, 286, 287, 288; and creation, 53–54, 59, 60, 63–65, 66, 67, 130; creatures' relation with, 44, 48, 205; decrees of, 2; and deism, 92, 108; delight in, 61; dependence on, 49–50, 54; diffusion of fullness of, 202; as direct existence, 61; as disposition, 61–62, 63, 65, 68, 131; disposition to communicate self, 202; and duality, 44; dynamic conception of, 201, 209n.19; effulgence of, 201, 203, 205, 209n.19; elect as one with, 67–68; and emanation, 54, 55, 56, 82, 202, 203, 204, 205, 206, 216; end in creation, 63–65, 67–68, 69, 130, 134, 145, 147, 153, 170, 201–2, 216, 226, 238–39; enlargement of, 70; eternality of, 201; and evil, 117, 126; excellency of, 4, 51–53, 93, 105, 140, 201, 238; exhibition of proportionate to believer's disposition, 201; existence dependent on perception of, 22; existence in mind of, 35, 37; as existing through himself, 35; experience of, 93; faithfulness of, 201, 202; Father as first true actuality of, 61–62; fear of, 201; as first and last, 44; flowing forth of, 64; foreknowledge of, 89, 170; fullness of, 68; glory of, 6, 54, 63–64, 70, 107, 144, 145, 169–70, 185, 191, 192, 200, 202, 203, 204–5, 216, 238, 246, 259; and good, 52, 54, 63, 124, 246; as harmony of Trinity, 76, 77; and history, 191, 232; as holy, 124; as holy society, 206; and human beings, 6, 44, 73–76, 93, 145, 205; human beings as dependent on, 6; human beings as participating in activity of, 60; human beings incorporated by, 55; human beings' infinite obligation to, 139–40; idea of, 46, 61; idea of self of, 44; identity in otherness, 52; identity of, 93; image of, 198, 258; immutability of, 65; increase in being of, 65, 66–67; and Indians, 262; indwelling presence of, 6; JE's boyhood questioning of, 2; and Jesus, 70; Jesus Christ as knowledge of, 54–55; as judge, 201; judgment of, 268; justice of, 141; and knowledge, 45, 46–47, 54–55, 61, 67, 68, 89, 112, 150, 201; and law, 293; and Logos, 80; and love, 44, 45–46, 48, 52, 54, 55, 69, 79, 103, 104, 147, 148, 149, 150, 156, 169–70, 201, 205; majesty of, 4, 201; marks of, 154; and material bodies, 35–36; mind of, 3–4, 35, 37, 77; and morality, 14; moral perfection of, 201; and nature, 131, 145, 205; nature of, 3; and objectivity, 77; omnipotence of, 255; omnipresence of, 201;

oneness of, 47; as only proper substance, 35; as only substance, 22; as own object, 203; as pattern of all, 44; perception of, 22, 93; perception of self by, 203; perception of through grace, 191; perfection of, 44, 59, 62, 65, 201, 202; and pleasure in creation of, 66; pleasure in presence of, 238; power of, 9, 150, 193, 201, 254, 255; preservation of world by, 173; primacy of, 131; as prime and original being, 44; providence of, 54, 92–93, 116, 117, 125, 150, 190, 193, 195, 239; rational reflection about, 92; reality as idea in mind of, 3–4; and reason, 108, 201; reconciliation to, 76; and redemption, 6, 49–50, 92–93, 119, 202, 203, 218, 232, 246; and religious affections, 103; repetition of, 59, 62, 64, 69, 70, 144; resistance to, 76; Richard of St. Victor on, 47; and saints, 69, 176, 238–39; self-contemplation of, 46; self-enjoyment of, 203; self-enlargement of, 59, 65, 67, 68, 69; sense from, 110; in sermons, 244; sinners as reliant on, 6; as society, 45, 47; as sole effective power, 150; as source, 195–96; sovereignty of, 2, 4, 6, 117, 118, 119, 130, 132, 193, 201, 254, 255, 293; and space, 68, 69; as space, 42n.4; and sufficiency, 54, 65, 66; superabundance of, 55; and time, 59, 63, 64, 66, 67, 68, 69; transcendence of, 193; and triplicity, 44; and truth, 38; understanding of, 46; union with, 44, 48, 53, 57, 76, 170, 206, 238–39; and unity of discourse, 200, 204; and unity of essence and existence, 35; as Unmoved Mover, 67, 68; upholding of physical laws by, 22; voice of, 93, 191, 205, 207; and war, 281; and will, 116, 117, 118, 119, 124, 150; will of, 46, 201; wisdom of, 296; word of, 46; and world, 59–70, 173; worship of, 169–70. *See also* Father; Godhead; Holy Spirit; Son; Trinity
Godhead: defined, 185n.6; emanation of divine fullness from, 216; Holy Spirit as fullness of, 179, 187n.16; as society, 203; as society of three persons, 48. *See also* Trinity
Godwin, William, *Enquiry Concerning Political Justice*, 295

Goen, C. C., 227, 241n.11
good: act of faith as, 138, 139, 141–42; and beauty, 77; Bible as, 93; duty to do, 151; as entity, 39; for friends and enemies, 151; and God, 52, 54, 63, 124, 246; objective vs. inherent, 246; and others, 148, 149, 151; and spiritual community, 77; and will, 121, 122, 124, 125
Gordon, A. J., 294
grace: in Aquinas, 131–32, 136, 142, 143; in Calvinism, 130; of charity, 131; and church, 168, 174; common, 154; common vs. special, 111; as conforming, 55; covenant of, 171, 197, 204, 274, 275; created, 131, 132, 136; double, 142; as enduring transformation, 131; and faith, 130, 136, 138; as gratuitous, 130, 132; holiness through, 142; and Holy Spirit, 130, 131, 133, 135, 144, 151, 204; as implanted, 136; infusion of, 205; and Jesus Christ, 55; and justification, 144–45, 146n.8; morality of, 154; and nature, 111, 150; as new disposition, 131; and perception, 191, 209n.19; and redemption, 130, 197; and regeneration, 131, 135, 136; and revivals, 154; as sovereign, 130, 132; transformation by, 204; and Trinity, 54; true vs. false signs of, 10; uncreated, 131, 132; and virtue, 132; Western theology of, 131
gratitude, 149, 158, 159, 162, 163
gravity, 23, 202, 206
Great Apostasy, 4–5, 118
Great Awakening, 8–10, 103, 168, 181, 182, 183, 220, 231, 260, 270, 294. *See also* revivals
Great Commission, 259
Great Earthquake, 277–78
Grotius, Hugo, 29
guilt, 137, 140, 299, 300. *See also* imputation

habit, 59–60, 135. *See also* disposition
Half-Way Covenant, 2, 182
Hall, David, 167–68
Hampshire Association, 24, 25
happiness, 63, 148–49, 158, 229, 237, 240. *See also* pleasure
harmony, 38, 40, 56, 77, 154, 155, 157, 194. *See also* proportion

Haroutunian, Joseph, 304–5; *Piety vs. Moralism*, 305
Harvard College, 18, 19, 297
Hawley, Elisha, 184
Hawley, Gideon, 12, 266, 270
Hawley, Joseph, 7
Hawthorne, Nathanial, 255, 257n.17
heart: and being in general, 41, 156, 160, 161, 163; and benevolence, 159; as disposition, 155; extension of, 156; and head, 105, 110; as inclination, 104; and JE's upbringing, 1; sense of, 93, 103, 105–6, 107–8, 109, 110; and sermons, 244; as spiritual center, 106; and virtue, 40; as will, 155
heart religion, 103, 109, 113, 151
heaven, 57, 70, 228, 229, 237–38, 240
Hebrews, Epistle to, 9
Heereboord, Adrianus, 18
Heimert, Alan, 227
hell, 54, 229, 238, 240, 278
Henry, Matthew, *Exposition of the Old and New Testaments*, 28
Herbert of Cherbury, 27
heresy, 21
heterodoxy, 4, 5, 10
history: and Bible, 28, 92, 96, 98; and church, 171; colonial, 220; continuance of, 69, 70; divine presence in, 191; and eschatology, 226, 228, 229, 231, 232, 235, 238, 239; God's control of, 232; God's voice in, 191; interpretation of, 217–18; as medium for creation, 216; and millennium, 217, 218, 221; Niebuhr on, 219–20; and ontology, 194, 195, 198, 199, 200, 204; and prophecy, 217, 218; and providence, 190, 193, 239; and redemption, 198, 204, 210, 211–16, 217, 222, 223, 236, 259, 262; religious expression in, 192; and revelation, 218; and revivals, 8; in sermons, 284; Son in, 55; sources of, 212, 213; as subject, 217; and typology, 97, 193, 194, 195, 196, 197, 199, 201, 204, 207, 217, 218, 223; as unitary process, 220, 221, 222; universal, 213
Hoadly, Benjamin, 25
Hobbes, Thomas, 92, 118
Hodge, Charles, 296, 299
Holbrook, Clyde, 127

holiness, 4, 53, 124, 137, 140–41, 142, 144, 145, 240
Hollis, Isaac, 263
Holy Spirit: in Aquinas, 135–36; assistance of, 110, 111; and church, 169; and community of spirits, 82; and conversion, 239; as disposition, 130, 131, 132–35, 136, 137, 145; and divine light, 106–7; and emanation/remanation, 56; and faculties, 108; and faith, 140–41; fruits of, 103, 104, 111, 239; as fullness of Godhead, 179, 187n.16; and general law, 135–36; gifts of, 56; God's communication by power of, 169; and grace, 130, 131, 133, 135, 144, 151, 204; in history, 213; and holiness, 145; honor of, 48; indwelling of, 55, 69, 130, 133–34, 135, 136, 144; and Jesus Christ, 82; knowledge made possible by, 69; in Lombard, 135; as love, 48, 50, 52, 53, 54, 62, 82, 203; in Mather, 46; and nature, 134; and natures of Jesus Christ, 79, 80; progress through, 239; reality of, 133, 134; and redemption, 54, 55, 296; and regenerate person, 69, 130, 132, 134, 135, 136; as relation, 82; and religious affections, 112; sealing of, 104; and timelessness, 67; in Trinity, 82, 203; and will, 135. *See also* Trinity
honor, 47, 48
Hooker, Thomas, 251
Hopkins, Samuel, 13, 22, 29, 87, 127, 215, 227, 296, 300; *System of Doctrine*, 293
Hosea, Book of, 178
human being(s): in Aquinas, 131; capacity to know God, 46–47; communion with God, 92, 93, 205; conviction of, 108; as dependent on God, 6; disposition of, 201; as dispositions and habits, 60; frailty of, 201; and glory, 204–5; and God, 93; God's exhibition of self to, 201; God's glory in, 145; God's incorporation of, 55; God's self-enlargement through, 59; image of God in, 258; infinite obligation to God, 139–40; love to, 147; merit of, 6; as natural man, 110, 150, 151, 154; natural vs. moral ability of, 295; as participating in God's activity, 60; prelapsarian, 205; preservation of, 161; relationship with

God, 6, 44, 73–76, 205; responsibility of, 293; self-identity of, 121; and self-love, 153; self-understanding of, 121; sinful nature of, 299; unity with Adam, 14. *See also* creation; creature(s)
Hume, David, 26, 161
Hutcheson, Francis, 150, 161, 222
Hutchinson, Abigail, 10
hypocrisy, 8, 11, 180, 183, 278–79

idealism, 4, 36–37; Emersonian, 194; and God's communications in nature, 194; and More, 42n.4; Neoplatonic, 200, 201; objective, 35; phenomenalistic, 37; and Trinity, 46
idea(s): agreement among perceptual, 38–39; defined, 105; and experience, 109; human vs. divine, 109; in Locke, 109; and reality, 77; of self, 61; Son as, 50; and words, 109. *See also* imagination
identity, 14, 52, 93, 121
illumination, 91
imagination, 40, 107, 159. *See also* idea(s)
immaterialism, 22, 193, 208n.7
imputation, 14, 74–75, 143, 144, 299, 300
inanimate things, 157
Incarnation, 172, 191, 259
inclination, 104, 121, 262, 263. *See also* disposition
Indians, 12–13, 119, 120, 235, 258, 260, 261–69, 279, 286, 295
intellect, 117, 121, 122
Isaiah, Book of, 2, 14, 28, 176, 181, 211
Israel, 218, 276, 279–81, 283, 287

James, William, 41, 107, 110
Jehovah, 50
Jenson, Robert W., 227
Jeremiah, Book of, 178, 283
Jesus Christ: atonement by, 55, 137, 140; beauty of God as manifest in, 70; beauty of union with, 139; and believer, 73–76; blood of, 175; as bridegroom, 69–70, 170, 171, 175, 178, 180, 186n.12; in Campbell, 303; and church, 69–70, 168–71, 172, 175, 178–80, 240; church as body of, 168, 169, 170, 171, 174, 177, 178, 179–80, 183, 184, 185; church as fullness of, 178–79; church as ingrafted into, 169; church as mother of, 172, 186n.10; church as risen with, 171; as church's head, 171; closing with, 73–76; communication in union with, 171; consciousness of, 80, 81; and creation, 78; death on cross, 78, 79, 303; and eschatology, 78; and faith, 138; and Father, 80; and final judgment, 237, 240; glory of, 197; God's communication through, 170; and grace, 55; and Holy Spirit, 82; and Indians, 261; indwelling of, 55; JE's focus on, 47; justification in, 170; knowledge of, 81; as knowledge of God, 54–55; life in, 171; and light, 197; and Logos, 79–82, 83; and love, 152–53; as mediator, 54, 70, 170; as moral actor, 125; natures of, 72, 73, 75, 76, 78–82, 84n.6; and necessity, 89, 125; in New Testament, 72, 81; as one hypostasis, 72–73; oneness of, 73; passion of, 184; and Princeton Seminary, 302; and redemption, 4, 54–55, 73–76, 78, 97, 213, 303; in "Redemption Discourse," 212; redemption offered by, 138; and regenerate person, 150; righteousness of, 74, 75, 143, 144, 170; sacrifice of, 4, 153; and saints, 168, 178, 200; and secular world, 169; self-creation of, 78; and sin, 74; in Smith, 302; and Son, 80; sorrow of, 304; soul's marriage to, 74; subordinationist views of, 50; suffering of, 137, 179, 303; sun as type of, 199; and typology, 97, 190, 191, 196–97, 199–200, 212–13; union through, 170; union with, 138–39, 145, 152, 170–71, 183, 184, 240, 258; as virtuous, 89; will of, 124–25. *See also* Logos; Son; Word
Jews, 172, 230
1 John, Epistle of, 230, 249
John, Gospel of, 178, 245
Johnson, Edward, 220
Johnson, Samuel, 3, 20, 21; *Dictionary*, 192
Johnson, Thomas, 23, 24
Jones, Jeremiah, *New and Full Method of Settling the Canonical Authority of the New Testament*, 28
judgment: and fast sermons, 277, 278, 279; final, 174–75, 237, 240, 277; by Jesus Christ, 237, 240; in sermons to Indians, 268; and will, 104
Judson, Adoniram, 294
justice, 141, 157, 159, 160, 163, 295

justification, 8; in Aquinas, 142–43; in Arminianism, 145; in Calvin, 140, 141, 142; as change, 143; and faith, 5, 74–75, 136–45, 146n.8, 172; forensic conception of, 139–45; and grace, 144–45, 146n.8; and holiness, 141, 142, 144; as imputation in court of heaven, 74; in JE's followers, 300; in Jesus Christ, 170; Rand on, 119; and revivals, 119; and *sola gratia*, 6–7; and Trinity, 53; as unmerited, 142

Kames, Henry Home, Lord, 295–96; *Essays on the Principles of Morality and Natural Religion*, 296
Kellogg, Martin, 266
Kierkegaard, Søren, 110
Kimnach, Wilson, 17, 21
1 Kings, Book of, 177, 230, 281
Kingsley, Bathsheba, 183
Kirkland, Samuel, 264
Kneeland, Samuel, 120
knowledge: agreement in, 38; of beauty, 112; and being, 35, 36; coherence of all, 96; and God, 45, 46–47, 54–55, 61, 67, 68, 89, 112, 150, 201; and Holy Spirit, 69; and interpretation of Bible, 96; and Jesus Christ, 54–55, 81; and logic, 18; mind's appetite for, 36–37; self, 121

language, 109, 163, 207
Lardner, Nathaniel, *Credibility of the Gospel History*, 94
last judgment. *See* judgment
latitudinarianism, 19, 20, 21, 25–26
law, 22, 59, 60, 63, 135–36
learning, polite, 19–20, 25, 26, 27
Lee, Sang Hyun, 48, 185n.6, 201, 209n.19, 227
Leland, John, *View of the Principal Deistical Writers*, 28
Lesser, M. X., 274
Leviticus, Book of, 281
liberalism, 20, 83, 202
libertarianism, 121
light, 3, 6, 106–7, 108
Lightfoot, John, 97
Lloyd-Jones, Martyn, 305
Locke, John, 4, 16, 17; and Bible, 27, 98; in Drummer's collection, 20;

epistemology of, 200, 205; *Essay Concerning Human Understanding*, 22, 38, 105, 108–9; *forma ab extra* in, 205; influence of, 22–23, 31n.16; on knowledge from perception, 38; language of, 202; Miller on, 192, 193, 220; Norris on, 23; and polite learning, 19; on psychology, 61, 192; reality in, 77; *The Reasonableness of Christianity*, 27; recent discoveries of, 3; as source, 106
Logan, Samuel T., Jr., 146n.8
Logos, 50, 54, 79–82, 83. *See also* Jesus Christ; Word
London Magazine, 25
Lord's Supper, 2, 11, 17, 119, 167, 168, 182, 184, 185, 235, 285
Louisbourg, fortress at, 281–83
love: and affections, 104, 104; in Aquinas, 132; and beauty, 155, 157; to being in general, 155, 156, 293, 295; and benevolence, 41, 151–52, 156; in Bible, 154; Christian, 111, 154; of complacence, 41; divine, 147, 148; and eschatology, 153; as excellence, 40; and Father, 52; fullness of, 153; and God, 44, 45–46, 52, 54, 55, 69, 79, 103, 104, 147, 148, 149, 150, 156, 169–70, 201, 205; and happiness, 148–49, 158; and holiness, 53; and Holy Spirit, 48, 50, 52, 53, 54, 62, 82, 104, 203; to human beings, 147; and imputation, 143; inordinate, 148, 153; and Jesus Christ, 152–53; JE's works on, 147; and morality, 158–59; and neighbor, 63, 148, 149, 152, 156; object of, 41; for others, 152; parent-child, 161, 162; partaking of divine, 150; as passion, 85n.28; as perfection of person, 47; reciprocal, 52; of self, 147–49, 153, 157, 158, 159; and selfishness, 152, 153; and Son, 52; and Trinity, 48, 52, 80; and true religion, 104; virtuous, 41; and will, 117, 132. *See also* charity
Lovelace, Richard, *Dynamics of Spiritual Life*, 305
Lowance, Mason, 208 nn. 9, 17, 234–35
Lowman, Moses, *Paraphrase and Notes on the Revelation*, 232
Lucretius, 117
Luke, Gospel of, 179, 230, 238

INDEX

Luther, Martin, 26, 74, 84n.10, 132; *Christian Liberty*, 74
Lyon, Mary, 294

machine/mechanism, 122, 124, 125, 127, 128
Malebranche, Nicolas, 193; *Recherche de la Vérité*, 23
marriage, 74, 170
mass, 202, 206
Massachusetts Bay charter, 2
Mastricht, Peter van, *Theoretico-Practica Theologia*, 19, 24–25
material body, 35–36
material universe, 60, 61, 63, 77, 118, 193, 238. *See also* creation
Mather, Cotton, 3, 17, 20, 21, 46, 220, 259; *Manuductio ad Ministerium*, 24–25
Mather, Increase, 3, 17, 21
Matthew, Gospel of, 8, 9, 112, 133, 173, 175, 176, 178, 181, 230, 248, 259
Mayhew, Jonathan, 50
McClymond, Michael, 51; *Encounters with God*, 222
McCulloch, William, 295
McDermott, Gerald, 27, 28, 222; *Jonathan Edwards Confronts the Gods*, 221; *One Holy and Happy Society*, 221
Medean paradox, 117
Melanchthon, Philip, 74, 75, 76
merit, 141, 142, 143
Messiah, 11, 28, 198, 199. *See also* Jesus Christ
metaphysics, 22, 35, 44, 45, 76–77
midwife, manual for, 12, 183–84
millennium, 231; approach of, 8, 191, 192, 193, 196; arrival of, 260–61; description of, 229, 236–37; emanation/remanation at, 206; and end of creation, 239; and history, 217, 218, 221; hope for, 9, 10; JE's writings on, 241n.11; Miller on, 220; and redemption, 239; and revivals, 8, 9, 232, 233–34, 239; and saints, 56–57, 237; and Trinity, 56–57. *See also* eschatology
Miller, Perry, 16, 17, 23, 29, 88, 222, 274, 305–6; on epistemology, 108–9; and eschatology, 227; and federal theology, 275; on free will, 127; on history, 220; *Jonathan Edwards*, 220, 304;

on Locke, 22; *The New England Mind*, 304; on typology, 192–93, 194, 207n.4, 208n.7
Miller, Samuel, 297
Mills, Samuel J., 294
mind: and appetite for knowledge, 36–37; and dissent to being, 36; enlargement of, 159; enlightenment of, 112; existence in God's, 37; of God, 3–4, 35, 37, 77; heart as inclination expressed in, 104; in Locke, 109; nature of, 3; operations of, 36; as plural, 36; and proportion, 38; and truth, 38
missions, 258–70, 294–95. *See also* evangelical movement; Stockbridge, Indian mission at
Mix, Elisha, 19
modernism, 202
modernity, 82–84
morality, 25; and beauty, 41, 112, 157; benevolence in, 154; Christian, 154; common, 111, 154, 157–62, 163; and conscience, 157; corporate, 275, 277, 278; in deism, 92; and determinism, 301; Enlightenment attitudes toward, 20; and excellency, 138; and God, 14, 201; and goodness, 162; of grace, 154; of Indians, 268–69; in JE's followers, 293; and love, 158–59; and nature, 154, 159; and necessity, 126, 296, 298; in Old Testament, 197; progression of, 153; reform in, 288; and religion, 163–64; and self-love, 158, 159; and virtue, 40, 163–64; writings on, 13. *See also* sin; vice; virtue
moral sense, 158, 159, 165n.14
More, Henry, 19, 20, 35, 42n.4; *Enchiridion Ethicum*, 18; *Enchiridion Metaphysicum*, 18
Morgan, Edmund S., 20, 274
Morgan, Thomas, 27
Morimoto, Anri, 135
Morris, William Sparkes, *The Young Jonathan Edwards*, 23
Morse, Jedidiah, 293
Moses, 191, 197
motion, 23
motive, 121–22, 128n.6
Murphy, Arthur E., 128
Murray, Iain, 16, 227, 305

natural law, 161
natural man, 110, 150, 151, 154. *See also* human being(s)
natural philosophy, 3, 14, 18
natural principles, 107, 110, 111, 162–63
natural religion, 91–92
nature: analogies with spirit, 193; beauty of, 37; and being, 36; and Bible, 194; calamities of, 277–78, 279; capacity of, 151; and deism, 108; and deity, 202; divine presence in, 191; divine uniformity of, 192; exaltation of, 192–93; God's actions through, 131; God's communication through, 193, 194; God's glory in, 145; God's self-enlargement through, 59; God's voice in, 191, 205; and grace, 111, 150; and Holy Spirit, 134; and Indians, 268; insufficiency of, 92; JE's writings on, 5; living things in, 39; morality of, 154; perfection in, 200; and providence, 150; relation in, 39; and religion, 1, 192; in sermons, 264; as shadows of being, 36; as shadows of spiritual things, 37; and typology, 97, 190, 191, 192, 193, 194, 195, 196, 199–200, 204, 205, 207. *See also* creation
natures, communication of, 78
necessity, 89, 122–23, 124, 125–27, 296, 298, 301. *See also* determinism; providence
Nehemiah, Book of, 248
neighbor/others, 63, 148, 149, 151, 152, 156, 159–60
Neoplatonism, 64, 68–69, 193, 200, 201, 202. *See also* Plotinus
Nettleton, Asahel, 293, 297
New Divinity theologians, 296
New England, 49, 239, 260; God's covenant with, 275, 276, 277–78, 279, 280, 282, 283, 284, 285, 286, 287, 288; sin of, 276, 277; war in, 281–83, 287
New England Congregationalists, 297
New England theologians, 296, 298, 299, 300, 301, 302
New Haven theologians, 294, 296, 298, 301
New School Presbyterians, 297, 301
New Testament, 95; and church, 171, 172; Jesus Christ in, 72, 81; and Old Testament, 152; revelations in, 191; and Trinity, 50; and typology, 97, 190, 198. *See also* Bible; *specific books*
Newton, Sir Isaac, 18, 77; divine uniformity of nature in, 192; in Drummer's collection, 20; influence of, 23; language of, 202; Miller on, 192, 193, 220; on optics, 37; and question of will, 118; recent discoveries of, 3; and sermons, 255
Nicole, Pierre, *La Logique, ou L'art de penser*, 18
Niebuhr, H. Richard, 88, 216, 221; *The Kingdom of God in America*, 219, 305; *The Social Sources of Denominationalism*, 219
Niebuhr, Reinhold, 16, 216
nihilism, 83
nominalism, 59
non-Christians, 221
Nonconformists, 25, 26
Norris, John, *An Essay towards the Theory of the Ideal or Intelligible World*, 23
Northampton. *See* First Congregational Church of Northampton
Numbers, Book of, 177, 247

object: beauty as, 41, 112; of consenting, 36; excellence of divine, 108; God as own, 203; of love, 41; and virtue, 40–41
objectivity, 77
obligation. *See* duty/obligation
occasionalism, 22, 23, 60
Old Lights, 10
Old School Calvinism, 301
Old School Presbyterians, 297, 298, 299–300
Old Testament: and church, 171, 172, 177, 195; and Gospel, 152; moral law of, 197; in "Redemption Discourse," 212; revelations in, 191; saints in, 171, 172; spiritual transformation in, 198–99; and Trinity, 50; and typology, 97, 190, 193, 197, 198, 212, 213. *See also* Bible
Oliver, Andrew, 263
ontological analogy, 199
ontology, 169; excellency in, 38; and history, 194, 195, 198, 199, 200, 204; and typology, 193, 194, 195, 196, 197, 199
optics, 3, 37
others. *See* neighbor/others
Owen, John, 24

pain, 150
Park, Edwards Amasa, 293, 299–300
Parrington, Vernon, 274
Paul, 103, 130, 139, 177
Pauw, Amy Plantinga, 29
Pepperell, William, 282
perception: in Aristotle, 84n.10; and blinding power of sin, 205–6; divine, 22; existence dependent on divine, 22; of glory, 204; and grace, 191, 209n.19; knowledge from, 38; multiples in, 38; and reality, 76–77; renewal of, 93; by saints, 205, 207; and virtue, 154. *See also* apprehension
perfection, 51, 140, 141, 200, 201
Perkins, William, 243
person, as term, 52–53
1 Peter, Epistle of, 112
2 Peter, Epistle of, 264, 268–69
Peter Lombard, 131, 135
phenomena, 36–37, 38–39. *See also* creation; nature
philosophy, 16, 21, 92, 96
physics, 3, 18, 22, 38, 96, 118. *See also* science
Pierpont, Benjamin, 89
pietists, 275
piety, 200
Piper, John, *Desiring God*, 305
pity, 159, 161, 162, 163
Plato, 116–17
pleasure, 38, 39, 109, 150, 157, 238. *See also* happiness
Plotinus, 65, 68. *See also* Neoplatonism
plurality, 34, 36, 40, 41, 52
Poe, Edgar Allan, 255, 257n.17
Pomeroy, Hannah, 183
Poole, Matthew, *Synopsis Criticorum*, 28
Port-Royal logic, 18
pragmatism, 127
prayer, 234
predestination, 117, 123
preordination, 2
Presbyterians, 2, 296, 297, 298, 299–300, 301
Prideaux, Humphrey, *Old and New Testaments Connected in the History of the Jews*, 28
Prince, Thomas, *Christian History*, 119
Princeton Theological Seminary, 296, 298, 300–301

print, culture of, 17, 29
prophecy, 11, 91, 95, 191, 201, 202, 217, 218, 234, 236
proportion, 34, 37–38, 39–40, 45, 194. *See also* harmony
Protestantism: and Bible, 91; commentarial tradition of, 28; and God's end in creation, 216, 217; grace in, 132; history in, 222; and JE's convictions, 23; JE's debt to, 29; and justification, 130, 136, 139, 144; and missions, 269–70; redemption in, 212, 215; scholasticism of, 21; Trinity in, 47; and typology, 193, 194, 218; and will, 117; at Yale, 19
providence, 54, 92–93, 116, 117, 125, 150, 190, 193, 195, 239. *See also* necessity
Psalms, Book of, 172, 175, 176, 181, 230, 265, 287
psychology, 3, 7, 16, 22, 61, 99, 192, 253, 255
Puritans/Puritanism, 45; and America, 221; and Bible, 17; changing status of, 2, 3; church in, 169; covenant in, 274–75; English, 222; and exegesis, 211; as frame of reference, 24; and history, 222–23; influence on JE, 16–17, 18; and JE's exaltation of nature, 192–93; in JE's library, 26; legacy of, 297; New England, 223; and sermon form, 212, 243, 253; and will, 118

Ramism, 250, 253
Ramsey, Paul, 147, 149, 153, 154, 164n.3, 305; "Heaven Is a Progressive State," 70
Ramus, Petrus, 18
Rand, William, 7, 119
rationalism, 22, 31n.16, 150, 276, 282, 285, 286
realism, 59, 169
reality, 35, 59–60, 76–77, 82
reason: in Aquinas, 131; assistance to, 107, 111; and Bible, 27; and Christianity, 14, 51; and deism, 51, 91; and emotion, 105; and Enlightenment, 20, 50; and God, 6, 108, 201; importance of, 1; and redemption, 93; sanctified, 107; secularized, 82–83; and Trinity, 50, 51; and will, 117
redemption: acceptance of, 138; assurance of, 10; and Bible, 213; in Campbell, 303; and church, 171, 217; and covenant,

redemption (*cont.*)
55–56, 135, 258; dependence in, 56; dependence on God for, 49–50; and elect, 69, 238; and faith, 4; and Father, 54; as glorification of God, 246; and God, 218, 232; and God's communication of self, 202, 203; and God's sovereignty, 119; God's work in, 6; and grace, 130, 197; and history, 198, 204, 210, 211–16, 217, 222, 223, 236, 259, 262; and Holy Spirit, 54, 55, 296; and Indians, 258, 262, 269; and Jesus Christ, 4, 54–55, 73–76, 78, 97, 138, 213, 303; and millennium, 239; and New England, 284; opposition to, 239–40; personal, 275, 288; personal vs. general, 197–98; progress of, 191; and prophecy, 236; and reason, 93; revelation concerning, 92–93; and suffering, 179; sufficiency of divine action in, 293; and Trinity, 48, 53–57; as undeserved, 137; as unmerited, 141

regenerate person(s): in Aquinas, 132; change in, 130; and grace, 136; and Holy Spirit, 130, 132, 134, 135, 136; and Indians, 262, 263, 264–65; natural powers of, 135; as new creation in Christ, 150; perception by, 205; sensibility of, 192; as spiritual, 133; and typology, 196. *See also* elect; saints

regeneration: and grace, 131, 135; as Holy Spirit indwelling, 69; reality of, 137, 145; and sense, 110

relation, 34, 39, 40, 45, 52, 53

religion, 10, 28–29, 104–5, 163–64, 230, 265

religious affections, 99, 103–13, 119

remanation, 54, 56, 205, 216

repentence, 280, 286

republic of letters, 19, 21, 25

resistance, 60, 70n.2, 76

revelation, 10, 11, 51, 88, 91–94, 95, 191, 218

Revelation (biblical book), 168, 178, 228, 230, 231, 232, 234, 236–37, 238, 249

revivals, 1–2, 6, 7, 8–10, 16, 29, 270; and Bible, 99; Chauncy on, 105, 113, 234; and church, 168, 169; and church membership, 181, 182, 183, 184; and eschatology, 231–32, 233, 235; expectation of, 260–61; and grace, 154;

Holy Spirit in, 111; and Indians, 258; JE's reputation concerning, 294, 295, 296, 297, 298; and justification, 119; and millennium, 232, 233–34, 239; and missions, 259; and redemption history, 218; and religious affections, 103, 112; in Scotland, 295; and Stoddard, 1–2

rhetoric, 17; and Bible, 90; in sermons, 243, 244, 245–46, 247, 249–51, 253–55, 264–65, 275–81; of Stoddard, 251–53

Richard of St. Victor, 47

Richardson, Samuel: *Clarissa*, 26; *Pamela*, 26

righteousness, 74, 75, 137, 170, 171, 237

Robe, James, 295

Rohault, Jacques, 18

Roman Catholic Church, 23, 26, 28, 142, 143, 194, 228, 230–31, 281

Romans, Epistle to, 248

saints: in Aquinas, 131; bodily perfection of, 229; church as, 168; and church membership, 183; communion of, 168; and community of believers, 206; election of, 170; encouragement for, 228; and God, 238–39; God's delight in, 69; as God's portion, 176; and grace, 136; and gracious affections, 154; happiness of, 229, 237, 240; in heaven, 228, 229, 237; holiness of, 140–41, 240; and Holy Spirit, 110–11, 130; increase in number of, 192, 198, 206; JE's reflections on, 53; and Jesus Christ, 168, 178; and Lord's Supper, 184; and millennium, 56–57, 237; and mixed multitude, 11; in new heaven and earth, 70; in Old Testament, 171, 172; perception by, 205, 207; remanation of, 206; righteousness of, 171; as select, 180; sense of divine in, 191; spiritual transformation of, 198; as types of Jesus Christ, 200; virtue of, 126

Saltonstall, Gurdon, 21

salvation. *See* redemption

sanctification, 8, 53, 142, 144

Sargeant, John, 12

Satan, 239. *See also* devil

Schafer, Thomas, 22, 167, 169

Scharlemann, Robert P., 132, 143

scholasticism, 21, 29, 132

science, 3, 18, 19, 22, 38, 96, 98, 116, 118, 191–92, 193, 202, 206, 208n.9, 277. *See also* empiricism
Scotland, 295, 302–3
self: love of, 147–49, 153, 157, 158, 159; reflexive idea of, 61
self-determination, 116, 125, 126
self-identity, 121
selfishness, 148, 152, 153
self-understanding, 121
sense, 39, 110
senses, five, 105–6
Separatism, 10, 12, 181
Sergeant, John, 265, 266, 267
sermons, 211, 243–56; Bible in, 98; Biblical interpretation in, 88; fast day, 275–81, 284–87; to Indians, 262–63, 264–65, 268; regular, 275; thanksgiving day, 276, 282–83, 287
Seven Years War, 13, 286
Shaftesbury, Anthony Ashley Cooper, earl of, 19, 20, 21, 222
Shepard, Thomas, 23, 24, 26
Sherlock, Thomas, 25
Sibbes, Richard, 23, 193
Simon, Richard, 92
sin: in Aquinas, 143; atonement for, 303, 304; blinding power of, 205–6; and character vs. action, 293; and divine light, 106–7; and fast sermons, 278, 280; forgiveness for, 170; freedom from guilt of, 137; infinite odiousness of, 141; and Jesus Christ, 74; and New England, 276, 277; in New England theologians, 299; original, 89, 285, 300; punishment of, 54; Reformed emphasis on, 47; remission of, 143; weakness from, 286. *See also* evil; morality
sinner: acceptance of redemption by, 138; holy disposition in, 142; and perfection, 140, 141; reliance on God by, 6; sermons on, 9; in *Sinners in the Hands of an Angry God*, 255; in *Wicked Men's Slavery to Sin*, 245–46
Skelton, Philip, *Deism Revealed*, 27–28
skepticism, 17, 27
Smith, Henry Boynton, 296, 301–2, 304; "The Relations of Faith and Philosophy," 302
Smith, John, 21
Smith, John E., 128, 304

Smyth, Egbert, 55
Solomon, 197
Son: Clarke on, 49; and community of spirits, 82; defined, 62; as disposition to communicate self, 62; divine nature of, 72; eternal generation of, 62; and Father, 82, 203; Father as one substance with, 49; Father loved by, 62, 76; as Father's idea, 46, 48, 62; as fullness of Father, 179; glorification of, 56; God's glorification in, 185; in history, 55; honor of, 48; hypostasis of, 72; as idea, 50; and Jesus Christ, 80; as Logos, 50; and love, 52; in Mather, 46; as repetition of Father, 48, 62; and timelessness, 67; as wisdom, 48, 50. *See also* Jesus Christ; Logos; Trinity; Word
Song of Solomon. *See* Canticles (biblical book)
soul, 74, 93, 131, 148–49, 198
sower, parable of, 9
space, 42n.4, 63, 68, 69, 97, 131, 144, 216. *See also* time
speech, divine, 191
Spencer, Elihu, 12
spider, image of, 9, 254
Spinoza, Benedict, 92
spirit, 4, 193
spirits, 77, 82
spiritual impulses, 10
spiritual sense, 93
Sprague, William, 294
Stapfer, Johann Friedrich, *Institutiones Theologiae Polemicae*, 29
Stearn, Lewis French, 301
Stebbins, Thomas, 7
Steele, Sir Richard, 19, 20; *Guardian*, 25; *Ladies Library*, 25, 26
Stein, Stephen, 28, 88, 97, 98, 208n.7
Stewart, Dugald, 295
Stillingfleet, Edward, 19, 20
Stockbridge, Indian mission at, 12–13, 119, 120, 235–36, 245, 261–69, 285
Stoddard, John, 12, 265
Stoddard, Solomon, 6, 11, 181; and admission to Lord's Supper, 17, 235, 285; *The Benefit of the Gospel to those that are Wounded in Spirit*, 251; *The Defects of Preachers Reproved*, 252; and Indians, 261, 271n.4; JE as assistant to, 5, 228; and revivals, 1–2; sermons of, 244, 250; works of, 17

Stout, Harry S., 304
Strict Congregationalism, 12
Sweeney, Douglas, 88, 99n.4
symbolism, 191, 193, 200
Synod of Dort, 117

Tappan, Henry Philip, 301
Taylor, Edward, 194
Taylor, John, 14, 21
Taylor, Nathaniel William, 294, 298, 300, 301
teleology, 64, 65
telescope, 191–92, 196
theism, 193
theology, 1, 90, 98, 99, 243, 245, 275, 279, 285, 288
Thomas Aquinas, 131–32, 135–36, 142–43
thought, 115, 117. See also idea(s); imagination
Tillotson, John, 19, 20, 26
time, 59, 63, 64, 66, 67, 68, 69, 97, 131, 144, 216, 226. See also space
Tindal, Matthew, 27, 28, 51
Toland, John, 27
Tracy, Joseph, 294
Trinity, 44–57, 61–62; and ancient philosophy, 29; in Augustinian tradition, 46; beauty of, 53, 54; and Bible, 47, 50, 51; as center of JE's faith, 45; consent of, 56; and conversion, 53; and creation, 61–62, 69, 203–4; equality of, 47, 48; and eschatology, 56; excellency of, 54; and glory, 53, 238, 258; God as harmony of, 76, 77; and Godhead, 185n.6; as God's disposition to communicate, 62; as God's overflowing wisdom and love, 48; grace in, 54; harmony of, 56; Holy Spirit in, 82; and idealism, 46; interdependence of, 48; and justification, 53; and love, 48, 52, 80; and millennium, 56–57; nature of, 3; perfection of, 51; person in, 52–53, 83–84; plurality in, 52; and reason, 50, 51; and redemption, 48, 53–57; scholarly interest in, 44; as society, 48, 56; source of, 203; union of, 54; and wisdom, 48, 54. See also Father; God; Holy Spirit; Son
tritheism, 52
Trumbull, Benjamin, 294; *History of Connecticut*, 250

truth, 11, 18, 28, 38, 83, 107, 108, 110–11, 157–58, 229
Turretin, Francis, *Institutio Theologiae Elencticae*, 25
Turretin, Jean Alphonse, 97
Tyler, Bennet, 293
typology, 101n.20; adumbration and fulfillment in, 196, 199; and antitype, 193, 197, 229; and Bible, 97, 190, 193, 195, 196, 197, 198, 212, 213, 229–31, 232, 233; and church, 177–78; conservative, 195, 196, 199; defined, 190; as divine speech, 207; and eschatology, 229–31, 232, 233, 238; evolution in, 198; and exegesis, 97; exemplary, 197; and history, 97, 193, 194, 195, 196, 197, 199, 201, 204, 207, 217, 218, 223; Israel in, 218; in JE's contemporaries, 193; and Jesus Christ, 97, 190, 191, 196–97, 199–200, 212–13; liberal, 193, 194, 195, 196; and Messiah, 11; Miller on, 192–93, 194, 207n.4, 208n.7; and nature, 97, 190, 191, 192, 193, 194, 195, 196, 199–200, 204, 205, 207; and New Testament, 97, 190, 198; and Old Testament, 97, 190, 193, 197, 198, 212, 213; and ontology, 193, 194, 195, 196, 197, 199; progressive perfection in, 198; prophetic, 197; repetition in, 199; and science, 193, 208n.9

understanding: and apprehension, 110; and experience, 105, 106; of head vs. of heart, 110; human vs. divine, 109; and illumination, 106; knowledge of God in, 150; Locke on, 22, 108; notional, 103, 104, 105, 110; and self-knowledge, 121; and sense of heart, 110; and sermons, 244; spiritual, 106, 107, 111; and will, 124
union: with being in general, 159, 161, 163; and benevolence, 159; with God, 44, 48, 53, 57, 76, 170, 206, 238–39; human desire for, 53; with Jesus Christ, 138–39, 145, 152, 170–71, 183, 184, 240, 258; with others, 149; real vs. relative, 170–71; of Trinity, 54; and ultimate reality, 44
Union Theological Seminary, 296, 301
universe, 60, 61, 63, 77, 118, 192, 193, 200, 217, 238. See also cosmology; creation

vice, 162, 286. *See also* fallen creature; morality; sin; virtue; wicked
Victorines, 47, 52, 106
virtue: of action, 126; and affections, 162; as agreement with truth, 157–58; in Aquinas, 132; and beauty, 40, 41, 154, 155, 156; and being in general, 40–41, 155; and benevolent being, 156; charity as, 147; and common morality, 157, 159, 163; defined, 40–41; end of, 147; and excellence, 154; faith as, 137; God's infusion of, 142; and grace, 132; and harmony, 154, 155; JE's works on, 147; and kind affections, 161; and moral beauty, 41; and morality, 40, 163–64; and natural principles, 162–63; and necessity, 126; and plurality, 41; true, 40–41, 111, 151, 154–56, 159, 160, 161, 162–64; and truth, 157; and will, 125, 154. *See also* morality
Voltaire, 222

war, 279, 281–83, 284–87
Warburton, William, 25
Wayland, Francis, 294
Wells, Edward, *Historical Geography of the Old Testament*, 28
Wesley, Charles, 8
Wesley, John, 8, 270, 295
Wethersfield, Conn., 18
Wheeler, Rachel, 264, 268
Whitefield, George, 8, 9, 10, 26, 119, 232
wicked, the, 237, 238. *See also* fallen creature; sin
Wigglesworth, Professor, 50
Wilkins, John, *Ecclesiastes*, 243, 250
will: and action, 104, 115, 117; and affections, 104; and apprehension, 110; in Aquinas, 131, 132, 143; and Arminianism, 118, 124; in Augustine, 117; in Calvin, 117; in Calvinism, 124; and causality, 116, 123–24; and choice, 104, 121, 123, 124; and compatibilism, 126, 134; definition of, 121; and desire, 115, 117; dissent of to being, 36; and evil, 125; and experience, 124;

freedom of, 11, 115–28, 143; and God, 116, 117, 118, 119, 124, 150; of God, 46, 201; and good, 121, 122, 124, 125; heart as, 155; and Holy Spirit, 135; and inclination, 104, 121; and indifference, 125; and intellect, 121, 122; and judgment, 104; and love, 117, 132, 150; and love of happiness, 148, 149; moral bondage of, 299; nature of, 115; and necessity, 122–23; and New England theologians, 298, 299; and predestination, 117, 123; and reason, 117; and self-knowledge, 121; as self-moving, 132; and sense, 110; as separate faculty, 104, 121, 123; and thought, 115, 117; and understanding, 124; and virtue, 40, 125, 154
Willard, Samuel, 17, 259
Williams, Elisha, 18
Williams, Ephraim, 267, 271n.13
Williams, John, 272n.18
Williams, Roger, 269
Williams, Solomon, 271n.13
Williams, William, 244, 256n.2
Williams family, 266, 268, 271n.13
Wilson, John, 195, 208n.15
Winslow, Ola E., 23, 127
wisdom, 48, 54, 157, 296
Wollaston, William, 157
Wollebius, Johannes, 259; *Compendium Theologiae Christianae*, 19
Woodbridge, Timothy, 267
Woolman, John, 269
Woolston, Thomas, 27
Word, 107, 108, 150. *See also* Jesus Christ; Logos
works, 137, 143, 144, 303
world, 59–70, 229. *See also* creation; universe
Wright, Conrad, 49

Yale College, 17–18, 20–21, 22, 23, 294
Yale Theological Seminary, 297, 301

Zakai, Avihu, 222–23; *Jonathan Edwards's Philosophy of History*, 223
Zechariah, Book of, 234